THEODORE ROOSEVELT'S GHOST

THEODORE ROOSEVELT'S GHOST

The History and Memory of an American Icon

MICHAEL PATRICK CULLINANE

LOUISIANA STATE UNIVERSITY PRESS

BATON ROUGE

Published by Louisiana State University Press
Copyright © 2017 by Louisiana State University Press
All rights reserved

Designer: Barbara Neely Bourgoyne
Typeface: Ingeborg

Library of Congress Cataloging-in-Publication Data
Names: Cullinane, Michael Patrick, 1979– author.
Title: Theodore Roosevelt's ghost : the history and memory of an American icon /
    Michael Patrick Cullinane.
Description: Baton Rouge : Louisiana State University Press, 2017. | Includes
    bibliographical references and index.
Identifiers: LCCN 2017002432| ISBN 978-0-8071-6997-1 (pbk. : alk. paper) | ISBN
    978-0-8071-6673-4 (pdf) | ISBN 978-0-8071-6674-1 (epub)
Subjects: LCSH: Roosevelt, Theodore, 1858–1919. | Roosevelt, Theodore, 1858–1919—
    Monuments. | Memorialization.
Classification: LCC E757.2 .C85 2017 | DDC 973.91/1092 [B] — dc23
LC record available at https://lccn.loc.gov/2017002432

The paper in this book meets the guidelines for permanence and durability of the Committee
on Production Guidelines for Book Longevity of the Council on Library Resources. ♾

For Claire, Sam, and Frankie

CONTENTS

ILLUSTRATIONS

following page 106

J. N. "Ding" Darling cartoon, "The Long, Long Trail" (1919)
Otho Cushing, "Apotheosis," from *The Teddyssey* (1907)
Edwin Marcus cartoon, "American" (1919)
Our Teddy, 1919 motion picture poster
John McCutcheon cartoon, "The Difference between F. R. and T. R." (1920)
Carl Akeley's memorial lion, clay model (1937)
WRMA collecting money for the construction of a replica of TR's birthplace
Reconstructed Roosevelt birthplace, opening day
Aerial-view drawing of Washington, DC
John Russell Pope's architectural model of proposed Roosevelt memorial
Gutzon Borglum's bronze bust of Roosevelt (1919)
J. N. "Ding" Darling cartoon, "A New Roosevelt Invades the West" (1932)
Walter Hoban cartoon, "The Copyright Owners" (1932)
Cover of comic book *Teddy Roosevelt and His Rough Riders,* by E. R. Kinstler
Ford pickup truck with Roosevelt centennial bumper sticker (1956)
Sidney Blackmer getting into costume as Theodore Roosevelt (1948)
Drawing of proposed bridge from E Street over the Potomac River (1954)
Drawing of armillary sphere by Paul Manship, the original memorial
    proposal for Theodore Roosevelt Island (1958)
Sagamore Hill, Roosevelt's home at Oyster Bay, Long Island (1933)
Pat and Richard Nixon with Alice Roosevelt
John Allen Gable and Hermann Hagedorn at centennial event, Roosevelt
    birthplace (1958)
Roosevelt's cabin at Pine Knot, Albemarle County, Virginia
Presidents' race at Washington Nationals baseball park (2013)

ACKNOWLEDGMENTS

Among the countless images of Theodore Roosevelt, Andy Warhol's screen print of him in Rough Rider attire is my favorite. The portrait is part of the artist's 1986 *Cowboys and Indians* portfolio, in which Warhol transformed America's frontier figures into pop icons, demonstrating how enduring their visual representations are. That Theodore Roosevelt pervades our consciousness is no less true today than it was in 1986, or 1919, for that matter.

Roosevelt can be found everywhere, and I am eternally grateful to the many people who helped me find him or shared their stories of their favorite image and explained how they remember him. I am particularly grateful to the many communities of Roosevelt commemorators. Among them, the Theodore Roosevelt Association deserves particular thanks. TR's great-grandson and TRA president Tweed Roosevelt provided invaluable understanding about the workings of the first incorporated presidential fan club, as did its vice president and *TRA Journal* editor Bill Tilchin. Sharon Kilzer and Clay Jenkinson at Dickinson State University's Theodore Roosevelt Center helped me access digital resources; they run an annual symposium that incubates budding researchers, and it was an honor to attend. Mike Amato at the Roosevelt birthplace made sense of a most unusual archive and memorial, and gave me an appreciation of a National Park treasure in a way only a longtime veteran of the US National Park Service can. Valerie Naylor kindly took me around Theodore Roosevelt National Park in the Badlands. More generally, the National Park Service staff at Theodore Roosevelt Island, Sagamore Hill, and the Inaugural Site provided stellar tours. Portrait artist Everett Raymond Kinstler, Sidney Blackmer Jr., and culinary genius Ed Engoron took time out of their busy schedules to help me understand the traditions and (sometimes wacky) ways in which people memorialized Roosevelt.

I am deeply indebted to the Arts & Humanities Research Council of the UK, which generously funded several research trips to the United States and provided financial support that allowed me to focus on this book. Harvard University's Houghton Library facilitated a month-long trip to Cambridge. Theodore Roosevelt Collection curators Wallace Finley Dailey and Heather Cole kindly showed me around the vast underground archive at Houghton and the TR corner in Widener Library; they were always attentive and ready to answer my endless questions. The British Association of American Studies and the Eccles Centre at the British Library underwrote much of the research that I could do in London, and the FDR Presidential Library and Roosevelt Study Center in Middelburg, the Netherlands, funded that which needed to be done elsewhere. Phil Davies, Cara Rodway, David Woolner, Bob Clark, and Leontien Joosse made working in these archives a joy.

I am privileged to have colleagues who took an interest in this research and offered advice. Kathy Dalton, Sid Milkis, Stacy Cordery, DeeGee Lester, and Hans Krabbendam filled in many blind spots. Even those not naturally inclined to study Roosevelt did so in aid of a friend. David Gleeson, Joe Street, Brian Ward, Sylvia Ellis, Iwan Morgan, Simon Rofe, David Haglund, Douglas Eden, Giles Scott-Smith, and David Ryan have listened to me rasp on about this project for so long that they probably shudder when they hear Roosevelt's name. Former colleagues at Northumbria University Lynn Dobbs and Don MacRaild deserve my everlasting thanks for seeing promise in an early career academic, and my thanks go to Charlotte Alston, Daniel Laqua, and Colin Reid for reading chapters in our writing group. Rand Dotson at LSU Press saw potential in this book and guided me through publication, and I owe Robert Cook my gratitude for suggesting Rand and LSU. One Roosevelt scholar deserves special mention: I met Serge Ricard in 2007 and decided that I wanted to write about TR. He remains an encouraging friend and source of great inspiration.

If friends are not tired of me bleating about Roosevelt, my family surely is. The Cullinane and Garry clans have nevertheless endured, and in some cases entertained, my fascination. I remember scouring Henry Pringle's biography of Roosevelt on my honeymoon. Poolside, on a balmy afternoon, I spent hours sticking Post-it notes in nearly every page of the book to mark where Pringle condemned his subject. Most partners would have reconsidered their vows at that point, but not Claire. She never complained. She has even taught the boys to support me without qualification, and to this gang I owe most.

THEODORE ROOSEVELT'S GHOST

INTRODUCTION

In the early hours of January 6, 1919, James Amos rested in a chair beside the fire, allowing the warm hearth to fend off winter's chill. He listened to the rhythmic breathing of his friend, former president Theodore Roosevelt. When the subtle, tranquil sounds of Roosevelt's respiration turned heavy and labored, Amos hastened to his bedside. He touched his friend's head; it felt dry and warm. Leaning in closer, Amos noticed him take deep gulps of air, followed by short shallow puffs. Fearing the worst, he fetched the nurse, but by the time they returned, Roosevelt's breathing had stopped entirely.

News of Roosevelt's death began to spread as the sun rose over his estate at Oyster Bay, Long Island. Only sixty years old and semiretired from politics, he remained one of America's most eminent and conspicuous personalities. Dying in bed was uncharacteristic, an act that belied his image as a man of boundless life. "Death had to take him in his sleep," Vice President Thomas Marshall eulogized, "for if Roosevelt had been awake, there would have been a fight."[1] On President Woodrow Wilson's orders, federal buildings draped black cloth from windows and lowered flags to half-mast. The houses of Congress adjourned, as did the Supreme Court, with "a deep sense of sorrow," according to Chief Justice Edward Douglass White.[2] In New York City, aldermen canceled the day's business. "One sentiment prevailed," the *New York Tribune* reported—"deep regret, tinged by a sense of personal bereavement." Observers from across the country reported a sky full of black crepe, comparable only to the sky the day Lincoln died, and one journalist beheld "strong men weep as they spoke to each other in the streets."[3]

Two days later, Roosevelt's family interred his body at Youngs Cemetery, a small graveyard near his estate, Sagamore Hill. The War Department offered to organize a full military service, but the family declined, citing Roosevelt's explicit request for a simple ceremony. His widow,

Edith, asked uninvited guests to refrain from attending the austere event, summoning only close friends and relatives. Nevertheless, travelers could not be discouraged. The heavy snowfall that carpeted New York slowed but did not stop the deluge of mourners journeying to Oyster Bay.[4]

In the few hours preceding the funeral, sculptor James Earle Fraser created the first posthumous image of Roosevelt by applying plaster to his lifeless face and casting a death mask. Fraser also struck plaster molds of Roosevelt's fingers and hands so that "authentic sculptural records" could inform the work of future artists. But funeral-goers renounced the mask as an unrecognizable likeness. Poet Frank Owen Payne studied the mold, pondered the mask, and recorded his impressions in verse:

> Can this be your face, this whose calm repose
> Portrays no presence, but cold, dreamless sleep?
> This is not you, this bit of smooth, still earth
> For you walked straightaway to the Throne above
> And asked God cheerily, "What's to do up here?"[5]

Fraser's death mask frustrated those who knew Roosevelt, many of whom complained that its contours lacked the subject's audacity, that it did not have Roosevelt's soul.

Such reactions to Fraser's clay cast resemble the public's discontent with other posthumous portrayals of Roosevelt. Undeterred by critics, Roosevelt commemorators produced a steady stream of controversial depictions. The press at home and abroad published vivid encomiums. Poets incanted exaltations. Artists prepared canvases, metalworkers poured bronze into casts, and politicians recited tributes. Philosopher John Dewey joined the grieving multitude and contributed one of the most noteworthy eulogies. Dewey had supported Roosevelt's 1912 campaign for president and admired elements of his life, yet did not worship him as infallible. He believed the American public would remember a personalized image of Roosevelt, one that venerated part, if not all, of him. The compulsion to recall only facets of his life rather than the totality, Dewey said, came from a natural urge to impose contemporary contexts and personal desires on the memories of the past. He defined commemoration as inherently subjective, an act that reflects the aspirations of those who remember. Dewey prophesized that a Roosevelt doppelgänger would emerge, created from idiosyncratic memorials rather than objective reality. "Of every man who goes into political life there gradually grows up a double," he declared. "The double consists of the acts of the original individual reflected first in the imagination and then in the desires and acts of other men." A Roosevelt double would grow particularly "immense" over time, Dewey assumed, because his "capture of the imagination of his countrymen was so complete."[6]

The growth and evolution of a Roosevelt double took no time at all. At the funeral, mourners paired grief with disappointment, finding the proceedings too prosaic. Publisher Lawrence Abbott said the service had a certain "solemnity," and naturalist Carl Akeley said it "seemed too casual," insisting that "Roosevelt was too great to be privately buried. He was our greatest man. He belonged to the nation, not Oyster Bay."[7] The absence of hymns, the truncated rituals, the simple gravestone, and the modest crowd gave Akeley the sense that the funeral services did not sufficiently celebrate the spirit of Roosevelt. Ferdinand Iglehart, pastor of New York City's Park Avenue Methodist Church, admitted that for those who knew Roosevelt personally, no monument was necessary, but he maintained that "monuments of stone, some large, tall shaft or figure" should be erected to "remind the coming generations of the great giant that lived and loved and wrought for them."[8] Discontent with the funeral and the natural tendency to craft a "towering" double, as Dewey put it, gradually inspired a century-long memorial campaign to preserve Roosevelt's legacy in a grander, more accessible, and permanent fashion.

Contemporary explanations of how we memorialize the past have not strayed far from Dewey's. "To remember something is to rework it mentally," historian Geoffrey Cubbit contends: "What is remembered is always reconfigured, and thus implicitly reinterpreted, never merely resuscitated or reproduced."[9] Or, as cultural historian Michael Kammen explains, "We arouse and arrange our memories to suit our psychic needs."[10] Memory inevitably yields personal impressions of the past, and, as a result, memories link the past to the present and fasten the present to the future. Likewise, subjectivity predisposes memory to omission and forgetting. The absence of memory or the failure to remember, whether conscious or unconscious, shapes perception.

The posthumous image of Roosevelt, dependent on these laws of remembrance, multiplied exponentially and in a manner that complicates easy interpretation. Countless retrospectives of Roosevelt exist, so many that to call Roosevelt's posthumous image a "double," as Dewey did, diminishes the scale of his reimagination. A more appropriate description of Roosevelt's legacy is "polygonal," a term coined by his friend and literary critic Brander Matthews.[11] Roosevelt has many sides, distinguished

by many memorials and myriad meanings. Pulitzer Prize–winning biographers Henry F. Pringle and Edmund Morris relied on Matthews's
description for their portrayals, and David McCullough called Roosevelt
"a man of many gifts and masks."[12] American Museum of Natural History
president Henry Fairfield Osborn presented Roosevelt's passing as an
opportunity "to look at his life as a whole" and a chance for observers to
"realize that he was not *one* man, but many great men, many personalities, combined and harmonized into one."[13]

How our memories conceive Roosevelt's angles, edges, and sides has
differed greatly over the century since his death, and yet the more complex his posthumous image becomes, the easier it is to glean meaning
from the representations. More often than not, the sources of Roosevelt's
legacy attempted to distill the many-sided man into an essence that can
represent some overarching narrative. For example, at the dedication of
Mount Theodore Roosevelt, Maj. Gen. Leonard Wood called his longtime
friend a many-sided man, then lectured the crowd about TR's special affec-
tions for the US military and the American frontier.[14] Wood's deployment
of Roosevelt's western legacy and notoriety as a soldier helped demonstrate to prospective voters in the 1920 Republican election, that he, like
Roosevelt, was a tough military man capable of harnessing the American
spirit. Wood's recollection did not diminish the polygonal image; it merely
drew upon certain elements to suit the political context and his personal
ambitions.

The subjective view reflects the desires of memorializers, and yet none
arrive any closer to an authentic image. This ambiguity is what makes
Roosevelt so interesting. Just as James Earle Fraser could not construct
a true portrait of Roosevelt from his lifeless face, no true Rooseveltian
legacy exists; there are only depictions and interpretations. The syndicated press cartoonist J. N. "Ding" Darling lamented this fact when he
attempted to draw a perfect caricature of Roosevelt immediately following
his death. Darling's editor requested a drawing within two hours after
the news broke, but the artist suffered an "emotional coma," confounded
by "a subject that demanded the supreme effort." He blanked, unable to
think of "anything at all."[15]

In Darling's effort to sketch the nation's loss, he drew Roosevelt from
a memory of their last meeting, riding colts in Oyster Bay. The illustrator penciled an ethereal figure on horseback waving goodbye. Somehow
it seemed unfitting, an informal image that only satisfied the author's
memories and lacked the myriad meanings of Roosevelt. Darling tossed

the sheet to the ground to begin on another. He discarded the next sheet, too, and every sheet after it. After hours of frustrated scribbling, the artist accepted defeat. Then, glimpsing the first sketch under the pile of abandoned cartoons, he reached an epiphany. The mounted Roosevelt pleasantly waving goodbye to Darling looked, on second inspection, more like Roosevelt gesturing farewell to the nation, perhaps the world.

Exhausted, Darling submitted the cartoon to his managing editor, who criticized it as insufficiently portraying Roosevelt's legacy. The editor opted instead to run a photo of Roosevelt framed by a thick black rim. But when he searched for a photo, he discovered that a fire had destroyed all images of Roosevelt on file. Left with no choice but to publish the cartoon, Darling rushed to produce a version with greater detail. He added clouds to the horizon and a trail of westward pioneers. In the background he situated the skyline of the nation's capital, a reference to Roosevelt's political achievements.

Neither Darling nor his editor expected the image to have much effect. The following day, however, Darling picked up the *Chicago Evening Post* and happened upon the familiar silhouette of a mounted apparition. "The Long, Long Trail," as it was called, was reprinted around the country, and demand for special copies, etchings, and book editions made the hurried sketch Darling's best-recognized work. The illustrator admitted his relief that his work captured some essence of Roosevelt, yet understood that no single portrayal could epitomize Roosevelt's legacy. Satisfied that his cartoon touched his fellow Americans, Darling confessed that it "wasn't what it should be." Even so, the image became emblematic because it adapted to public fascination. To this day, the public sees Roosevelt as it wants to.[16]

The notion that we cannot reproduce a true depiction of the past underlies this book's analysis of Roosevelt's legacy. Reflected and refracted through the eyes of memorializers, Roosevelt has acquired a subjective meaning, and, no matter how slightly our perception varies, each imagination of him raises questions about how we contemplate the past. To understand Roosevelt's image requires a comprehensive investigation of memorializers, their motives for remembering, and how these memories circulate. Unfortunately, researching every mode of remembrance and each commemorative community is impossible. Over three hundred biographies of Roosevelt crowd the historiographical field, not to mention thousands of academic monographs and journal articles. Countless artistic portraits, Rooseveltiana, sculptures, theater productions, commercial advertisements, television shows, films, and documentaries inundate the cultural landscape. Every US president since Warren G. Harding has invoked Roosevelt's legacy. Sites of memory—utilitarian and aesthetic alike—exist in locations around the world. The scope of the remembrance makes comprehensive analysis impossible, but we can make an inclusive examination of the most representative imagery. Although every artistic sketch and political co-option contributes to Roosevelt's enduring legacy, only some reach national audiences, and, of those, only a portion have an enduring influence. By identifying the communities of commemoration and the individuals who set interpretive trends through widely distributed portrayals, a reliably detailed account of Roosevelt's legacy can be achieved.[17]

Who, then, are the agents of presidential legacy? Fan clubs and memorial foundations, media producers, family, authors, historians, politicians, and architects produce vital portraits. In Roosevelt's case, men's and women's memorial associations emerged soon after his death, intent on preserving and extending his legacy. These associations collected books, manuscripts, and motion pictures; financed and designed monuments; and built partnerships with museums, universities, and commercial businesses to venerate Roosevelt. The associations stood at the center of commemorative activity, often hand-in-hand with the Roosevelt family, perpetuating a positive image. Partners that joined their campaigns often did so for reasons other than sheer admiration. Advertisers and entrepreneurs found commercial value in Roosevelt's recognizable and affable profile. One businessman who, with the help of the memorial associations, opened a chain of TR casual-dining restaurants said he chose the "Roosevelt brand" because he could relate to it and because "people easily identified him."[18] It is little surprise that officeholders of all parties cast themselves as disciples of such a popular politician. Local and state government played a part in supporting and sometimes stalling memorial activity, and local and state interest groups assumed a comparable role.

Communities of commemoration swayed public perception and apotheosized Roosevelt, but at times, individual acts of memorialization made a comparable impression. The historian or biographer is perhaps the best example. Tucked away in dusty archives, the solitary researchers who authored accounts of Roosevelt's life profoundly affected public opinion. For instance, Henry Pringle's 1931 biography, a negative portrayal of Roosevelt that stemmed from the author's disdain for politicians, lingers as a subjective individual memory that shaped public impressions for a generation. Poets, novelists, and artists, inspired by eclectic ambitions, contributed other views.

Analysis of the historical context provides an additional angle in understanding the myriad perspectives of Roosevelt. The agents and "vehicles" of memory, independent or collectively arranged, summoned the past from a particular sociocultural framework, making commemoration a product of its time.[19] The memory of historical figures and events varies by generation and is affected by political turns, social disruption, or cultural trends. Historian Clifford Geertz urged scholars to think of context as a vital circumstantial paradigm, rather than a causal force.[20] Context helps to make sense of human action, and, as historian Lynn Hunt contends, memory studies that traverse generational periods "connect individuals with society and culture more generally."[21] Understanding the sociocultural context in which memorializers have conceived Roosevelt's legacy over the last one hundred years, while carefully avoiding oversimplification of any given era, can provide insight into the broadest commemorative tendencies. For example, context can explain why Roosevelt's detractors refused to attack him in the days following his death. National bereavement made doing so socially inappropriate. Similarly, we can ask what effect the cultural context of the Cold War or the Great Depression had. Situating individual and collective memories in the mise-en-scène provides valuable perspective and explains how commemorative trends develop and endure.

Aside from its obvious significance for understanding how we conceive Theodore Roosevelt historically, the examination of his posthumous image set against an evolving contextual backdrop offers a unique view of American history in the twentieth and early twenty-first centuries. Beginning with Roosevelt's death and the tributes that immediately followed, this book chronologically investigates how memorializers conceived his legacy. As the centennial of his death approaches, it is possible to see the cadence of memory, the myths that arise and disappear, and the positive, negative, indifferent, or ambiguous portrayals. It is possible to take stock of Roosevelt's reputation, understand memory's changing tenor over time, and consider how subsequent generations will interpret him.

When Roosevelt's grandchildren visited Sagamore Hill, they sensed his ghost in every corner of the big house and believed his spirit looked over them as they played. "He just had too much vitality to die and leave all those grandchildren deprived of his companionship," grandson Archie Roosevelt Jr. said.[22] Born less than a year before TR died, Archie never knew his grandfather, but he felt his presence and "asked him to help me be worthy." He modeled his life on a particular conception of his grandfather and his grandfather's expectations. "We knew him only as a ghost," Archie related, "but what a merry, vital, and energetic ghost he was. And how much encouragement and strength he left behind to help us play the role Fate has assigned us for the rest of the century."[23] Conjuring Roosevelt's ghost reveals the roots of these memories, the modes and motives of remembrance, and the enduring legacy of an American icon.

[CHAPTER ONE]

CONSTRUCTING A LEGACY

oosevelt's death inspired an outpouring of adulation. Poet Rudyard Kipling, for one, christened him "Great-Heart," a fawning reference to the spiritual guide in John Bunyan's *Pilgrim's Progress*. William Allen White, a journalist in the Roosevelt White House and a prominent social commentator, bestowed near-biblical status upon Roosevelt, calling him "a great agitator like Isaiah and Elijah." And a drawing by syndicated cartoonist Otho Cushing of Roosevelt joining the ranks of Ramses, Caesar, Achilles, and Alexander in Valhalla was widely reprinted.[1]

Irrespective of the spiritual tradition to which memorializers alluded, these early tributes typically portrayed a fabled Roosevelt whose example carried a lesson for the living. Such exaltations also came from beyond the United States. Kipling's eulogy is a case in point. The poet had developed a close relationship with Roosevelt in the 1890s and cast him as Britain's dearest friend in the years of World War I.[2] At the time of his death, Roosevelt stood in stark contrast to President Wilson, whose policy of neutrality isolated the United States until 1917. Roosevelt opposed Wilson's diplomatic negotiations for "peace without victory" and expressed doubt about the Fourteen Points. In turn, Kipling credited Roosevelt with stimulating Allied support in the United States and impressed upon British diplomats that Americans like Roosevelt shared British apprehensions. When European leaders met in Versailles to find peace, redraw boundaries, and exact vengeance on the vanquished, although Roosevelt was absent, the spirit of his political message remained.[3] Allied delegates voiced their hostility to Wilson's Fourteen Points by invoking Roosevelt's hesitations.

Effusive tributes to Roosevelt after his death came from Allied leaders, crowned heads of state, and the European intelligentsia. They praised Roosevelt as the chief advocate of American intervention and preparedness. One Parisian evening newspaper called him the "Champion of the cause of the Entente," declaring him a heroic ally who supported the French "without waiting for the decision of his fellow citizens."[4] Across the English Channel, the sentiment was equally complimentary. In life, as in death, Kipling told Sen. Henry Cabot Lodge, Roosevelt was "too big to be 'discreet,'" and although he represented "the greatest of your people's line of great men," he belonged to the world.[5]

Not all deaths elicit the same level of public interest and arouse global attention like Roosevelt's did. Nor do all presidents prompt the same veneration. What galvanized international esteem for Roosevelt was the value his life held for commemorators. Roosevelt as Great-Heart provided specific meaning to a specific context, and the early memorials play a particularly important role in his long legacy because they set the tone for future generations. Roosevelt is remembered everlastingly as Wilson's adversary, in part because he challenged Wilson in life, and in part because after his death, his legacy continued to frustrate the sitting president. If we examine Roosevelt's legacy during the first year of remembrance, we find that six interrelated dimensions came to dominate his image. By examining the early tributes, it is possible to identify the wellspring of his public memory.

The principal theme to emerge in early tributes was Roosevelt's legacy as a patriotic figure. His political popularity, demonstrated by the electoral majorities he commanded and the legions of followers he inspired, convinced many that his stature matched that of the most esteemed Americans, namely, George Washington and Abraham Lincoln. Rabbi Joseph Krauskopf of Philadelphia could recall the deaths of Ulysses S. Grant, Grover Cleveland, James A. Garfield, and William McKinley and, profound as the public mourning was, "especially in the case of the latter two, it was a sorrow different from that which swayed the American people when told of the death of Roosevelt." Only Washington and Lincoln compared to Roosevelt, Krauskopf insisted, and "not since the days of Washington has a one-time Chief Executive held so conspicuous a place in the esteem of the people." Krauskopf knew of no other president that "stood as close to the people as Roosevelt has stood to us."[6]

Politicians commemorated him in similar tones. Republican senator William Kenyon of Iowa ranked Roosevelt as "the greatest American since Lincoln," as did former president William Howard Taft, who called him "the most commanding personality in our public life since Lincoln."[7] Less superlative compliments still effervesced with adoration. New York City preacher Leighton Parks predicted, "Roosevelt will not stand in our national Pantheon beside Washington and Lincoln" but "will be one in the triumvirate of creative Presidents, with Jefferson and Jackson."[8] Long before Arthur Schlesinger Sr. asked scholars to rank American presidents, public opinion placed Roosevelt in an elite class of national leaders—if not great, then near great, and undeniably transformative.

A quiet crosscurrent of antipathy ran beneath the seemingly ubiquitous praise. Unlike Washington, who after death became a "marble man" dehumanized by myth-making memorializers, and Lincoln, who kept a degree of humanity but was honored in somewhat impregnable and omnipotent ways, Roosevelt remained vulnerable to critics. His detractors initially concealed their unfavorable opinions. Walter I. Smith, a midwestern Republican congressman and appellate court judge, avoided public comment. He privately wrote Taft about his mixed emotions: "Of course I am sorry he had to die but am afraid, my dear Judge, I am not quite as forgiving as you are."[9] A stalwart conservative, Smith found it impossible to pardon Roosevelt for splitting the Republican Party in 1912. Perennial Democratic candidate for president and political adversary William Jennings Bryan said Roosevelt had inspired "a multitude of devoted followers" that subsequently created a counterforce, which "naturally arrayed against him a host of opponents, but his death puts an end to controversy and he will be mourned by foe as well as by friend."[10] As Bryan predicted, the country was swept up in public mourning, a force that overwhelmed those who did not admire Roosevelt's achievements or ideology.

One explanation for the widespread positive regard was that Roosevelt's image transcended American sectionalism. The *Chicago Daily News* eulogized him as having "the culture of the East, the breeziness and independence of the great West, and the chivalry and warmth of the South."[11] "He could appeal, as no president could since the Civil War, to all sections of the country," retired New York senator Chauncey Depew eulogized: "Harvard gave him an eastern culture and ranch life on the western plains brought him into contact and close association with those pioneers who have discovered, developed, and peopled our territories, from the Mississippi to the Pacific."[12] Of course, Roosevelt cultivated this image throughout his life. A New Yorker at his core, he embraced his mother's southern roots and regularly emphasized his time spent in the West.

To be remembered as the national conglomerate was a powerful trope in 1919, when the idea of Americanism peaked in the national consciousness. Loosely defined, Americanism signified a set of national ideals and values such as democracy, free enterprise, individualism, and civic equality. After World War I, it stood for national fidelity and patriotic vim, combined with public distaste for communism and immigration. The first Red Scare coincided with Roosevelt's death and fused his legacy with anti-communist hyperbole and xenophobic discourses. Unquestionably, Roosevelt's deployment of such rhetoric in political speeches facilitated these posthumous invocations. He belittled "hyphenated Americans" during the Great War and particularly immigrants from non-Allied nations, like Ireland and Germany, who split their allegiance between a mother country and their adopted nationality. Americanism and US citizenship, he insisted, required deference to the United States. Although Roosevelt did not take this assertion to its logical end to preclude immigrants from joining the "American club," he often employed "an odious and unnecessarily cruel" rhetoric that relied on racial stereotypes to identify immigrants as "others." Only by assimilating and casting off the features of a nonnative identity, Roosevelt believed, would the foreign born become full and equal American citizens.[13]

Beyond the anti-communist and anti-immigration elements of this Americanism, memorializers celebrated Roosevelt as a generic, benign signifier for patriotism and national identity. From his pulpit at the First Baptist Church of North Adams, Massachusetts, Rev. Daniel Clare called Roosevelt "the incarnation of the American spirit," a man as recognizable as Uncle Sam, and one who "typifies America in the eyes of the world." Foreigners agreed. Danish journalist Johannes Jensen said Roosevelt "touches upon the history of all America and marks trait by trait, the highly developed, energetic, inexhaustible people of this day between the Atlantic and Pacific." Buenos Aires newspaper *La Nacion* eulogized him as "the most representative type of American," an icon interchangeable with the essence of the nation.

Perhaps not surprisingly, Roosevelt received abundant tribute on the Fourth of July. In Chicago, Twelfth Street was renamed Roosevelt Road, and a parade float of girls dressed as Lady Liberty led the celebrations in his honor. At the Cathedral Church of St. Paul on Tremont Street in Boston, Rev. Edward Sullivan used his Fourth of July sermon to proclaim Roosevelt the "greatest private citizen" amid a chorus of national anthems. *New York Times* cartoonist Edwin Marcus sketched Clio, the muse of history, struggling to compose a suitable epitaph for Roosevelt. Crossing out numerous inscriptions, the muse settled on "American" as most apt.[14]

As frequently as tributes cited Roosevelt's Americanism, they also associated him with the West, portraying him as an American cowboy.[15] This affiliation strengthened the theme of Americanism because it conveyed national exceptionalism through the myth of the cowboy, a paragon of rugged manliness set against the backdrop of the western continental frontier.[16] The 1890s and 1900s produced a particular cultural iconography of the cowboy which occurred at the same time that Roosevelt was working to construct his own public image as a frontiersman. At the turn of the twentieth century, the cowboy appeared as the personification of intense masculine morality and heroic nationalism in books like Owen Wister's *The Virginian,* in staged shows like Buffalo Bill's Wild West, and in academic treatments like Frederick Jackson Turner's "frontier thesis," which embodied the intellectual basis of American exceptionalism. The frontier, according to Turner, produced unique character traits in the American people that enhanced their fitness for survival. It created a new race. On the prairies, the range, and across peripheral western towns, democracy was seasoned. There Americans built their capacity for self-government and formulated plans to expand their civilization. The cowboy became an evolutionary figure, representative of American liberty roaming the free and open spaces of the West, seeking to establish law and order in untamed lands, and symbolic of the country's transition from rural nineteenth-century pastoralism to twentieth-century modernity.[17]

Roosevelt unquestionably contributed to this definition of the frontiersman. In his four-volume tome *The Winning of the West,* which proposed an identical thesis to Turner's, Roosevelt constructed an image of the mythical cowboy. Moreover, during his three-year stint as a rancher in the North Dakota Badlands, he crafted a self-image as a cowboy by wrestling cattle, leading a posse, and sleeping rough on the prairie. Off the range he reinforced this image in staged photos in which he wore dandified cowboy outfits.[18] In politics, at the end of the nineteenth century, he supported overseas expansion, using the frontier metaphor to promote the acquisition of territory in the Caribbean basin and the Pacific. Beckoning American men to rejuvenate the nation's martial spirit, Roosevelt heeded his own call and led the 1st Cavalry Volunteers, better known as Teddy's Rough Riders or Teddy's Cowboy Contingent. The regiment stormed Cuba's San Juan Heights, brought military glory to Roosevelt, and fortified his fabled celebrity as a frontiersman. Wister, Buffalo Bill, and Turner manufactured the cowboy myth, but Roosevelt was the living prototype.

Roosevelt's cowboy persona persisted long after the War of 1898 and was evoked most regularly when describing his foreign policy. During his presidency, Roosevelt often spoke of the evolutionary progress of human beings and the advancement of global civilization, contending that the fittest societies would survive and expand at the expense of so-called tribal people. Like the cowboys of the frontier, he believed the United States could develop the Far East and Latin America in collaboration with other imperial nations tasked with the same "White Man's Burden."[19] His statecraft became known as "big stick" diplomacy, after Roosevelt's penchant for quoting an alleged West African proverb, "speak softly and carry a big stick." The proverb advised diplomacy—speaking softly—backed with a willingness to use force—the big stick. Political cartoonists habitually depicted him in Rough Rider costume or cowboy gear, wielding a club as an imperial tool for tutoring, or herding, foreigners.

The first posthumous tributes extended this image. Sen. Warren G. Harding of Ohio, then a Republican candidate for president, made much of TR's Americanism and cowboy spirit. "Men thought of him first as a warrior"; within him existed an "extraordinary" martial spirit, an "appealing, vigorous, fearless, American manhood." These characteristics, Harding said, derived from Roosevelt's ranching experience "in the freedom of the West," an adventure that reverberated throughout his life. "He revealed it as the soldier in the world's first war for humanity. He revealed it in administrative and executive office, in his vaster responsibilities, and it was the conspicuous side of him in the retirement to which he could not retire." Harding presented the Panama Canal as the greatest evidence of Roosevelt's cowboy spirit; the modern engineering feat, he said, was the product of an "aggressive Americanism and our Republic's capacity to do big things."[20] Or, as one poet pronounced, "His was the sturdy heart / Of the untamed pioneer."[21]

A latent dualism existed within the cowboy myth. On one side, rugged chivalry and persistent enthusiasm were the hallmarks of the virtuous frontiersman, the crusading moralist who served national interests and identity. On the other side, the myth signified the recklessness of a man on the border between civilization and barbarism, an outlier in close proximity to the lawlessness of the backwoods and in regular contact with racially inferior populations. Life on the borderlands produced a man willing to use violence in order to achieve his ends, and, rather than exemplifying a patriot, this cowboy figure symbolized rebelliousness, instability, and adolescence. Sen. Marcus Hanna voiced this best when he famously called TR "that damned cowboy," fearing the Rough Rider had a short temper and an untamable hastiness. Hanna based his opposition to Roosevelt on the undesirable aspects of the cowboy myth, and while the first posthumous tributes wholly depicted Roosevelt as the virtuous type of cowboy, the dichotomy already inherent in that myth indicates how different interpretations would take shape.[22]

Corresponding to the American cowboy image was that of the American progressive. Whereas the cowboy looked outward toward the frontier as a place to spread the American dream, the progressive peered inward at domestic deficiencies. Roosevelt put himself at the fore of defining and characterizing the progressive movement. Early in his career he forged a reputation as a reform-minded New York assemblyman who fought Tammany Hall and Wall Street corruption. His six years as the bipartisan federal civil-service commissioner and as the anti-vice chair of New York City's police commission confirmed his status as a reformer. As president, Roosevelt earned the nickname "trust-buster" for executing the first successful lawsuit against an interstate monopoly, and he supported the Pure Food and Drug Act, which mandated higher standards for the consumer goods industry. Had these historic steps not already established him as a reformer, his 1912 candidacy for the White House—first as a Republican and then as the leader of the Progressive Party—gave his memorializers an even firmer foundation for their position. The Progressive platform included advocacy for women's suffrage, the recall of elected officials, direct election of senators, a national minimum wage, tax reforms, a greater role for government in public health, and the prohibition of child labor.

In their attempts to mend the nation's social and political ills, progressives often spoke of their activism as typically American, such as when Carl Schurz described progressive Americanism as tenacious fairness: "My country right or wrong; if right, to be kept right; and if wrong, to be put right."[23] And, much like the cowboy, progressives imagined themselves as warriors of righteousness. Roosevelt's western attire in political cartoons needed no changing; his riding chaps and big stick fit the image of a progressive crusader fighting corporate greed and political plutocrats.

The progressive movement formed an amorphous group of self-professed activists with diverse social reforms, and it remains difficult to pin down a definitive identity.[24] Roosevelt personified a constituency of progressivism, especially when he founded the Progressive Party, but far-left groups, like the Socialist Party, who also adopted the progressive moniker qualified their praise, deeming Roosevelt not progressive enough. "Goodbye, Teddy," the socialist *New Appeal* mournfully waxed after his passing: "You didn't know anything about Socialism, and you wrote many stupid and cruel things about Socialists; but you did know *something* about the malefactors of great wealth."[25] On the opposite side of the political spectrum, conservatives saw Roosevelt's reforms as government meddling, and although these detractors praised his cowboy spirit and patriotic Americanism, they censured his political principles as dangerously radical. For example, Senator Harding called Roosevelt's decision to bolt from the Republican Party in 1912 his "greatest blunder" and refused to accept the progressive legacy as authentic. Harding remembered him as "less the radical than he at times appeared" and as a man who "sometimes spoke radically against his own judgment."[26]

For those who admired Roosevelt's progressivism, his influence on the national consciousness remained categorical. Harold L. Ickes, a Progressive Party delegate in 1912 and Interior secretary in Franklin Roosevelt's cabinet, credited TR with restoring the American merit system, and in his 1919 encomium he asserted that TR's tenure in the White House permanently transformed the way successive presidential administrations approached social reform.[27] A similar tribute came from labor relations lawyer Merle Vincent, who maintained that Roosevelt's progressivism "inaugurated a change in our ideals and habits of thinking and practicing."[28]

Less dispute surrounded Roosevelt's conservation legacy. His affection for flora and fauna began in youth and matured throughout his life, leading him to engage intellectually and tangibly with the outdoors. Roosevelt devoured ecology scholarship and befriended leading naturalists of the day, including John Muir, John Burroughs, John Jay Chapman, and Gifford Pinchot. He contributed to the scholarly literature by publishing critically acclaimed essays on birds, evolution, and hunting, and he legislated for preservation as governor of New York. As president, he approved regulations that preserved forests, stopped industrial dumping, provoked Congress to build federal dams, and established the US Forest Service. In 1906, he signed the Antiquities Act, which preserved hundreds of bird sanctuaries, game preserves, and woodlands. Above all, he longed to be outdoors. Roosevelt hiked mountains, tracked wildlife, and studied nature up close, particularly in his post-presidential safari in Africa and his exploration of the Brazilian rainforest.

Conservation belonged to the same class of social issues that progressives worked to reform by way of government regulation, and although

Roosevelt's activism reflected his legacy as a progressive, those who recalled his affair with ecology typically did so by excluding references to other legacy themes. The Boone and Crockett Club—the first American wildlife and conservation society, cofounded by Roosevelt—saw progressivism and the cowboy spirit as "incidental" legacies. The club remembered TR "on the common ground of a common interest—the love of outdoor life"—and fêted him as "the ardent hunter and the field naturalist."[29] David Starr Jordan, the president of Stanford University, lamented that politics had "spoiled a good naturalist" but acknowledged that "the naturalist was never submerged in the exigencies of the statesmanship."[30] For environmentalists, Roosevelt's conservation legacy distinguished him as a chief executive without comparison. While those celebrating his patriotism compared him to Washington and Lincoln, and the cowboy and progressive legacies put him in league with Jackson and Wilson, the environmentalists knew that no president had done more than Roosevelt to conserve natural resources, raise awareness of natural sciences, or establish preservation societies. Pinchot, the first chief of the US Forestry Service, demanded that any future memorial pay its respects to Roosevelt's conservationism above all other dimensions of his career and personality.

Two further legacy themes emerged in the first tributes: Roosevelt as the man of letters and as the preacher of righteousness. "He is best known to us as a publicist," agricultural expert Henry C. Wallace said; "when all is said and done, it seems to me the greatest contribution to the good of humanity was made in his character as a preacher of righteousness."[31] Not surprisingly, many caricatures of Roosevelt include his toothy grin. Those who listened to his speeches often applauded the force and vigor with which he enunciated his convictions and snapped his jowls. "The voice persisted even when his lips were sealed," progressive comrade William Allen White said.[32] In addition to his iconic oratory, Roosevelt was a prolific author of more than fifty books, among them groundbreaking history monographs, travelogues, compilations of public speeches, and political editorials. His vast oeuvre of publication pales, however, in comparison to the estimated 150,000 letters he composed to family, friends, and foes—a record amount of correspondence for any American president. "We may think of him as preeminently an outdoor man, and such he was, of course; but he was also an indoor man," Brander Matthews eulogized; Roosevelt was as much "a denizen of the library, as he was an explorer of the forest."[33]

The "preacher of righteousness" image fits with Roosevelt's oratorical and literary legacy while intimating a religious bent. As a parishioner at the New York Dutch Reformed Church and an affiliate of his wife's Episcopal church, Roosevelt was a servant of God. Clergy bolstered their homilies with references to Roosevelt's faith, proclaiming that it was the foundation for his political convictions. In a simple eulogy, Episcopal priest Leighton Parks said that Roosevelt combined "scripture with politics." Others dwelled further on his religiosity, as when Presbyterian Rev. William Henry Huber compared Roosevelt to Jesus Christ, his philosophy to the Golden Rule, and his moral compass to the Bible. Rev. William E. Barton of the First Church of Oak Park chose a secular interpretation, saying that Roosevelt "was never so happy and never so effective as when he was able to define his issues in terms of right and wrong, and then preach the gospel of the right as he saw it."[34]

Americanism, the cowboy myth, progressivism, conservationism, the man of letters, and the preacher of righteousness themes became the memorial taxonomy for classifying Roosevelt. On a national day of mourning observed on the Sunday one month after Roosevelt's death, eulogies across the country drew together these interrelated themes. Ministers and priests restaked claims to Roosevelt's spiritual legacy and invited prominent parish members to convey personal memories that focused on the preacher-of-righteousness theme.[35] Meanwhile, state legislatures heard speeches admiring Roosevelt's progressivism, his role in transforming American politics, and his Americanism.[36] At the Century Association, a private and elite New York City social club dedicated to the arts, former secretary of state Elihu Root remembered Roosevelt as a tender friend who loved literature and history. Rough Rider veterans met and celebrated TR's cowboy credentials, his triumph in Cuba, and the warrior spirit. Overseas, the archdeacon of Westminster Abbey demonstrated TR's global legacy by displacing the choral ritual of evensong for the first time in the church's history.[37]

Commemorations combined in an official crescendo when Sen. Henry Cabot Lodge, a close personal friend and political ally of Roosevelt, delivered the official state eulogy. At a joint session of Congress, swollen beyond capacity with attendees from the Supreme Court, the executive branch, and hundreds of foreign dignitaries, the senator soberly recounted his friend's influence on American society. Throngs of sympathizers had turned out to bid farewell to the popular president, and Lodge insisted that the crowd give "serious consideration" to Roosevelt's unusual personality: "What a man was is ever more important than what he did, it is upon what he was that all his achievement depends and his value and meaning to fellow man must rest." Over the course of his speech, Lodge recited the themes already enunciated by others in a manner that would fasten them in the public consciousness: "There was no hour down to the end when he would not turn aside from everything to preach the doctrine of Americanism . . . in the Spanish War or on the plains among the cowboys, he was always vivid . . . Roosevelt was always advancing, always struggling to make things better, to carry some much needed reform . . . The early love of natural history which never abated had developed into a passion for hunting and for life in the open . . . Moreover, he always looked for an ethical question." Reciting the themes, Lodge offered them as the ultimate meaning of Roosevelt's life. In conclusion he pleaded for Americans to repeat them often, so that "when the future historian traces Theodore Roosevelt's extraordinary career he will find these embodied ideas planted like milestones along the road over which he marched."[38]

To assist this pursuit, memorial associations organized in the days after Roosevelt's death, even before Lodge's speech. A group of New York City's most influential socialites called on the nation's women to propose or design a fitting memorial, and the response revealed a wide range of ideas. Some suggested an annual holiday celebrated on Roosevelt's birthday; others called for scholarships to enable young people to study a variety of subjects that reflected the primary themes of his legacy. Further ideas included a community education center to teach Rooseveltian values or a dedicated public space to teach Americanism. Schemes for monuments outnumbered all others. The most popular proposal was a statue of Roosevelt to be erected in Central Park, a recommendation that gathered momentum quickly among the wealthy women who lived along the park's boundaries.

An investigating committee, comprised of a small contingent of the New York social set, considered the feasibility of the proposals. Despite the demand for a Central Park statue, the all-female group determined it "too great an undertaking for women" because it required extensive political lobbying. Instead, the committee wanted to reconstruct Roosevelt's birthplace at 28 East 20th Street in the Flatiron District of Manhattan, a task less politically challenging but logistically impractical. It obliged them to raze a commercial property that occupied the site before undertaking the construction of a replica antebellum brownstone.[39] Notwithstanding the extensive project management required, the women settled on the plan and purchased an option on the property which restricted its acquisition by other buyers. Then, the women hastily incorporated as the Woman's Roosevelt Memorial Association (WRMA).[40]

The decision to register as a New York corporation reflected the homogenous demographics of the WRMA executive. Memorial ideas came from every part of the country, but the association's forty directors hailed from New York City, and each came from a wealthy background.[41] Among the Vanderbilts and Whitneys, the association also counted eminent personalities like Louise Wood, wife of Republican presidential hopeful Leonard Wood, and Martha Bacon, wife of the former secretary of state Robert Bacon. While its leadership was solidly New York, however, the WRMA was an influential network that, as one activist said, "could not be kept local." Within months of the establishment of a national office, branches opened in two dozen states, and expatriates organized chapters in such places as Cuba, Puerto Rico, the Philippines, and Panama. The pace of recruitment intensified in the months following Roosevelt's death, and the association took advantage of public sympathy to collect donations.[42]

Independent of the women, a group of men simultaneously organized a commemorative campaign. Gathering in Chicago three days after Roosevelt's death, the men organized a nonpartisan national association called the Roosevelt Memorial Committee. They secured a salubrious headquarters in the plush executive library of the Metropolitan Life building in midtown Manhattan, and, like the WRMA, the membership represented society's upper crust. In short order they filed for federal incorporation as the Roosevelt Memorial Association (RMA), received a congressional charter, and named mining magnate and Republican fundraiser William Boyce Thompson as chairman. The members assumed Thompson's experience with nongovernment organizations like the American Red Cross would help the association build a sustainable campaign.[43]

The executive committee of the RMA held its first meeting on March 24, 1919, and, to keep pace with the WRMA, turned its attention to commemoration schemes. Hermann Hagedorn, a writer and biographer who befriended Roosevelt long after he left the White House, used the first meeting to present an array of proposals collected from correspondents not affiliated with the RMA. The association had received hundreds of suggestions, including ones for a Roosevelt national holiday, memorial trees, a national highway, national and local parks, a hunting reserve, clubs, museums, hospitals, children's homes, monuments, agricultural endowments, educational scholarships, an American cemetery in France, and a foundation for teaching American values. Hagedorn told the assembled committee members that the majority of correspondents favored Americanization projects, particularly the establishment of a foundation for teaching American values.[44] Not without bias, Hagedorn personally called for settlement houses in major cities to teach American history and literature, provide legal aid for the foreign born, and assist the assimilation of non-Americans. Underlying the Americanization plan was a set of prejudiced assumptions that immigrants would become socialists, anarchists, or antidemocratic rabble-rousers if not educated in American traditions.

Despite the scheme's apparent popularity, the RMA executive rejected Hagedorn's proposal, a decision that owed much to Elihu Root's opposition. Root had served as secretary of war and secretary of state in Roosevelt's cabinet and held the de facto status of club dean among RMA trustees. In a poignant speech at the first meeting, he steered the association away from memorials that reflected contemporary politics:

> The needs of today have disappeared tomorrow. A memorial should be for all time to come. Each development of character and interest in that many-sided man may furnish memories to us and incentives to enterprise and devotion for the public good, but no one of them can be an adequate memorial of the man. In all projects of utility, even at the beginning, the useful purpose tends to attract and concentrate the attention of mankind, and as the years pass more and more the name that is attached to the institution or the enterprise grows dim, and the purpose becomes all in the minds of men. I think there is no way in which an institution of charity or education or usefulness can be made a memorial to a man, except that the man himself founds it.[45]

Root insisted that public art, with its capacity to be interpreted, was the only tribute capable of transcending generational divides. Artistic representation would make Roosevelt comprehensible in future contexts, whereas political projects would fix him to a particular era.

Root persuaded RMA trustees. He could not, however, influence the activities of the WRMA. The women adopted the Americanism theme and anticipated that the reconstructed birthplace would become a center for patriotic education, a plan that closely resembled Hagedorn's proposal for an Americanization foundation. The decision drove a wedge between the associations and particularly annoyed Root, as did the WRMA's decision to resurrect a long-destroyed house and present it as Roosevelt's Mount Vernon. Roosevelt's homestead was located in Long Island, at Sagamore

Hill, and while the Roosevelt family still lived there, Root expected the house would eventually fall into the public domain and become a fitting memorial. For many RMA trustees, a replica Manhattan brownstone housing a political message seemed entirely inappropriate.

The divergent approaches to commemoration bred friction, but the men and women grew especially estranged over fundraising. The WRMA's construction expenses for the replica brownstone ran to nearly $1 million, excluding the extensive price tag to duplicate the antebellum decor and furnishings. Realizing that the deep pockets of the city's elite could not alone finance the project, the women instigated a publicity drive. Trustees borrowed from philanthropic experience gained during World War I, a period that transformed the concept of charitable giving and the way Americans considered community activism. The establishment of community chests and welfare councils familiarized Americans with fundraising, as did the growth of nongovernmental organizations that introduced new schemes of public appeal. One such innovation relied on shifting from national drives to provincial campaigns by setting a donation quota or collection goals for local chapters. During the war, the Red Cross and YMCA had successfully employed quota campaigns, and, after the war, private organizations including colleges, churches, the Boy and Girl Scouts, and the American Federation of the Blind adopted quotas with similar success. Rudimentary as the tactic was, it revolutionized charitable giving and produced results, instilling local responsibility and ownership by drawing on the culture of community empowerment that fostered movements like rationing and victory gardens.[46]

At first, the WRMA attempted to arbitrarily introduce collection quotas, relying on the experience of their members rather than external experts. They established a publicity committee and a state organizing team. Results were mixed. Kentucky was the first to organize a WRMA chapter and returned nearly $7,000 before the summer. By autumn, eighteen states and overseas committees in Cuba, Argentina, China, London, Puerto Rico, and the Philippines introduced quotas.

The first wave of contributions subsided in the summer of 1919 as Roosevelt's death ebbed from public consciousness, leading the WRMA in September to hire public relations expert Ivy Lee to refresh the drive. Lee, often described as the founder of modern marketing, was an appealing hire for the women because he did not demand a percentage of their funds, only a set fee and expenses. Other firms asked for 3 to 8 percent as compensation. Lee had earned distinction working with the Red Cross,

Princeton University, and the Young Women's Christian Association, and he brought a new style and professionalism to the WRMA. Under his direction, the association "planted" assistants at rallies to "arouse the meeting" and kick-started pledge drives in states where publicity flailed. He organized for hotels and department stores to host subscription desks, and he produced new publicity literature aimed to lure wealthy bankers and patrician families outside New York City. By the end of the year, the WRMA's treasurer announced over $100,000 in donations, half of which had come after Lee started.[47]

The men invested even more in publicity. RMA chairman Thompson appointed professional consultants Charles Sumner Ward and Harvey J. Hill to build the association's financial reserves as soon as the ink on the congressional charter dried. Ward and Hill brought extensive experience working with the Red Cross, the YMCA, and the US Food Administration, but Thompson also hired Arnauld C. Marts, a former vice president of Standard Life Insurance and church fundraiser, to direct the campaign on a full-time basis. Marts co-opted two publicity advisors from nongovernmental charities to execute the campaign, rounding off a highly trained and competent team of promoters that significantly outnumbered the WRMA's operations. The men concocted four aims: first, "invite citizens of financial means" to contribute; second, create a membership scheme with incentives; third, launch an executive publicity committee to promote fundraising activities; and fourth, encourage regional activity by imposing fundraising quotas. The PR team quickly filled the RMA's social calendar with events at Oyster Bay and Carnegie Hall, as well as a pledge week that coincided with Roosevelt's birthday.

In the first month of fundraising, Marts announced the publicity campaign's overwhelming success. Forty-eight states organized committees led by distinguished chairmen. Nearly thirty cities did the same, and the RMA secured cooperation from the governments of at least three European countries.[48] Despite organizing in similar fashion, the size of the men's campaign exceeded the women's, and, consequently, they collected considerably more—$1.5 million in their first year. The RMA did not split the market on charitable giving; they commandeered it. Greater purchasing power gave the men an advantage, and they produced glossy magazines and attracted famous speakers to grand events.[49]

It was a man's world, WRMA trustees complained. Many were the wives of wealthy men, and while they requested donations from their husbands, the very same men donated more generously to the RMA.

Although women would vote nationwide for the first time in 1920, the WRMA counted no secretaries of state or congressional representatives on their executive. Leading periodicals favored the men, providing the RMA with full-page advertisements strategically placed at the front of magazines, while the women's ads, always of reduced size, went to the back. Unquestionably, a gender bias existed that explains, in part, the disparity between the associations. The funding gap also stemmed from their memorial plans. The men worked exclusively on fundraising in the first few years, whereas the women fixed on an established memorial objective. The WRMA aimed for $1 million in funds and focused their attention on replicating Roosevelt's birthplace, while the men vaguely aspired to build an artistic national monument of undetermined proportions. In the summer of 1919, the RMA set its fundraising target at $10 million, with half of that amount earmarked for building a "monumental memorial" in Washington, DC, and half for establishing a permanent Roosevelt foundation and a memorial park at Oyster Bay.

By the end of 1919, it became evident to both groups that public generosity was reaching its limit. Day by day, public recollections of Roosevelt receded, and, as the attention naturally waned, memorial associations struggled to generate contributions. The women collected less than 15 percent of the necessary donations needed to rebuild the birthplace, and the men revised their fundraising targets by half. On certain days, public interest renewed somewhat. Roosevelt's birthday (October 27) and the anniversary of his death (January 6) generated awareness, if only fleetingly, and the memorial associations organized events to capitalize on those moments. In a rare act of collaboration, the associations worked together to finance a week of birthday celebrations in 1919 and observance of the anniversary day of Roosevelt's death in 1920. The occasions proved anomalous. The RMA made a half-hearted inroad at rapprochement with the WRMA, proposing the associations merge in the summer of 1919, but the women declined. A clear division existed on the matter of commemorative themes—specifically, the RMA's reluctance to focus on Roosevelt's Americanism.[50] One of the WRMA vice presidents said of her male equivalents that they "so lean[ed] towards socialism" that the two associations could never cooperate entirely, an insult the men received in the manner it was intended. The remark permanently marred the RMA's opinion of their female counterparts.[51]

Although the memorial associations clashed over how to portray Roosevelt, they agreed that visual culture would play an important part in constructing the image. From the outset of their campaigns, the WRMA and RMA used motion pictures to stimulate public interest and inspire contributions. The women included an auditorium for screening movies in the design of the birthplace, and the men ambitiously proposed producing a series of short "two-reel" movies.

The greatest champion of using the motion picture medium to commemorate Roosevelt was Hermann Hagedorn. The son of German immigrants who fled Europe in the mid-nineteenth century, Hagedorn regarded mass-media literature as the force behind the public uprisings that sparked the 1848 revolutions and compelled political change in Europe. As a young novelist during World War I, he harnessed the power of mass-media literature to promote Americanism and, in 1916, cofounded the "Vigilantes," a short-lived poetry syndicate that published pro-Allied propaganda. The Vigilantes worshiped Roosevelt as a heroic patriot, and, in return, the former president endorsed the literary circle and began a cordial relationship with Hagedorn. In 1918, Hagedorn published his first book-length tribute to Roosevelt, a biography for juvenile audiences called *The Boys' Life of Theodore Roosevelt,* based on personal letters and writings held at Sagamore Hill. It mawkishly told of TR's triumph over asthma, his heroics up San Juan Heights, his hunting prowess, and his political prescience. "He had something of the prophet Ezekiel in him," Hagedorn wrote, pitching Roosevelt as a man of "the Heroic Line" with characteristics of literary, mythical, and historical warriors, "something of Natty Bumppo, something of Hildebrand . . . something of Olaf the sea-king, something of Cromwell, something of Charlemagne." Worshiping Roosevelt as a friend and chronicler, Hagedorn obsessed that one "cannot explain him any more than you can explain electricity or falling in love."[52]

After Roosevelt died, Hagedorn lobbied RMA trustees to invest in the production of memorial films and personally took up the task of directing a short documentary of Roosevelt's life in the Dakota Badlands. Originally, the novelist had planned to shoot in Oyster Bay and interview family and friends on Long Island, but after giving the project more thought, he chose the western landscape of North Dakota. The setting served two purposes: first, it coincided with Hagedorn's research for a biography on Roosevelt's time as a rancher; second, the Badlands allowed him to present Roosevelt as a rugged American cowboy, extending the Americanism legacy without the disapproval of hesitant RMA trustees like Elihu Root.[53]

The movie, a two-reel, thirty-minute silent film called *Through the*

Roosevelt Country with Roosevelt's Friends, reached small-town theaters
and select audiences in the last months of 1919. It provided a virtual tour
of Medora, the bucolic one-horse town in western North Dakota where Roosevelt lived in the 1880s. In the film, the town's residents, many of whom
knew Roosevelt, mingled inaudibly amid the director's sweeping shots
of the barren plains, bucking broncos, and grazing bison. Hagedorn's
Medora appeared as the stereotypical Wild West, with desolate scenery
designed to mesmerize unfamiliar audiences and conjure up a bygone
era.[54] The portraits of hardy ranchers civilizing the foreboding "waste
spaces" of the frontier evoked Frederick Jackson Turner's thesis and
reinforced the portrait of Roosevelt as an American cowboy. Hagedorn's
interviews cast Roosevelt as a tough, common man who "sat in the sad-
dle forty-eight hours" and went "hungry for longer than that." Narrated
frames interspersed with the silent cinematic landscape emphasized,
indeed greatly exaggerated, Roosevelt's place on the frontier. Hagedorn
claimed that TR "won the fight for law and order and by his example the
whole northwest became law abiding."[55]

   Through the Roosevelt Country was not the only film to promote Roosevelt's Americanism. McClure's Productions, a media venture of the
McClure Publishing Company, cemented Roosevelt's heroic image in a
feature-length biopic. Frederick L. Collins, managing director of Mc-
Clure's, had invested heavily in the nascent film industry and produced
several films from 1912 to 1919, most of which failed to make a return.
Collins hoped that Roosevelt's popularity would reverse the studio's fortunes and, in the final year of the former president's life, convinced him
to sign a film contract, share biographical details with screenwriters, and
exclusively promote the production. Roosevelt demanded the right to
amend the final cuts before distribution, a condition that demonstrated
his awareness of film's ability to shape public impressions.

   Collins intended to focus on Roosevelt's political opposition to Wilson
during World War I, as well as to celebrate his son's military service in the
war. He originally called the film *The Fighting Roosevelts* and designed
posters with the faces of each "fighting Roosevelt" set against blue stars.
Quentin, who perished in battle, was distinguished with a gold star. After TR's death, Collins opted to change the movie's title to *Our Teddy* to
reflect the national grief, and he marketed it as a tribute to TR's patriotism. Screenwriters Charles Hanson Towne and Porter Emerson Browne,
admirers of Roosevelt's Americanism, wrote a script that emphasized his
dedication to that idea.

The sixty-minute film begins with a young, sickly, asthmatic Roosevelt who reconditions himself through sheer will into a tough cowboy, serving in the cavalry, charging up San Juan Heights, and rising through the political ranks as a gritty reformer. The final twenty minutes concentrate on Roosevelt's post-presidential years, his unsuccessful attempt to enlist in the Great War, and his sons' service at the front. Director William Nigh enlisted British stage actor E. J. Ratcliffe, a performer known for dramatic flair, to portray Roosevelt. The silent movies of the early film era obscured Ratcliffe's cockney accent, helping to preserve the image of Roosevelt's Americanism. Critics deemed *Our Teddy* "thoroughly characteristic of the patriotic and noble-hearted Roosevelt," and thought that the film demonstrated his cowboy spirit and political dexterity.[56] Although the producers contended that the film made "no attempt at analysis or delineation of character," *Our Teddy* unquestionably portrayed an image of Roosevelt akin to that in the prevailing tributes that emphasized his nationalism.[57] The film omitted elements of Roosevelt's life that complicated the heroic image, excluding references to his wealthy Knickerbocker family and entirely overlooking the persistence of his asthma. To become "our Teddy," Roosevelt was shown as having a high degree of self-sufficiency and was divested of any shortcomings. Towne and Browne scripted the film in the same way other memorializers aimed to enshrine Roosevelt's legacy. Although *Our Teddy* earned widespread praise and attention, it failed to resurrect McClure's Productions. The studio produced only two more movies before permanently ceasing operations.

The new and exciting medium of film provided but one means of visual commemoration. Memorializers also devised grand public exhibitions, perhaps the most notable of which opened at Columbia University's Avery Hall on May 10, 1919, and closed with the college's commencement ceremonies in early June. Designed by Hagedorn and the RMA, the exhibition brought together a variety of artwork, costumes, mementos, and historic objects, including letters to and from Roosevelt, trophies from hunting trips, portraits, sculpture, and literary works.[58] The foremost attraction was Roosevelt's ranch outfit and cowboy relics, another testament to the public interest in the mythical cowboy. Less appealing was James Earle Fraser's death mask, which continued to confound observers' sense of the departed man.

Frank Owen Payne's review of the exhibition condemned some objects as mediocre, but he also identified "one or two others which deserve more than a passing mention."[59] His otherwise tepid appraisal of the exhibition singled out Frederick MacMonnies's sculpture of Roosevelt on horseback and J. Massey Rhind's stately bust, significant because they contributed to an image of Roosevelt as "the most extraordinary of all American citizens." Nicholas Murray Butler, president of Columbia University, helped conceive the exhibition as such a tribute, an initiative that complemented Columbia's Center for Americanization that opened in 1918. The exhibition simultaneously served Butler's personal ambitions, which included the presidential nomination of the Republican Party in 1920. His platform rested almost solely on advocating Americanism, and Hagedorn was only too pleased to assist. He endorsed Butler, penned a short biography of Roosevelt that emphasized his patriotism, and made the pamphlet freely available to visitors at the exhibition.[60]

Despite Butler and Hagedorn's efforts, Americanism did not dominate the show. The artwork and material culture revealed "a versatile character," and artists and audiences approached Roosevelt from a variety of perspectives. "What appears to be the most striking characteristic to one artist," Frank Owen Payne judged, "may be ignored by another who will lay special stress upon an entirely different trait." The *New York Tribune* called the show a parade of "personal souvenirs" donated by old friends and associates to honor Roosevelt's life in countless ways. "The occasion is full of suggestion [and] invites reflection."[61] Roosevelt's distinctive many-sidedness precluded any single aspect of his life from dominating the exhibition as a whole, and despite the curatorial design, numerous friends and family found alternative aspects of Roosevelt more captivating than his Americanism.

The first year of tribute closed with a week-long celebration of Roosevelt's birthday. The RMA estimated that the number of public gatherings held during the week reached more than 350,000. In California, the associations distributed memorial propaganda to nearly every public school in the state; in Minnesota, Roosevelt devotees organized between five and six hundred autumn fêtes; in Ohio, memorializers screened motion pictures; and on Boston Common a marine band played all week while meetings and speeches paid respect.[62] The scale of the festivities was remarkable. A variety of commemorative campaigns, public exhibitions, and movies cast Roosevelt in multiple roles—as the quintessential American citizen, prototypical cowboy, progressive politician, enthusiastic conservationist, man of letters, and preacher of righteousness. These roles, or themes, were not mutually exclusive. Memorials might lay stress on one theme at the expense of another, but the composite depiction included all strands.

The immediate shock of Roosevelt's death also produced a single, celebratory tone. The atmosphere of mourning allowed him to escape criticism, and tributes of all sorts overlooked undesirable characteristics in favor of pleasant remembrances, effectively canonizing Roosevelt and adding him to the pantheon of great Americans.

CHAPTER TWO

PROMETHEUS UNBOUND

During Roosevelt's presidency, impulses to lionize or pillory him oc-curred in equal measure. Biographies particularly swung between these poles. One editorialist wrote that after President McKinley succumbed to his assassin's bullet, the newspaper biographies depicted Roosevelt as a president who "would shoot the lights out and live on top of Washington's monument, letting himself down by a lasso to shake hands with the people." Before long, that impression shifted, giving way to a mythology that "he was never born. His mother found him one day with his gun in his hand charging barefoot through the cactus bed and yelling for more thorns." In actuality, the editorialist concluded, the true portrait was somewhere in between: "Teddy is alright. He will make as good a president as 9,000,000 other men in the United States will make . . . We get disgusted, not at him, but at the fool newspapers who . . . try to make a little god out of a good enough common man."[1]

Biographers in the 1920s did not take such a measured view. They dispensed with negative impressions and deified Roosevelt as the greatest figure of his generation. The biographer who made the nearest compari-son to godliness, William Roscoe Thayer, canonized Roosevelt, comparing him to Prometheus, the tortured Greek demigod who disobeyed Zeus by bringing fire to mankind. For his transgression the gods sentenced Pro-metheus to endless torment, chained to a rock where an eagle fed daily on his liver. In Thayer's assessment, Prometheus symbolized Roosevelt's nonconformity, a trademark he honed during the Taft and Wilson presi-dencies. For his punishment, the Republican Party and President Wilson ostracized Roosevelt in various political maneuvers. Death, Thayer wrote, "unbound Prometheus" and elevated him to a timeless being whose "blem-ishes due to misunderstanding" fade away. The biographer predicted, "the world will see him as he was" and come to "appreciate him more and more."[2] For more than a decade, that premonition proved true.

The deification of Roosevelt coincided with a revolution in biographical writing. In the early twentieth century, biography went from a practice of learned intellectuals trained in the skill of expository writing to an amateur hobby of nonliterary professionals seeking to express personal narratives through historic characters. Scientists, artists, engineers, and clergy wrote popular profiles during the interwar years, and while some fashioned eloquent and meaningful investigations, others published watery drivel. The "old ignominy," British literary critic Edmund Gosse warned, "seems to be that no one is too great a fool, or too complete an amateur, or too thoroughly ignorant of composition to undertake 'the life' of an eminent person," and if readers did not resist such texts, biography would become "a dust-heap which no one will dare to disturb, a vast receptacle of useless matter irredeemably devoted to oblivion."[3] As Gosse pointed out, poor biographies sacrifice historical context in their effort to detail the personality of an individual. At worst, this sort of storytelling results in hagiography, a narrative that lacks critical analysis and opts for an overly reverential depiction. The best biographies extol "not the complete person or the complete society," historian Oscar Handlin maintains, "but the point at which the two interact." Or, as biographer David Nasaw explains, "it is the task of the biographer to disentangle, to prioritize, to attempt to understand how, in a given time and place, a 'self' is organized and performed."[4]

The first Roosevelt biographies typically tended more toward hagiography rather than the professional practice Handlin and Nasaw describe. By the end of 1919 more than a dozen dueling Roosevelt biographies appeared in bookstores, and by the end of the 1920s the total climbed to nearly eighty. Each new account glorified Roosevelt, and all too often they assessed him independent of his context, but despite their scholarly shortcomings, they played an important role in shaping his legacy. Their abundance demonstrated the demand for literary portraits of Roosevelt, a circumstance that allowed publishers to release multiple interpretive accounts, confident they would sell. Publishing houses gave Roosevelt's biographers carte blanche to compose personalized sketches and subjectively portrayed characterizations.

In addition to the "unofficial" biographies, Roosevelt handpicked Joseph Bucklin Bishop to write his official life story, a decision that, to a certain extent, reflected the trend toward nonliterary raconteurs. Bishop worked as a reporter at the *New York Tribune* and *New York Evening Post* until Roosevelt appointed him executive secretary of the Isthmian Canal

Commission, managing the day-to-day operations of the Panama Canal Zone. Despite being an investigative journalist by trade and an experienced writer, Bishop never wrote a book until 1913. While in Panama he resolved to do so, and less than a year before he returned to the United States, he published *The Panama Gateway*, based on his experiences on the isthmus. Acclaimed as an authoritative and comprehensive account of the remarkable engineering feat, Bishop's book won him distinction as a masterful author capable of avoiding partisan politics or dumbing down a complex subject. The praise led him to believe he could transition from working as a government administrator to being a biographer.[5]

The timing was fortuitous. Bishop's first book arrived just as Roosevelt returned from Brazil, where he had explored the River of Doubt. The death-defying adventure in South America prompted the former president to consider his legacy, and, at this contemplative moment, the idea of an official biography took root. "I know what I wish you would do," Roosevelt told Bishop: "Write the story of my public life. You know it almost as well as I know it myself." The former president promised to turn over his private correspondence for analysis, and two years later he fulfilled that pledge by donating a cache of documents to the Library of Congress.[6] Bishop alone had access.

Not until the autumn of 1918 did Bishop avail himself of the archive, and work on the first chapters went slowly. "The material was virtually inexhaustible," he lamented. Sifting through the presidential years would take a particularly long time. Nevertheless, he managed to draft a considerable portion of the book before Roosevelt died, making it nearly halfway through chronicling his presidency. The pace owed much to Roosevelt's assistance. When Bishop slowed or found historical episodes complicated, he simply contacted the protagonist to fill in any blanks, and Roosevelt obliged. After Roosevelt's death, however, Bishop was without his muse. He began to search through the storage space at Sagamore Hill for revealing documents, a quest that compounded his workload when he uncovered nearly double the number of letters originally donated to the Library of Congress.[7]

While the world waited for Bishop's official biography, competing writers without access to Roosevelt's private papers satisfied the public appetite with accounts that relied on personal recollections or interviews. Lawrence Abbott, the editor of *Outlook* magazine, a weekly that had employed Roosevelt as a correspondent after the 1912 election, published his *Impressions of Theodore Roosevelt*, a 300-page book that relied on Abbott's personal memories. It detailed his friendship with TR, beginning with their acquaintance in the New York legislature before jumping to Roosevelt's tenure at the New York City police commissioner's office and their mutual interest in Roosevelt's 1909 African safari. Abbott's *Impressions* ignored broad periods of Roosevelt's life when the two men did not collaborate, skimming along at such a pace as to obscure significant episodes. Most notably, the section on the presidential years lacked insight.[8]

Other biographers succumbed to the same style. Pastor of New York's Park Avenue Methodist Church Ferdinand Iglehart published *The Man as I Knew Him,* emphasizing the "moral courage" and Christian values of Roosevelt, and tracing his progressive politics to a faith in God. "Everybody knows that Theodore Roosevelt was intensely religious," Iglehart maintained: "he did not hesitate, on all proper occasions, to announce publicly his faith in the fundamental doctrines of Christianity."[9] Iglehart identified faith as a common denominator, a point at which his life intersected with Roosevelt's. Likewise, Roosevelt's trekking guide William Sewall penned a biography that underscored TR's relationship with the outdoors and recounted their shared experiences hiking through the Maine forests and riding in the Dakota Badlands. His account endowed Roosevelt with remarkable fortitude, alleging he could withstand regular exposure to heat up to 125°F in the summer and freezing temperatures of -65°F in the winter. For Sewall, Roosevelt's political success derived from his ability to "put into practice the principles he had expressed when he was a boy in Maine and when he was a young man in Dakota."[10] Whether written by the trail guide, the pastor, or the journalist, these personalized biographies favored individual legacy themes that, not coincidentally, provided a unique marketing angle for publishers. Only collectively did they illustrate the polygonal image of Roosevelt.

In addition to these personalized hagiographies, three ostensibly more objective books preceded the publication of Bishop's official biography—trade writer Frederick Drinker's *Theodore Roosevelt: His Life and Work,* Dean of the University of Pennsylvania Law School William Draper Lewis's *The Life of Theodore Roosevelt,* and professional biographer William Roscoe Thayer's *Theodore Roosevelt: An Intimate Biography.* All three "were almost uniformly bad," historian Richard Collin contends; "only Lewis's is vaguely respectable historically."[11] Each relied on Roosevelt's *Autobiography* and failed to critically question that source. Although few archival resources existed outside the impenetrable collection at the Library of Congress, each of these books alleged to be a "truthful portrayal of the life" and an "impartial, non-partisan history." In truth, they exemplify the undulating worship of Roosevelt in "one long secular sermon, delivered in ringing, oracular terms, in a kind of poetic prose, and with a singleness of purpose."[12]

The literati nearly unanimously panned the first biographies. H. L. Mencken called them "feeble, inaccurate, ignorant and preposterous," complaining that "in all of them I found vastly more gush than sense."[13] Praise for Thayer and Abbott came from the *New York Sun,* which named their biographies among the books of the year, although the newspaper's readers described them in editorials as hollow portraits.[14] Reviewers for the *Mississippi Valley Historical Review,* the forerunner to the *Journal of American History,* bemoaned that the biographies generated "a sense of disappointment." The scholarly community called for "a more comprehensive study," and Pulitzer Prize–winning historian James Ford Rhodes accused the biographers of making Roosevelt "a saint, which he was not."[15]

For the many faults of these biographies, their authors produced accounts that echoed the eulogistic context. They indulged the prevailing idolatry because to do otherwise seemed incomprehensible. The other major problem for these biographers was inadequate access to archival records. Critics could complain about the hyperbole and overstated achievements, but the embellishment was a substitute for information that simply was not available. The Roosevelt Papers at the Library of Congress remained closed, and biographers faced threats from TR's family when they proposed to publish personal letters. Roosevelt's wife Edith and eldest son Ted, who served as executors of his papers, insisted on severe restrictions and limited the publication of correspondence, including documents outside the Library of Congress collection. The legal basis for such stringent control was questionable, but TR's old friends did not want to strain relationships with the family. When Lawrence Abbott applied to Edith to publish letters in his possession, she at first refused. Gradually, she softened her stance, permitting him to include the letters only if published in their entirety, so as not to misrepresent her husband. Once Abbott convinced her that his edits enhanced TR's reputation, she acquiesced.[16]

Edith and Ted's strict interpretation of copyright even extended to family. TR's sister Corinne published personal recollections of her brother in 1924, using letters in her possession. Ted called her decision "audacious" and a "thoroughly irritating" act of insubordination.[17] Baffled by the restrictions, Corinne told friends, "It's all a mystery to me. I feel there must be some screw loose about the whole thing." She insisted that no one, "Mrs. Roosevelt or anyone else," could stop her or other biographers from "quoting, in a sketch, from personal letters received."[18] In Corinne's case, Edith and Ted did not pursue legal action, but they threatened others with that recourse. Thayer felt uncomfortable disobeying the Roosevelt family's wishes but persistently and politely petitioned Edith to allow him to quote from letters he had received. Yet, no matter how graciously he pleaded for access to the Library of Congress papers, Edith and Ted refused, rigidly obeying TR's wishes.

Locking researchers out of the archives bred animosity, and the choice of Bishop as the official biographer amplified the frustration of his rivals. Thayer particularly criticized the decision, in some degree out of jealousy. He privately grumbled that Bishop "seemed overwhelmed by his colossal task" and questioned his decision to "learn the difficult and elusive art of biography" at the age of seventy-one. Thayer received letters of sympathy from Roosevelt's friends. Abbott and Hagedorn believed that he deserved the job, that only he possessed the skills and flair to produce an enduring account. Hagedorn predicted sarcastically, "Bishop's book will undoubtedly contain material of the greatest interest, but I strongly suspect that the presentation of this material will not be such as to rob anybody of his accustomed pre-midnight slumber."[19] When asked his choice of biographer, Thayer proposed Sen. Henry Cabot Lodge, whose relationship with Roosevelt had begun in the 1880s with his political career in the New York Assembly. Lodge also had written widely admired biographies of Alexander Hamilton, George Washington, and Daniel Webster. Thayer believed him the natural choice, but as the chair of the Senate Foreign Relations Committee and the man responsible for steering the Treaty of Versailles through the ratification process, Lodge could not devote time to the chore of another biography and refused.[20]

Notwithstanding the contempt and jealousy of his peers, Bishop published *Theodore Roosevelt and His Time* in 1920 to a mixed chorus of praise and criticism. Thayer predictably found fault. "Whatever importance attaches" to the book, he proclaimed, came as a result of it being "the 'official biography' of a great man." He remarked that "often 'official' lives are not finally accepted as the true lives" and refused to believe that "this one will be." He contended grudgingly that Bishop's greatest contribution was to publish many of Roosevelt's letters, and "it must always remain the first source or quarry from which readers and later historians will draw." Despite this acknowledgment, Thayer took aim at the way Bishop sifted through the material at the Library of Congress. There seemed too little correspondence, especially given the breadth of Roosevelt's communication with leading lights of his day.[21] Other reviewers also picked up on this deficiency. "It is unfortunate that Mr. Bishop was not a trained historian," one writer groused: "Of all the letters written" in Roosevelt's early career, "Mr. Bishop has given us extracts from only eight, although he finds space to quote from newspapers more than thirty times."[22] Detractors scrutinized the way *Theodore Roosevelt and His Time* presented the correspondence, blaming Bishop for dropping letters into the text without considering the wider historical frame in which they were written. Thayer declared Bishop an amateur, "not having either by nature or by training a biographer's endowment," and he complained that the biography "raises no edifice, but leaves his material heaped up in separate blocks awaiting the coming of a builder."[23] In his attempt to let Roosevelt's letters speak for the man, Bishop had separated the subject from his environment, blurring the circumstances surrounding TR's life. Fellow biographer Nathaniel Stephenson wittily roasted Bishop, saying his book should be renamed *The Concealment of Theodore Roosevelt,* and William Allen White wrote Ted that the biography "embalmed" TR in a portrait of a "middle-aged, middle-classed gentleman who had a rather remote and passionless interest in the passing show."[24]

On the other hand, numerous reviews hailed the work as praiseworthy. Lodge succinctly called it "very admirable." The critics at the *New York Tribune* stated that "Mr. Bishop deserves high praise," and Roosevelt's immediate family embraced the book as a "marvel." Edith complimented it as thoroughly gratifying. "I do not wish to flatter, but who else could have done it?" she wrote Bishop.[25] The popular consensus settled somewhere between the elation of the Roosevelt family and Bishop's harshest critics. Most readers assented to Thayer's viewpoint, believing the book would have inestimable value for historians, even if it failed to set the literary world aflame.

None of the early biographies, Bishop's included, impartially examined Roosevelt. Thayer even criticized his own book, believing that readers would disapprove in the future, deeming it "not a biography but a paean."[26] Lord Charnwood, the British biographer of Lincoln, admitted "avowing a hero worship of long standing" before embarking on his Roosevelt biography. James Amos, Roosevelt's personal servant who tended him until death, wrote a memoir of a man he considered more than an employer, "my dear friend to whom I could go always with my most personal and private troubles." J. W. McSpadden "tried to avoid hero worship" in his biography, recognizing it as "a common fault of most books extant upon Roosevelt to-day." And yet he could not fail to practice it. "Those who had called him a superman were not far wrong," he declared.[27] The first literary depictions produced an "undoubtedly partisan" view that ushered in a decade of unqualified praise for Roosevelt's policies and personal convictions.[28]

The trend of bestowing unqualified praise also found its way into the era's political rhetoric. The 1920 presidential election was the first since 1880 in which Roosevelt did not run as a candidate or campaign on behalf of one. For nearly forty years he canvassed in local elections, and, had he lived, he would have influenced the Republican nomination in 1920. In fact, speculation abounded that Roosevelt intended to throw his hat into the ring for another presidential run. "It was pretty generally believed that had Father lived he would have been the nominee of the Republican Party," daughter Alice Roosevelt Longworth intimated in her memoirs.[29] Economist Raymond Robbins had alleged before Roosevelt died that Republicans would "nominate TR in 1920 by acclamation" but that former progressive Republicans, like him, would "nominate him by assault."[30] Such conjecture endures. Biographer Edmund Morris believes that the "nomination would [have been] his if he wanted it." But Roosevelt's poor health and diminishing commitment to barnstorming suggests that a run would have been unlikely and entirely hypothetical.[31] At the very least, however, we can say that Roosevelt would have wielded considerable influence in the selection of the Republican nominee.

The unpopularity of Woodrow Wilson and the political calamity that failed to ratify the Treaty of Versailles raised the prospect of a Republican landslide. With the odds in their favor, a dozen GOP contenders announced their candidacy. Some ran as favorite sons, like Massachusetts's Calvin Coolidge, New York's Nicholas Murray Butler, Illinois's Frank Lowden, and Ohio's Warren G. Harding; others like Leonard Wood, Hiram Johnson, and Herbert Hoover had nationwide name recognition. Individually, the candidates represented the party's various blocs and held remarkably diverse views on domestic and foreign policy. Other than calling themselves Republicans, they had little else in common. One thing did unite them: each invoked Theodore Roosevelt as his political idol. The three leading candidates—Maj. Gen. Leonard Wood, Illinois governor Frank Lowden, and California senator Hiram Johnson—ran competitive campaigns that eagerly recited their connection to Roosevelt and avowed their policies as Rooseveltian.[32]

The favorite for the nomination was Leonard Wood. With a popular national profile and a list of exploits as legendary as Roosevelt's, Wood captivated the early attention of Republicans. A graduate of Harvard Medical School, he had served as a medical officer on the last expedition to capture Geronimo. There, under the strain of allergic anaphylaxis, he delivered important dispatches through enemy territory and took command of a detached platoon of soldiers. His tenacity earned him the Congressional Medal of Honor and caught President Cleveland's attention. In 1895 he moved to Washington to serve as the president's personal physician; President McKinley retained him in the same capacity until 1898.[33] During his time in the McKinley White House, Wood met Roosevelt and discovered they had much in common. Both had attended Harvard and were entranced by the American frontier. Wood and Roosevelt reveled in adventure and physical feats of strength, and exuded an enthusiastic view of American nationalism. Politically they saw eye to eye, advocating US intervention in the unfolding Cuban humanitarian crisis. They believed the projection of American power in the Western Hemisphere would promote social progress, and, as war with imperial Spain neared, Roosevelt called for the establishment of a volunteer cavalry regiment. Wood was appointed colonel, and Roosevelt his lieutenant. The infamous Rough Riders played a key role in the Cuban campaign and earned both men national acclaim. McKinley promoted Wood to brigadier general and Roosevelt to colonel. After the war, Roosevelt returned to New York to run for governor, while Wood remained in Cuba as the island's military overlord until 1902.

As Roosevelt climbed the political ladder, Wood rose through the ranks to major general. When World War I broke out in Europe, they had an opportunity to join forces once again. As outspoken critics of President Wilson's neutrality policy, they spoke in favor of war preparedness, and Wood opened a civilian training corps. Atrocity stories from Europe impelled them to oppose Wilson's foreign policy, and for their insubordination the president refused them a part in the war. Roosevelt petitioned for command of a volunteer regiment, a request denied by Wilson, and Wood was ordered to remain in Kansas as a training specialist.[34]

Wood's relationship with Roosevelt prompted the political rumor mill to surmise that, had he lived, Roosevelt would have endorsed the general's campaign. That suspicion intensified when TR's immediate family backed

Wood. Alice said, "It was taken for granted that Father's family would be for General Wood. It was quite natural that we should be. Since 1897, he and Father had been friends and associates. We had a real affection for him, and moreover, a satisfying degree of confidence in his position on public questions."[35] TR's youngest sister Corinne touted Wood as her brother's living successor and seconded his nomination at the Republican National Convention. "It is not because Leonard Wood was my brother's friend that I am so strongly behind his candidacy," she told convention delegates; it was "because he is essentially the *type* of my brother."[36] Roosevelt's handpicked presidential successor, William Howard Taft, the best-placed person to recognize the process of anointing a replacement, eloquently quoted Hamlet, saying it felt as though "the funeral bake meats had furnished forth the feast for the heir."[37]

Wood's candidacy pleased conservative Republicans, but the general held little appeal among progressives. Labor unions opposed Wood because he lined up with big business and supported the relaxation of industry regulations. His campaign tried to portray the major general as the most labor-friendly candidate by emphasizing his part in a 1919 military intervention that avoided a lockout and riot. From the unions' perspective, however, the "employment of the military forces in strikes has no supporters in the ranks of workingmen," and they raised questions over a general's suitability to be chief executive. Oswald Garrison Villard, editor of the left-leaning periodical the *Nation,* described Wood as a "dogmatic military authority," an opinion held by other progressives who prompted Wood's campaign managers to urge their candidate to resign his army post, believing it would enhance his image as a common citizen. Other handlers argued that his military background distinguished him as the only candidate sufficiently experienced to take on Bolsheviks, immigrants, and radicals.[38] Ultimately, Wood decided to keep his commission, and he maintained his place in the polls, a lead that pundits believed rested largely on his relationship with Roosevelt and the support of TR's family.

Hiram Johnson, one of Wood's chief rivals for the nomination, also pinned his hopes on depicting his candidacy as an extension of Roosevelt's legacy. Johnson began his career as a California lawyer and quickly rose to fame in 1908 after successfully prosecuting San Francisco's mayor for bribery and extortion. The trial won him statewide attention as an anticorruption progressive, and less than two years later he won the California governorship with promises to take on special interests. The

California Republican Party, with Johnson at its helm, represented the most progressive policies of the day, espousing ideas that would come to embody the platform of Roosevelt's 1912 presidential campaign. Common political ambitions drew Johnson to Roosevelt, and the California governor sometimes referred to Roosevelt as a "father-confessor." Johnson seconded Roosevelt's nomination at the Republican Convention in 1912, and, when he failed to win, Johnson made an equally fierce speech in denunciation of the GOP.[39] The two formed the Progressive Party, and Johnson was nominated as the Bull Moose's vice-presidential candidate. Roosevelt carried six states, one of which was California, where Johnson's relentless canvassing helped deliver the narrowest of victories.

Johnson did not dwell on the Progressive Party's loss. His participation in the campaign propelled his reputation and marked him as a political acolyte of America's most compelling statesman, a connection that benefited him throughout his career. Progressives fled the Bull Moose Party in 1916, including Roosevelt and Johnson, who assimilated into the Republican fold. For Johnson, the transition seemed to come full circle when he ran for California's open Senate seat as a Republican. He won over 60 percent of the vote, one of the largest GOP victories that year.

Complete reconciliation proved more elusive. Johnson habitually complained about the party's conservatism and continued to push for TR's nomination for president. When Republican stalwarts successfully nominated Charles Evan Hughes, Johnson half-heartedly endorsed him. As a result, Hughes refused to campaign for Johnson, and Johnson refused to help Hughes in California. The political row likely handed Wilson a slim majority in the Golden State and denied Hughes the White House.[40]

After the 1912 and 1916 elections, Johnson found it difficult to convince the Republican faithful of his commitment to the party. "Hiram Johnson would have enjoyed the French Revolution," one Republican said; he "is not a revolutionary. But revolution has a fierce attraction for him."[41] Such sentiment dogged Johnson in the 1920 nomination contest. What sustained him was the fight against Wilson's League of Nations. Classed as an "irreconcilable," or one of the more than a dozen US senators on both sides of the aisle that refused to support the Treaty of Versailles, Johnson used the ratification as an opportunity to rebrand himself as an adversary of Wilsonianism. Giving the president the power to execute war at the behest of the League of Nations sidestepped congressional approval and defied the checks and balances of the Constitution, he argued.[42] He shadowed the president as he toured the nation in an effort to sell the

League idea to the American public, a trip that afforded Johnson the opportunity to promote his name in unfamiliar states and raised his profile in the months before the Republican primary campaign.

When the Republican nomination race began, Johnson attempted to neutralize the Roosevelt family's endorsement of Wood by publishing correspondence from Roosevelt to a Californian who purported to support Johnson. In the letter, TR wrote, "I am trying to keep in touch with Hiram Johnson, for of all the public men in this country, he is the one with whom I find myself in most complete sympathy. You are perfectly safe in following his lead."[43] Wood's spin doctors declared the 1916 note anachronistic, claiming it merely demonstrated Roosevelt's support for Johnson's Senate campaign four years earlier and not his presidential bid in 1920. The front-runner's campaign also pointed out that Roosevelt "referred to 'men in public life,' which of course, excluded Gen. Wood, who was in the army and no sense public life."[44] Johnson's attempt to summon TR's endorsement from the grave also outraged Roosevelt's family. Ted discounted the letter and, on a cross-country campaign for Wood, criticized Johnson. Corinne also reiterated her endorsement of the major general.

Yet, on the issues, Johnson made a substantiated connection to Roosevelt's legacy. At an assembly of adoring TR fans he said, "Theodore Roosevelt would oppose ratification of the League of Nations pact, were he alive," and in Minnesota he hollered at crowds, "O, if Roosevelt were only here . . . his red blooded Americanism would have made short work of the un-American thing which Mr. Wilson seeks to foist upon us." It had taken seven months, Johnson claimed, for him to finally "control his emotions sufficiently to pay tribute" to his deceased father-confessor, a moment that conveniently came during a campaign stop in Chicago. There he felt enlivened enough to declare that if "any man, I care not who he is, tries to tell the American people that Theodore Roosevelt would have favored this League of Nations, that man lies."[45]

Again, the Wood campaign rebutted Johnson, adamant that Roosevelt would not have classed himself an "irreconcilable." The public, however, remembered Roosevelt as an outspoken opponent of Wilson, with close political friends in the irreconcilable camp. The political context made Johnson's allegation plausible, at least, and Alice Roosevelt Longworth helped his cause. Although she supported Wood, her dogged activism to keep the United States out of the League of Nations and her fearless support of the irreconcilable senators gave Johnson's claim greater credibility. She even proposed that the Roosevelt family release a statement attesting her father's opposition to the League, but Edith refused to be drawn into the political maelstrom.[46] What the foreign policy issues of the 1920 campaign made clear was that Wood did not have a monopoly on Roosevelt's legacy.

Frank O. Lowden of Illinois proved equally troublesome for Wood. Elected governor in 1916, Lowden earned a reputation as an outstanding administrator, adept at political maneuvering and able to unite the broad interests of the state's Republicans. In his first year as governor, he re-organized the unwieldy state government from hundreds of agencies to nine departments, all of which answered directly to him. He instituted a budgetary system for appropriations that saved taxpayers millions and allowed him to cut taxes. These initiatives made him popular and helped make Illinois one of the best-prepared states for World War I.

Lowden was a centrist who, at first glance, appeared a member of the conservative "Old Guard" Republicans. Machine bosses supported his campaigns, and Lowden amassed an incredible fortune from wise investments in farming and his marriage to Florence Pullman, an heiress to the Pullman railway car estate. Because the Pullman Company did not employ union laborers, Lowden's reputation among working men suffered, but his affiliations with great wealth and corrupt politicians did not stop him from courting progressives. His policies, if not his as-sociations, demonstrated a reform-mindedness that progressive Illinois senator Medill McCormick declared "a truly progressive message."[47] Be-yond supporting government reform and transparent budgeting, Lowden also favored women's suffrage, shorter working days, and greater public control of utilities.

The tumultuous factions of the Republican Party made Lowden partic-ularly attractive to those who wanted to permanently mend the rift. What hindered him was his negligible relationship with Roosevelt. In 1912, he unenthusiastically supported Taft, refusing to abandon his party, but he never demonized Roosevelt for the decision to bolt and attributed the split "to a quarrel over party leadership rather than to a disagreement over issues." That distinction "drew faint applause from the Bull Moosers" and effectively kept Lowden out of the tumult.[48] In 1916, Roosevelt endorsed Lowden's candidacy for governor, and two years later he invited him to a meeting in Oyster Bay.[49] The get-together fueled speculation that Roosevelt was considering him as a vice-presidential candidate in 1920, gossip that may well have contained a germ of truth. In an intimate letter to his son, TR disclosed his great confidence in Lowden as a unifier. "If the nomination were made tomorrow, I should have to be leader, but the Germans, Sinn Fein Irish, pacifists and the like, will soon hold up their heads again and the best of them may support my principles but not me," Roosevelt wrote. "In that event, we shall be lucky if we can put some man like Lowden through."[50] Roosevelt's letter should not be read as an open endorsement, especially as his correspondence made similar comments in favor of Wood and Johnson. That aside, the mark of respect he paid Lowden—in private correspondence—demonstrates that he believed the party would be well served by the Illinois governor.

After Roosevelt's death, Lowden's campaign began to take shape. He denied any intention to run, but without TR on the stump, Lowden became his state's favorite choice. Like Johnson's campaign, Lowden unearthed a supportive 1916 letter from Roosevelt: "I earnestly hope you will now assume a position of leadership," Roosevelt told the Illinois governor; "you shall help bring the Republicans far enough forward to enable us to hold the progressives far enough back to keep a substantial alignment."[51] The letter, like the one Johnson had used, came under criticism for being taken out of context. Opposing Republican candidates, including Johnson, cried foul, and Lowden never again attempted to co-opt Roosevelt's legacy. The governor satisfied himself by quietly steering the Illinois Roosevelt Memorial Association and spoke about TR as a political hero, avoiding the intense competition for a posthumous endorsement.

At the Republican National Convention, Wood (the anointed heir), Johnson (the progressive reincarnation), and Lowden (the distant admirer) failed to win a majority of the convention's delegates, and each candidate refused to release his supporters to his rivals, leaving the party in deadlock. Ohio senator Warren G. Harding filled the vacuum in a suspenseful conclusion to the convention—an end that his campaign manager Harry Daugherty correctly predicted would finish in a smoke-filled room in the wee hours of the morning. Indeed, it was Republican Party bosses who jostled delegates into nominating Harding, and what distinguished the eventual candidate from the others was that he shared no significant personal or political connections to Roosevelt. Despite this, the Republicans actively promoted Harding as quintessentially Rooseveltian.

The Ohio senator mustered little excitement during the primary season or the convention. He "managed to pick his way warily" through the Ohio political morass, moving to the top of the state's favorite son list because competing Republicans coveted his Senate seat. When TR visited

Ohio in the autumn of 1918, Harding's competitors touted him as a vice-presidential candidate, an odd prospect because Harding and Roosevelt had famously fallen out in 1912.[52] Harding had publicly blamed Roosevelt for destabilizing the GOP that year, and at the party's 1912 convention he officially nominated Taft in an alliterative and histrionic speech: "Progression is not proclamation nor palaver. It is not pretense nor play on prejudice. It is not of personal pronouns, nor perennial pronouncement. It is not the perturbation of a people passion-wrought, nor a promise proposed. Progression is everlastingly lifting the standards that marked the end of the world's march yesterday and planting them on new and advanced heights to-day. Tested by such a standard, President Taft is the greatest progressive of the age."[53] The speech defined Harding as a conservative stalwart, a stance that became more obvious after the victory of Woodrow Wilson. Harding berated the Bull Moose as that "mad Roosevelt," impugning his loyalty and condemning him for the Republicans' defeat. Even after the political din settled, Harding seethed: "The eminent fakir can now turn to raising hell, his specialty along other lines." He called progressives "wreckers" and vowed that "Stalwart Republicans are so incensed politically that years will not reconcile them."[54]

He was wrong. It took four years for Republicans and Progressives to rejoin forces. When the next presidential campaign kicked off in 1916, Harding and Roosevelt appeared to mend their relationship. At the national convention, Harding served as chairman, gave the keynote address nominating Charles Evans Hughes, and navigated the delegation through the reconciliation process, allowing both sets ample stage. He also did his best to keep Roosevelt from being nominated. A full settlement between the men came in 1917, when Harding introduced legislation that would allow Roosevelt to raise a regiment of troops to fight in World War I. "The one man who would be able to raise these divisions alone would be Colonel Roosevelt," Harding told the Senate: "He is known in Europe as is no other American."[55] The gesture pleased Roosevelt enough to invite the senator to Oyster Bay; in Harding's recollection, "then and there we agreed to work together and we buried the past and we conferred often thereafter to the time of his death."[56]

After Roosevelt's death, Ohio Republicans began considering who to nominate. "I think very likely the death of Col. Roosevelt will somewhat change the plans of some Republicans in Ohio," Harding wrote a political ally; "we are going to be able to organize without any serious friction."[57] Roosevelt's death made invoking him easier as well. "In any appraisal Colonel Roosevelt's name will be inseparably linked with the finding of the American soul," Harding related in his eulogy. "Here was a great American and courageous American, who called to the slumbering spirit of the Republic."[58] Avoiding the acrimony of 1912, he campaigned on an Americanism platform, claiming to be a disciple of Roosevelt. He fended off Wood in Ohio's primary election by a small margin, keeping his chances of nomination alive as a compromise candidate at the convention.

When the Republican bosses chose Harding to break the deadlock, Roosevelt's close friends and family voiced their regret. Wood campaigners deemed it an affront to Roosevelt's memory, and progressive Republicans took the news worst of all. William Allen White recalled Harding's nomination as the moment "the Republican party bade farewell to the twenty years of liberalism which had grown up under the leadership of Theodore Roosevelt." White sensed that the crowd of cheering Republicans at the national convention "danced on the grave of the Colonel who had been my leader and my friend for a quarter of a century." Gifford Pinchot, conservationist, founder of the Forestry Service, and a convention delegate from Pennsylvania, pledged to oppose Harding. He called the Ohioan a "reactionary," aligned against reform, and a man "entirely unfit to be President." Kentucky progressive and newspaper editor Desha Breckinridge privately wrote that Republican regulars like Harding "hated and feared Roosevelt living" and at the convention "dishonor him dead."[59]

The intense disappointment among many Republicans led Harding and his advisors to fear that unhappiness with his nomination could trigger a schism like that of 1912. But the progressives did not bolt, chiefly because Harding worked diligently to court them. He approached Johnson to gauge his interest in the vice presidency, but well before any serious negotiation could occur, the convention nominated Calvin Coolidge by acclamation. After the convention, Harding sought out Johnson as a surrogate and entertained his isolationist positions on the League, even if he had no intention of adopting an "irreconcilable" stance. He wrote to White, imploring the editor to consider his election manifesto as that of a "rational progressive," and he urged Pinchot to content himself that a vote for him would be a protest against Wilson.[60] Eventually, Pinchot capitulated. He released a statement endorsing Harding, admitting that they had "been on opposite sides of many questions . . . But these things are past" because if the Democratic nominee won, then "the most vicious political machines in the country" would take over the White House.[61] On the other end of the Republican spectrum, the conservatives and big business interests who supported Wood easily fell in behind Harding. The *Boston Globe* argued, "The Senator from Ohio is so distinctly on the conservative side that many of the industrial centers of his own state gave primary pluralities to Gen. Wood on the ground that the Gen. was more of a liberal."[62]

Roosevelt's family also rallied for Harding. Ted met with him two weeks after the convention and issued an official endorsement. "In Senator Harding we will have," Ted testified, "a man who will represent and unite the entire party." TR's namesake lost little sleep over Wood's demise, once grousing to his brother Archie, "Confidentially, he gives me a pain."[63] Harding used Ted in the campaign to remind the wider public of his connection to TR and shared the stage with him when he officially accepted the nomination. The newspapers reported "very little evidence of Rooseveltian 'reflex' in Harding's acceptance speech," but the personal support of the Roosevelt family bolstered his image. Corinne Roosevelt Robinson, who had enthusiastically supported Wood, begged the country to rally behind the Buckeye senator and dismissed the differences once so apparent between him and her brother. Even Edith endorsed Harding. Although still grieving and not inclined to wade into political campaigns, TR's wife pronounced, one month before Election Day, that the "country's vital need is the election of the Republican candidates."[64]

With the Roosevelt family on board and the harmony of the Republican Party ensured, Harding took liberties with TR's image. His campaign biography contained an entire chapter on their relationship, claiming that after 1916 "there was perfect personal and political accord between Colonel Roosevelt and Senator Harding," and that "the family of Theodore Roosevelt regarded Harding as a friend true-blue." A vote for the Ohioan was a vote for Roosevelt, or, as the biography put it, "The spirit of Roosevelt goes marching on!" Campaign literature even touted Florence Harding and Edith Roosevelt as classic examples of the "American wife": "Like Mrs. Theodore Roosevelt, Mrs. Harding believes that her husband belongs to the public, and in order to help him in his work maintains that her duty is first to the home." The Republicans recirculated thousands of copies of Harding's eulogy of Roosevelt and added to the pamphlet Ted's official endorsement.[65] Taking advantage of new methods like motion pictures, audio recordings, and celebrity testimonials, Harding revolutionized modern presidential campaigning. He enlisted Hollywood A-listers like comedian Al Jolson, who sang a short ditty that would become the campaign's anthem:

> We think the country is ready for another Teddy.
> One who's a fighter through and through.
> We need another Lincoln to do the nation's thinking.
> And Mr. Harding we've selected you.[66]

The lyrics originated in GOP headquarters, and Jolson's act was framed by a banner that read "A Man like Teddy." Editorialist James Hollomon ridiculed the scene: "The verse is much further than the comedian imagined or intended. Harding is as much like Roosevelt as mud is like marble; as a house cat is like a panther; as a carp is like a trout; as sap pine is like hickory."[67]

Roosevelt's political legacy was further complicated when the Democrats selected Assistant Secretary of the Navy Franklin Delano Roosevelt as their vice-presidential candidate. TR's fifth cousin hailed from Hyde Park, outside Poughkeepsie in upstate New York, and his branch of the family belonged to the same wealthy social set as their Long Island relatives. "Strange how history dances around the circle," the *New York Times* reported; "a mere twenty years sees another Roosevelt from New York running for Vice-President."[68] But the Democrats' nomination of Franklin came as no coincidence, and it effected both a minor political controversy and a major family feud.

From his youth up until his venture into national politics, Franklin admired his cousin. Stories of the exuberant young Teedie building a natural history museum in his bedroom inspired Franklin to shoot birds on his estate and to consider the outdoors as a realm of wonder. News of TR's heroics at the Battle for San Juan Heights inspired Franklin's boyhood, and when he was old enough he bought a pince-nez to wear in "open emulation." When Theodore ran for governor of New York, Franklin joined the Harvard Republican Club, notwithstanding his father's life-long affiliation with the Democrats. In 1905, he married Theodore's niece, Eleanor, a marriage that brought Franklin "closer to the charmed circle" of Oyster Bay. Theodore, then president, gave away the bride and invited the newlywed couple to several engagements at the White House during his second term. For Franklin, whose father died early in his life, Theodore became an idol. He mimicked and admired his cousin "more even than other young men of his generation."[69]

That esteem gradually translated into political imitation. In his first campaign for elected office, running as a Democrat for a seat in the New York State Senate, Franklin sparked comparisons to TR when he used language often association with his cousin. "Dee-lighted," he roared at campaign stops, and along the Hudson River he was heard saying, "Bully." So often did Franklin use TR's bon mots that the press sometimes confused the men, and Franklin felt compelled to declare, "I'm not Teddy."

Once elected to the state senate, Franklin modeled his political philosophy on the reform record of his illustrious relative, attacked Tammany Hall, and called himself a progressive Democrat. When President Wilson tapped him as assistant secretary of the Navy, Franklin abided by the naval philosophy of Capt. Alfred Thayer Mahan, an ethos that reflected Theodore's strategic thinking. During World War I, Franklin even ventured to keep his cousin informed of naval operations, a perilous thing to do, given Theodore's criticism of the Wilson administration. It appeared, at times, that Franklin's admiration for and loyalty to his family was stronger than his political affinity for the Democrats and Wilson. One Washington insider said that from a "brief exchange on the subject of T.R." with Franklin in 1913, he could see that the assistant secretary made "constant appraisal . . . of his relative to guide his conduct."[70] Franklin avoided presenting himself as a carbon copy but aped particular traits and attributes of TR's that appealed to him. Over time, he stopped imitating the "superficial aspects of TR's personality," which never entirely fit his disposition. But he retained the qualities of Theodore that also "were naturally part of his self."[71]

Generally, the Hyde Park and Oyster Bay clans regarded each other highly until Franklin's nomination as the Democratic vice-presidential candidate in 1920. The campaign soured relations and created a rift that would last over sixty years. At the center of the dispute were the political aspirations of Ted and the ostensibly dueling ambitions of Franklin.

Sensing the responsibility of being TR's namesake, Ted sought to equal his father's achievements. He earned distinction fighting with the US Army in France and returned home in 1919 with a view to winning political office. He founded the American Legion and won a seat in New York's Assembly—as luck would have it, his father's first political position. With the help of Alice, who took up the role of Ted's political advisor, his reputation among Washington Republicans brightened at every social event. Although the Oyster Bay Roosevelts backed the wrong primary candidate in General Wood, Ted's support for Harding was so unequivocal that most pundits presumed he would have a place in a Republican administration, and, in 1921, he succeeded Franklin as assistant secretary of the Navy.

Ted felt that Franklin's nomination to the Democratic ticket usurped his place as the inheritor of his father's legacy. So did Alice, who complained that to "see Franklin following those same footsteps with large Democratic shoes on was just too terrible to contemplate!" Defeating him became a personal crusade for the Oyster Bay clan. "There we were," Alice recalled many years later, "the Roosevelts—hubris up to the eyebrows, beyond the eyebrows, and who should show up but Nemesis in the person of Franklin."[72]

The Democrats almost certainly nominated Franklin because of his name. When James Cox, the Democrats' presidential nominee, was asked about Franklin's potential, he replied, "His name is good." Franklin preferred to ignore his family brand, however, and insisted that the party focus on his service as assistant secretary of the Navy, which he believed distinguished him for high office. Once nominated, however, Franklin was advised to make greater use of the Roosevelt appellation. Journalist Stephen Early, acting as Franklin's advance man on the campaign trail, investigated demographics and hot issues at each stop. His dispatches to Franklin reveal how much the Roosevelt name mattered in Democratic strategy. On Franklin's first tour west of the Appalachian Mountains, Early relayed, "The Boss should take good here. They like his name and his kind. It was a T.R. state and I hope it will be an F.R. state next." On foreign policy questions, Early advised Franklin to "go [the] limit" when "pointing [out] Theodore Roosevelts support of [the] League [of Nations]." Early even encouraged Franklin to emphasize the vocabulary Theodore used, like "bully" and "splendid." At one stump speech Franklin declared, "T.R. and I were the best of friends."[73]

The Democratic campaign also sought to tie Franklin to his cousin's progressive legacy. Franklin frequently reminded audiences of Theodore's split from the Republicans in 1912. "Progressive sentiment in Oregon overwhelming," Early telegrammed headquarters: "Harding known as a reactionary and his fight against TR in 1912 recalled."[74] From the outset of the campaign, Franklin emphasized Harding's rift with TR, and in his acceptance speech he made an audacious play for Republican votes by co-opting his cousin as a modern-day Democrat. Praising the "fine citizenship which goes into the rank and file of the Republican Party," he took aim at progressive Republicans by condemning the party leadership, calling them "a group of selfish men" who sought to "gain control of the Party machinery" for their own nefarious gain. Taking Early's heed, Franklin reminisced on TR's political career and beseeched Republicans to remember the party schism only eight years prior:

It was in this very city that was born the movement of protest that, in the election of 1912, received the majority of the votes of the old Republican Party. That vote was given to a great American leader, but it was even more than support of Theodore Roosevelt, the man; it was the voice of insistence that the Party control be taken out of the hands of selfish men, of men who had not discovered that the world was moving on. Among those . . . who hurled bitter and insulting abuse at the Progressive Leader, was the present Republican nominee . . . These men do not represent True Republicanism . . . Join with [the Democrats] in a sincere effort to help our beloved land in this year of years [and] make possible in the future a restoration of the Republicanism of Lincoln and Roosevelt by striving to defeat those who were responsible for the acts of this Chicago convention.[75]

In Helena, Franklin asked crowds not to forget "the men in 1912 who thwarted the will of the majority." In Cincinnati, he called on Ohioans to oppose "the type of men whom Theodore Roosevelt fought in 1912." And in West Virginia, he told listeners, "I do not profess to know what Theodore Roosevelt would say were he alive today, but I cannot but help think that the man who invented the word 'pussy-footer' could not have resisted the temptation to apply it to Mr. Harding." One newspaper summarized Franklin's crusade as drawing "liberally on the record of the late Col. Roosevelt in his attempt to show the Republican party of today is not in tune with the Republican party of his day."[76] Franklin breathed new life into the Democratic campaign by co-opting TR in much the same way his Republican counterparts did. It led eminent Bull Moosers like Harold Ickes to endorse the Democratic ticket.

FDR's whistle-stop tour incensed the Oyster Bay clan. Alice and Ted found the comparison to Theodore an "imposture rather than homage," and, to rectify it, they reached out to their cousin. Communicating through their aunt Corinne, Ted and Alice accused Franklin of misappropriating the Roosevelt name for partisan gain. "I bitterly resent the adroit way in which he is bringing Father in and making him sponsor for all the democratic depravity which he fought," Ted wrote Corinne. Eleanor rushed to her husband's defense. "I do see how annoying it must be to have people saying and thinking Franklin is a near relation of Uncle Ted's," she responded, and she trusted that Ted and Alice understood that "we personally never sail under false colors." Franklin made certain to clarify his relationship to TR when directly asked, saying "he's a distant cousin." But his supporters encouraged the comparison. Journalist J. W. Holcombe advised him to "broadly proclaim that you are the political and spiritual heir of Theodore Roosevelt, that he was an essential and fundamental democrat." Poets brandished literary comparisons, cartoonists bequeathed Franklin his cousin's "big stick," and one supporter deemed Franklin "the only man who can ever quite take the Colonel's place." Such analogies infuriated Ted.[77]

In actuality, there was little confusion on the campaign trail. No matter how much mimicry or political invocation Franklin employed, voters made the distinction. In the Dakotas, Republican audiences recognized the dissimilarity straight away. "Franklin is as much like Theodore as a clam is like a bear cat," a local daily reported. In Minnesota, journalists said that Franklin had "a pleasing personality but seems to lack the punch of his distinguished and very distant relative, Theodore." In Colorado Springs, the mayor called him "Franklin Rosenfelt," apparently unaware of the famous last name altogether.[78] No matter how high the expectations of Democrats who thought that FDR would be mistaken for TR, or how much Republicans feared that prospect, the American public generally recognized the difference.

Not prepared to take any chances, the Harding campaign directly attacked Franklin's heredity by commissioning Ted to shadow his speaking tour. After Franklin passed through a town, Ted arrived and delivered the Republican message and refuted Franklin's connection to his father. The tactics at first "galled" Franklin, and before long they led to a "bad feeling." When the western press parodied Franklin as a phony, nominated only because of his name, Ted obliged journalists with a quotable one-liner about his cousin: "He is a maverick—he does not have the brand of our family." The jibe made it into the national press overnight. Ted failed to grasp how the slight would be received and professed to his aunt Corinne that it did not constitute a personal attack: "If they bring up the question of Franklin from the audience I am going to treat him as a joke. I will say east of the Mississippi words to the effect that every family has a skeleton in its closet and that it is not polite for people to taunt them about it in public."[79] Ted rationalized his invectives as merely political; Franklin took them personally.

Political supporters urged Franklin to "heckle young T.R." Prohibitionist William H. Anderson recommended that the Democrat criticize Ted's probusiness record in the New York Assembly. "The mere spirit of 'Theodore Roosevelt, the Real' who being dead yet speaketh, will count for infinitely more than anything that can be said by a son who has turned traitor to much that the father stood for," Anderson avowed.[80] Still, FDR avoided direct confrontation. He made indirect jibes, choosing to target Harding, reminding voters that in 1912 Harding had referred to Theodore Roosevelt as the Republican Benedict Arnold and insisting that the insult was "one thing, at least some members of the Roosevelt family will not forget." The *New York Times* dismissed Harding's "ancient acid remarks" but accepted that Franklin's constant prompts to "remember 1912" affected public perception. "Every time [Harding] mentions Mr. Roosevelt's name he evokes dangerous memories and dissimilitudes," the newspaper testified.[51] Clearly, Franklin's remarks struck a chord.

The family feud reached a climax when Ted mocked Franklin's decision to remain in the Navy Department during the war. "There was not a male representative of the close official family of the national Democratic Administration who . . . was within range of a gun fired," Ted blasted. The barb stung his cousin, who regretted his decision not to enlist. From that moment, Franklin and Eleanor put considerable personal distance between themselves and their Oyster Bay relatives. "I have heard that a silly young man is going about the country trying to make the people believe the Republican Party won the war," Franklin mocked. It was a rare attack; he typically allowed the Democratic press to stage the counterattack. "Mr. [Franklin] Roosevelt thinks it very essential to have somebody here at Headquarters who can follow up these things," a memo from the vice-presidential campaign revealed, as "he and Governor Cox are not in a position to answer statements made by men like . . . young 'Teddy.'"[52]

On Election Day, almost 27 million voters turned out, and over 60 percent of them cast a ballot for Warren G. Harding and Calvin Coolidge. The Republican landslide endures in American history as the largest margin of victory in the popular vote. Harding made no significant missteps and appealed to women voters, who exercised the franchise nationally for the first time that year. He led a rejuvenated and united Republican Party by reaching out to the various factions through a purposeful, if unrealistic, invocation of Roosevelt. The Democrats summoned the same spirit, channeled through Franklin. Their campaign sparked personal animosity between Ted and Franklin, which evolved into a lasting family feud over who was TR's rightful political heir. Ted and Franklin personified the competing interpretations, but the two major political parties perpetuated the feud, demonstrating the widespread reach of TR's ghost. Theodore Roosevelt's name and image carried considerable political weight and in 1920 inherited a bipartisan legacy that would reverberate for a century.

After the news of Harding's conquest settled, Roosevelt biographer William Roscoe Thayer wrote TR's sister that the election "was really *Theodore's* victory."[83] The ubiquity of his image and the collapse of the Democrats, Thayer believed, vindicated TR's opposition to Wilsonianism. But Harding's position was so at odds with Roosevelt's that historian Kathleen Dalton aptly calls him a "false claimant" to the "Bull Moose mantle."[84] The election did not represent a Rooseveltian victory, as Thayer suggested, but rather a triumph for conservatism. It marked the end of a long period of progressive reform in domestic politics, an era instigated by TR and sustained by Taft and Wilson. Harding's election also revived isolationist tendencies in US foreign policy. He abandoned international interventionism and Roosevelt's foreign relations ideology in particular. The election prompted a new era in American political history, one that Harding called a return to "normalcy," and a period that lasted almost an entire decade through the Republican presidencies of Calvin Coolidge and Herbert Hoover. During that time Theodore Roosevelt's image was used in presidential rhetoric to craft the Republican administrations of Harding, Coolidge, and Hoover as Rooseveltian, despite their countervailing political positions. Harding, Coolidge, and Hoover called for limited American leadership in world affairs, government deregulation at home, and the reduction of executive power. Although their electoral majorities in 1920, 1924, and 1928 constituted a victory for TR's political party, it did not represent a victory of his ideals. More than anything, it demonstrated the docile and elastic nature of his legacy.

CHAPTER THREE

THE FIRST MONUMENTS

S ites of memory differ from other forms of commemoration. While Henry Cabot Lodge's eulogy, the first Roosevelt biographies, and the exhibitions of Rooseveltiana lingered briefly in public memory, their effect dissipated quickly. Successive generations have read new biographies, visited different exhibitions, and understood political invocations in evolving contexts. Sites of memory or public monuments, however, afford a degree of consistency over time. Because such sites are immobile and set, generations of observers experience them in largely the same manner. For example, today's tourists gaze upon the Lincoln and Washington memorials in much the same way as tourists of a previous generation. Perhaps, over the years, the landscape changes, or the interpretive accents at the site vary, but Washington's obelisk and Lincoln's temple persist. Sites of memory like these produce a shared experience, and while elements of memorial sites may change over time, the aesthetic remains generally constant.[1]

The first monuments dedicated to Theodore Roosevelt attempted to romanticize his virtues, ignore his faults, and reiterate the familiar themes found in tributes and hagiographies. Conservation dominated early efforts to remember the former president. Environmental activists lobbied federal and state governments to purchase parkland in his honor. North Dakotans petitioned their state legislature for a massive national park in the Badlands in memory of TR's time as a rancher. In California, activists sought to rename Sequoia National Park as Roosevelt-Sequoia. In New Jersey, the wealthy Wall Street financier Malcolm S. Mackay donated land in the sprawling suburban township of Tenafly for a garden, pool, and double-sided limestone bas-relief that celebrated Roosevelt's love of the outdoors.

The Roosevelt family applauded these activities. Edith and Ted made known their disapproval of statues, preferring interpretive images if commemorators insisted on artistic memorials. The project they most encouraged was naturalist Carl Akeley's sculpture of a giant lion. Akeley began work shortly after Roosevelt's death on a clay model, hoping that when scaled to a larger size the sculpture would grace some secluded space in Washington's Rock Creek Park. For friends and family, the lion and the site had important symbolic meaning. TR's "tennis-cabinet," the nickname for his closest advisors during his presidency, gave their chief a golden lion in 1909 in honor of his retirement. Their recognition of Roosevelt as the king of the political jungle, an image often imitated in political cartoons, was echoed by his family, who revered him as a patriarchal "old" lion. Akeley, who had been on safari in Africa with Roosevelt, affectionately remembered the lion hunt in his sculpture. Setting it in Rock Creek Park, a place Roosevelt cherished during his presidency, would celebrate the location as a unique public refuge from the bustling metropolis. In sum, the lion embodied a range of themes, from conservation to politics, and allowed audiences to draw their own understanding of Roosevelt from the otherwise abstract figure. Support for the memorial grew among RMA trustees and Roosevelt's family, but Akeley's commitments to other pursuits in natural history distracted him from the project, and his sudden death in 1926 doused hope for the sculpture's completion.[2]

The Roosevelts endorsed other projects, including plans to build a park and public plaza along Oyster Bay's three-mile shore. The RMA agreed to finance the park and facilities for an outdoor auditorium, pool, fountain, baseball diamond, and boat slip. In addition, TR's cousin W. Emlen Roosevelt donated to the National Association of Audubon Societies twelve acres of land, adjacent to Youngs Cemetery, where the nation's leading ornithological society would build a bird sanctuary and fountain directly opposite TR's gravesite.[3] The grave itself became a place of pilgrimage. On the second anniversary of TR's passing, a small group of RMA executives met in Oyster Bay and arranged for an annual procession to the burial ground. Admirers made a "solemn reaffirmation of their allegiance to the leadership of Theodore Roosevelt" and pledged to "take such action as will serve best to keep alive vital interest in his principles and policies." One observer described it as "a strange scene" of devotees "longing to renew an inspiration at its source."[4] Indeed, between the park, the bird sanctuary, and the annual pilgrimages, the town of Oyster Bay became a veritable holy land for Roosevelt disciples.

Across the country, other sites sprang up. On Independence Day, 1919, a gathering of Roosevelt admirers climbed Sheep Mountain in Deadwood, South Dakota, singing patriotic anthems until they reached the summit. There the crowd dedicated a newly built thirty-foot stone tower and officially renamed the butte "Mount Theodore Roosevelt." The stone fortification, better known as the Friendship Tower, symbolized Seth Bullock's relationship with Roosevelt. Bullock had guided Roosevelt on wilderness treks through the Dakotas and later served with the Rough Riders regiment during the Spanish-American War. When he spoke at the tower's dedication, his face took on a look of "infinite sadness" before he admitted that neither he nor the country could begin to understand the implications of Roosevelt's absence. The mountaintop tower would stand, he declared, as a silent mark of Roosevelt's friendship with the Dakotas and the wider American West. It evoked themes of conservation, Americanism, and the cowboy spirit, which Bullock declared was the "unquestioned heritage, of the spirit of that great soul."[5]

Proposals for national highways linked Roosevelt's progressive legacy with projects to modernize travel networks. The National Highway Association of Long Island produced working plans for a multilane expressway from Queens to Montauk Point, billing the road as a modern marvel of engineering that would serve the country's economic needs for decades to come. Advocates invoked Roosevelt as the "Progressive of Progressives" and told how the highway would enshrine his memory by replacing the antiquated roads of the past and advancing a new age of travel.

Despite promising a speedier trip across Long Island, the proposal failed to muster support, in part because the Roosevelt image had so saturated utilitarian memorials that a national highway won the privilege of using his name. Almost immediately after his death, a national auto trail, or series of associated interstate roads, was dedicated the Theodore Roosevelt Memorial Highway. The tarmac network connected Portland, Maine, to Portland, Oregon through twelve states and a portion of Canada. Commemorators declared the route quintessentially Rooseveltian, taking motorists past "real live Indians and crying paposes [sic]" without any need to forge water, "sand-storms," or "mountain grades." The route promised travelers an opportunity to fish for trout along the way and facilitated a "pilgrimage" for nature lovers "through Roosevelt country." It took nearly ten years to complete and forced other road works to abandon the Roosevelt moniker.[6]

Universities joined the frenzy. Colleges renamed themselves "Roosevelt" and introduced Roosevelt scholarships. At Harvard, Roosevelt's alma mater, former classmates invoked his memory as a man of letters and in 1923 erected a plaque on the house where he had lived as a student. Charles Washburn, a Roosevelt biographer and classmate, eulogized him at the unveiling by recounting the many "departed spirits" that once had walked the same streets and now radiated a "mysterious and almost magic power of memory." Among the spirits Washburn encountered was TR-the-scholar, who had penned his first draft of *The Naval War of 1812* as an undergraduate and pugnaciously challenged his professors. Washburn remembered him as "the most illustrious member" of Harvard's class of 1880 and declared him an emblem for classmates in much the same way Rough Riders upheld him as their colonel. Fellow classmates planned, but could not accomplish, the construction of a "Roosevelt House" on the campus. They more successfully endowed artwork, including a portrait of Roosevelt, and dedicated a stained-glass window in Memorial Hall to him. Later, his classmates installed a simple stone marker along the exterior wall of Harvard Yard.[7]

Roosevelt's legacy as a "preacher of righteousness" was visible in several religious memorials. Episcopal priest William Lander of Forest Hills, New York, dedicated a new parish church and steeple on Roosevelt's birthday. At the ceremony, Director of the RMA Hermann Hagedorn compared Roosevelt to a biblical archangel. "In giving the name of Roosevelt to the church," he praised the parish, "you bring into intimate contact with your daily lives, not . . . the spirit of some holy mystic . . . but the spirit of one whose peculiar gift it was to stir the first elementary spiritual longings in men who had never known spiritual impulse before."[8] At Grace Reformed Church in Washington, DC, where he had worshiped as president, the parishioners installed a "Roosevelt Room" for public meetings and to display a sizable collection of Rooseveltiana.

Cult-like commemoration of Roosevelt in public spaces reached its apex during the 1920s. Sites of memory extended across the nation and echoed the well-established legacy themes, but of these memorials, three captured and sustained the attention of the American people for over a generation. These include the birthplace in New York City, the planned national memorial in Washington, DC, and Mount Rushmore in the Black Hills of South Dakota. Each inspired controversy, each demanded reinterpretations of Roosevelt's legacy, and each attracted enormous public audiences in a way that other sites did not.[9]

The first of these to be completed was Roosevelt House, a four-story brownstone at 28 East 20th Street in the Gramercy Park neighborhood of Manhattan's Flatiron District, where Martha Bulloch Roosevelt had given birth to her son. Named after his father, young Theodore lived in the city mansion until he turned fourteen. Then, in 1874, the Roosevelts moved into a new house, bigger and uptown, away from the crowded Lower East Side. Although he vacated his birthplace long before entering the world of politics, it remained a family property until 1899, when his sister sold it.

TR's election as president in 1904 prompted admirers to convert the old brownstone into a memorial. Because he was the only president born in New York City and because he spent most of his childhood at the site, devotees considered the house of great historical importance. A Roosevelt Home Club organized to conserve the house. Upon hearing the proposal, Roosevelt wrote the Home Club that he "felt very uncomfortable about the effort" and terminated their campaign by sanctioning the house's demolition in 1916. The site's new owners replaced the terraced residence with a commercial building.[10]

The WRMA revived the Home Club's idea in 1919, despite Roosevelt's disapproval and the absence of the original building. "The whole plan is so sensible and practical," an internal WRMA memo reported, "I'm sure were [Roosevelt] able to do so he would give us his warmest approval."[11] To validate the birthplace project, the WRMA engineered a myth that Edith Roosevelt desired the restoration. According to WRMA publications, on the day before TR's funeral, Edith privately recounted her hope that activists rebuild the house. Yet no proof of such a conversation exists, and conflicting evidence demonstrates that she did not encourage the memorial. After her husband's funeral, she took a transatlantic voyage to visit the grave of her youngest son Quentin in France. Edith purposely distanced herself from memorial activities until she returned. More than five months after the birthplace idea took root in the minds of WRMA trustees, Edith beckoned the group's president to Oyster Bay to provide information about the project and explain the purposes of the memorial to the family. WRMA minutes indicate that the family had ambivalent feelings about the project and recalled TR's aversion to it in the past. They supported the WRMA only after the association composed a suitable charter that clearly defined the memorial's objectives and WRMA chair Emily Vanderbilt Sloan (Mrs. John Henry Hammond) personally assured Edith that, in championing the house project, the association had her husband's best interests at heart.[12]

Even with Roosevelt family support, some WRMA activists continued to resist the birthplace memorial. Among the wealthy New York socialites that joined the association, several disputed the neighborhood's aesthetic value. The Gramercy Park neighborhood had changed considerably since the 1850s. Situated in the heart of Manhattan's bustling retail and trade offices, the residential community had developed into a commercial hub, and the elite residents who once called it home had moved northward. Florence Bayard Lockwood, the wife of notable New York City architect Christopher Grant La Farge, complained that "East 20th Street no longer represented the place where Colonel Roosevelt had lived" and protested the monument because "it would be difficult to recreate his atmosphere there." Louisa Lee Schuyler, the great-granddaughter of Alexander Hamilton and renowned city philanthropist, insisted that Manhattan "had so changed" since Roosevelt's time "that its significance as a memorial site had gone."[13] These women recommended an annual Roosevelt Day event or Roosevelt statue in nearby Central Park.

The birthplace garnered strong support from women who desired an education center, and the prospect of such a "living" memorial swung the vote in their favor. Opponents like Florence Bayard Lockwood and Louisa Lee Schuyler staged a final challenge before the WRMA approved the plans by putting forward a motion for the association to work with the RMA on all sites of memory. Their hope was that cooperation would lead to an alternative tribute at Sagamore Hill, but the majority of WRMA trustees feared an alliance with the RMA and believed cooperation would diminish their control. The decision to rebuild the birthplace as a center for Americanism dashed the hopes of some women, although it also established the WRMA's autonomy.[14]

Gender divided the WRMA on other aspects of the memorial. The association determined that the birthplace must reflect female interpretations of Roosevelt. It also decided that "all things being equal, women be employed" to construct the house, a mandate that included the architectural design. That eliminated from consideration the all-male Trowbridge and Livingston group, one of the most accomplished and prestigious architectural firms of the day. Trowbridge and Livingston applied to rebuild the house, but despite their renowned work in New York City—they designed the classical Beaux arts–style JP Morgan Building on Wall Street and the St. Regis Hotel—the WRMA appointed Theodate Pope Riddle, an amateur architect with little professional experience. Pope Riddle had restored several colonial farmhouses and a few nonresidential properties in the Northeast. Her first substantial contract was the construction of Westover School, an elite Connecticut boarding academy; she got the contract because her friend, neighbor, and Westover headmistress, Mary

Hillard, recommended her. The commission for the birthplace followed a similar pattern of patronage. Pope Riddle lived near TR's sister Bamie, who suggested her to the WRMA. Although Pope Riddle had no experience with urban buildings, memorials, or Victorian architecture, Bamie's endorsement carried significant weight.[15]

Using city records and family accounts, Pope Riddle designed a replica brownstone, intended to be a "humble house in which the entire country" could experience the "sacred memory" of Theodore Roosevelt and a dwelling that could match, simultaneously, the grandeur of Washington's Mount Vernon and the humility of Lincoln's log cabin. The plans, she insisted, gave the house a "distinctly monumental character" and manifested Roosevelt's values in a variety of ways. A large open space in the basement club room was reserved for storytelling. A drawing room and library, "restored practically as they were in 1858," gave the public access to volumes of Roosevelt's writings. A second-floor museum and collection of Rooseveltiana exhibited the narratives of his life and legacy. And a three-hundred-seat auditorium on the fourth floor provided a space for the public to learn from lectures and motion picture shows. Pope Riddle also drew plans for an adjacent building that included a reference library for rare manuscripts and an administrative center for the WRMA.[16]

Pope Riddle's design accorded with the WRMA's Americanism agenda. The architect subscribed to Roosevelt's brand of patriotism and deployed it in her plans. Her prior work typified the trend toward the Colonial Revival style, one that she believed celebrated America's heritage, and although the Victorian-style exterior of Roosevelt's birthplace reflected a distinctly foreign elegance, she engineered the interior to exhibit Americanism. Pope Riddle imagined the library as a teaching resource where foreign nationals could learn American values, the club room basement as a place to indoctrinate through storytelling, the museum of Rooseveltiana as a temple of "sound American doctrines," and the auditorium as a venue for communicating the virtues of American democracy. Her interior design transformed the house into a foundation "for instruction in American citizenship and civic service," a living memorial and place for the WRMA to convert "pacifist, radical idiots," socialists, and Bolsheviks. The foundation would make them "Roosevelt minded Americans."[17]

To more firmly establish Americanism as "their work," the WRMA amended their constitution to guarantee the permanent maintenance of an "educational institution for instruction in American citizenship and civic service." They regarded femininity as a natural defense against communism. "The education of the child falls naturally into the hands of the woman until well along the road to maturity," the association insisted, and "the problem of molding" and developing a public resistance to communism was one that "only women understand."[18] They planned for the birthplace to prescribe "sound American doctrines" to inculcate in "our children during their formative years," so that "later in life they will be impervious to such anti-social, anti-national forces as now threaten the established order of society."[19] The WRMA regarded fighting communism as woman's work and education as their weapon.

The association purchased the sites and buildings at 26 and 28 East 20th Street on May 26, 1919. They quickly arranged for the commercial structure that replaced the original birthplace at number 28 to be demolished, and on the second anniversary of Roosevelt's death, they invited thousands of visitors to a ceremony at the vacant lot to celebrate the groundbreaking of the replica house. After a raucous crowd-led rendition of the "Star Spangled Banner" and a salute to the flag led by the Manhattan Council of Boy Scouts, WRMA president Emily Hammond introduced several eminent speakers, all of whom mentioned Roosevelt's Americanism and anticipated how the house would reflect his patriotic legacy. "Classes on Americanism, lectures on what he believed, will be in this house the order of the day," Corinne Roosevelt Robinson declared. President-elect Warren G. Harding wrote to apologize for being absent and asked Hammond to announce his support of the WRMA's "work of perpetuating his splendid American spirit." Invited foreign speakers also identified with Roosevelt's Americanism, including former French ambassador Jules Jusserand and ambassadors from Italy, Belgium, Panama, Cuba, the Netherlands, and Brazil. Jusserand told the gathering that when the French president heard of the birthplace idea, he immediately recognized its importance. Patriotism, Jusserand said, was "a sentiment, a state of mind, a state of heart which [the French] greatly appreciate and admire."[20]

The birthplace also anticipated the changing political dynamics of the American polity in the 1920s and the rise of women's activism. Beyond promoting Americanism, Roosevelt House would provide a command center from which to advance women's rights and invigorate women's interests. The leaders of the WRMA, including Roosevelt's sisters, exemplified this new class of political activist, and the birthplace was to stand as a monument to advancements in gender equality. Additionally, by showcasing Roosevelt's humanity through his boyhood trials, the WRMA sought to produce a shrine that differed greatly from the marble, male-designed memorials of other former presidents. The women promoted a heroic depiction but confronted Roosevelt's social privilege as a child of wealthy Knickerbockers and his vulnerability as a sickly boy confined to his bedroom whenever an asthma attack flared. Vice president–elect Calvin Coolidge congratulated the WRMA on this aspect of the house's design: "Men build monuments above the graves of their heroes to mark the end of a great life but women seek out the birthplace and build their shrine not where a great life had its ending but where it had its beginning, seeking with a truer instinct the common source of things not in that which is gone forever, but in that which they know will again be manifest."[21] The house would familiarize visitors with Roosevelt's upbringing. In his bedroom, one would imagine his bookish curiosity taking shape. The gym and children's porch would show visitors where the young boy trained, built his strength, and conceived a strenuous living philosophy through emulating his father's adherence to muscular Christianity. What distinguished the WRMA's work and Pope Riddle's design was that they relied more on public empathy with the past and less on Roosevelt's intrinsic greatness.[22]

At the dedication of the site in 1921, Leonard Wood laid a ceremonial cornerstone and dedicated the memorial "to Americanism." He pronounced the site a place of pilgrimage where visitors could learn "to do good work for country and humanity." The WRMA executive stood behind Wood as he spoke, next to a heap of old bricks recovered and authenticated as having belonged to the original brownstone. The bricks surrounded a small time capsule filled with the minutes of the first WRMA meeting, coins from the year of Roosevelt's birth, newspapers from the early days of his career in New York, and the WRMA emblem. After Wood finished his speech, he lifted a silver trowel, scooped a heap of mortar, and smoothed it around the pile of bricks to an ovation that filled the entire city street. No sooner had the ceremonial stone begun to set, then the masses cleared and the excitement subsided. The empty lot behind Wood and the small pile of bricks revealed what a daunting task was still at hand. With no house, no museum, no auditorium, and only the promise of Pope Riddle's design, the excited crowd retreated in the hope that all the grand assurances of a memorial to TR's Americanism would come to fruition.[23]

In the following months, the WRMA received news of "unavoidable difficulties" in the construction plans. Contractors required additional engineering reports before they could erect the exterior, a delay that would last months. Meanwhile, the trustees collected decorations, furnishings, and artifacts for the interior. The Roosevelt family, particularly TR's sisters and wife, helped locate furnishings that had once adorned the rooms. His niece Eleanor donated china, a coat of arms, and a tea set. The family also helped the WRMA by drawing diagrams of the rooms as they existed in Roosevelt's youth. The WRMA located TR's original bedroom set and sourced identical wallpaper and carpets, an embroidered bedspread, and bespoke silk curtains. They purchased the original portrait of Martha, TR's mother, that had hung over his fireplace. Where originals could not be found, the association acquired replicas or period decorations.[24] As part of the collection efforts, the women gathered books for the library and movies to screen in the auditorium. Acquisitions proved expensive and tapered in frequency as fundraising dried up. The WRMA attempted to raise money with a "brick" campaign that asked for sponsors to contribute to the house's construction costs, one brick at a time. They sold advertisements in their newsletter, held town hall collections across the country, and hosted a Roosevelt festival every summer. Despite their tireless efforts, income never matched expenses.

By 1922, it became clear that the birthplace's construction would cost nearly double the original quote, and the association had no choice but to ask the RMA for help. On February 13, 1922, a select group of RMA representatives met a negotiating team from the WRMA to identify the basis for cooperation. The women required money, which the men had, and the men required space, which the women had. Both associations collected books, films, and Rooseveltiana, but the RMA had acquired substantially more and had limited storage space. Months of negotiation ended with a mutually beneficial settlement. The RMA made a contribution of $150,000 to the WRMA, and in return the women leased the men the second and third floors of the adjoining building (26 East 20th Street), where the RMA established a library and administrative headquarters. The organizations would share the ground floor and basement, transforming these spaces into a fireproof storage area and Roosevelt museum.[25]

Some WRMA trustees resisted the idea of working with the RMA, and all WRMA members worried that an injection of capital would make their campaign appear a failure, but the RMA did not expect recognition for the cash or meddle in the plans for the birthplace. Even the plaque on the exterior walls displayed only the WRMA's emblem, and the RMA never sought to dissuade them from Americanization work. As such, the women saw the settlement as favorable, not only because it secured the construction of the birthplace but also because it halved their overhead costs for decades to come. The RMA committed to share the cost of utilities and maintenance of the properties, and the men acquired ownership of the entire collection of memorabilia, bore the cost for its conservation, and finally settled into a permanent headquarters.[26]

With the WRMA bank account fortified, the building's Victorian façade was completed and the interior decorated. The WRMA held its first meeting at the house in the summer of 1923, and on October 27—Roosevelt's birthday—the birthplace held its grand opening. The auditorium filled with Roosevelt's friends and colleagues, and the street flooded with more than two thousand spectators. The following day, the house welcomed its first public visitors, reporting that twelve thousand people poured into the building, each paying 25 cents to see the restored rooms and antique furnishings, and to have a chance to sense Roosevelt's ghost in the reconstruction of the room in which he was born.

During the same period, the RMA faced its fair share of obstacles. President William Boyce Thompson ordered a committee of architects and sculptors to select a site in Washington, DC, for their proposed "monumental" memorial. The committee, chaired by New York architect Christopher La Farge, set about organizing an investigation of possible sites for a national shrine, but to Thompson's disappointment, La Farge took a year to examine a number of locations around the capital. In their official reports, the RMA told supporters that planning required extensive reflection and explained that La Farge's work progressed "the only way in which such a project can ever safely progress, which is slowly and steadily." Privately, however, trustees grumbled about the delay.[27]

During the long wait for the La Farge committee's report, the RMA kept busy with publicity work. Hagedorn convinced trustees to establish a Bureau of Roosevelt Research and Information that issued press releases and pamphlets and made "a sound and complete case for the Roosevelt memorial." The bureau produced and distributed motion pictures, collected the works and papers of Roosevelt, promoted hagiographies, and managed events that coincided with key legacy dates. Fundraising successes made the bureau's work easier. By 1921 the RMA held over $1.9 million in its reserves, largely from donations by wealthy patrons and the efforts of quota campaigns among state committees. The trustees invested the donations wisely, mainly in high-yield Liberty bonds that ensured a regular income from the interest on the principal. The accrued interest was so abundant, that it alone funded the association's running costs.

Under Hagedorn's stewardship, the bureau expanded its role, becoming a clearinghouse for Rooseveltiana.[28] As a reward for the remarkable collection he amassed and in recognition of his dedication to the task of memorializing Roosevelt, the RMA hired Hagedorn full-time as executive director. The appointment allowed him to focus on creating original RMA publications and cinematic productions. In his first years as director, he wrote a short biography for mass publication, as well as a monograph on Roosevelt's time in the North Dakota Badlands. He advised Hollywood director Victor Fleming on the 1927 blockbuster film *The Rough Riders* and began editing a collection of Roosevelt's works.[29] If the RMA was a "cult of worshippers," as historian Richard Collin called them, Hagedorn was its prodigious high priest.[30]

The executive director kept the RMA relevant until the monumental memorial plans gained traction. In 1923, the La Farge committee identified two suitable Washington, DC, sites for a monument: one near Pierce's Mill in the northern part of the city, adjacent to Rock Creek Park, and another in the south, at the Tidal Basin. The Tidal Basin site had considerable appeal because, as the last vacant position in eighteenth-century city planner Pierre L'Enfant's cruciform design for the Federal City, it had the potential to commemorate Roosevelt's memory in a way that no other site could. L'Enfant had designed the National Mall so that key buildings would occupy the points of a cross. In 1800, the Executive Mansion, now the White House, dotted the northernmost point. By 1863, the Capitol came to completion at the easternmost location. The first memorial added to L'Enfant's plan was the Washington Monument, completed in 1885 at the intersection of the cross, and in 1914 the construction of the Lincoln Memorial began on reclaimed land at the westernmost point. The only remaining space was to the south of Washington's obelisk, where the sprawl of the Potomac River meets the Washington Channel and an inland reservoir surrounds the fringe of the city. Because a memorial at the Tidal Basin would bestow a significant national honor, the RMA opted to pursue construction there. Trustees concluded that "the Pierce's Mill site would abandon the idea of placing Colonel Roosevelt with the great historical figures" of the United States.[31]

As the Tidal Basin was the most significant unused space on the National Mall, Congress received multiple propositions to build there. The city's planners favored moving the Supreme Court building so as to position all three branches of government in L'Enfant's design, while other proposals with substantial popular support included calls for a memorial to the Founding Fathers and Thomas Jefferson. RMA trustees possessed considerable political clout and used their insider knowledge of governmental procedures to speed the process through Congress. They wrote a draft joint House and Senate resolution for permission to explore the Tidal Basin as the site for a Roosevelt memorial, and only three months later Senator George Pepper of Pennsylvania introduced the legislation in the Senate.[32] The RMA's proposal advanced in typical fashion to a Joint Committee on the Library, where legislators gave it further consideration and the first apprehensions about the plan came to light. Congressmen feared the resolution would "commit" the government to constructing a memorial before enough time had passed for the public to consider Roosevelt's place in history. The choice of the Tidal Basin struck the committee as particularly audacious, given the short period since Roosevelt's death, and although the original resolution allowed Congress to veto any design, it did grant construction rights. In order to take a more cautious course of action, the joint committee recommended that the resolution restrict the RMA's construction rights and concede only the option to start a design competition.[33]

The reworded resolution frustrated RMA trustees, and none more than the chair of the RMA's monument committee, James R. Garfield. Namesake of the former president, Garfield had taken a leading role in Roosevelt's "tennis cabinet" and had supported the 1912 Bull Moose campaign. In 1914, he unsuccessfully ran as the Progressive Party candidate for governor of Ohio, a defeat that led him to permanently resign his political ambitions and return to the Republican Party in 1916. He worked diligently behind the scenes to elect the party's candidates and restore his influence among the Republican faithful. In 1924, when Thompson resigned the presidency of the RMA, Garfield accepted leadership and labored almost as tirelessly as Hagedorn to memorialize TR. He was instrumental in the annual pilgrimage and led efforts for the national memorial. The Library Committee's misgivings about the Tidal Basin site only intensified his efforts.

Working with Hagedorn in what he called "a little missionary work," Garfield organized a support network of Roosevelt devotees to raise awareness of the national memorial. "We are going to need public support," Hagedorn told Garfield; he worried that Roosevelt's political opponents would endorse alternative proposals to sink the RMA's plans. Woodrow Wilson's death in 1924 had instigated considerable public reflection on the Progressive Era, and Hagedorn believed Democrats coveted the

Tidal Basin for a memorial to Wilson. Relatively little time had elapsed since the most bitter fights between Roosevelt and Wilson, a reality that made the RMA's proposal appear intensely partisan. Wilson disciples in the House and Senate opposed all efforts by the RMA to build at the Tidal Basin and ceaselessly denied that the twenty-sixth president's stature resembled the greatness of Washington or Lincoln.[34]

Editor of the *Nation* Oswald Garrison Villard aggressively opposed the RMA's memorial plans as the delusions of fanatics. In an editorial akin to Mark Twain's satirical writing, Villard imagined the association as a corporate legacy firm called "Creating Reputations Ltd." The company provided "services of the wisest propaganda, publicity, and advertising experts . . . Laboring in connection with the ablest literary lights, college professors, historians, and professional biographers" to reimagine the past. It "will build up or develop reputations or refurbish tarnished ones," and "nothing whatever will be left to chance or to history." Villard condemned the RMA as a team of whitewashers. "Unfortunate happenings will be presented in the best possible light or explained away altogether after a series of consultations by the expert group" and any "improper criticisms" relegated to obscurity to "insure the gradual obliteration [of] known inconsistencies." Angered by Villard's insinuation that the RMA falsified history, Hagedorn publicly repudiated any intention to build "a false tradition" or "shine up a halo" for Roosevelt. "The fact is," Hagedorn charged, "we have collected the anti-Roosevelt material with even more enthusiasm [because] it is rarer, for one thing, and often much more amusing."[35]

Political opponents like Villard represented the growing public concern about the proposed memorial. The brief duration between TR's death and his canonization raised eyebrows, especially when the memorial association compared him to Washington and Lincoln. It took nearly fifty years after the deaths of those presidents before Congress erected their respective memorials. "The verdict of history on Roosevelt has not yet been delivered," complained a Democratic editorial in the *New York World*. Even Republican-friendly editorials in the *New York Times* proposed to "preserve [the site] until the welter of political and personal passions died down." Then, and only then, would Roosevelt's historical legacy become clear to posterity.

By the end of 1924, the Library Committee passed the revised resolution for the RMA to hold a memorial competition and forwarded it to the Senate and House for open debate. In each chamber, the trepidation

about the memorial grew clearer. Rep. Robert Luce, a Republican from
Massachusetts and supporter of the RMA memorial, was forced to clarify
the remit of the joint resolution as "a study of the facts [that] goes only to
the extent of official permission to survey and examine further a possible
location." When pressed on the RMA's rights to build at the site, Luce
maintained that the resolution "commits the Government in no way" and
insisted on this exactness of language to ensure the resolution's passage.
The House and Senate approved the resolution, and the RMA scored a
minor victory, but it had failed to convince Congress to grant construction
rights or make any formal commitment to the site as a definite location
for a Roosevelt monument. The bill went to President Coolidge for final
approval, and he promptly signed it on February 12, 1925.[36]

By the 1920s, memorial design competitions involved a standard procedure based on recommendations made by the American Institute of
Architects. The RMA applied the criteria to its competition, drafted a
schedule, appointed a qualified independent jury, and made plans for an
illustrated publication of the designs. Once the legislation passed granting
them permission for a competition, the RMA invited the nation's leading
architects, sculptors, and landscapers to imagine what a memorial at
the Tidal Basin would look like. The association dictated that it must be
artistic rather than utilitarian, and the Roosevelt family requested that
designers avoid statues. The jury included one RMA nominee, one nominee chosen by the competitors, and one chosen by the two nominees. They
were directed to pick a designer, rather than a design—an instruction
that left open the possibility to develop the memorial "after the selection."
The RMA permitted applications until October 1, 1925, and promised a
decision in less than six months.[37]

More than a dozen designers submitted schemes, and the jury took
only a day to deliberate. On October 4, 1925, they announced John Russell
Pope the winner. An architect of growing renown, Pope had established a
New York firm that designed homes for the Vanderbilt family, Richmond's
Union Station, the House of the Temple masonic lodge in the capital, and
Baltimore's Museum of Art. He was acclaimed by his peers as one of the
foremost Beaux arts–style architects. The RMA delighted in the choice
of Pope, although they initially disliked his design for the memorial.
Pope's drawings envisioned a white granite island with a central fountain
surrounded by two semicircular colonnades. In the center, a fountain,
or what Pope called a "living shaft of water," shot up into the air more
than two hundred feet above the vast sprawl of the circular plaza. At four

equidistant points around the fountain, Pope fixed statues of sea vessels crafted in a classical style, contributing to the shape of a giant compass. The design, the architect said, revealed the reach and global significance of Roosevelt's message and values.[38]

The design troubled the RMA leaders, most notably Garfield, Hagedorn, and Root. Its size, the fountain, and the sea of white marble "seemed to lack unity," they complained. In a letter to Hagedorn, Edith Roosevelt also admitted her disappointment. "Don't bring Mr. Pope's designs" to Sagamore Hill, she requested; "I just can't look at them."[39] Despite their misgivings, the RMA officers and Roosevelt's family endorsed the drafts and publicized them as appropriate, primarily because the competition stipulated that the final design could be reconsidered. In the official press release, Garfield announced that Pope chose a spout of water to "show through confusing details of a multifarious life how clearly and powerfully the living radiating spirit of [Roosevelt's] Americanism grows." The fountain represented "that source of inexhaustible vitality and boundless energy that Roosevelt was noted for." Of course, the water could also symbolize his progressive and cowboy spirit, Garfield admitted. Pope's design allowed interpretive flexibility, an artistic goal Elihu Root long supported.[40] The memorial, Garfield said, gave future generations a role in crafting Roosevelt's memory.[41]

Architectural reviews celebrated Pope's creativity and the scheme's aesthetics. Even so, they questioned the site's suitability, reigniting resistance to honoring Roosevelt at the Tidal Basin. As one architect related, Pope's memorial "will be a thing of beauty," because Pope was the nation's most skilled architect, "but it is a grave question whether it should be located at the end of the cross axis of the mall opposite the White House."[42] Even the cost, revised up to $5 million from the initial $2 million estimate, did not trigger as much criticism as the RMA's decision to bid for the last cardinal point on the National Mall. Henry Stoddard, editor of the *New York Evening Telegram,* reported to the RMA that "whisperings" among Washington correspondents who wielded "considerable influence over public opinion" alleged that a great hostility existed in relation to the site. In private correspondence, Hagedorn and Garfield admitted that the opposition required the RMA to intensify their publicity campaign.

Shortly after Pope's design reached the public, the memorial association commissioned a scale model to go on display in the Corcoran Gallery in Washington, DC, so that media correspondents could see the dimensions of the memorial. Hagedorn reported that the correspondents reacted positively, accepting the memorial's artistic merits and gaining a better perspective of its place in the capital. He assumed the association had averted a public relations disaster.[43]

The RMA submitted the designs to Congress, emphasizing the beauty of Pope's work. They deliberately avoided any suggestion that the memorial elevated Roosevelt to a status akin to that of Washington or Lincoln. Instead, the association seized on Roosevelt's support for L'Enfant's vision and made a case that he had played a central role in the city's planning and therefore deserved a place at the Tidal Basin. During Roosevelt's presidency, a report of the Senate Park Commission had reconsidered L'Enfant's cruciform design of the National Mall. Roosevelt, despite RMA suggestions, played only a minor role. Often referred to as the McMillan Plan after chair of the commission Sen. James McMillan, the redesign included a new layout surrounding Lafayette Park, the construction of a modern railway station, and several upgraded public recreation facilities. Roosevelt ardently supported the plan as conceived by the Park Commission, for which the RMA gave him substantial credit. Hagedorn declared him, not McMillan, the chief advocate of the capital's reconstruction. Root advised against using this tactic when lobbying Congress, but Pope and a majority of RMA trustees believed this approach offered an effective rationale for building at the Tidal Basin. "His unwavering support" of the city's redesign, the RMA wrote in a press release, makes it "particularly fitting that his memorial should be an important factor in the realization of the plan."[44]

In Congress, complaints about the memorial hardly touched on Pope's design or the tenuous link to Roosevelt's support of the McMillan Plan. Instead, anxiety stemmed from the all-too-fresh political disputes between Roosevelt and Wilson.[45] Soon after the RMA supplied legislators with the details of Pope's design, Wilson's allies protested. "I have no purpose to disparage the achievements of Mr. Roosevelt," progressive Democratic senator William Henry King said, "but I respectfully submit that it is an ill-advised, if not audacious, plan which contemplates the placing of Roosevelt's name alongside that of Washington and Lincoln, and the creation of a great national triumvirate." King pointedly assured the RMA that no senator "will object to a suitable monument erected to the memory of Theodore Roosevelt; indeed, there will be general approval," but placing a memorial at the Tidal Basin would "indicate a purpose to apotheosize Mr. Roosevelt and declare to the world that the three immortal figures in our history are Washington, Lincoln, and Roosevelt."[46] Most RMA trustees ignored King's criticism and similar invectives from Wilson devotees. Hermann Hagedorn could not. "Washington founded the Republic, and Lincoln united it," he wrote in an open letter to the *New York Times;* "so did Roosevelt consolidate and revitalize it."[47] For those congressmen who clashed with Roosevelt in life, memorializing him on the mall as a leader akin to Washington and Lincoln was impossible. Other opponents to the plan included the American Institute of Architects and the Washington, DC, Commission on Fine Arts.

The steady dissent from a broad base of political and nonpolitical stakeholders took a toll, and in April 1926 the RMA accepted defeat. The group refused to publicly acknowledge that its campaign had collapsed, however, and at executive meetings the trustees held out hope for a change in political will and public perception. Throughout 1927 they officially deemed the proposal "still pending." Privately, though, they admitted it was doomed and unofficially ceased all efforts. Trustees reasoned that further insistence would produce a political quarrel in Congress that would scuttle future considerations about an appropriate memorial at any location in the capital.

The RMA's proposed memorial design unintentionally stoked public interest in memorializing another US president at the Tidal Basin. The year 1926 saw the July 4 centennial of Thomas Jefferson's death and the sesquicentennial of the signing of the Declaration of Independence. These anniversaries and the RMA proposal prompted fresh consideration of Jefferson for the cardinal spot at the Tidal Basin. The Jefferson Foundation had recently purchased and reconstructed the third president's Virginia home, Monticello, and the publication of his papers had led to considerable interest in a national memorial. With Congress resolved against a Roosevelt memorial on the site, momentum gathered to celebrate Jefferson in his place. Construction of the Jefferson Memorial did not begin until 1938, but popular support swung behind the idea as early as 1926.[48]

By 1930 the RMA had officially abandoned the Tidal Basin and requested an alternative location from the city's planning committee. As the central objective of the RMA's mission, the effort to build a public monument on the National Mall haunted the trustees and foreshadowed the turn Roosevelt's legacy would take in the coming decades. Yet, even as opposition to a national memorial increased, plans to enshrine Roosevelt in an audacious monument in the Black Hills of South Dakota were taking shape.

On September 24, 1924, Gutzon Borglum, a sculptor of moderate renown, met South Dakota historian and local politician Doane Robinson.

Impressed with Borglum's enormous carving of Robert E. Lee on Georgia's Stone Mountain, Robinson invited the sculptor to visit South Dakota to plot a colossal monument in the Black Hills. The two men traveled to Rapid City via Custer State Park to the top of Harney Peak and through winding unpaved trails that passed tall, eroded granite pillars the locals call "needles." At first, Robinson proposed that Borglum transform the needles into statues of American heroes such as Washington and Lincoln, or Meriwether Lewis and William Clark. South Dakotans protested that to do so would defile the area's natural beauty, and Borglum gradually came to see Robinson's notion as aesthetically distasteful. He called it "totem pole" art.[49]

After three years of scoping mountain facades, Borglum settled on Mount Rushmore, a granite peak northeast of the needles, as the place for a colossal sculpture of American presidents. In time, he would carve busts of George Washington, Thomas Jefferson, Abraham Lincoln, and Theodore Roosevelt.

Construction began in the summer of 1927. Although it was a privately funded artistic venture, Borglum had considerable support from powerful politicians. President Calvin Coolidge made the journey to South Dakota to dedicate the inaugural stone cutting and celebrated the installation as apt: "Here in the heart of the continent, on the side of a mountain which probably no white man had ever beheld in the days of Washington, in territory which was acquired by the action of Jefferson, which remained an unbroken wilderness beyond the days of Lincoln, which was especially beloved by Roosevelt, the people of the future will see history and art combined to portray the spirit of patriotism."[50] The scale of the project reflected the ambitious nature of Americans and the vast accomplishments of the nation to date, the president professed. Immediately following the speech, Borglum scaled the mountain and scored the first holes in the granite.

The dedication ceremony demonstrated an obstinate insensitivity toward Native Americans, particularly the Lakota Sioux, who protested the carving as vandalism of territory they considered historically and spiritually significant. South Dakota's Native American tribes held the US government responsible for broken treaties, decades of war, and forced resettlement. They judged Borglum's memorial an added insult to these injuries, as it ignored the story of Native American dispossession and rejoiced in European settlement and imperial dominance. Environmentalists joined the concert of disapproval, complaining that the memorial disrupted the area's natural beauty. Despite these objections, the big idea of Rushmore carried on, powered by speculation about an economic boom in tourism, infrastructure improvements, and the support of wealthy out-of-state patrons charmed by Borglum's bold design.

The construction of the memorial took fourteen years and demanded a collective effort of thousands of laborers and engineers to chisel the granite and erect the infrastructure; it also required a coterie of lobbyists to win funds from the federal and state governments and, in time, the oversight of the National Park Service to ensure the interests of taxpayers. Notwithstanding the many years of work and thousands of contributors, Mount Rushmore's design started and ended in the minds of three men: Borglum, Robinson, and South Dakota's senior US senator Peter Norbeck.

The question of who should appear on the mountain dominated the planning in 1925. Borglum and Robinson questioned whether the memorial should be restricted to sculptures of American presidents or if they should include military heroes like John Frémont or the explorers Lewis and Clark. At one point Robinson even suggested a Native American figure, but he opposed carving more than two statues and abandoned the idea. Initially, Robinson believed Borglum would carve the figures from head to waist, but Borglum convinced Robinson that busts of great white "Americans" would make a compelling artistic spectacle. Robinson continued to advocate for a two-man memorial, recommending Washington and Lincoln as the subjects, but Borglum came to insist that Thomas Jefferson join the pair as the president responsible for the Louisiana Purchase, the nation's largest territorial expansion. In a flurry of excitement, Borglum even floated the idea of adding Theodore Roosevelt, Grover Cleveland, and William McKinley, a second tier of presidential greats. If the donations and workload permitted, he hoped to add their faces to the mountain.[51]

In the end, the addition of Roosevelt was the result of Norbeck's urging.[52] While Borglum and Robinson admired Roosevelt as a great president, they balked at his inclusion on Rushmore for the same reasons others had opposed TR's memorial on the National Mall: it was less than a decade since Roosevelt's death, and the verdict on his legacy remained unclear. Norbeck dismissed their apprehensions and pushed his collaborators toward the conclusion he had already reached—that Roosevelt deserved a place on Rushmore more than anyone else for pragmatic and historical reasons.

"I did not dare tell Doane Robinson that I am trying to talk Borglum out of his Washington-Lincoln Siamese Twin idea," Norbeck wrote a close friend in January 1925, when the deliberations on Rushmore's design intensified. "I told him they would be quite appropriate if the mountain were located on the plane of Ohio, but that neither of them belonged to the west."[53] Roosevelt's experience in the Badlands of North Dakota and his political campaigns throughout South Dakota made him the only president who had engaged with the region, a connection Norbeck felt compelled to defend and enshrine. Roosevelt, he asserted, was the only true westerner.

Norbeck's admiration sprung from personal experience, what Rushmore historian Gilbert Fite has called his "Horatio Alger" upbringing. An astute young man raised in the poverty of the rural Midwest, Norbeck built a fortune selling water wells. His charismatic personality earned him a reputation as an honest broker, a status that launched his political career. Inspired by Roosevelt in his early career as a state senator, he joined the Republicans, kept a close affinity with the progressive branch of the party, and, in 1912, supported Roosevelt's breakaway bid for the White House. Using his influence among South Dakota voters, Norbeck helped deliver the state's electoral votes to the Progressive Party. In 1916, when Roosevelt rejoined the Republican Party, Norbeck followed suit and won statewide election to become South Dakota's first native-born governor.[54] Like other Republicans who fled the party in 1912, Norbeck saw himself as a progressive and the issue of conservation as inherently Rooseveltian. After one term as governor, Norbeck won election to the US Senate and, during his three terms, championed conservation at the national level. With his support, the federal government preserved the area surrounding the iconic Black Hills and created the Custer State Park and Game Sanctuary.[55] When Norbeck insisted that Roosevelt appear on Rushmore, it reflected his own life's work as a progressive reformer and environmental conservationist.

Enshrining Roosevelt also served a practical purpose for Norbeck. He believed each man represented on the monument would elicit patronage from particular regions, projecting that Pennsylvania donors would fund Washington's likeness because "Washington did so much, suffered so much and is tied up with the Keystone State." Funding for Jefferson would come from "a southern group of fine men" Norbeck recruited to "look after" the Virginian. "I want Chicago Illinois to take care of Lincoln," he said, and as for Roosevelt, "Root, Thompson, and Pinchot," the leaders of the Roosevelt Memorial Association, would contribute: "Theodore's old friends will take care of him."[56] Robinson, who feared the local South Dakota community could not fund the project, was reassured by Norbeck's confidence that Roosevelt's friends would underwrite some of the construction. Robinson imagined Mount Rushmore as a thing of value, a means of encouraging a tourist industry and stabilizing the volatile agricultural economy of his state. He cared considerably less about the artistic and interpretive rationale of the project. Roosevelt's popularity and Norbeck's conviction that his presence would attract wealthier patrons persuaded Robinson to go along with the plan.

The RMA, however, much to the disappointment of Robinson, Norbeck, and Borglum, refused to support the sculpture at Rushmore. Already inundated with requests to support countless memorial ideas, the RMA strictly declined to fund or endorse any scheme over which it did not have complete administrative control.[57] When this came to light, the deliberations about which presidents to include were done. Roosevelt was in. Without donations from the RMA or substantive fundraising assistance from the association, Norbeck and Borglum were forced to lobby Congress for federal financing. Indeed, the government became the primary guarantor of the memorial.

Over time, Borglum warmed to the idea of Roosevelt's inclusion on the monument. The two men had shared a close personal and political relationship that stretched back to the 1880s, when Roosevelt had worked for the New York City police. They had sustained a friendship throughout Roosevelt's tenure as president, and Borglum had unveiled some of his most acclaimed work at the White House. One carving, a huge bust of Lincoln, stayed on display at the Executive Mansion for so long that when it moved to the Capitol Rotunda, Roosevelt said he "missed seeing it around."[58] In 1912, when Roosevelt ran for president as a Progressive, Borglum took the helm of the Connecticut Bull Moose campaign, and like so many faithful supporters, called for Roosevelt to run for president in 1916 after his reconciliation with the Republican Party.

In the 1916 nominating contest, though, Borglum and Roosevelt had a falling out. Roosevelt promised he would support Leonard Wood's speculative candidacy, but when it became clear that the general lacked the delegates necessary to win the nomination, TR moved to support Henry Cabot Lodge and later gave his endorsement to the eventual nominee Charles Evans Hughes. Borglum censured Roosevelt as a crafty sycophant, lacking the high-mindedness that had characterized his Bull Moose candidacy only four years earlier. Despite this unpleasant political episode, the rapport between the men did not end. "I think I disagreed with him half the time," the artist reminisced after Roosevelt's death. "What does it matter?" he asked. "I think I annoyed him as much he annoyed me, he liked me none the less, and so I admired him the more."[59]

When the two men met for the last time in 1918, Roosevelt related his pride in the acquisition of the Panama Canal, counting it as his most significant contribution to the nation. According to Borglum's wife, that revelation deeply affected her husband's view of Roosevelt and, in turn, his vision for Rushmore.[60] Borglum met with Archie Roosevelt shortly after TR's death to discuss casting a sculpture of his father. Familiar with Borglum's work, Archie hoped that a combination of the artist's memories and access to James Earle Fraser's death mask would produce an exceptional sculpture.[61] Borglum accepted the offer and invited the press to his studio during the sculpting. The *New York Evening Telegram* reported that as he shaped the clay, "Borglum told of many incidents of his acquaintance with Teddy." Often, when it appeared the sculpture had neared completion, he would suddenly cleave off part of the face. "I've got to put the soul there," the artist exclaimed, "his soldier's soul!"[62]

The bronze Borglum created included the soldier's soul and more, one art critic declared. Reviews credited him with adding elements of the statesman and the western cowboy, declaring his bust of Roosevelt as among 1919's best artwork. "You live," Rev. Joseph Fulford Folsom exclaimed in a sonnet about the bronze, "for Borglum found you amid the throng Invisible, and brought you back to light."[63] When the RMA organized a public art exhibition in late 1919, Borglum's bust took center stage. In the display cases installed along Broadway at the office buildings of Gorham Manufacturing, Tiffany & Company, and Scribner's, the RMA exhibited photos, painting, and other sculptures. Prominently positioned was Borglum's bronze.[64]

The artist's close friendship with Roosevelt made him amenable to Norbeck's idea for Rushmore; moreover, the image of Roosevelt fit seamlessly with Borglum's plans to enshrine the myth of manifest destiny on the mountainside. A massive sculpture nestled in the Black Hills appealed to Borglum's affinity for the expanding American frontier and rugged prairie, where he, like Roosevelt, believed that the American people had forged their unique traits and distinguished the character of their nation. Mount Rushmore would honor continental expansion as the wellspring of American democracy. As an adherent of Frederick Jackson Turner's frontier thesis, Borglum imagined the grand sculpture as a memorial to the American people.[65]

Setting Rushmore in this background, he called the monument a shrine to America's "Empire builders," a memorial to the men who shaped American identity by expanding national boundaries and civilizing the barbarian West. Borglum declared Washington's place on the mountain "inevitable." He symbolized "the rock on which the republic was founded—the plumb line to establish its direction." The 1803 Louisiana Purchase, the nation's "first step westward," gave Borglum reason to include Jefferson. Lincoln was "the savior of the republic," the man who saved the Union and extended the reach of the Constitution. Lincoln also belonged, Borglum stated erroneously, as the "president under whom Alaska was acquired." (Secretary of State William Seward actually devised the purchase of Alaska after Lincoln's death.) Finally, Roosevelt's contribution to empire came with "cutting the Panama Canal," an act that put him among the other great American imperialists. Roosevelt "accomplished the dream of Columbus and opened a sea-way from Europe to Asia and his name was closely linked with territorial expansion following the war with Spain."[66]

Borglum wrote to the RMA trustees: "Whatever there was of opposition to Roosevelt, his great essential virtues cheered every true American . . . In him lived and grew . . . our national spirit . . . A freedom that must become tangible, concrete and understood, because in it and through it, alone can America grow and fulfill her promise and free herself from the vanities of the older civilizations." Roosevelt stood as an American "dreadnaught, the star of empire in its western course," and his place on Rushmore fit "the genius of America" as a "Big Brother in the world."[67] In the heart of hallowed Native American lands, Borglum carved four faces in celebration of American imperialism and called it a "shrine of democracy."

Despite decades of work, the eccentric sculptor never realized the full extent of his vision. Expanding costs and Borglum's death in 1941 cut short the work. The sculptor sought to carve an entablature in the shape of the Louisiana Purchase alongside the busts, a slab of flat granite bearing a five-hundred-word history of the United States. Borglum also proposed and began construction on a Hall of Records designed as an interpretive visitor's center. Set into the back of the mountain, the hall was to tell the artist's version of manifest destiny and act as a time capsule, showcasing copies of the major relics of the nation's history, including the Declaration of Independence and the Constitution. Neither the entablature nor the hall came to fruition.

Without these additions, Mount Rushmore appears to most tourists to be a tribute to four great presidents. In the 1920s, when Roosevelt's public reputation ranked alongside that of Washington and Lincoln, that seemed reasonable, but as Roosevelt's reputation retreated in the 1930s, it appeared less so. What had actually earned him a place on Rushmore was Norbeck's affinity for his western attributes and like-minded progressivism. That Roosevelt's public memory carried multiple meanings made his addition to the South Dakota mountainside possible, even as the country disputed his place on the National Mall. These first monuments demonstrate the elasticity of legacy and show how closely connected Roosevelt's was to historical contexts.

The birthplace, the national memorial, and Mount Rushmore relied on themes that had been developed in the first tributes and, with the exception of the national memorial that was never realized, extended Roosevelt's legacy along similar lines. The birthplace was a memorial to Americanism, Roosevelt's New York upbringing, and his progressive morality. The vast collection of Rooseveltiana stored at the house and museum illustrated other facets of his legacy, and in this regard the WRMA achieved remarkable success, despite the absence of financial reserves necessary to do so independently. The infusion of RMA money helped finish the birthplace, but the women still needed a loan to cover the operating costs of the house. They took out a mortgage and paid it off before the end of the decade, but financial woes would bother them for years to come. This difficulty confined the WRMA's work to New York City and restricted their activities outside the birthplace.

Nevertheless, the house stood as proof of their resolve, their commitment to women's issues, and their determination to lead the promotion of Americanism. Conversely, the RMA's botched plan to erect a memorial at the Tidal Basin, while disheartening for trustees, did not wreck their long-term plans. They maintained a robust bank balance and evolved as a powerful force in the memorialization of Roosevelt around the country and globally. Most successfully, Mount Rushmore emphasized Roosevelt's presidential greatness, a controversial matter in the 1920s and one that separated his nemesis Woodrow Wilson from the class of Jefferson, Washington, and Lincoln. Even if Congress, and particularly the Democrats, refused to admit that comparison was warranted, Mount Rushmore stands as a permanent reminder that many considered Roosevelt among the most important US presidents.

The tributes of 1919, the hagiographies, the hero worship in motion pictures, the memorial associations, and the first monuments exemplify the appreciation that some Americans had for Roosevelt in the years following his death. The first backlash against this deification came when Congress refused to erect a national memorial at the Tidal Basin and demonstrated the limits of public admiration. "The opposition which Mr. Roosevelt, living, stirred up was never tepid," Hermann Hagedorn admitted to RMA president James R. Garfield: "People were either 100% for him or 100% against him, and I suspect that situation still holds."[68]

[CHAPTER FOUR]

THE OTHER ROOSEVELT

The Roosevelt family feud that erupted during the 1920 election intensified over the course of the decade. Consumed by the partisan spirit of the day, the Oyster Bay and Hyde Park branches used their relationship with TR to propel their political ambitions. Ted and Franklin especially entrenched themselves. As an unwavering Republican, Ted billed himself as the namesake, while Franklin cast himself as the Democratic simulacrum. Pitted against each other as rival political patriarchs, they waged a zero-sum battle to be designated TR's rightful heir. As nemeses, one's political success typically paralleled the failure of the other. The New York gubernatorial elections became a battleground for their disputes, with a Roosevelt running in 1924, 1928, and 1930. Franklin's decision to run for president in 1932 brought the family feud to national attention. TR biographer Edmund Morris argues that Franklin's rise gave the Hyde Park clan an opportunity to overshadow the Oyster Bay Roosevelts and that Franklin's regular co-option of Theodore's legacy diminished by 1933, allowing him to "make his own imperious way" as a historical figure.[1] But the reality is more complex. Franklin continued to co-opt Theodore's legacy throughout his presidency, and because this was a time when Ted Roosevelt receded in popularity, Franklin kept Theodore in the public's mind.

After his defeat in the 1920 election, Franklin descended into political limbo, neither valued for his contribution to the Democratic ticket nor blamed by party faithful. The election had launched him as a national figure, made him familiar in once-unfamiliar places, and helped him transcend the accusation of being "a Democratic echo of Theodore Roosevelt." Even so, the crushing defeat by Harding and Coolidge had arrested Franklin's career and crushed his confidence. Worse, he contracted infantile paralysis in the summer of 1921, a condition that literally crippled his ability to run for office or stand for election. Intent on recovering from an illness without a cure, Franklin focused on medical treatment and physical therapy rather than politics.[2]

Meanwhile, the Oyster Bay Roosevelts flourished. Ted won reelection to the New York State Assembly by the largest margin his district ever delivered, then resigned his seat to fill Franklin's shoes as assistant secretary of the Navy. Ted believed the junior cabinet post would launch his national profile in the same way it had his father's and his cousin's.[3] While Franklin convalesced and retrained his body to walk with crutches and braces, Ted hosted dinner parties and poker games with Washington's elite. Ted's political network owed much to his sister Alice and brother-in-law Nick Longworth, who would become speaker of the House in 1925 and who connected Ted to influential politicos within the Republican Party and the Harding administration. Whether winning or losing at poker, Ted made valuable political friendships with Washington heavyweights like Secretary of State Charles Evans Hughes, Secretary of Commerce Herbert Hoover, and Treasury Secretary Andrew Mellon. Outside the cabinet he met progressive Republicans like William Borah, the lion of Idaho, who would illegitimately father Alice Roosevelt Longworth's only daughter. In 1924, Borah pressured Republicans to add Ted to the national ticket as Harding's vice president, a move that would replace the austere Calvin Coolidge.[4] His machinations failed, however, and Coolidge eventually succeeded Harding. The effort nevertheless illustrated Ted's soaring popularity in the party.

At the Department of the Navy, Ted made a particularly significant contribution. The 1921 Washington Naval Conference, a meeting of nine countries organized by Secretary of State Hughes to promote disarmament after the war, gave Ted an opportunity to showcase his diplomatic acumen. He chaired a panel of naval experts and pressed world powers to reduce their navies. The so-called Five Power Treaty—a flagship agreement that concluded the conference—came about, in part, due to Ted's vigilant statecraft. The treaty limited fleet sizes and decommissioned some existing battleships, easing security tensions in Asia and soothing war-weary budgets. International relations experts hailed it as a significant step on the road to global peace and bestowed considerable praise on Ted.[5]

Ted took his political cues from prominent Republicans in Harding's administration, a strategy that accelerated his career and, in equal measure, irreparably damaged it. Hoover, Hughes, and Mellon made positive contributions, but corruption and scandal also plagued the Harding administration and affected Ted's reputation. There was bribery in the Justice Department, profiteering at the Veterans Bureau, and widespread bootlegging that flagrantly subverted the new Prohibition laws. But no crime sullied the administration's credibility more than the Teapot Dome affair, a scandal in which administration officials sold oil-rich federal lands to drilling companies without a competitive bidding process.

Authority for the strategic federal land sales originally had rested with the Navy Department until President Harding transferred power to the Interior Department, led by Albert Fall. Ted resisted the reallocation of authority and protested the sale of the land on the grounds that it acted as an oil reserve for the Navy, but his immediate superior, Secretary of the Navy Edwin Denby, authorized the handover without consulting his assistant. Unbeknown to Harding, Denby, or Ted, Interior Secretary Fall accepted more than $400,000 in bribes or gifts from the oil industry to hasten the sale of these lands. When his transgressions came to light, Congress voided the sale and returned authority to the Navy Department. A congressional investigation uncovered the full extent of Fall's offenses, which led to his indictment, criminal conviction, and incarceration.[6] Harding escaped interrogation and impeachment when he died in 1923, and Denby avoided trial by resigning his cabinet post.

The Teapot Dome scandal put considerable strain on Ted as assistant secretary of the Navy. His reputation as an honest politician was tarnished, and his longstanding relationship with Sinclair Oil, one of the companies indicted in the affair, intensified the negative public impression. Harry Sinclair, the company's founder, was accused of "loaning" Fall $100,000. Ted had worked as a director of Sinclair Oil after World War I, before entering politics, and maintained a close relationship with Harry Sinclair. He had even asked Sinclair to hire his brother Archie, who became vice president of the company in 1923. Ted and Archie's association with the company fueled speculation that the Oyster Bay Roosevelts had a cozy relationship with prominent Teapot Dome co-conspirators. Adding to the list of circumstantial evidence, Ted held a sizable portfolio of Sinclair Oil stock until December 1921, a few months before the scandal hit the headlines. The timely sale smacked of insider trading; actually, it came about after his wife took over the family finances. No matter how innocent, though, the fortuitous investment strategy appeared duplicitous.[7]

To clear his name, Ted testified before the congressional committee investigating the scandal. After two days of giving evidence, he expected exoneration, but South Carolina representative William Francis Stevenson sensed a political opportunity. Declaring that Ted had "had a part" in the deceit, Stevenson introduced a congressional motion to force his resignation. Ted's high-powered friends like Nick Longworth rushed to his defense and helped him withstand the barrage of allegations. After the investigatory committee heard all the testimony, it formally exonerated him.[8] Nonetheless, the affair unnerved Ted, who believed it permanently damaged his dream of following his father's footsteps. That suspicion was seemingly verified when President Coolidge refused to appoint him to a cabinet position made vacant by the scandal. "My political career is over and done with," he wrote his wife: "People will . . . never believe the truth."[9]

But redemption came sooner than Ted expected. In 1924 he won the Republican nomination for governor of New York, and much to his surprise the nod came on the first ballot. Suddenly, he had an opportunity to move beyond Teapot Dome and the confines of bureaucratic Washington politics. It was a chance to chart the path taken by his father, who had won the governorship in 1899.

As New York was the most populous state in the Union and a bellwether of national sentiment, its governor's race commanded widespread attention. Empire State governors often succeeded in winning their party's nomination for president, and in 1924, Democratic governor Al Smith aspired to that office. In running against him, Ted faced one of New York's most formidable politicians. Born in Manhattan, Alfred Emanuel Smith identified with the city's immigrants and built his political network on their patronage. He won gubernatorial races twice, in 1918 and 1922, by portraying himself as an urban populist. While that message had appealed to New Yorkers, Smith's campaign throughout the country required a centrist message that reached out to rural people and social conservatives. Such a rebranding exercise required a campaign manager capable of attracting these audiences, and Franklin Roosevelt nicely fit the bill. As an upstate Democrat and Protestant, Franklin distracted from Smith's Catholic faith and city slicker persona, and their collaboration united New York Democrats. For Ted, however, Franklin's return to state politics was a threat.

After three years of physical therapy, Franklin's recovery had plateaued and forced him to retrain his attention on his career, rather than his body. His decision to reenter politics also reflected his awareness of Ted's decision to run for governor. A Republican victory in New York, Franklin supposed, would perpetuate his political dormancy, and he staged a comeback on the grandest platform possible, making his first public appearance in three years at the Democratic National Convention in New York City. With help from his son James, a discreet pair of crutches, and supportive metal braces hidden under his trousers, Franklin shuffled up to the central podium, buoyed by the rapturous applause of the Democratic delegates who packed Madison Square Garden.[10] Channeling the spirit of William Wordsworth while clinging to the podium, he declared Smith the "Happy Warrior," a rare politician who "speaks with the voice of America" and "burns with the fire of divine humanity." To the undecided crowd, Franklin insisted, "with him we can win."[11]

The speech energized the convention and dramatically boosted Smith's appeal. As an opponent of Prohibition and an urban, working-class Catholic, Smith did not naturally inspire rank-and-file Democrats, but when balloting began, he came second, not far behind the former Treasury secretary William McAdoo. After eighty-seven ballots, the national convention gave Smith the lead, although not a majority. Unable to sway McAdoo's contingent, the nomination eventually went to compromise candidate John W. Davis of West Virginia, a man who lacked the necessary charisma to restore the enthusiasm sapped by the Smith-McAdoo standoff. The *Chicago Tribune* reported on the day's weather as representative of the Democratic mood, observing that driving torrents of rain "sent thousands scurrying for shelter" and that Davis's boring speech hastened the crowd's dispatch "into the surrounding shadows of the surrounding meadows."[12] Party leaders could not manufacture passion for their nominee, and in November, Davis mustered less than 30 percent of the popular vote. Despite the rout, Franklin Roosevelt counted the 1924 election as a victory. He had reignited his career and demonstrated his political dexterity in spite of his severe physical limitations.

With Smith out of the presidential campaign, the Hyde Park Roosevelts focused on securing his re-election as governor. Eleanor played a substantial role. She began working with political maestro Louis Howe, who urged her to stump for state legislative candidates and to take leadership of the state's women. She transformed campaign fieldwork and fundraising but presumed her role would diminish after her husband returned to New York as a booster for Smith. It did not. Howe pushed her to continue, and she proved instrumental in attracting New York's women to Smith's candidacy.[13] At the 1924 New York Democratic convention, she successfully won the right for women to name their own delegates, largely because Smith supported her, and in return Eleanor introduced a resolution that all New York delegates at the national convention must support Smith as the state's favorite son. A powerful speaker in her own right, Eleanor matched Franklin's oratorical prowess when she endorsed Smith's nomination at the state convention. Biographer Joseph Lash described her as "one of the convention's high points."[14]

Eleanor's political ferocity was most apparent on the campaign trail. She orchestrated a full-frontal assault on the Republican candidate, remarking after her cousin Ted's nomination that Smith's victory was all but guaranteed: "How can he help it when the Republican convention yesterday did everything to help him?" Eleanor respected her cousin as a "personally nice man" before criticizing him as politically corrupt and "willing to do the bidding of his friends." Throughout the autumn months she traveled the breadth of New York, often following Ted in much the same way he had followed Franklin in 1920. She gave speeches along the way, ridiculed him in radio broadcasts, and emphasized the Teapot Dome allegations. Louis Howe organized for a massive papier-mâché teapot to be built around the chassis of Eleanor's seven-passenger campaign car. Dubbed the "singing teapot," the kettle-car spewed real steam from its spout and became a talking point that drew attention from the campaign's substantive issues. Given Ted's exoneration in the affair, her Oyster Bay cousins protested Eleanor's antics as unfair and decried the attack a "vicious" smear. Only in retrospect did Eleanor admit that it was a "rough stunt." At the time, it seemed entirely legitimate to her.[15]

Franklin also got involved. He called Ted's Teapot Dome testimony "a pitiable spectacle" and implored New Yorkers to read the congressional investigation reports. "The Republican candidate has a splendid war record," he told voters: "He has, on the other hand, a record in public office which is wretched."[16] At one campaign stop, Franklin told a gathering that TR would not have accepted his son's "gross stupidity" as assistant secretary and "would have dismissed" him for being "tainted with gross incompetence."[17] Howe told Eleanor that Franklin had "been waiting to get even for a long time."[18]

"And so the silliness went on," Alice Roosevelt Longworth said. The family feud made headlines and fanned gossip among New York social circles, but Ted's campaign had bigger problems. Teapot Dome had hurt his credibility, and his time away from New York as assistant secretary of the Navy had distanced him from local electoral issues. His campaign team proved amateurish, working from bad information. Consequently, Ted made several blunders, including one at Colgate University, where he praised the football team's victory over Cornell. Colgate had lost—to Nebraska.

The crowd of students roared abuse, and in the commotion Ted barked at his aides, "Who told me that?" The press widely recounted the incident, which Smith parodied. With a "gold-toothed grin" the Democrat mocked Ted's cluelessness, punctuating each campaign promise with the punchline, "Who Told Teddy That?"[19] The governor's political cunning, personal charisma, and masterful team of operators handily dispensed with his opponent, and Ted failed to distinguish himself on the big issues like labor relations, the KKK, or public utilities. Prohibition divided them to some degree—Ted was a nominal "dry" and Smith an unyielding "wet"—but much of the campaign came down to character and political machinery.

At the ballot boxes, Smith triumphed. The result, at first glance, appeared narrower than it really was. Ted lost by just over 100,000 votes. However, the defeat came in a year when Republicans swept Democrats in most states. Calvin Coolidge crushed John W. Davis throughout the country, and in New York he won by nearly 1 million votes. That means the Empire State opted for the Republican presidential candidate, then defected to the Democrat for governor, a trend that bucked the nationwide pattern of voting the straight party line. In fact, Ted was the only New York Republican candidate to lose statewide. Even his lieutenant governor won.[20] Conversely, the election represented a watershed for the political fortunes of Hyde Park. Franklin's revival and Eleanor's arrival set in motion one of the most powerful duos in American political history.

The Hyde Park ascendancy continued in 1928. Franklin nominated Al Smith for president once again, and when Smith won the Democratic nomination, Franklin earned his blessing to run for governor of New York. Smith ultimately lost to Hoover in the general election, but in the Empire State Franklin narrowly won against a countercurrent of Republican victories. His incredible campaign success led political analysts to rumor that he might run for the White House in 1932.

Like his father, Ted escaped the spotlight after losing the election by traveling abroad to explore and collect rare animal specimens for American museums. When he returned, the extent of his political decline became evident. New York Republicans snubbed him in 1926, and Ted never again ran for elected office. In 1929 he accepted President Hoover's offer of the governorship of Puerto Rico, a post that distinguished him as an adept executive and government administrator. Three years later he accepted the position of governor general of the Philippines, where he served until 1933. Alice Roosevelt Longworth recalled the 1920s as a period of awkward transition. "There was this family feeling which I didn't brood about, but which was definitely there," she said. "Ted had been brought up by my father to follow in his footsteps . . . and to see Franklin follow in those same footsteps with large Democratic shoes on was just too terrible to contemplate!" She proclaimed the Oyster Bay clan "*the Roosevelts*" and referred to Franklin as "Nemesis."[21] Corinne Roosevelt Robinson was more sanguine. She wrote Eleanor, "You are both certainly fine soldiers. How I wish we were fighting for the same leaders . . . I often think what joy it would be to me, caring for you both as I do, to be lined up side by side!"[22]

The high-profile dispute between the Hyde Park and Oyster Bay families failed to shatter the cult of personality that enveloped TR's image. If anything, Ted and Franklin enhanced the hero worship by seeking to emulate TR. Dartmouth College history professor Charles R. Lingley said that TR had cast a "spell of personal magnetism" that created "a vacuum" in public memory. Among scholars, Lingley complained that poor archival research "and technically inadequate material" led to sweeping deification; there was "too much interpretation and not even an attempt at documentation."[23] TR became a "self-parody" of never-ending hagiography, a faultless image that continued to glimmer in 1930.[24] Owen Wister, author of *The Virginian,* published an effusive personal memoir of Roosevelt that year, as did diplomat Lewis Einstein, who lionized Roosevelt as "half legendary."[25]

Such sustained idolatry presented an opportunity to correct the historical image, and Henry Fowles Pringle seized on it, single-handedly shifting the paradigm in 1931 with a new kind of biography. Born in Manhattan the same year as TR's youngest son Quentin, Pringle enlisted in the army when the United States entered World War I. After the war he enrolled in a journalism course at Cornell University, graduated in 1920, and began work immediately as a beat reporter for the *New York Sun.* Two years later, the promising young writer joined the staff of the *New York Globe* before being recruited by Herbert Bayard Swope, the chief editor of the city's notoriously investigative *New York World.* There, Pringle's writing style matured.

He delved into the city's gritty underbelly to uncover corruption, vice, and the illicit sale of alcohol, relying on local personalities to lend color to his muckraking. He developed a faithful readership that relished his scrupulously psychological portraits, and his aptitude for such writing led to his resignation in 1927, when he resolved to pursue fame and fortune as a freelance biographer. Aligning his style with a class of authors called "debunkers," he was contemptuous of biographical portraits "yanked down from Olympus," and he set out to expose hero worship as fraud.[26] William E. Woodward, a literary critic who in 1923 popularized the term *bunk* as historical deceit, led the avalanche of revisionism with his 1926 biography of George Washington, a book that flattened the American hero. Pringle admired Woodward's passion and imagined debunking as a kind of academic honesty. Many scholars complained that the practice relied on an author's subjectivity and smacked of opportunism. After all, Woodward "recast the adult Washington in the image of a pragmatic Wall Street tycoon of the 1920s" to appeal to modern audiences. Debunking thus contained a contextual perspective, creating a subjective account that aimed to bring the past into the present in a manner that captivated the public imagination.[27]

While writing for the *World,* Pringle compiled voluminous research on Al Smith and his 1924 reelection campaign. Setting out to sketch the governor as a tough party boss and Tammany bootlicker, Pringle chose a living subject with no historiographical lineage. Consequently, the book regurgitated stories of a familiar personality and uncovered few surprises. One reviewer even thought that Smith "emerges from the debunking process more human, more credible, and more admirable."[28]

Critical, but not captious like Woodward, Pringle experienced muted success with his first book. For his second effort, he sharpened his literary talons. In 1928 he published *Big Frogs,* a book that did not disappoint the public appetite for defamation. Pringle dissected the nation's most prominent men by locating in each of his subjects an unpleasant personality trait and exploiting it in pseudo-psychological analysis. First, he sketched presidential candidate Herbert Hoover, known best as the "great humanitarian" of World War I and co-architect of the decade's economic prosperity. In *Big Frogs,* Hoover devolved from an administrative mastermind into a laborious orator and social dolt. New York City mayor Jimmy Walker, known as the savior of the Big Apple's sanitation crisis, came across as an egotist with little intellectual dynamism. Public relations innovator Ivy Lee went from being seen as a modern-day advertising genius to a temperamental narcissist. Theodore Roosevelt Jr. fared worst of all. Pringle called him a "thick-headed" errand boy for the Republican Party. Not surprisingly, *Big Frogs* sold exceptionally well, and despite being sensationalist it earned rave reviews, establishing its author as one of the foremost political writers of his time.[29]

In 1930 the untarnished image of former president Theodore Roosevelt caught Pringle's attention. After more than a year of research in the Library of Congress and associated archives in the Roosevelt birthplace, resources made available by the RMA and the Roosevelt family, Pringle steadily released his biography as a series of articles in *Outlook* magazine. In sixteen parts issued over the course of the autumn and winter of 1931, the author traced Roosevelt's life from birth to the collapse of the Bull Moose Party and his political clash with Woodrow Wilson. When the series concluded, Harcourt Brace published an edited and unabridged version of Pringle's research as a book.

Among academic and popular audiences, the biography initiated new conversations about Roosevelt, and praise for Pringle came in many forms, including a Pulitzer Prize for best biography in 1932. The Pulitzer board called it "a vitalized portrait," one that resuscitated Roosevelt from the caricature of previous expressions. In general, historians hailed it as a "first-rate contribution" that made use of archival materials "with a scholarly thoroughness, judgment, and detachment."[30] The combination of academic professionalism with an exceptional narrative set Pringle's portrayal apart from others. Unlike William Roscoe Thayer, Pringle had full access to Roosevelt's papers from childhood to the presidency, and although he did not read Roosevelt's post-1909 manuscripts, the biography utilized the most current research available. In contrast to Joseph Bucklin Bishop, Pringle had the artistic flair and literary creativity of a gifted scribe. And unlike the personal memoirs of TR by Owen Wister, Lawrence Abbott, or James Amos, Pringle's account gained a patina of objectivity because of his distance from his subject.

The book's success confirmed how overdue a reassessment was, yet Pringle's depiction did not escape its own kind of self-parody. Regardless of the accolades it won, Pringle's book was a revisionist account that relied on overemphasizing a single character trait in the same way that Wister celebrated Roosevelt's masculinity or Abbott highlighted his reform-mindedness. For Pringle, Roosevelt radiated adolescence. On nearly every page, he emphasizes Roosevelt's juvenile nature, perhaps most in the years surrounding the War of 1898. Roosevelt's service in the Rough Riders presents as childish enthusiasm, and his "frantic appeals for the Medal of Honor" come across as vainglorious. In youth, childish behavior and an energetic immaturity hardly seem out of place, yet Pringle depicts Roosevelt's exuberance as unique and almost menac-

ing, seeding the "first green . . . shoots of a germinating ego." He relates
the romantic story of Roosevelt's triumph over asthma not as a tale of
overcoming adversity but as an episode that set in motion a "hysterical
calling" to enter politics. TR's young adulthood and the pre-presidential
years become a whirl of frenzied, impulsive, and infantile moments that
Pringle defines as overcompensation for personal demons, such as his
asthma and his father's failure to serve in the Civil War. Describing Roosevelt's political career, Pringle portrays an immature adult exhibiting an
"overly enthusiastic" attitude and an unreasonably high "estimate of his
services." Whether he was governor of New York, vice president, or president, these qualities pervaded Roosevelt's style of management, which,
Pringle argues, served to soothe his self-worth.[31] Even without access to
Roosevelt's post-presidential papers, Pringle represents the "Roosevelt of
later years" as remarkably like his Roosevelt of all other years, "the most
adolescent of men."[32]

TR's friend and journalist William Allen White complained that Pringle's impression left the reader looking at "every unpleasant side and
angle," a fair observation that nevertheless obscures the fact that Pringle
relied on the same exalted themes as TR's hagiographers. Nationalism,
virility, progressivism, and ecological mindfulness stand out in this 1931
account as much as they did in earlier books. Pringle qualified these
themes with the proposition that Roosevelt's adolescence and ego mo-
tivated the pursuit of genuinely beneficial political causes. So, a fault
existed in Roosevelt's personality rather than in the ends he championed.
Pringle lampooned Lewis Einstein's 1930 biography that described TR as
a renaissance man "in no way a typical American," saying that Einstein's
portrayal was "true, at least in a sense": Roosevelt did campaign for
righteous ideals, but only "when he was not busy" aggrandizing his ego.[33]
For the debunker, Roosevelt's intentions had considerable bearing on his
legacy. Pringle reduced progressive reform, patriotism, and conservation
to acts of a flawed character, and Harcourt Brace advertised the book as
an opportunity to discover Roosevelt's faults.[34]

In some measure the revisionist biography sprang from the author's
personal dislike of politics. Pringle found it almost "impossible to accept
the political calling as an honorable one" and as a consequence "could not
have written a sympathetic book on any successful politician," let alone a
man who held as many offices as Roosevelt.[35] Pringle associated the desire
to win elections with narcissism, neuroticism, and jealousy, concluding
that "no great reforms burned in Theodore's breast as he began the career

that he was to follow with few interruptions until he died." His virtues came about "accidently," a product of ego and a yearning to have "a hand in everything that was going on."[36] The neurotic and covetous image recedes during a three-year interruption of TR's political career, when he lived in the North Dakota Badlands, but it never disappears entirely. Even on the range, Pringle's TR is a man "whose riding, recklessness, and exhibitionism" among the cowboys reflects his hubris and conceit.[37] The book determines that Roosevelt won the respect of the plainsmen because he instinctually emulated them, an interpretation that suggests fraud, and Pringle maintains that Roosevelt's true identity was that of a refined New York Knickerbocker.

To that point, no single biography had changed Roosevelt's popular memory as definitively as Pringle's. He turned hagiography to bunk and took TR from deity to demagogue. In fact, the image was so convincing that few new biographies appeared in the 1930s, and none challenged the dominance of Pringle's. If anything, popular culture echoed his view. The most exaggerated depiction of this image of TR came in Joseph Kesselring's comedic play *Arsenic and Old Lace*. The play follows the homicidal activities of the Brewster family. The protagonist, Mortimer Brewster, discovers a dead body at the home of his elderly aunts Martha and Abby, who offer free room and board to lonely men before poisoning the lodgers with elderberry wine spiked with arsenic. The "mercy" killings of woeful travelers are covered up by Teddy Brewster, Mortimer's brother, who lives with his aunts and buries the victims in the basement. He also believes he is Theodore Roosevelt.

Kesselring wrote the play in 1939, and it opened in theaters two years later. In 1944, Frank Capra directed a film adaptation starring Cary Grant as Mortimer. While the farcical plot contains several twists and an abundance of characters, the antics of Teddy, played by John Alexander on stage and screen, generate the satirical absurdity that drives the plot. Close in age to his dapper brother Mortimer, Teddy dresses in Rough Rider uniform and screams "Charge!" each time he climbs the stairs, imitating Roosevelt's pursuit of Spanish soldiers up San Juan Heights. When forced to explain his khaki outfit, shovel, and long periods in the basement, he tells his brother, "I'm off to Panama . . . a new lock for the canal you know." The play reaches a crescendo when a psychiatrist diagnoses Teddy as delusional and commits him to an asylum.

While other Capra films like *Mr. Smith Goes to Washington* and *It's a Wonderful Life* convey clear political messages, film critics have tended to

treat *Arsenic and Old Lace* as "sheer entertainment without any real sub-
stance."[38] Yet Capra's adaptation of the play emphasized certain elements
of Kesselring's set and dialogue so as to illustrate how political myths
contradict reality, a point Capra made in several of his films. *Arsenic and
Old Lace* demystifies, even debunks, the Brewster family. The audience's
first impression of aunts Abby and Martha as charitable pillars of society
twists into shock when Mortimer unearths their murderous nature. At
the end of the film, Mortimer discovers they adopted him. The revelation
brings relief to Mortimer, who now can distance himself from the Brew-
sters and dismiss the growing fear that he will follow in their footsteps.
As with the rest of the characters, Teddy Brewster gradually changes.
At first he appears a lovable, deluded dunce, but as the play goes on, he
becomes a dark and menacing figure who buries seventeen houseguests.

In making the film, Kesselring and Capra crafted an image of TR that
relied on the psychological caricature Pringle devised, and echoed his
effort to demystify an American icon. When theater companies staged
the play, they told actors playing Teddy to think of TR as Peter Pan, as the
boy who never grew up.[39] The emotionally adolescent Teddy Brewster demands the audience's attention by shouting, thundering around his aunts'
house, trumpeting a bugle, and pretending to hold cabinet meetings.
Traits that initially seem innocent—loudness, juvenile enthusiasm, and ig-
norance—evolve into the faults of a dangerous and unhinged collaborator.

Arsenic and Old Lace ran on Broadway for five years, and the film met
with widespread praise. Initially, the Roosevelt memorial associations did
not grasp the significance of these depictions of TR as infantile. The RMA
classed the 1930s as "difficult days" and recognized that TR's image "suffered" in public memory. In fact, the RMA bears some responsibility for
the revisionist image. Director Hagedorn had encouraged the association
to give Pringle access to the Roosevelt Papers, and after the biography was
released, he was slow to denounce its negative representation. Hagedorn
took a brief leave of absence from the association in the 1930s, and trustees chose to focus on building the national memorial in Washington.[40]

Pringle's biography came at a time of dramatic change for American
society. The irrational exuberance that had characterized the 1920s collapsed into a lasting economic depression so ruinous that agricultural and
industrial production stagnated for more than a decade. Unemployment
rates soared to 25 percent; international trade declined by half; inequality,
homelessness, and poverty crushed Americans' hopes for a swift recovery.
A political realignment followed. The Republican presidencies of Hard-

ing, Coolidge, and Hoover received much of the blame for a golden-calf culture that encouraged individual wealth seeking without scrupulously considering the economic consequences. The 1930 congressional elections depleted once-dominant Republican majorities and instigated a long decline for the party.

The Oyster Bay Roosevelts observed the implosion of Republican power with trepidation and "silent dismay." The decline overlapped with personal losses that devastated the family.[41] Nick Longworth—TR's son-in-law, who once called FDR a "denatured Roosevelt" because of his physical affliction—resigned as speaker of the House in 1931. He died a month later. His death swung political control of the House to the Democrats for the first time since 1919. TR's eldest sister, Anna "Bamie" Roosevelt Cowles, who had criticized Eleanor for her vitriolic campaign against Ted, died later that summer. And TR's youngest sister Corinne, once a Republican heavyweight who championed women's suffrage, was no longer physically able to campaign.[42]

TR's children also felt the strain. Politically exiled to Puerto Rico and later the Philippines, Ted remained largely absent from the partisan discourse. He watched the rise of Franklin and Eleanor with disdain, holding them responsible for his truncated career. Kermit, the only Oyster Bay Roosevelt to maintain cordial relations with Hyde Park, began a long descent into economic and emotional depression, in part due to his shipping company's financial losses.[43] Ethel, TR's youngest daughter, escaped the Depression by taking her family to Europe, where their dollars went further.[44]

In contrast, the Hyde Park Roosevelts thrived. As governor, Franklin shepherded New York's financial recovery and relieved the state's impoverished citizens by opening National Guard armories to the homeless, commissioning a review of unemployment insurance, and enacting a progressive state income tax. In 1930 he won reelection by more than 700,000 votes, double his own predicted margin of victory and an achievement that led many in his party to consider him the frontrunner for the 1932 presidential nomination. Praise came from around the country. Burton K. Wheeler, a liberal Democratic senator from Montana, announced his support for FDR as president and stimulated an outpouring of support in the West. Boosters from the South and North advocated for Franklin, due to the forward-thinking strategies of Louis Howe, who had continued to correspond with regional party leaders after Franklin's 1920 vice-presidential campaign.[45]

Speculation about FDR's reentry into national politics ended on January 22, 1932, when he confirmed his intention to seek the Democratic nomination for president. At that moment, Americans had not entirely disambiguated TR from FDR. One Nevada resident told Howe that "five million people in the west who do not know T.R. is dead" would vote for Franklin, and just as he had done in 1920, Howe quietly encouraged the association.[46] The Roosevelt name brought instant recognition and led editorial cartoonists to sketch the two Roosevelts together. Illustrators who supported Franklin drew him as a virtuous cowboy following a trail through "Teddy's Romping Ground" or referred to him as "a modern Teddy." The romanticized cowboy image fit Theodore's enduring legacy, but Franklin had no comparable experiences, a fact that led critical cartoonists to picture him as an eastern aristocrat far removed from the masculine persona of TR. Franklin appeared in many caricatures as an urban dandy making unrealistic promises to rural America. For example, in 1932, J. N. "Ding" Darling resurrected his iconic image of TR's ghost from the "Long, Long Trail" and contrasted the heroic cowboy image with a foppish "New Roosevelt Invading the West."[47]

These conflicting impressions first appeared in newspapers in the West, where the Democratic primaries gave the first hint at a candidate's political strength. "The Roosevelt name doubtless is an asset," the *Oklahoman* reported, but the association with the mythical cowboy mattered less to westerners. Franklin could not be expected to live up to TR's cowboy image, the newspaper explained, because a "man in a wheelchair is not a heroic figure in a national crisis." Likewise, the *Oklahoman* observed, a cowboy cannot offer relief from the global economic depression. Franklin's campaign offered a new hope and greased the wheels of the Democratic machinery out West, two factors that "nominated more candidates than all the color, personality and daring" associated with the mythical cowboy.[48] In North Dakota, Franklin won by a two-thirds majority, but not because he emulated TR or shared the same name, although these things hardly hindered him; rather, he won the policy contest and appealed to voters on the issues. After North Dakota, he took Wisconsin, South Dakota, Nebraska, and Oregon and swept the southern primaries.

At the Democratic National Convention, Franklin secured the lion's share of delegates and took only four ballots to win the nomination.[49] Breaking with tradition, he addressed the convention and accepted the glory in person. His speech balanced the political sensibilities he stressed on the campaign trail with a direct plea to those progressives formerly aligned with TR. He may have explicitly praised the last Democratic president Woodrow Wilson for implementing a progressive political transformation, but he refused to malign Republican progressives, and he cast his ire at the "Republican leadership" in much the same way he did in 1920. FDR stimulated a spirit of political harmony for the sake of national progress. Implicitly, he credited TR with cultivating a progressive wing of the Republican Party and sought to attract those reformers to the Democrats. Formally courting "nominal Republicans" and former Bull Moosers "who find that their conscience cannot be squared with the groping and the failure of their party leaders," Franklin laid fault for the economic downturn with corporate giants who hoarded wealth and shirked public responsibility. Also to blame were the laissez-faire policies of conservative Republicans who encouraged greed and market speculation at the expense of progressive proposals for public works, agricultural sustainability, and financial security. Having billed himself as a progressive in all of his previous campaigns, Franklin never feared to echo TR's rhetoric, and at the national convention he proposed new federal responsibilities for relief, declaring a "new deal for the American people" based on an "equitable opportunity to share in the distribution of national wealth."[50] The New Deal imitated his cousin's "Square Deal" in linguistic style and ideological spirit. In short, FDR sought to complete the political realignment that TR had begun in 1912.[51]

To accomplish this goal, FDR enlisted academics like Raymond Moley, Rexford Tugwell, and Adolf Berle, who "traced their inspiration" for corporate regulation and trustbusting "back to the New Nationalism of Theodore Roosevelt." Likewise, advisors Harold Ickes and Donald Richberg joined FDR's team as "veterans of the Bull Moose crusade" who had "never abandoned the dream" that Theodore Roosevelt planted in their imagination.[52] These progressives became FDR's closest advisors, the so-called Brain Trust. If the New Deal sounded like the Square Deal, it was because it hailed from the same intellectual source and was promoted by many of the same advocates. Editorials picked up on the similarity, conceding that Franklin struck a "calmer and less impulsive" tone than TR.[53] Such observations gave further weight to Pringle's portrait, condemning TR's personality while exalting the virtues of his political crusade. Franklin represented sensible progressivism, they argued, a movement descended from the wily adolescent reform of TR but more mature and composed.

"I was furious," Alice Roosevelt Longworth said about the comparison. "I was jealous about my father's position . . . I had this resentful feeling

that my admired and respected parent was going to be forgotten with the
new [Roosevelt] coming up."[54] Infuriated with Democratic appropriation
of Theodore's ghost, the Oyster Bay Roosevelts retaliated. TR's widow
Edith, who after 1920 had never actively campaigned for any presidential
candidate, did so for Hoover in 1932. In a letter to Ted, Edith maintained
that Franklin made "deliberate propaganda of the name Roosevelt" and
complained that "ignorant people" will "vote for him under a false apprehension."[55] Publicly, she called Franklin "nine-tenths mush and one-tenth
Eleanor" and maligned the New Deal as a dangerous experiment.[56]

Ted considered returning to the United States from the Philippines
to attack Franklin, but the governor general's office had never been po-
liticized in such a manner. Hoover, after careful consideration, decided
not to recall Ted for the campaign, but TR's namesake opted to give a
live radio broadcast from his office in Manila. "In every corner of our
land individuals have been preaching panaceas," Ted declared, including
communism, dictatorship, and subversive populism: "I do not accuse the
Democratic standard-bearer of advocating all of these theories[;] however
they are all held in a lesser or greater degree by component elements that
are backing him."[57] Ever the believer in the Republican Party's capacity
to solve the nation's ills, Ted condemned Franklin as a reactionary.

The daily editorials paid little attention to the animosity of the Oyster
Bay Roosevelts and their attempt to discredit Franklin. Public opinion
perceived their attacks as sour grapes, a sentiment pithily summarized
by baseball poet George Phair:

> Little Teddy, always ready
>   To advise the humble mob;
> Little Teddy, always steady
>   On a governmental job,
> Raised his voice and rooted thus:
>   "Roosevelt! Roosevelt! That means us!
> We may have our poor relations,
>   But we own the copyright,
> So beware of imitations
>   On the next election night."[58]

Rather than depict Ted as heir to TR's legacy, editorial cartoonists portrayed him as a ventriloquist's dummy controlled by Hoover. Edith's
speeches similarly rebounded, provoking public contempt for her treatment of a fellow Roosevelt. "They all seem to know what father would

do under the present conditions," she wrote her son, "and vilify me for doing otherwise."[59]

Despite arousing "the full venom of the Oyster Bay Roosevelts," Franklin and the Democrats swept to power.[60] The country's mood shifted so palpably in the wake of the Great Depression that 42 of 48 states and over 57 percent of the popular vote went to Franklin. Not since Harding's election had a presidential candidate won so decisively. Editorials applauded the return of a Roosevelt to the White House, and cartoonists once unsure of how to cast Franklin in relation to Theodore now illustrated him walking in his predecessor's footsteps, greeted by TR's specter as he moved to accept the presidential throne. Even Franklin made the association, telling a White House correspondent, "You know how it was when Uncle Ted" lived there, "how gay and homelike! Well, that's how we mean to have it!"[61]

The comparison continued throughout his presidency, most frequently in FDR's first one hundred days. But as Franklin became a familiar progressive, more so than even Theodore, artists dispensed with showing his cousin. The connection lingered, however, through symbols like the "big stick." Illustrators sometimes called it "the old symbol" or the "Roosevelt Tradition." It represented progressivism as much as political forcefulness. With Democrats in control of all branches of government and confronted with a crisis unlike any other in American history, Franklin directed a plethora of progressive measures through Congress, which one Republican congressman characterized as having "an atmosphere of hysteria." In his view, major decisions about the nation's future zipped through legislative procedure without typical considerations, and "bills originating in the White House were passed almost daily."[62] No previous administration had acted with such urgency in the first days of its tenure, and, consequently, the New Deal gave rise to editorial criticism about expansive executive power. TR had earned comparable censure during his presidency, but many illustrators ranked Franklin's authority as even more sweeping. In cartoons, TR's big stick shrunk when compared to Franklin's, and other caricatures had him whittling his own, larger than his cousin's.

The big stick never disappeared from editorial cartoons during Franklin's twelve years in office. Certainly the most popular symbol used to connect FDR to TR, it was, however, not the only association. Cartoonists drew Franklin in safari costume stalking prey in the "economic jungle" or shooting big game that represented the social and economic symptoms of the Great Depression. When Congress passed forest conservation measures and the Emergency Conservation Work Act, creating the Civilian Conservation Corps, Theodore's ghost reappeared in cartoons to congratulate Franklin on extending the family's conservationist legacy. During the fight to pass the National Recovery Act, Franklin's most controversial New Deal program that allowed government to intervene in private enterprise and set fair trading conditions, illustrators portrayed the president dressed in Rough Rider gear imploring the American public to charge "San Juan Hill—1933." Even the Teddy bear, an iconic image of Theodore created by artist Clifford Berryman in a 1902 cartoon, seeped into drawings of Franklin. At the end of 1933, Berryman drew Franklin directing the country out of the dark economic wilderness flanked by Uncle Sam and the Teddy bear.

As often as editorial cartoons emphasized FDR's connection to TR, the president reinforced it in speech. In his second fireside chat, Franklin explained his plan for national solvency, outlining new employment schemes, farm-relief legislation, public works projects, transportation reform, and, should all of these fail, the reauthorization of beer sales. The range of reforms, he said, came about in a spirit akin to Theodore's strenuous life philosophy. "I have no expectation of making a hit every time I come to bat," Franklin said, but he took comfort in something his cousin once said: "If I can be right 75 percent of the time I shall come up to the fullest measure of my hopes."[63]

For every speech in which Franklin drew from Theodore's legacy, the Oyster Bay Roosevelts retaliated with accusations of plagiarism, and they attacked the New Deal as "a pack of cards thrown helter skelter." Ted called FDR "faithless," charging that his policies "usurped the function of Congress" and defiled the "sacred oath taken on the Bible."[64] Edith wrote friends that Theodore's Square Deal "in no way resemble[d] the policies of the present Administration."[65] And Alice, after watching the Senate vote to take the United States off the gold standard, staged a protest by arriving at a White House function draped in blue velvet and gold pendants, gold watch, gold earrings, and gold hair combs. She made "nasty" personal remarks about Franklin's disability and his affair with Lucy Mercer, and called Eleanor a "Trojan mare."[66]

Alice and Ted presumed that they could preserve a particular memory of their father's legacy, but it was the Democratic Roosevelt who captivated public attention and redefined "Rooseveltian." Historian Richard Collin argues that Franklin's presidency relegated TR to the position of a "forgotten man," that FDR produced a "historical obliteration" of TR, but this claim does not ring true. Franklin eclipsed Theodore, and Henry Pringle's critical biography certainly revised the historical impression, yet TR endured, even thrived, in public memory. FDR and Pringle changed TR from a "unique, isolated" presidential icon "beyond confusion with anybody else" into a puzzling figure with a political association with Franklin.[67] Hardly obliterated, TR's ghost adapted and remained pertinent in a new context.

A good example of this transformation occurred when New York State memorialized TR at the American Museum of Natural History in uptown Manhattan. At two o'clock on the afternoon of January 19, 1936, in the museum's freshly decorated entrance hall, dignitaries gathered to pay tribute. After the traditional benedictions, Franklin delivered the keynote address to museum patrons, consecrating the memorial as "typical of Theodore Roosevelt. It reflects the universality of his mind and his interests . . . his life, his work, and his play."[68] The president spoke only briefly about TR's conservation record despite it being the central focus of a memorial at an institution devoted to education about environmental sciences. Instead, in a short punchy speech, FDR fixated on TR's statecraft. Asking the crowd to remember TR not "as an abstract being, dwelling apart on the heights, but rather a friendly soul pervading this very hall," Franklin effectively incarnated himself as Theodore's heir. Although the address was brief, Franklin found space to cite no less than five speeches delivered by Theodore from 1901 to 1907. Each quotation extolled the virtues of the Square Deal and commemorated Theodore's pioneering progressivism. Rattling off adages and terms invented by TR, like "the wealthy criminal class," the "lunatic fringe," "speak softly and carry a big stick," and "muckraker," Franklin co-opted his cousin's slogans to celebrate the accomplishments of his own administration. For all intents and purposes, the speech kicked off his 1936 reelection campaign and was a defense of the New Deal.

Ted sat listening "with keen attention," waiting to make his own speech. A chorus of New York Democrats preceded him, including New York governor Herbert Lehman. Republican mayor of New York City Fiorello La Guardia also spoke. After they finished, Ted could not resist recounting to the crowd the irony that "most of them opposed [TR] during his life." Feeling he needed to make a unique contribution to the memorial, Ted avoided politics or conservation and spoke about the "intimate sides" of his father. No other dignitary at the inauguration, Franklin included, could recount the same memories, other than Alice, who sat beside Ted's empty seat on stage and silently lamented her family's political decline. She admired Ted's sensitive ovation vaunting the human and masculine sides of the man they so loved. For the most part, the newspapers ignored Ted's comments. Predictably, they focused instead on the president, progressivism, and the 1936 election. Alice recalled the moment some years later, saying, "We were out. Run over."[69]

In spite of Franklin's speech, TR's progressive legacy was absent from the memorial's design. New York legislators intended the museum to depict his "humanitarian influence" on the city and state, and in that sense Ted's speech captured the intended meaning of the memorial far better than FDR's. John Russell Pope, the architect who designed the national memorial, also designed the memorial at the American Museum of Natural History and declared the giant archway entrances symbolic of "the scientific, educational, outdoor, and exploration aspects of Theodore Roosevelt's life." Inside the museum's memorial hall, murals celebrated TR's interest in the Panama Canal and arbitration of the Russo-Japanese War, casting him as a great American statesman. Mural artist William Mackay said the paintings paid tribute to his patriotism and sheer Americanism. For years to come, the museum would represent TR's contribution to ecology and scientific exploration, but at its dedication the political context blurred that memory and made for a many-sided impression of TR.[70]

Franklin billed the 1936 election as a referendum on the New Deal and targeted progressives of all political persuasions in an effort to see through the revolution he started in 1933. For their part, Republicans nominated TR's political descendant Alf Landon, who had campaigned for Roosevelt in the 1912 election and staged a progressive insurgency in Kansas. Landon won the Republican nomination in 1936 precisely because his progressivism compared favorably to FDR's and TR's. In fact, all three candidates for the Republican nomination that year—Landon, William Borah, and Frank Knox—could make genuine claims to be descendants of TR's progressive bloc. Borah, at seventy-one, seemed to the party faithful too old and remained too radical. Knox erroneously "convinced himself that there was a deep anti–New Deal groundswell throughout the nation" and campaigned against social welfare, a miscalculation that cost him the nomination."[71] Republicans chose Landon because he accepted much of the New Deal as sound national policy, although he renounced FDR's legislative methods as unconstitutional. Landon promised to continue the domestic reforms, but with Congress as a partner rather than a rubber stamp.

Progressive Republicans felt conflicted with the choice between Landon and FDR. William Allen White, one of TR's allies in 1912, wrote Ted in 1932 that the new president, "your distant relative," was an unknown factor and "may develop his stubbornness into courage, his sense of superiority into statesmanship." Presidential responsibility, White told Ted, "is a winepress that brings forth strange juices out of men." By 1936, White acknowledged the merits of the New Deal and Franklin's leadership style. "I am afraid I am convincing myself that he is more right than wrong," he conceded to Ted: "I was jealous of the name Roosevelt and was mean about it in my heart." Nevertheless, White endorsed Landon and nominated his fellow Kansan at the Republican National Convention, feeling that a vote for FDR would betray his personal loyalties. Franklin ridiculed White's position and, when he visited Kansas on a reelection tour, glibly thanked the journalist for his "generous" support in "three and a half years out of every four."[72]

The Republicans' choice of Landon led Franklin to double down on his progressive record, invoking TR. On the very day Republicans nominated Landon, FDR spoke informally at a Dallas luncheon about his cousin. One night, at a White House dinner in 1905, Franklin recalled, Theodore "was visibly perturbed and was stamping up and down in front of the fireplace in the Oval Room." Recounting his frustration with getting progressive legislation passed, TR said, "Sometimes I wish I could be President and Congress, too." Franklin sympathized, and, with perfect political pitch, told the Dallas crowd, "I suppose if the truth were told, he is not the only President that has had that idea."[73] When he sought legislative help "from someone whose integrity and knowledge I could trust," Franklin admitted to another audience in Pennsylvania, he recalled Theodore. And when defending the New Deal in Chicago, FDR relied on TR's definition of malefactors of great wealth to describe a "minority which includes the type of individual who speculates with other people's money [and] says that popular government cannot be trusted." Even his final campaign speech invoked TR. In a radio broadcast on the eve of Election Day, Franklin quoted directly from TR's "Man in the Arena" speech, portraying himself as the man "whose face is marred by dust and sweat and blood; who strives valiantly; who errs, who comes short again and again, because there is no effort without error and shortcoming."[74]

FDR's campaign was faultless. He increased the number of electoral votes and the margin of popular votes from his previous landslide. The victory earned him a fresh mandate for the New Deal and bolstered his claim to be the true political inheritor of TR's progressive legacy. FDR did not obliterate TR; rather, he cemented TR's place in history by co-option.

Franklin's unprecedented reelection to a third term in 1940 set him apart from other chief executives. Indisputably popular, he transformed the party system that had dominated American political culture since the Civil War, and his management of the Great Depression assured him a prominent place in the history books. The looming war in Europe and the Pacific tested his diplomatic mettle before Pearl Harbor thrust upon him what Theodore Roosevelt called "the great occasion," for which a president "has the chance to develop great qualities."[75] TR had faced no comparable conflict, and yet Franklin and his political allies continued to invoke his legacy to justify their foreign policies. Nowhere does this connection appear more regularly than in the era's motion pictures. And no studio used TR's image to reflect FDR's foreign policies more than Warner Brothers.

Warner Brothers Entertainment operated, in part, as a propaganda vehicle for the FDR administration. Founders Jack and Harry Warner campaigned for Franklin in 1932, despite having previously supported only Republican candidates. After Jack met Franklin on a train to Los Angeles, the movie mogul called the Democrat "a vital and enormously magnetic man" and said that the day-long train journey "began a friendship that endured to the day he died."[76] Meeting Warner gave FDR an appreciation of film as a medium for shaping public consciousness, and Warner promised to make "a good picture about America every now and again" to support Franklin's domestic and foreign-policy agendas.[77] Before war consumed Europe, the studio had unashamedly dubbed itself "A New Deal in Entertainment," producing films that lionized progressive activism. *Black Fury* (1935) depicted a Pennsylvania coal town divided between trade unions and mine operators, and Warner Brothers came down in favor of unions so obviously that the Motion Picture Association of America determined that the studio had breached the production code by glorifying class struggle.[78] More allegorical was Warner's production of *Road Gang* (1936), which depicted life in a prison camp to caricature the harsh social inequalities of Depression-era America. Again, the Production Code Administration restricted the studio by deeming the original script too graphic a portrayal of social injustice. The final production of

Road Gang limited the depiction of political corruption and social disparity, but the censorship had only tempered the political slant; it did not remove it.[79]

When it came to films about foreign affairs, Warner Brothers initially clashed with the president's official policy. Jack and Harry ranked among the most ardent antifascists in Hollywood, in part because they had experienced, firsthand, the violent and xenophobic tendencies inherent in ultranationalist totalitarianism. In 1936, Nazi brownshirts allegedly murdered the studio's German-Jewish salesman Joe Kaufman in a Berlin alleyway.[80] In retaliation, Warner Brothers ceased distribution in Nazi Germany and produced several antifascist movies, including *Confessions of a Nazi Spy* (1939), which "aroused . . . official disfavor" from the White House. The film censor said it "unfairly represented" German chancellor Adolf Hitler, and FDR believed that it threatened to fracture the already shaky diplomacy that kept Europe from war.[81] When Germany invaded Poland and the Allies declared war, Franklin announced a strict neutral position. He quietly asked Warner Brothers to shelve any explicitly anti-Axis films, and this request, coupled with the uproar caused by *Confessions of a Nazi Spy,* convinced the studio to stop producing such films until the United States officially joined the Allies in 1941.

The studio's political position nevertheless showed through in films about national defense, and Theodore Roosevelt played a key role. In October 1939, six months after the success and clamor of *Confessions of a Nazi Spy,* and one month after Britain declared war on Germany, Warner Brothers released a short historical dramatization entitled *The Monroe Doctrine.* Part of a wider series of two-reel films about American patriotism, the film commemorated President Monroe's 1823 declaration of American isolation from European conflicts and the legacy that act had on successive presidential administrations. Sidney Blackmer played Theodore Roosevelt, speaking as the last American president to certify the merits of hemispheric isolation. By co-opting TR's legacy and the legacies of other former presidents, such as Polk and Cleveland, Warner Brothers attempted to bolster Franklin's policy of neutrality and portray him as the latest defender of American security.[82]

One year later, in the aftermath of France's military collapse and the Battle of Britain, Warner Brothers released *Teddy the Rough Rider,* an entirely different short that again starred Blackmer. It traced the career of the young TR from his stint as president of the New York City Police Commission up until the time of the McKinley assassination. The movie's technical achievements won it a 1940 Oscar for best short, and Blackmer's portrayal earned critical praise. Cinematic reviews aside, the short took a much different approach than *The Monroe Doctrine* to US foreign policy. Rather than advocate American isolation, TR promoted the merits of intervention by demonstrating personal valor and bravery at San Juan Heights. Warner Brothers studded the scenes with an energetic soundtrack of patriotic music as TR charged up the hill and won glory for the United States. Other than the studio's 1942 production of *Yankee Doodle Dandy,* an unapologetically jingoistic biography of composer George M. Cohan, no other movie exhibited the virtues of intervention more than *Teddy the Rough Rider.*[83]

Warner Brothers' films reflected the public disagreements over the future of America's foreign policy. Interventionists, led by the Committee to Defend America by Aiding the Allies, lobbied FDR to join the British, French, and Russians against the Axis Powers. Isolationists organized the America First Committee and petitioned to stay out of the war. Opinion polls showed that the majority of Americans favored neutrality until 1940, a judgment the Oyster Bay Roosevelts shared. Alice was convinced that Franklin was moving the country closer to war on a daily basis in order to amplify presidential power and extend the New Deal. She called FDR's diplomacy "needling" the Axis Powers, and said it served only to buttress the president's political position at home, "which has been slipping so rapidly." She submitted "that only war can divert attention from his sweeping failures," and Ted joined Alice in organizing the America First Committee. Ted, however, also judged isolationism a "doomed good cause."[84] Conflicted, he eventually abandoned America First in 1941 and took up command of his former army division.[85]

Until the attack on Pearl Harbor, Franklin charted a course of cautious neutrality by keeping the United States an official nonbelligerent nation while assisting the Allies with preferential trade and financing. The National Press Club defined FDR's statecraft as comparable to his cousin's. They gifted him a "big stick" for upcoming negotiations with Japan, declaring, "Never since Mr. Theodore Roosevelt have we needed [one] as much as we do today."[86] In an effort to create a unity government, Franklin enlisted Republicans who had built political reputations during TR's lifetime. Henry Stimson, TR's close friend throughout World War I and Taft's Secretary of War, returned to the War Department in 1940. Frank Knox, a former Rough Rider and progressive Republican, took over the Navy Department the same year. The appointments, designed to remove any perception of partisanship in the cabinet, also reflected the reach of TR's interventionist legacy. Stimson and Knox called for military preparedness, just as they had in World War I alongside TR and Leonard Wood.[87]

After the Japanese attack on Pearl Harbor, the Oyster Bay Roosevelts put aside their grievances to join the war effort. Archie's disagreement with Franklin turned to warm regard throughout the war. The president approved Archie's request for reenlistment, despite his disabled status. Stationed in southwest Asia by the army, Archie fought in New Guiana before returning to the United States as the only soldier classified as entirely disabled by combat wounds in each world war.[88] Kermit, after being discharged from the British Army as mentally and physically un-fit, undertook a four-month detox treatment and, with FDR's help, was admitted to active service in the US Army. Kermit was posted to Fort Richardson, Alaska, in order to keep him away from the fighting, but he committed suicide shortly after arriving there.[89] The family so feared Edith's grief that they told her Kermit died of heart failure.

Another world war and another dead son compelled the Oyster Bay matriarch to relinquish her grudge against Franklin. She related her appreciation to him for admirably leading the nation through the crisis and gradually came to see his domestic reforms as measured, not radi-cal.[90] Even Ted reconciled. In 1941 he was promoted to brigadier general when hostilities began, and he shipped out to England in 1943. He fought campaigns in North Africa and Italy, and helped organize the Allied invasion of Normandy. On D-Day he led the charge across Utah Beach, the only American general to command his troops from the frontline. His leadership earned him the Congressional Medal of Honor, but less than a month later, before he could accept the commendation, Ted suc-cumbed to heart disease. He had suffered several bouts of cardiac arrest throughout the war, successfully keeping the medical condition from his commanding officers. Before departing for his last major battle, deeply aware of his mortality, he wrote FDR and buried the hatchet: "I wanted you to know that to me" your administration's policy "seems excellent." The first cordial communication between the cousins in more than a decade was cathartic, Ted confessed, an exercise he undertook "to relieve my mind."[91]

Of TR's immediate family, only Alice remained bitter. "Everyone is so terribly amiable," she hissed: "No one really hates anymore."[92] She campaigned against Franklin in 1940 and 1944. Her political enmity notwithstanding, World War II ended the more-than-twenty-year family feud. When Franklin died in 1945, the entire Oyster Bay clan, including Alice, sent heartfelt condolences to Eleanor.

FDR had overshadowed his cousin and predecessor in the 1930s and 1940s, but in doing so he had relied heavily on TR's public memory. By regularly co-opting him and encouraging comparison (or not discouraging it), FDR kept TR relevant and enhanced his legacy. Likewise, Henry Pringle's biography and other similar cultural portraits of a juvenile Teddy Roosevelt transformed the perception of TR's personality, while reiterating the prevailing memorial themes. Pringle failed to diminish what Dewey called the towering double and, in attempting to assassinate his character, only demonstrated the lasting influence of TR's progressivism.

When the war ended in 1945 and the Allies neared the German border, Secretary of War Stimson organized a group of generals and politicians to meet at his office to commemorate the twenty-fifth anniversary of Theodore Roosevelt's death. Reading Elihu Root's tribute from 1919, Stimson told the gathering that he "couldn't hope to explain or describe Roosevelt," and he hoped that Root's speech would accomplish this. Stimson confined his words to personal reminiscences, and Frederick Trubee Davison recalled the moment as "a most impressive thing . . . an emotional experience" that gratified busy men like George Marshall and Hap Arnold. Later that evening, Stimson read Root's eulogy to Supreme Court justice Felix Frankfurter over dinner. It received a comparable hearing.[93] Davison and Frankfurter never said whether the meeting had any bearing on wartime policy or exactly how the eulogy touched them, but both considered the greatness of Theodore Roosevelt a powerful exemplar. FDR sensed this as well.

It is indisputable that TR's legacy fell out of the limelight it had enjoyed during the 1920s, but it never disappeared altogether. In the halls of power, like Stimson's office, and in cultural representations, like *Arsenic and Old Lace,* Roosevelt loomed large. Even if reminiscences did not accurately match the facts of history, the enormity of Roosevelt remained apparent.

J. N. "Ding" Darling cartoon, "The Long, Long Trail" (1919), drawn
immediately after news of Roosevelt's death broke. Printed in newspapers
across the country, this cartoon became Darling's best-recognized work.
(Courtesy National Park Service, Manhattan Historic Sites Archive)

Otho Cushing, "Apotheosis," from *The Teddyssey* (Life Books, 1907).
(Author's collection)

Edwin Marcus cartoon, "American" (1919).
(Courtesy National Park Service, Manhattan Historic Sites Archive)

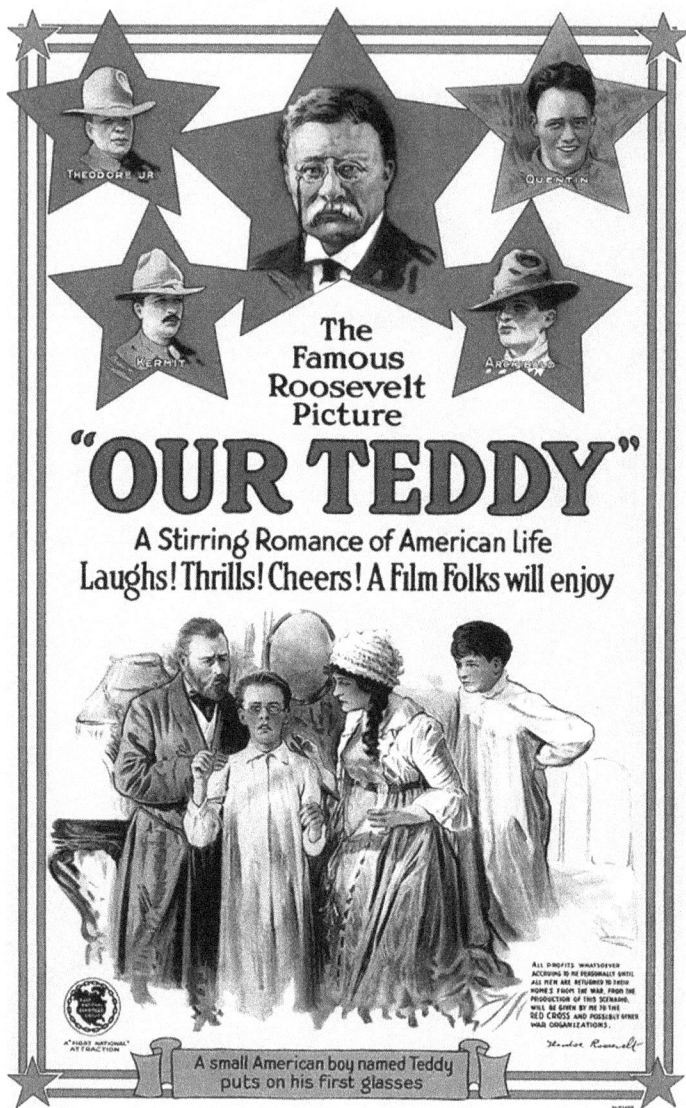

Our Teddy, 1919 motion picture poster.
(Author's collection)

THE DIFFERENCE BETWEEN F. R. AND T. R.

John McCutcheon cartoon, "The Difference Between F. R. and T. R.,"
Chicago Tribune, July 9, 1920.
(Franklin Delano Roosevelt Papers, FDR Presidential Library)

Carl Akeley's memorial lion, clay model (1937).
The project had widespread support but was never completed.
(Frank Ross McCoy Papers, Library of Congress)

Members of the WRMA collecting money for the construction of
a brownstone replica of TR's birthplace.
(*WRMA Bulletin,* 1921, courtesy National Park Service,
Manhattan Historic Sites Archive)

Reconstructed Roosevelt
birthplace, opening day.
(*WRMA Bulletin,* 1921,
courtesy National Park
Service, Manhattan
Historic Sites Archive)

Aerial-view drawing of Washington, DC, with labels of cardinal points in
Pierre L'Enfant's cruciform city plan (enhanced by author).
("RMA Competition for a Roosevelt Memorial," published for Congress, 1926)

John Russell Pope's architectural model of proposed Roosevelt memorial (1926).
(Courtesy Houghton Library, Harvard University)

Gutzon Borglum's bronze bust of Roosevelt (1919), found in
Mount Rushmore National Monument archives.
(Courtesy Theodore Roosevelt Center, Dickinson State University)

J. N. "Ding" Darling cartoon, "A New Roosevelt Invades the West,"
New York Herald Tribune, April 21, 1932.
(Basil O'Connor Papers, FDR Presidential Library)

Walter Hoban cartoon, "The Copyright Owners,"
New York American, August 22, 1932.
(Basil O'Connor Papers, FDR Presidential Library)

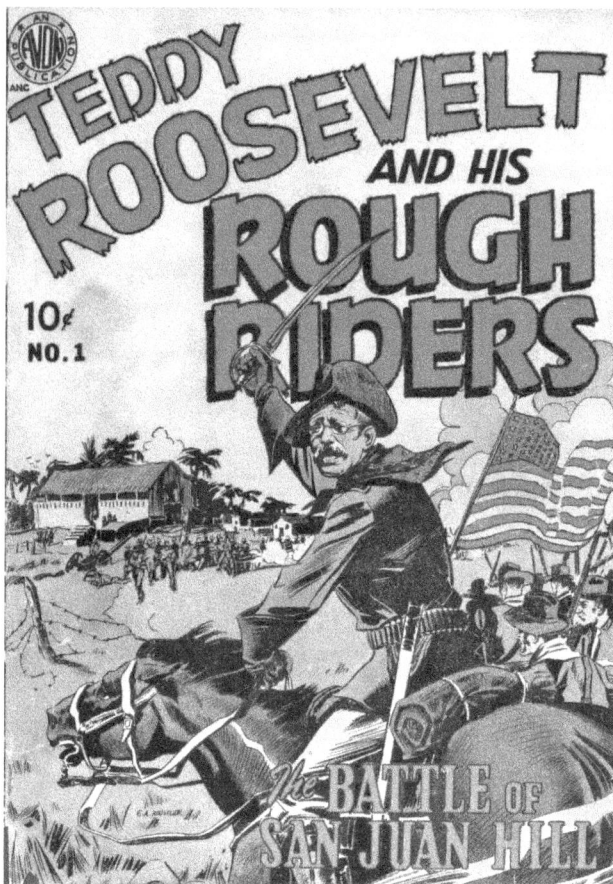

Cover of Avon comic book *Teddy Roosevelt and His Rough Riders*,
by E. R. Kinstler (enhanced by author), 1950.
(Courtesy E. R. Kinstler)

Ford pickup truck with Roosevelt centennial bumper sticker (1956).
(Courtesy National Park Service, Manhattan Historic Sites Archive)

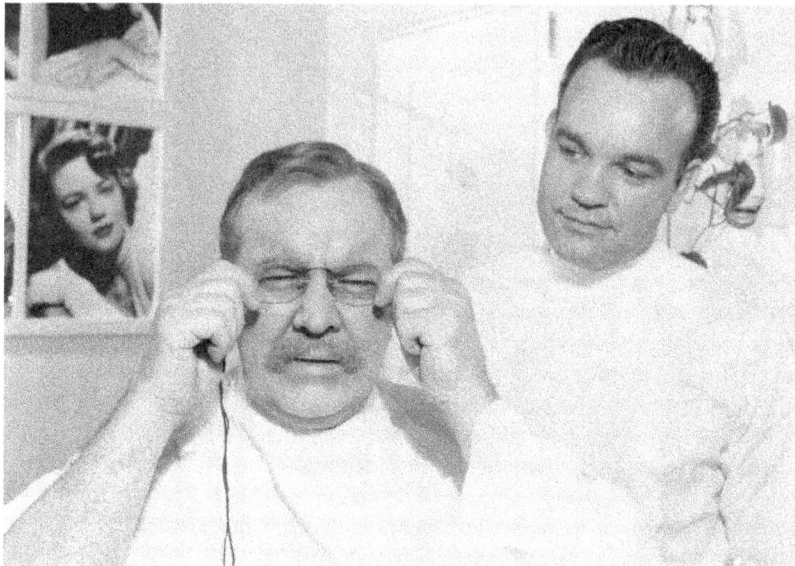

Sidney Blackmer getting into costume as Theodore Roosevelt (1948).
(Courtesy Jonathan Sidney Blackmer)

Drawing of proposed bridge from E Street over the Potomac River (1954),
Department of Highways, District of Columbia.
(Theodore Roosevelt Island National Memorial Archive)

Drawing of armillary sphere by Paul Manship, the original memorial
proposal for Theodore Roosevelt Island (1958).
(Theodore Roosevelt Island National Memorial Archive)

Sagamore Hill, Roosevelt's home at Oyster Bay, Long Island (1933).
(Library of Congress)

Pat and Richard Nixon with Alice Roosevelt (*center*), 1973.
(Photo by Jack Kightlinger, courtesy Richard M. Nixon Presidential Library)

Future executive director of the TRA John Allen Gable (*left*) with former executive director Hermann Hagedorn at centennial event, Roosevelt birthplace (1958). (Courtesy National Park Service, Manhattan Historic Sites Archive)

Roosevelt's cabin at Pine Knot, Albemarle County, Virginia.
(Courtesy Virginia Department of Historic Resources)

Presidents' race at Washington Nationals baseball park (2013).
(Photo by John McDonnell/*Washington Post*)

COLD WAR REVIVAL

n the summer of 1941, the trustees of the Roosevelt Memorial Association
began a campaign to revivify TR's public memory. As the United States
confronted the Axis Powers and Franklin Roosevelt earned his stripes
as a war president, Edith Roosevelt regretted that "there are but few
who think of Theodore's life, work, and aspirations for his country."[1]
RMA director Hermann Hagedorn described the state of commemorative
activities as having declined to the point of desperation. Regardless of
what "happens to Europe in the coming year," he wrote colleagues, the
RMA faced "a very dark future." No one would "take much interest in
memorials," he conceded. The only way to rescue Roosevelt's fame from
the precipice of insignificance, Hagedorn believed, was to formulate a
new approach to memorialization.[2]

During the war years, in order to secure its financial future, the association divested itself of assets that carried a high annual expenditure.
Particularly onerous was the impressive library, housed at the birthplace,
that cost nearly $3,000 a year to maintain and had grown so large that
it overflowed the shelves and spilled into an adjoining room. Keeping
the stacks filled with the latest publications added to the association's
economic burden, as did the salary of Nora Cordingly, the full-time librarian who curated the collection. Hagedorn approached Columbia and
Harvard Universities to gauge their interest in acquiring the archive. Both
institutions recognized the library's value, but Columbia balked when it
estimated the long-term expenses. Harvard took ownership in June 1943
and split the collection, moving books and newspapers to Widener Library and manuscripts to Houghton Library. Cordingly reluctantly agreed
to accompany the archive and smooth the transition, helping students
and visiting researchers navigate the unique trove of documents.[3]

Moving the library was more than a cost-saving exercise, however. The
RMA expected that depositing these resources at Harvard would inspire a

new generation of scholars to revise the historiographical image of Roose-velt. Soon after the move to Harvard, Cordingly approached the faculty to encourage them to use the collection, but the timing, professor of history Arthur Schlesinger Sr. told her, was terrible. Much of the able-bodied faculty had gone to fight Hitler. For the same reason, undergraduate en-rollments had decreased, and graduate students proved scarce. Cordingly told the RMA trustees that few Harvard staff or students visited. "For the most part," she reported to Hagedorn, her time was spent cataloging the books and manuscripts, a chore "buried in deadly routine."[4]

But determined to kick-start an era of historical revisionism, the RMA commissioned new reference works. In 1941 the association published the *Roosevelt Cyclopedia,* a volume designed to quickly allow readers to identify TR's views on all manner of issues through his speeches, public papers, and writings. The idea originated with Harvard professor Albert Bushnell Hart, who discussed the matter with Hagedorn as early as 1923. Hart joined the RMA's memorial crusade as chair of the Cambridge Bureau of Roosevelt Research and showed a keen interest in the association's activities. He began work on the *Cyclopedia* in 1926 after retiring from regular teaching. Then, he envisioned an expansive two-volume tome that would contain over 2 million words spread across 2,400 pages in an alphabetical catalog classified by "self-evident entries." Working with veteran indexer David Maydole Matteson, Hart set a project timeline of two years and estimated the total cost at $15,000, largely to cover his fee. Initially, the RMA considered the project too expensive and "too specu-lative," but when publisher Charles Scribner's expressed an interest, the trustees voted to subsidize production of a manuscript.[5]

It took Hart three years to submit a draft, rather than two, and the finished product was decidedly smaller than anticipated. Upon inspection, the RMA secretary found "upwards of 1,000 errors," including improper page references and incorrect dates. Hagedorn gave the manuscript a closer analysis and concluded that Hart had "badly arranged" the quota-tions and had duplicated entries. He refused to present it to Scribner's and feared confrontation with Hart about the matter. Because of his age, the professor would certainly not "give the manuscript the drastic editorial overhauling which it needed" and might even decide to "take the manu-script back," Hagedorn warned the RMA's trustees.[6] Hart's carelessness and Hagedorn's anxiety paralyzed the project until the autumn of 1938, when the RMA director proposed an academic conference to relaunch the undertaking. Hart, by then eighty-four, agreed to attend, but failed to turn up and provided no explanation. Whether his absence was due to senility or a snub, the RMA considered its arrangement with the Harvard professor annulled, and Hagedorn took over the project. The RMA director enlisted Herbert Ferleger, a Columbia University PhD candidate, to complete the manuscript, and within three months Ferleger produced a revised digest with over four thousand Roosevelt quotations on more than one thousand subjects.

The laborious effort to finish the *Cyclopedia* was almost for naught. When presented with Ferleger's draft, Scribner's rescinded its contract, citing the long delay and Ferleger's modified scheme, which the publisher said made the book less attractive.[7] Deeply disappointed, the RMA elected to print and distribute the volume independently, a decision that proved unwise. The *Cyclopedia* sold poorly, and the association failed to recoup its costs on the paltry 450 copies they managed to shift. Even when they reduced the price, the book did not sell. By 1943 the association distributed 1,300 of the remaining 1,500 copies for free.[8] Financially, the venture weighed on the RMA's balance sheet and on trustees' minds, but while it demonstrated the danger of ignoring professional opinions, the *Cyclopedia* also represented a new beginning for Roosevelt scholarship. As Hart had expected, academics turned to the *Cyclopedia* as their first point of reference, a fact that encouraged the RMA trustees' belief in their capacity to influence scholarship.

When Hagedorn discovered that the purple carbon ink on TR's onion-skin letter books at the Library of Congress was fading to the point of illegibility, he lobbied RMA trustees to support a project to microfilm the papers. Ferleger's work on the *Cyclopedia* made him the natural choice to oversee the preservation, and the idea gained support within the RMA, but a variety of circumstances stalled progress.[9] First, the microfilming, still a nascent technology, took longer than expected. (The Library of Congress and Harvard University had only begun using microfilm in the mid-1930s.) Second, tempting a publisher to produce a Roosevelt reference book seemed unlikely after the disappointment of the *Cyclopedia*. Scribner's and Doubleday, two companies with close relations to RMA trustees, refused to consider the letters project as viable. Several trustees also complained that the project risked depleting the RMA's already shrinking capital resources. And finally, Ferleger terminated his employment with the RMA to enlist in the army, leaving the association with no choice but to postpone publication.[10]

The association continued to microfilm Roosevelt's papers during the war, and after V-J Day it announced the preservation of more than 60,000 pages of correspondence, an achievement that resuscitated the idea of a bound volume. With the help of Harvard professor Frederick Merk and Columbia professor Allan Nevins, the RMA lured Professor Elting Morison to the editorial role. Morison had previously worked as assistant dean at Harvard before joining the Navy during the war. He returned to academia as professor of humanities at the Massachusetts Institute of Technology, building his reputation with an acclaimed biography of Adm. William Sims. An able and energetic editor, Morison secured a commitment from Harvard University Press to publish a selection of Roosevelt's letters and prodded the RMA to ante up to $100,000 for a staff of highly skilled academics. His team produced *The Letters of Theodore Roosevelt*—eight volumes of more than six thousand letters. Harvard University Press released the first two volumes in 1951 and the last two in 1954. Morison predicted that the reference books would encourage the postwar generation of scholars to reevaluate Roosevelt's place in American history.[11]

The cost of the project exceeded the RMA's expectations, and some trustees viewed it as disproportionate when memorials, like the one in Washington, remained unfinished. Others considered it money well spent. President of the RMA Gen. Frank Ross McCoy called it "the most important thing we're doing," and when trustee Mark Sullivan read the first volume, he felt "strongly conscious of a revived thrill."[12] The real measure of success, Morison asserted, came not from the amount of royalties the association could tally but from the scholars who would devote time to researching the volumes. Only time would tell if the *Letters* made an impression on the academic community, Morison warned.

In fact, academics reached a verdict quickly. Reviews praised the project and the editor's attention to detail and arrangement, if not the selection of correspondence. Historians suggested "many additions and subtractions" from Roosevelt's trove of 150,000 letters, a criticism that seemed almost inevitable, given the sheer breadth of material. Beyond that, scholars concluded almost unanimously that the *Letters* provided new resources that would lead to reinterpretation.[13] Some academics, like Dewey Grantham, believed that presenting Roosevelt in his own words gave the former president an "indescribable humanness that warms and captivates the reader."[14] For Grantham, readers need not wait for the updated historical narrative; they could glean a fresh portrait directly from the letters.

By the time Morison's last volumes reached bookshelves, the scholarship on Roosevelt had increased conspicuously. Pringle's image of a truculent and juvenile man who opportunistically chose to endorse progressive policies retreated.[15] Perhaps the best example of this transformation comes from the work of Columbia professor Richard Hofstadter. His seminal book, *The American Political Tradition and the Men Who Made It* (1948), describes Roosevelt as a "tardy" and "opportune" convert to progressive politics. During his presidency Roosevelt subscribed to a centrist ideology, Hofstadter maintains, one that paralleled a trend in national politics and traced its roots to the American Revolution. In short, Roosevelt was no radical. Hofstadter classes him as a chief executive who perpetuated the status quo and only made changes at the periphery of American society. Indeed, most residents of the White House, he argues, did not exceed the boundaries of well-established traditions.

The Columbia historian dubs Roosevelt "Conservative as Progressive" and defines his 1912 election campaign as an anomaly in an otherwise moderate career. *The American Political Tradition* recites Pringle's version of a "desperate" man—"pitiable," unable to salve an insatiable ego, and with a personality that "did not usually cut very deep." At times, Hofstadter claims that Roosevelt displayed "qualities of recent authoritarianism" and describes him as "Mussolini lite."[16] University of Wisconsin professor Howard K. Beale criticized the interpretation. "It is obvious you do not like Theodore Roosevelt, in fact, that you have an intense hatred of him," Beale wrote Hofstadter: "I suspect that you are just another product of the student generation of fifteen years ago" that relished Pringle's biography as the final word.[17]

But after reading Morison's *Letters*, Hofstadter changed his view of Roosevelt.[18] In his 1954 book *The Age of Reform*, Roosevelt's progressive wit earns unexpected praise from Hofstadter, who recognizes moments of political genius during TR's presidency. His position on the 1912 campaign is softer, and *The Age of Reform* observes less ruthless opportunism in TR's personality.[19] This change aside, Hofstadter holds fast to the basic thesis of his previous book, which sets Roosevelt within the centrist stream of American politics. By 1962, however, after digesting all eight volumes of the *Letters*, Hofstadter categorically abandoned his initial interpretation. In *Anti-Intellectualism in American Life* (1963), a book that won the Pulitzer Prize for nonfiction, he determines that Roosevelt "paved the way for Progressivism" and that he displayed an intellect that exceeded others of his age. TR, he concedes, "attracted into public service a vigorous and dedicated type of man not much seen in government for well over a generation." Hofstadter even refutes Pringle by suggesting that the exuberance of TR's early career appeared at odds with his presidency and that his pure adolescent persona in youth matured until Roosevelt became "a very bright man with some practical ideas."[20]

John Morton Blum agreed. His book, *The Republican Roosevelt* (1954), dismisses the image of an overly adolescent Roosevelt and pronounces him an astute, able, and conscientious chief executive. "In describing Roosevelt as a madman," Blum writes, the scholarly class "erred" and inappropriately exaggerated certain traits. Also, Blum complained, the transformational nature of New Deal politics encouraged a disproportionate amount of attention on TR's progressive legacy at the expense of other characteristics. As Morison's assistant on the *Letters* project, Blum had read vast swathes of TR's correspondence and discovered a man whose political ethos rested on the idea of political fairness based on the "gospel of good works." Roosevelt, in Blum's estimation, sanctioned neither the radicalism of some progressives nor the "sterile conservatism of *laissez faire*" patrician classes.[21] Instead, he bridged conservative and progressive extremes. Rather than a man consumed by ego and ambition, Roosevelt was, for Blum, an intellectual polymath capable of prodigious feats of judgment.

Likewise, George E. Mowry's *The Era of Theodore Roosevelt, 1900–1912* (1958) portrays TR as a pragmatist who adopted trustbusting and corporate regulation to keep the nation in touch with its democratic customs. Working within the same paradigm as Hofstadter and Blum, Mowry swept away the extreme images depicted by Pringle and the hagiographers by reinforcing the trend toward consensus that "played down the newness of the New Deal" and fastened TR's legacy to the *longue durée* of American political history.[22]

Hofstadter, Blum, and Mowry relied on Morison's *Letters* to homogenize TR's place in political history, as did a growing field of scholarship on the Gilded Age and Progressive Era. At least twenty monographs, forty scholarly articles, and a broad cohort of doctoral theses examined Roosevelt's place in this period of American history.[23] Some gushed, like the hagiographies of the 1920s. For example, Carleton Putnam's *Theodore Roosevelt: The Formative Years, 1858–1886* (1958) presented an "unduly flattering" image and deliberately aimed to endear Roosevelt to the postwar generation. Putnam's obvious affection for TR polluted his objectivity. Reviewers commended the book's methodical study of Roosevelt's youth, marriage to Alice Lee, and remarkable career in the New York Assembly but also said it all-too-purposely disregarded the ego and bluster that Pringle had documented.[24] The majority of historians, however, adopted a synthetic portrait that acknowledged elements of the hagiographies and Pringle's research.[25] These accounts examined TR's influence on individual states and regions, his role in legislation like the Pure Food and Drug Act, his part in labor disputes, his thoughts on race relations, his campaign rhetoric, his ancestry, the New York governorship, the vice-presidency, and his work toward civil service reform.[26] Morison's *Letters* allowed historians to delve deeper, to find examples of Roosevelt's many-sidedness.

The abundance of fresh research also coincided with escalating Cold War tensions. In his introduction to the *Letters,* Morison appreciated the "relevance" Theodore Roosevelt's correspondence had for the citizens "of this country in 1950."[27] Without directly mentioning international relations, Morison alluded to the contextual parallels between Roosevelt's lifetime and the postwar period. The US membership in the United Nations and the creation of the North Atlantic Treaty Organization resembled the early twentieth-century advocacy for a League of Nations and League of Democracies. The anti-communist sentiment that dominated public consciousness after World War I had abated only to intensify again after 1945, when McCarthyism gave rise to a second Red Scare fueled by hyperpatriotic Americanism. The two primary political parties accepted the rise of expansive executive power, a phenomenon that had begun with TR and increased throughout FDR's administration. The Soviet threat trumped all other issues in the postwar period, and Congress deferred management of the national security state to the White House.

The circumstances of the Cold War prompted midcentury scholars to construct a historical pathway from Theodore Roosevelt's era to their day. Beale led the way with his 1956 book *Theodore Roosevelt and the Rise of America to World Power.* Deeming society to be in a "desperate state" of existence "that threatens to destroy civilization itself," Beale explains how American foreign policy "started down this road" with TR. According to Beale, as the twentieth century's first American statesman, Roosevelt normalized the practice of power politics in US diplomacy and set the precedent for presidential leadership in international affairs. Moreover, Beale contends that Roosevelt demonstrated the importance of personal relationships with foreign diplomats to achieving political ends while appearing flexible. Commending Roosevelt for a nuanced and complex set of policies that "symbolized and gave voice to widespread American attitudes," Beale discloses an "admiration for Roosevelt's ability, his energy, and his devotion to his country's interests." His statecraft, the historian insists, revolutionized American international relations and proved to be ahead of its time, a compliment qualified by the author, who also believed, in hindsight, that Roosevelt's foreign policies revealed "a sense of tragedy." Beale observes that TR's overestimation of China and of that nation's capacity for democracy, along with his miscalculation about the decline of British power and his subscription to an ideology of imperialism that injected American interests into every international crisis, led directly to the eruption of World War I, the rise of Japanese militarism, and even the Cold War. Beale ultimately judges Roosevelt's diplomacy a failure because it took four decades and two world wars to sway Americans against a deep-seated tradition of isolationism.[28]

Diplomatic historians like Beale called Roosevelt an early proponent of realism, the school of thought that favored hard-nosed calculations of state-to-state relations based on power and the advice of professional diplomats "that understood the architecture of global balances."[29] Leading this realist school was George Kennan, the State Department's first head of policy planning, who devised the containment policy to ensure the preponderance of American power after the war. Kennan's diplomatic philosophy emphasized the global balance of power and encouraged strong international relationships as the best means to make informed strategic decisions. In 1951, after he retired from the State Department, Kennan published *American Diplomacy, 1900–1950,* a collection of lectures and writings that castigated foreign policies like the open door as too economic-minded and criticized Woodrow Wilson's internationalism as needlessly idealistic. Kennan rebuked elements of TR's foreign policy, particularly his administration's extension of the open-door idea and the maintenance of a colony in the Philippines, but he also acknowledged Roosevelt's disillusion with those endeavors, conceding that TR had wished "we could be rid" of the Philippines.[30] As an accidental president, Roosevelt had inherited McKinley's policies and cabinet, circumstances that Kennan believed excused him from complete responsibility. Like Beale, as a policy wonk, Kennan admired TR's realism and drew a line from Roosevelt's foreign policies to his own, occasionally using the former president's legacy to advocate his own position. After Mao Zedong's communists threatened to invade Formosa (Taiwan), Kennan recommended the United States establish a provisional protectorate with a "ruthlessness and self-assurance," which he described as "the way Theodore Roosevelt might have done it."[31]

The burgeoning fear of communism as a dire threat to America's political traditions dominated interpretations of Roosevelt and led public

figures to exalt him as a symbol of patriotism, law and order, and necessary vitality. Director of the FBI J. Edgar Hoover said that TR had "special meaning" for those in law enforcement. "The America of 1949 has a
need—a great need—for the convictions and ideals of Theodore Roosevelt," he declared, because "America today is under attack by powerful
antagonists" identical to those that threatened in Roosevelt's day, namely,
a criminal army of revolutionary communists. Employing Roosevelt as an
example of how to withstand communist infiltration, Hoover applauded
the former president's "moral strength" as a force that gave the current
generation of Americans "renewed energy" to fight subversives. Lucius
Clay, commanding general of the US Army in Europe and organizer of
the Berlin Airlift, urged American youths to emulate Roosevelt's patriotism and compared the anti-communist *Voice of America* broadcasts
to the roar of Roosevelt's oratory.[32] Even Eleanor Roosevelt, who rarely
invoked her uncle's name during the war, felt the need to do so afterward.
Unencumbered by her political office as First Lady, she enlisted TR's
ghost as a soldier in the Cold War, predicting that Americans would see
his legacy as one that "moved us forward along the lines of social justice
and humanitarian interests, which are today the areas that furnish us
with the only alternative to Communism."[33]

The RMA quickly recognized the value of the Cold War context, and no
trustee wished more to commemorate TR's Americanism than Hagedorn.
When the memorial campaigns had begun in 1919, the RMA's trustees
resisted depictions of Roosevelt that seemed overly political and declined
to emphasize the ideology of Americanism. Hagedorn, on the contrary,
embraced that theme. In 1954, he celebrated thirty-five years as RMA
director and his seventy-third birthday. Despite his age and long service, he showed no sign of fatigue. Rather, the Cold War reinvigorated
his commitment to memorializing TR as a national icon. In 1956, he
published a collection of Roosevelt's writings, edited to emphasize social
responsibility, public order, and the genius of American political institutions. Hagedorn called it *The Free Citizen: A Summons to Service of the
Democratic Ideal* and believed it would inspire those grappling with the
threat of communist aggression by showcasing Roosevelt as the nation's
foremost advocate of personal liberties, social cohesion, and democratic
internationalism.[34] The book became the intellectual foundation for
Hagedorn's revival of TR's Americanism legacy.

Never single-minded, the RMA director produced public exhibitions,
including a collaborative show with the New York City Police Department

that displayed Roosevelt's influence on criminal justice.[35] He successfully petitioned the post office for a memorial stamp that commemorated TR's statecraft, he wrote scripts for radio and television programs on TR's civic ideology and family life, and he encouraged Roosevelt's friends and family to recount personal memories that resulted in an oral history project.[36] Although many of these tributes relied on diverse themes such as the cowboy, the reformer, and the conservationist, Hagedorn made a point of stressing TR's Americanism in each.

The persistent emphasis on Americanism affected relations between the RMA and WRMA. The women, who promoted patriotism as a gateway motif for understanding the complexities of TR's legacy and intended the birthplace to enshrine this theme in architectural form, long refused to work with the RMA because the men did not feel as strongly about the patriotic theme. With the exception of Hagedorn, the men's association endorsed artistic representations as interpretive memorials that could endure regardless of the political context. However, the ambition to remain apolitical ended with the Cold War. The prevailing anti-communist mood kindled the RMA's desire to commemorate Roosevelt's nationalism, and that conversion signaled a newfound point of agreement between the associations.[37]

The RMA and WRMA discussed cooperative ventures before the Cold War, entering into the most serious dialogue just prior to the attack on Pearl Harbor. Then, small pockets of resistance to the idea made merging impossible. Even so, most of the women saw amalgamation as "desirable and inevitable."[38] A few trustees resisted because it would almost certainly erase their organization's distinctive identity, and a handful of these trustees wrecked reconciliation during the war by spreading rumors that the men had mismanaged their accounts by making sizable investments that never succeeded financially, namely, the publication of the *Cyclopedia* and Morison's *Letters*. The gossip enraged RMA members, who denied the speculation as incendiary and counted these publishing projects as fundamentally successful, if not financially practical. Hesitant RMA trustees set aside plans for integration, but the end of World War II and the death of Franklin Roosevelt hastened the need for rebranding the groups.[39] FDR's admirers proposed yet another "Roosevelt Memorial Association," and TR enthusiasts, realizing that a legal battle to preserve their name would cost more than it would afford, accepted the need to qualify which Roosevelt they commemorated.

In 1946 the RMA and WRMA added a "T" to their names, an adjustment that proved slight. The WTRMA and TRMA sought nearly identical ends and continued to splinter public interest. The women found it difficult to raise funds beyond their circle of wealthy New York socialites, and by the 1940s they could not balance their expenses with income. They faced a budget deficit that by all expectations would increase in years to come. The men, contrary to speculation, kept healthy bank balances, due to wise investment strategies, and built a national network of supporters. When the TRMA embraced Americanism as a memorial theme, there appeared little reason for the groups to remain independent. Lawyers advised the WTRMA that the most likely prospect was absorption by the TRMA because the men had a congressional charter that uniquely accredited them for nationwide activism, and in 1949 a joint meeting of the associations considered ways they could cooperate.[40]

Because Hagedorn was held in high regard by the WTRMA membership, he led negotiations and pressed for the birthplace to realize its potential as a center for good citizenship and patriotic education. He reported to the TRMA's executive that, combined, the associations would build "an agency which shall, affirmatively and with clear vision, rally the public to a renewed ardor for an understanding of America and the American spirit."[41] Relaunching the birthplace paved the way for a permanent merger. On May 21, 1953, the TRMA changed its name to the Theodore Roosevelt Association (TRA), a neutral, pithier label the men and women equally favored. Hagedorn continued to correspond with the WTRMA and orchestrated the logistics of amalgamation, including a new governance structure. By 1954 the men and women signed an agreement-in-principle, and on January 6, 1955, the thirty-sixth anniversary of Roosevelt's death, the women made the merger official by publicly announcing the dissolution of the WTRMA. Over the course of 1955, the TRA absorbed the assets of the former women's association, steadfastly adhering to the promise to develop the theme of Americanism.[42] Women joined the TRA's executive committee and ensured that promise was met.

The merger bolstered the women's campaign, even if it came under the auspices of a new joint association. They no longer faced the burden of a hemorrhaging bank account or the insecurity of constant comparison with the men. Rather, they focused on remodeling the birthplace and celebrating the renaissance of Americanism as a popular discourse. To that end, the TRA curated the birthplace as a center for Americanism and opened to New York public schools and universities, offered rooms for military enlistment and recruitment drives, provided exhibition space for

political campaigns, acted as a clearinghouse for information on citizenship, and hosted receptions for naturalization ceremonies.[43] Managed by a
"House Committee" consisting of male and female trustees, the birthplace
reported broad success. By the end of the first year, it had distributed
more than four thousand copies of a short play about TR's patriotism,
welcomed over 2,200 students, presented a "lively and popular" American art exhibit, and organized several successful fundraising benefits for
veterans.[44]

The enthusiasm of the former WRMA trustees touched Hagedorn. The
successful merger inspired him to organize a nationwide celebration of
Roosevelt's one-hundredth birthday in 1958, and with the permission of
the TRA executive he lobbied numerous US congressmen to establish a
government-sponsored centennial commission. At the heart of the centennial plans was Roosevelt's legacy as a patriot, a theme drawn from
the Cold War context, as well as from the women's influence on the TRA.

Hagedorn wore out his shoe leather as he tirelessly walked the corridors
of the Senate Office Building promoting his vision. This was his pitch:

> To the majority of [Americans] TR is only the Rough Rider and the Big
> Stick, they may be inclined to ask, "What's the fuss all about? Born a cen-
> tury ago? President, fifty years ago? Run along and play. We are living in a
> different world. We have the hydrogen bomb to worry about, communist
> infiltration, war, survival as a free people, survival even as individuals.
> What is your man to us?" Such a query would be wholly reasonable, and
> constitutes a challenge which any plan we may develop must take into
> account. If the observance of TR's centenary is to be worthy of the man we
> seek to commemorate, it must do more than stir nostalgic memories in the
> surviving few who directly or indirectly felt the impact of his revitalizing
> spirit. It must waken a response in the millions to whom TR has hitherto
> been only a fading echo of far-off trumpets; it must raise a tide of emotion
> in the nation, strike sparks of aspiration, bring the spirit of TR to life in
> men's hearts . . . Americans are frightened, confused, and suffering under
> dangerous tensions. World leadership has been thrust upon them, and
> they don't know what to do with it; and don't want it anyway. They are
> dismayed—and have a right to be—by evidence of disloyalty in places of
> influence and power, in the threat of war and what war might mean. The
> jittery among us take their panic out in suspicion, distrust and heresy hunts,
> shying at shadows because they have lost their hold on that "substance of
> things hoped for" that is faith in God, faith in their fellow-countrymen, faith
> in America, faith in freedom itself. It is that faith that TR represents in all
> its fire and dynamism. Dramatized in the actions of a great life, his words

furnish a gospel that the American people need supremely today—America as affirmation, courage, the zest for new frontiers, new directions, new resolves, new achievements; America as world-leader and world-inspirer; America to be loved and served, kept strong and righteous, and true to her destiny. Such a gospel created the nation, distinguished it, saved it in time of crisis and can maintain it and lift it to new highs in the years to come. We are trustees, then, not only of a great memory but of a reservoir of potential energy, capable of bringing light and power to darkened hearts, terror stricken spirits, and mutually distrustful groups. Why not then seize the opportunity that the Centenary gives us to lift the man TR to the level of a symbol (which itself would be an enormous, and wholly justified, service to his memory); and to give the American people in a dark hour, a spiritual rallying point and prophet-voice? TR, the symbol of an assured, joyous, undaunted, dynamic Americanism—isn't that natural, the inevitable keynote for the Centenary? TR was many things . . . But when he died, the designation applied to him most often and most feelingly was THE GREAT AMERICAN.[45]

After six months of near-constant petitioning, the idea of the Theodore Roosevelt Centennial Commission (TRCC) gained traction. In the spring of 1955, Sen. Irving Ives (R-NY) introduced legislation, and later that summer President Dwight Eisenhower approved it. Receiving the full support of the government, the commission was chaired by the president and supported by a bipartisan executive of elected officials including Vice President Richard Nixon and Speaker of the House Sam Rayburn. These policy makers served a powerful ceremonial purpose and lent political weight to commemorative activities, but the real direction came from eight "at-large" commissioners appointed by the president. At the helm of that group, unsurprisingly, was Hermann Hagedorn.[46]

Not since Roosevelt's death had the impulse for commemoration arisen so intensely, and, as it had in the 1920s, the insatiable fear of communism colored the memorial activities. The TRCC's official statement of purpose recognized the Cold War as the catalyst for celebrations, it being "a time less to indulge happy recollections of an earlier age than to summon the resources of the past to help men face the challenge of the present." The remembrance of TR would inspire good citizenship, the TRCC asserted, and furnish Americans and American institutions an exemplary model.[47] Hagedorn anticipated a citizenship education program for the nation's primary and secondary schools, the completion of Theodore Roosevelt National Park in the North Dakota Badlands, and collaborative ventures with women's organizations, youth clubs, veterans, ecological associations, and religious institutions based on five designated fields of tribute: family life, adventurous living, responsible citizenship, conservation, and the moral foundations of free societies.[48] In many respects these commemorative themes disguised the emphasis on Americanism, but upon closer inspection the effect of the Cold War and surge in public support for patriotic nationalism is evident.

The proposals to celebrate Roosevelt's family life stressed the importance of domesticity as a bulwark against communist infiltration. Pamphlets on TR's relationship with his children, distributed by the Federation of Women's Clubs and the Boys Clubs of America, reflected what Nixon called the "kitchen war." The vice president suggested often—most famously in his 1959 trip to Moscow—that American superiority began at home, in the kitchen, and that American affluence demonstrated the superiority of democracy and capitalism. The wealth of consumer goods and quality family time spent in the abundant space of residential living rooms substantiated the American way of life.[49] In similar fashion, the TRA and TRCC impressed upon the public a simplified image of Roosevelt's family life to reflect this Cold War ideal. For instance, the syndicated *Cavalcade of America* radio series sponsored by DuPont and broadcast by CBS dramatized Roosevelt's family life as idyllic, a paradise nestled in the suburban neighborhood of Oyster Bay. TR's children, Ethel and Archie, called the script "pretty terrible" and deemed it "sentimental tosh." Ethel criticized the pseudohistorical narrative as almost totally at odds with reality, yet the Roosevelt family admitted that the program probably appealed to the "American public who listen to stuff like this," and, given the Cold War milieu, Ethel and Archie rationalized that the "spirit was right."[50] Listeners wanted to hear about "folksy" families with rising affluence, and although the Roosevelts hailed from a social class that was hardly folksy and already wildly affluent, they represented a cohesive, affectionate family unit that Americans could appreciate and emulate.

Closely associated with espousing this domestic ideal was the centennial committee's promotion of "adventurous living" as a means to deter antisocial behavior among American youth. The postwar boom in prosperity increased leisure time and generated disposable income for teenagers. This social transformation drove speculation that idle hands would make the devil's work and that youth culture would lead to juvenile delinquency. As the next generation came of age, social commentators presumed that the youth entered "the group mind world of the enemy."[51] Young adults would find themselves ideologically subverted or at least susceptible to communist indoctrination. To counter the trend, youth organizations collaborated with the TRCC to sponsor wilderness excursions and recreational activities that would allow adolescents to expel their energy in a socially acceptable manner. The TRA dabbled with new mediums to reach juvenile audiences, including comic books that used TR's cowboy legacy to praise the qualities of individuality typically associated with the American frontier. Special-edition comic books as well as popular comics like *Dennis the Menace, Mighty Mouse,* and *The Adventures of Winky Dink* depicted the former president as a heroic icon of the strenuous life, symbolizing an ethos that implored children and young adults to embrace hard work, physical fitness, and traditional American social mores.[52]

The adventurous-living campaign inherently related to the campaign to promote TR's conservationism. Comic books and television programs depicted Roosevelt as a "guardian of nature," and the TRCC worked closely with ecological and ornithological societies to commemorate his legacy on public holidays and at utilitarian shrines. Several states encouraged citizens to plant a "Teddy Roosevelt tree" on Arbor Day.[53] The secretary of the Interior spoke at public events on Roosevelt's conservation legacy, and President Eisenhower called him the father of the environmental crusade.[54] The TRCC produced twenty-five thousand pamphlets on the subject and in collaboration with the National Parks Service distributed them to park visitors around the country. At North Dakota's Theodore Roosevelt National Memorial Park—officially opened in 1947—rangers completed extensive research on TR's achievements as a naturalist and began long-term projects to restore the Badlands. Had the theme of Americanism not overwhelmed the centennial, "'Conservation' would have stolen the show," Hagedorn reported.[55]

Another distinct field of tribute derived from Roosevelt's contribution to upholding the moral and spiritual values considered foundational to the United States. Working with churches and religious institutions, the TRCC circulated leaflets on TR's "Nine Reasons for Going to Church" and reprinted sermons from prominent clergy. Portraying Roosevelt's devotion to the Christian faith was only a small aspect of this theme, however. Methodist bishop and social activist G. Bromley Oxnam, an advocate of Americanism who ironically stood accused of being a communist at times because of his work with labor groups, called Roosevelt the vanguard of "freedom's holy light" and celebrated his oratorical advocacy for social justice.

The TRCC attempted to inject Roosevelt's legacy directly into social movements like the African American freedom struggle by making placards for public events. One poster quoted Roosevelt: "To me, the question of doing away with all race and religious bigotry in this country is the most important of all."[56] But African American civil rights leaders did not seek to apply Roosevelt's legacy because of his mixed record as an advocate of the African American freedom struggle. Although Roosevelt had invited Booker T. Washington to dine with him in 1901, a radical act of social equality at the time, he had also injudiciously discharged a regiment of black soldiers as punishment for a crime they did not commit. The TRCC attempted to remind Americans of his dinner with Washington, but civil rights groups of the mid-twentieth century found Roosevelt's language on race odious and his record as president mixed, at best.

The TRCC found greater success promoting Roosevelt among political leaders pledged to social justice. The commission invited Sen. John F. Kennedy to North Dakota in 1958 to pay tribute to Roosevelt's "moral and spiritual imperatives." Kennedy noted that TR had written an important biography of Thomas Hart Benton, the Missouri senator who valiantly resisted the forces of slavery. In his speech the future president likened Benton's ethical spirit to Roosevelt's legacy, declaring that both had striven ceaselessly for righteous causes, guided by a faith in American institutions, at a time when being a politician afforded limited rewards. Benton and Roosevelt stood as examples of a social responsibility that Kennedy would make the hallmark of his 1960 presidential campaign.[57]

Despite the diversity of subthemes, Americanism remained the core feature of the centennial. Accordingly, the 1958 celebrations of the Fourth of July took on particular importance for memorializers. "Dictatorships," the TRCC reported, "parade guns, tanks, and planes. Let us . . . bring in procession before our fellow Americans, on floats and placards, symbols of the basic liberties guaranteed in the Bill of Rights, and the basic responsibilities laid upon the free citizen to keep those rights alive and unimpaired."[58] To that end the commission planned countless events around the country. A special lighting at Mount Rushmore emphasized TR's place among the presidents, and public forums on the radio broadcast TR's achievements to millions. President Eisenhower made special mention of Roosevelt's birthday in his annual Independence Day proclamation. Adm. Chester Nimitz paid tribute to TR's naval legacy in a July 4 showcase of the Pacific Fleet in San Francisco Bay.

The summer of 1958 witnessed an explosion of Rooseveltiana and commemoration. New York City taxi drivers slapped centennial stickers to their bumpers. Theater companies organized plays with Roosevelt as a leading character. Fashion designers crafted "Rough Rider" hats for women. Speaking competitions, church sermons, public bonfires, and reenactments occurred around the country. From the opening of centennial activities in October 1957 until the close of the campaign a year later, the TRA and TRCC orchestrated thousands of anniversary events that brought their man to the minds of Americans in a way never accomplished before. Not since 1919 had the public experienced such an inundation of commemorative activity. And never before had the focus of memorial activity fixated so exclusively on a single theme. The purpose of the centennial was to extol the virtues of patriotic Americanism, democracy, and free enterprise and apply them "to the struggle for the survival of the free spirit in a divided and harassed world."[59] Theodore Roosevelt's legacy, the TRCC believed, would help the United States contain the Soviet Union and liberate those benighted by the autarky and tyranny of communism.

Independent of the TRCC's commemorative activities, the motion picture industry during World War II and throughout the 1950s began rethinking TR's image as a patriot. Actors like Sidney Blackmer and John Alexander, who had portrayed Roosevelt before the war, returned to the role, often cast in westerns, the era's most ubiquitous genre and one that exuded patriotic Americanism. From 1943 to 1955, Hollywood studios produced nearly three hundred feature-length films set on the American frontier, a total that represents almost 30 percent of studio output. That trend continued until 1962, when the production of westerns decreased dramatically. Network television productions mirrored the big-screen trend. From 1955, TV westerns captured over one-third of the average viewing audience until 1961.[60]

Explaining the popularity of westerns relies on comparing the frontier and the Cold War. Visually, these motion pictures mythologized continental expansion and necessarily invoked the allegory of the cowboy as an icon of America's national institutions and collective values. Although scholars in the 1940s and 1950s dismantled Frederick Jackson Turner's frontier thesis, his image of the West as the wellspring of American democracy continued in popular culture. Tales of the frontier provided a distinct parallel to the Manichean struggle between capitalist democracies and socialist republics. Cowboys epitomized virtuous Americans and Indians the foreign "other." An airplane pilot at thirty thousand feet who dropped an atomic bomb mirrored the gunslinger whose precise aim won the high-noon duel. The frontier townspeople who prayed for a cowboy to intervene and save their civilization compared with citizens of a mythologized third world resisting the tyranny of Soviet communism. The frontier myth even adroitly prepared uneasy Americans for the prospect of annihilation by reminding them that the nation once before had endured this sort of crisis and, in that fight for survival, had forged the country's identity. The pioneers' expedition westward could have destroyed the germ of American liberty, which in order to thrive required constant vigilance, an obligation to intervene in righteous battles, and recognition that American leadership preserved American blessings.

Before World War II ended and McCarthyism became a household word, the western bridged the gap between historical aversion to global leadership and the inherent realities of an interconnected world that required constant American engagement to counter real and perceived threats to national security. The director John Ford pioneered this kind of multilayered storyline in films like *Stagecoach* (1939), *My Darling Clementine* (1946), *Fort Apache* (1948), *She Wore a Yellow Ribbon* (1949), *Rio Grande* (1950), and *The Searchers* (1956). His films stressed vigilance and survival in a zero-sum struggle with Native Americans that traced a common American identity over time.[61] John Wayne became the symbol of American exceptionalism in Ford's films and the advocate of total mobilization, absolute strenuousness, and a brinkmanship that resembled the US standoff with the Soviet Union.

Ford was the era's most prominent director of westerns that explored the contemporary state of international relations, but other filmmakers, some funded by the Department of Defense, crafted similar narratives.[62] The abundance of westerns reinforced the likelihood that public interpretations of the Cold War filtered through these frontier tales. Historian Richard Slotkin argues that producers offered the genre with every expectation that audiences would either "buy or refuse" the films and storylines. The industry would react accordingly, and so what "emerges at the end is a body of genres and formulas whose appeal has been commercially validated."[63] The creative forces in Hollywood used the western to make sense of their time, the federal government favored it because of the frontier's trusted patriotic symbols, and the American public endorsed the metaphor, which led the motion picture industry to respond with more of the same.

Theodore Roosevelt's legacy easily fit the stereotypical formula of Cold War westerns because he had contributed directly to the myth of the American frontier and symbolized nationalism in his self-promoted image as a cowboy. Roosevelt had encouraged expansion and called for the "winning" of the West, declaring it the duty of white settlers to convert the continent's "waste spaces" to outposts of civilization. Only by doing so in a strenuous and consistent manner, Roosevelt explained, would the world realize the blessings of American liberty. He had also embodied the transformational narrative as a visitor to the West who shed the traits of an effete easterner by becoming a Dakota rancher. Elsewhere, the cowboy image pervaded his public persona, including in tales of his leadership of the assorted "western" characters that comprised the Rough Riders regiment and in reports of excursions through the wilderness. Yet Roosevelt's image as an American cowboy rarely made it to screen. More often, studios opted to dress him as a statesman who would mediate the conflicts. They cast him as the voice of the national conscience, an image that inherently invoked the cowboy, without the costume.

Republic Pictures, a studio that specialized in the western genre and gave stars like Gene Autry and Roy Rogers their start, used Blackmer as Roosevelt for their 1943 movie *In Old Oklahoma* (re-released under the title *War of the Wildcats*). Set in 1906, the movie features John Wayne as Daniel Somers, an army veteran who returns to the frontier and stumbles into a community that mutinies against the town's plutocratic oil baron, Jim Gardner. The town appoints Somers to lead a rival renegade and amateur oil-drilling outfit. Gardner attempts to block Somers's band of locals by appealing to President Roosevelt. Using his wealth to get an audience with the president, Gardner makes a case for his plan on the basis of expertise, but TR hears that Somers also wants the mineral rights. "Daniel Somers?" Roosevelt asks. The president sidesteps the millionaire Gardner to seek out his competition, and the audience discovers that the upstart Somers earned his military reputation with the Rough Riders. The president considers him one of his regiment's ablest men and consequently gives Somers the rights, although not without a twist. Somers has four months to transport ten thousand barrels of oil to market, a test that will prove the merit of his ambitions. Otherwise, Roosevelt will cede the oil rights to Gardner. In a short soliloquy, Blackmer as Roosevelt recites the frontier myth: "Our country owes all of its progress to a small detachment of pioneers, men who asked only for the chance to take a chance. That spirit is the essence of America."[84] Naturally, Somers succeeds against all odds in delivering the oil, vindicates Roosevelt's decision, and fortifies the frontier myth of intrepid pioneers.[65]

Television westerns mimicked the cowboy image found in feature-length films, although the small screen often relied on a family setting rather than focusing on the cinematic loner roaming the wild range. The different situation nevertheless provided a narrative that equally fit the Cold War zeitgeist. The frontier family promoted "the values of a modern pluralistic social order, a benign, legalized justice tempered with mercy and tolerance."[66] Network series like *Gunsmoke, Little House on the Prairie,* and *Bonanza* mythologized the frontier to emphasize American exceptionalism, if not American individuality. These shows illustrated how domestic life contributed to the frontier struggle and, circuitously, how the modern family underwrote the Cold War's ideological showdown. In much the same way the TRCC commemorated Roosevelt's family values, television depicted TR as a down-to-earth and approachable figure, while ever the man of action. Rather than don a top hat and jacket as a statesman, TR appeared in chaps, hunting gear, or Rough Rider costume in western TV dramas.

The 1956 season of CBS's *My Friend Flicka,* a show about a fictional Wyoming ranching family, the McLaughlins, brought in Roosevelt as a fisherman seeking a quiet vacation in the Rockies. Ken McLaughlin, a precocious schoolboy, teaches Roosevelt how to catch fish in a nearby pond. Because he does not recognize the president, he unwittingly saves the family farm by telling a story about neighbors who are gradually destroying the grazing common. The show plays into Roosevelt's record as a conservationist and outdoorsman, and touches on the cowboy image through the character of Rob McLaughlin, the family patriarch. Like John Wayne's Daniel Somers, McLaughlin served in the Rough Riders and automatically earns Roosevelt's ear when the matter of grazing arises.[67] Ultimately, Roosevelt arbitrates the dispute in favor of McLaughlin.

The cowboy image appeared in several other shows. The 1959 series *Law of the Plainsman* paired TR with Native American US marshal Sam Buckhart to bring thieves to justice, and NBC's 1962 adaptation of Owen Wister's *The Virginian* starred Karl Swenson as Colonel Roosevelt of the Rough Riders. Television developed a slightly different slant than film, but the frontier and its cultural undertones remained important in both mediums. Roosevelt symbolized the "moral exceptionalism" of the United States and "represent[ed] the culmination of the mythic ideological project."[68]

Although the western genre dominated the motion picture industry until 1962, the studios also used Roosevelt in dramas to tackle political issues that challenged American identity. The 1948 film *My Girl Tisa,* a story about foreigners living in New York City at the turn of the twentieth century, plunged TR into the controversial immigration debate. Anxieties over foreign arrivals soared in the postwar period, stoked by conservative Republicans and southern Democrats who joined together to play on public apprehensions about welfare fraud and communist infiltration. By 1952 these political forces legislated, over the veto of President Truman, the McCarran-Walter Act, which extended the system of quotas that had regulated immigration since 1924. The "national origins quota" system limited the number of immigrants by country to the percentage of that nationality already resident in the United States. The quotas disadvantaged immigrants who were not from Western Europe and continued the decades-old practice of excluding Asians.

Against this backdrop, *My Girl Tisa* recounted a tale of hard-working Eastern European immigrants determined to achieve the American Dream. Tisa, a Hungarian, works to bring her father to New York City but innocently depletes her savings, falls into arrears with unseemly characters, and winds up in jail. She relies on her boyfriend to redeem the situation. He breaks up a parade to gain the attention of Theodore Roosevelt and begs the president to pardon Tisa. Roosevelt obliges when he hears her sad story.[69] Critics applauded the performances, including Blackmer's penultimate portrayal of Roosevelt. On the immigration issue, however, critics found no consensus and debated the authenticity of Roosevelt's legacy.

Liberal critic Richard L. Coe, writing for the *Washington Post,* found it hard to disparage "a picture in favor of all the human virtues including patriotism and Teddy Roosevelt."[70] Coe admitted that the plot seemed "sticky" and unlikely, but he interpreted Blackmer's portrayal as generally accurate. Coe's review insinuated that Roosevelt, had he lived, would have disapproved of the McCarran-Walter Act. To the contrary, Edwin Schallert of the *Los Angeles Times* called the representation anachronistic in its attempt to connect the Cold War era with "a period when immigration laws were less restrictive than now, and when many people came to America to seek their fortunes rather than to save them in the modern manner."[71] Schallert found Roosevelt's intervention "about as unlikely an incident as one might witness" and recalled a president more prone to bristle at immigration and race mixing. The debate over *My Girl Tisa* reflected the pliability of Roosevelt's political legacy, which could be interpreted as favoring the progressive tradition of an American "melting pot" as well as the conservative tradition that sought to exclude foreign others in order to maintain traditional American values.[72]

Despite the disagreement on TR's political leanings, his image in Cold War motion pictures remained continuously American. Almost always given the role of mediator, either as a statesman or cowboy, Roosevelt was depicted as a symbol of the long-standing patriotic traditions of the United States. Films and television shows synthesized the perspective that consensus historians, public figures, and the memorial associations promoted. Roosevelt became a nostalgic link between a bygone era that had witnessed the rise of American influence and contemporary validation of national ideals in the Cold War era when the United States reached its apogee of global power. Motion pictures acquainted the public with the nationalistic and selfless image of Roosevelt, which had dwindled for a generation after Henry Pringle's biography. Along with the centennial tributes and the shifting historiography, the motion picture industry laid the groundwork for a permanent revival of Roosevelt's image.

CHAPTER SIX

UNFINISHED BUSINESS

Roosevelt's revival in public memory inspired new modes of memorialization. For example, television, radio, and print advertisers opted to use his image to sell a variety of consumer goods. While not unusual for Madison Avenue to deploy Roosevelt or any former US president, the rise of consumerism increased the frequency of presidential images in advertising. Images of the presidency served a nostalgic purpose, expressing patriotism, reliability, and trustworthiness. Lincoln, the most often co-opted chief executive, typically appeared as "Honest Abe" and became the icon of the Lincoln Motor Company and the Lincoln National Life Insurance Company, which relied on the self-descriptive slogan, "Its name indicates its character." Likewise, the myth that George Washington chopped down a cherry tree became an integral part of Fowler's Cherry Smash cola, and because Thomas Jefferson had brewed his own beer, Budweiser counted him a spokesperson. Tennessean Andrew Jackson sold bourbon, and chain smoker Ulysses S. Grant hustled cigar tobacco.[1]

With the exception of Lincoln and Washington, few chief executives appeared so regularly in advertisements as Theodore Roosevelt. Coffee maker Maxwell House relied on a dubious story that Roosevelt, on his visit to Nashville in 1907, declared their brew "bully good to the last drop." Hammermill Paper, A.B.A. Travelers Cheques, and the National City Bank of New York also regularly deployed Roosevelt as a company representative. He fronted advertisements for products and services as various as groceries, energy companies, life insurance, optometry, banks, candy, rifles, and Cracker Jacks.

Although some ads made scant reference to Roosevelt's biography, most linked consumer products to aspects of his life and legacy. Winchester firearms used his cowboy persona and outdoorsman reputation to entice the modern hunter. Sinclair Oil paid reverence to Roosevelt's conservation legacy in an effort to change its public image as a polluter.

Dromedary devil's food cake mix was marketed as a taste of Roosevelt's home life, and the company paid the TRA to stock its products at memorial sites. The Hancock Life Insurance Company billed its policies as a sensible security precaution by comparing them to TR's proactive statecraft.[2] And the intrepid art patron Walter Paepcke of the Container Corporation of America (CCA), the nation's largest manufacturer of cardboard boxes, distinguished his uninteresting and unglamorous product as integral to the postwar consumer era by releasing a series of artistic advertisements that celebrated Roosevelt's Americanism. The ads depicted Roosevelt as a great thinker, not unlike the designers of the CCA's boxes. The golden age of advertising in the 1950s and 1960s furnished many new and unanticipated impressions of TR.[3]

Representations of Roosevelt in fine art also flourished. Italian-American artist Vincenzo Miserendino's statue of Roosevelt speaking from a rocky plinth was erected in Boone, Iowa, in 1948. In 1954, Georg John Lober, an apprentice of Gutzon Borglum, presented a bust of Roosevelt to New York University's Hall of Fame. And, in 1957, the Theodore Roosevelt Centennial Commission (TRCC) reproduced Russian-born artist Gleb Derujinski's bust of Roosevelt for mass-market sales.[4] Curator of the Roosevelt Collection at Harvard Robert Haynes organized art exhibitions at Widener Library and coordinated with the Library of Congress to display their holdings of Roosevelt cartoons and ephemera. Rooseveltiana shows were featured at Macy's department store in midtown Manhattan, the New York Public Library, the New York City Police Department headquarters in Little Italy, uptown at the American Museum of Natural History, at IBM's head office in Armonk, and at the Metropolitan Life Insurance building across from Madison Square Garden. Not since 1919 had artists and curators taken such interest in Roosevelt.

New Roosevelt literature also proliferated. The New York State Department of Education reprinted its school guide to TR's presidency. The TRCC circulated millions of booklets and pamphlets highlighting the centennial theme of Americanism and good citizenship. Roosevelt's *Autobiography* was reprinted, as was Henry Pringle's biography and a photographic coffee table book. Literary scholar Edward Wagenknecht produced a centennial biography that presented Roosevelt as a legendary American occupying seven "worlds" of Action, Thought, Human Relations, Family, Spiritual Values, Public Affairs, and War and Peace.[5]

Several works of historical fiction considered Roosevelt and his legacy. Ambrose Flack, a contributor to the *Saturday Evening Post* and the *New*

Yorker, wrote *A Room for Mr. Roosevelt* (1951), about a family that hangs a portrait of TR in their house and obsesses about his morality. The household models their actions on TR's legacy, asking themselves, "What would Roosevelt do?" Flack's story enchanted television producers, who adapted it for prime-time audiences in 1952.[6] Other novelists capitalized on TR, like adventure writer Will Henry, who dramatized the Spanish-American War in *San Juan Hill* (1962); Oakley Hall, who unnecessarily fictionalized the true story of Roosevelt's time in *Bad Lands* (1978); and historian H. Paul Jeffers, who transitioned to fiction in a sensational hallucinatory tale called *Stalwart Companions* (1978), which paired Sherlock Holmes with Roosevelt as crime fighters in Gilded Age New York. Writers targeted juvenile audiences with depictions of Roosevelt as an overgrown kid exploring the outdoors.[7] The Cold War revival that had begun with academic reconsideration now advanced into centennial celebrations, motion pictures, political invocations, and an outpouring of cultural productions, but the TRA still had unfinished business—namely, its failure to erect a national memorial in Washington, DC.

The aborted plans to build at the Tidal Basin left TRA trustees to consider alternative locations. City planners offered two suggestions; neither matched the prominence of the location on the National Mall. Chairman of the Commission on Fine Arts (CFA) Charles Moore proposed the parkland area east of the Capitol that runs alongside the Anacostia River, where Robert F. Kennedy Memorial Stadium stands today. Trustees rejected it because the area was too far from the mall. Also, a housing development had gone up on the parkland in 1928, and it remained unclear how the neighborhood would mature. As an alternative, city planners at the National Capital Park and Planning Commission (NCPPC) recommended acquisition of Analostan Island, a seventy-seven-acre landmass that straddled the Potomac River due west of the Lincoln Memorial between the Francis Scott Key and Arlington Memorial Bridges. The location offered scope for new interpretations and innovative memorials, the NCPPC assured and, after careful consideration, the TRA concurred.[8]

Analostan Island grew from centuries of sediment accumulation. As the Potomac River swept silt along its banks, several small barrier islands surfaced. In the colonial era, Analostan was a mere twenty acres of mud, an atoll barely large enough to attract traders and travelers. By the time Theodore Roosevelt occupied the White House, Analostan had expanded to seventy acres, and it became a public recreation space. Evidence of the island's growth bares itself in the long marsh that scars its southern half.

When high tides and floodwaters swell, the Potomac reclaims the marsh and plows through the island's eastern interior. Opposite the swampy lowlands, a steep ridge rises and plateaus toward Analostan's southwestern coast, terminating in a semicircular cape. Here, a small ancillary atoll known as Little Island shares a legal boundary with Analostan and punctuates the headland. The northern half of the island features a second plateau that overlooks the Georgetown shoreline, and this area often served as a transit point to Virginia. Here the Algonquians traded with the roving Five Nation Iroquois and white colonialists.

Analostan did not have its first settled residents until 1792, when John Mason, son of the anti-Federalist founding father George Mason, built a seasonal vacation home on the island. The Masons held social parties in the balmy summer before ferrying back to Georgetown in the winter. Except during the Civil War, when Union troops occupied the island, Analostan mainly attracted sports and leisure enthusiasts. In the Gilded Age, when TR worked in the capital as civil service commissioner, the Columbian Athletic Club hired grounds on the island and built sports facilities, including a baseball diamond, tennis courts, a track for running and cycling, and a grandstand. In the same period, a boat club opened, and the island hosted medieval festivals with jousting tournaments.[9]

At the end of the nineteenth century, the island welcomed industry to its shores, a development that made it less attractive for recreation. The Great Falls Ice Company built cold-storage facilities and began cutting ice from Analostan's southern banks. Not long after, the sports facilities fell into disrepair. When the boathouse burned down in the early twentieth century, the club closed and never reopened. The Washington Gas and Light Company purchased the island in 1913 and proposed building an energy plant and gas storage facility, but the island's history as a park site generated protest from city planners and a nostalgic public. Dissent eventually prompted the utility company to look elsewhere, leaving the island to lapse into a state of wilderness that provoked persistent speculation about its future.

The Washington Gas and Light Company ignored development proposals for a sports stadium, an amusement park, and apartments during its period of ownership. The CFA and NCPPC accused the company of stalling the city's expansion projects. Intent on maximizing Washington's few green spaces, these government agencies instigated condemnation proceedings that, if carried out, would have purchased the island for public use. The Justice Department began appraising Analostan's value in 1931;

in the meantime, the TRA commenced negotiations to purchase the island from the energy company as a memorial location. The TRA made a final offer of $364,000 after nearly fifteen months of negotiations. Washington Gas and Light, however, valued the land at $400,000 and rejected the offer. The TRA's bid represented three times what the company had paid only twenty years earlier, and the association shrewdly refused to meet the company's demand. Trustees waited to learn the Justice Department's appraisal, and when the condemnation hearings valued Analostan at $250,000 ($100,000 less than the TRA's bid), the utility company quickly reversed its position and accepted the memorial association's offer.[10] On January 8, 1932, the TRA officially took possession of the island.

The association never intended to retain ownership, however. It struggled to maintain Oyster Bay Park, TR's gravesite, and other sites of memory, and so planned to transfer title to the island to the National Park Service (NPS) while maintaining the right to validate or veto any proposals for memorials there. Attorney General William DeWitt Mitchell advised President Hoover that the land transfer should be unconditional and that the NPS, rather than the TRA, should dictate the island's development. City planners at the CFA and NCPPC disagreed with Mitchell's advice but urged the memorial association to devise its own plans before passing along the title to ensure the government would accept the gift under clearly defined terms. To accomplish this, the TRA hired Frederick Law Olmsted Jr., the most prolific landscape architect in American history. Olmsted had helped his father design Chicago's White City for the 1893 World's Fair, served on the McMillan Commission that redesigned the capital, and counseled the nascent NPS on park management. Olmsted's experience and reputation gave his designs immediate credibility. The TRA also hired John Russell Pope, the architect of the original design contest for the Tidal Basin, hoping that he would design an architectural shrine on Analostan.

Pope's credibility rivaled Olmsted's, but over the course of the summer it became clear that a monumental memorial on the site lacked political and aesthetic favor. Olmsted determined that the island should become a natural "sanctuary," devoid of traffic and safeguarded from the bustle of Washington. Should a memorial become desirable in the future, Olmsted wrote the TRA, an outlook point for taking in panoramic views of the National Mall would set Analostan within a wider context of the city's commemorative features, while maintaining its natural beauty.[11] Olmsted's plan for a nature reserve won congressional approval largely on the grounds that it would not include a monument. "It is intended that there shall be nothing of a monumental nature erected," Congressman Robert Luce, chair of the Library Committee, said; "the island shall be kept as nearly as possible in a wild state." Luce considered it "fittingly testifying" to a conservationist president.[12] The island itself was the memorial.

On December 12, 1932, the island officially became the property of the United States, and President Hoover renamed it Roosevelt Island. Presiding over the ceremony from the East Room of the White House, the lame-duck Hoover joined TRA president James R. Garfield, Alice Roosevelt Longworth, and Secretary of State Henry Stimson to inaugurate the site and declare its "appropriateness" as a memorial. It associated "a bit of nature within the boundaries of the city" with a man driven to enjoy the outdoors, and it revived hopes that the island would again become a recreational space forever free from industrialization.[13] Edith Roosevelt, the family's most outspoken advocate for conservation memorials, called it "a dream come true."[14] Two months after the dedication ceremony, Congress renamed it Theodore Roosevelt Island to distinguish the memorial from incoming president Franklin Delano Roosevelt.[15]

After the dedication ceremony Olmsted began implementing his design. His work adhered to an ethos that public space, where possible, should protect wildlife of all kinds for future generations. Throughout his long career in landscaping, which spanned baroque Gilded Age to austere Depression-era public works, a singular mission had pervaded his work: respect for nature. With that mission in mind, he attempted to return Theodore Roosevelt Island to its "primeval" state, close to how the Potomac Valley was thought to have looked before white settlers developed it. He submitted a preliminary report to the TRA in 1934 and called for a long-term commitment to cultivate "a real forest" that would cover most of the island and constitute the "dominant landscape feature."[16] He proposed clearing the nonnative foliage and planting a variety of old and young trees to give a sense of an evolving natural habitat. At the southern plateau, the highest ground on the island, Olmsted sought to clear an outlook terrace to allow visitors to absorb "the superb views from the ridge . . . across the River toward the Lincoln Memorial and downstream toward the [Arlington] Memorial Bridge and beyond."[17]

The NCPPC and CFA approved the scheme, and Congress authorized the appropriations. The Civilian Conservation Corps (CCC), the New Deal agency that hired unemployed laborers to complete outdoor public works,

began clearing and replanting the island according to Olmsted's directions. By 1935 the undesirable vegetation was gone, and the CCC planted
trees to simulate a mature forest. With the exception of the marsh land,
which Olmsted decided not to fill with soil and plants, due to the excessive
cost and the detrimental effect it would have on the bird population, his
proposed restoration finished on schedule by 1936. The CCC banished
invasive species, carefully staked visitors' paths, destroyed potential fire
hazards, and reforested the island with thousands of new trees, shrubs,
ferns, and herbaceous plants.[18]

Timely progress of the landscaping gave the TRA and city planners
every expectation that the island would open to tourists by the spring of
1938, but the design for an outlook terrace, visitor amenities, and safety
precautions delayed the grand opening. The terrace caused the most
difficulties. Olmsted envisioned a rounded terrace at the southern plateau, fashioned from a retaining wall affixed to the ridge and flanked by
steps that would blend into the surrounding foliage. Some TRA trustees,
however, changed their minds about a monument, and because Olmsted
believed the terrace could accommodate a small sculptural feature of
some sort, the association began deliberating about how to utilize the
space. Disregarding Congressman Luce's insistence that no monument
mar the island's natural beauty, the TRA revisited long-discarded plans
to erect Carl Akeley's lion atop the outlook.

Hermann Hagedorn reintroduced the idea, and TRA president Gen.
Frank Ross McCoy endorsed it. "I had not seen [the lion] in a dozen years
or more," Hagedorn told McCoy, "and got the same thrill from it that I got
during the years that I was seeing it develop under Carl's hand." Hagedorn
lamented the absence of a monument: "We can say what we want about
the Island itself being the best possible memorial, but it is a memorial
without a point of focus, and, for the majority who visit it, it will be a
place of recreation and nothing else," he assumed.[19] Such sentiment
prompted the TRA to order a recrafted model of Akeley's lion and enlist
sculptor James Earle Fraser to create the final carving. For a time it appeared as if the lion monument was a certainty, but when Akeley's wife
saw the new model, she called it "a snarling beast, with its ears back and
chin forward." The original, she insisted, was designed as an elderly lion,
"noble in aspect and alert."[20]

Olmsted also resisted the sculpture, recalling that Akeley's original
intention was to set the lion "in the midst of the woods." The outlook

terrace, an open space atop a ridge, offered an entirely different location. Fearing that the "two goals" of an outlook vista and Akeley's lion "could never be reconciled," the TRA abandoned the sculpture.[21]

Tourists began visiting the island in 1938, but the TRA never formally inaugurated the island's opening in the manner Olmsted expected. The National Park Service held up the opening by demanding a water gate for the western banks of the island to protect visitors against high tide. In the 1940s, World War II absorbed all public funding. The construction of an outlook terrace and the necessary safety amenities stalled. The government interned the island, and, with the TRA's permission, the Office of Strategic Service (precursor to the CIA), the FBI, and the army trained there. Two temporary pontoon bridges connected the Georgetown coast from the northern point of TR Island to Virginia and formed an emergency military roadway. At the conclusion of the war, the bridges were removed, cutting away a tract of land and permanently scarring the topography.[22]

Years of neglect allowed invasive botanicals, once eradicated by the CCC, to reemerge. Overgrown brush crowded footpaths, igniting concern about wildfires. The proliferation of weeds wrecked the once well-groomed trails. Olmsted related his "distress" to the TRA and continued to lobby for an outlook. In 1947, he composed a final report that reiterated the core elements of his design; with the exception of a few visitor facilities carefully integrated into the surrounding nature, he said the island should in no way show a human imprint. The resolve to create Olmsted's expansive primeval landscape still existed, and the initial forestation had been completed years earlier, but the chronically underfunded NPS could not muster enough financial and administrative resources to implement the design, and the island's development remained dormant until a "dangerous situation" arose in 1952 that threatened the integrity of Olmsted's vision.[23]

After nearly four years of research, the capital's regional highway survey published a $96 million plan to radically reduce traffic and streamline the flow of commuters around the city. The report concluded that widening streets, introducing a one-way system, and building new bridges would siphon cars from congested exit points and help motorists avoid downtown. The western edge of the capital, the report noted, was particularly choked by traffic, despite the relatively new Arlington Memorial Bridge. The report's engineers proposed a multilane bridge connecting Washington to Virginia over Theodore Roosevelt Island. Naturally, the

TRA protested. "I am very disturbed," McCoy told reporters: "The association presented the island to the Government with the stipulation that it
must be maintained as a 'natural park for the recreation and enjoyment
of the people' and any plan for its development must be approved by the
association."[24] McCoy called the report "the raping of the park system,"
and Hagedorn denounced it as a "breach of faith" that would destroy
Olmsted's primeval forest.[25] It so plainly defied the ecological basis of
the memorial that the TRA presumed city planners would eventually
backtrack on the proposal.

To fight the construction plans, the TRA enlisted former chair of the
city planners Ulysses S. Grant III. They also recruited Park Service director Newton Drury and well-known conservationists like Audubon Society
president Irston Barnes, who wrote two open letters on the uniqueness
of the island. "It is a fitting memorial to a President who awakened the
conservation conscience, and it is a personal invitation to his people to
live fully and to learn the joys of the outdoors," Barnes avowed.[26] Alice
Roosevelt Longworth lobbied congressmen to keep true to the original
intention of the island, and Hagedorn organized a "back to the people"
marketing campaign to attract tourists.[27]

Believing they had veto power over any plan inconsistent with the
island's purpose, the TRA hired attorneys to challenge the city's planners. The rise in visitor numbers and anecdotal feedback from residents
gave them every hope the island would avoid being sullied. Legislators
signaled their support as well. Everett Dirksen (R-IL), chair of the Senate
subcommittee on the District, told TRA lawyers, "We are not going to let
them hurt you fellows."[28]

Meanwhile, the city's engineers devised four possible bridge routes,
each bisecting the island, and the capital's chief executive announced that
"no legal bar" existed that could hamper the plans. Technically, the TRA
had given the island without conditions, but the Interior Department's
legal counsel advised the city that the US government must "pay just compensation" for an act that so clearly violated the purpose with which the
island had been donated.[29] Sensing that political momentum had swung
in favor of the TRA, the city drafted plans for a tunnel, an idea that gained
support from the White House but ultimately faltered on the grounds that
it would cost nearly double that of a bridge.[30] The deadlock continued
until 1954, when Congress sanctioned the bridge to cross the Potomac
just south of Little Island. The TRA kept out of that debate, declaring it a
minor victory because the bridge bypassed the island, but realized that

the new site meant the bridge would unquestionably blemish the view of the capital from Olmsted's proposed outlook terrace. The TRA was forced to concede that, at some point, a bridge would cross the river near the island's general vicinity. Desirous to keep Olmsted's outlook unspoiled, the TRA voted to allow construction across the northern expanse.[31] The press reported the compromise as a magnanimous defeat.[32]

In actuality, the memorial association considered opposition to the bridge a losing battle and identified significant benefits if they conceded to the city's planners. Hagedorn reported to the executive committee that allowing the construction of the bridge across the northern acreage would take "the White House off an increasingly uncomfortable hook" with Congress. "If we refuse this request," Hagedorn hypothesized, "we go against the wishes of our best friends, including the President."[33] Not coincidently, the same month the TRA stopped resisting the bridge, legislative and presidential support for the TRCC gathered traction. Relinquishing opposition to the bridge was strategic in Hagedorn's negotiations for centenary celebrations.

Also, accepting the bridge forced the city to heed TRA-dictated conditions, including naming the bridge after Theodore Roosevelt, providing pedestrian access to the island, building a parking lot for visitors on the Virginia side, and planting several large evergreens to conceal as much as possible the bridge's edifice and to mute noise from traffic.[34] The compromise offered the TRA an opportunity to rebrand the island, a fact made evident when the city proposed moving the site of the bridge only a month later to the southern expanse, directly over Olmsted's terrace. The TRA relented almost immediately, demonstrating the complete collapse of its commitment to preserving the island's natural beauty. Trustees rationalized the decision as one that would maintain the panoramic views from the Lincoln Memorial to Arlington Memorial Bridge, but they abandoned the fight to preserve the island's habitat.[35] "It will only be a matter of time before the hot dog and frozen custard stands spring up," one Georgetown local complained, making the point that conservation no longer dominated the island's memorial narrative.[36]

Instead, the island became a shrine to TR's Americanism. The TRCC focused heavily on Independence Day, 1958, as a key date in the yearlong centennial celebrations and organized a fireworks display from Theodore Roosevelt Island. Six hundred guests gathered at the southern plateau to watch the rockets light up the night sky, and hundreds of thousands more watched from Georgetown and the mall. Maryland governor Theodore

McKeldin delivered a public address to officially dedicate the island as a monument to Roosevelt's enduring Americanism.[37] Patriotic observance was the order of the day, yet the transformation of Olmsted's tranquil primeval forest into a bombastic lightshow represented the total collapse of the conservation theme. Irston Barnes, a former ally in the movement to preserve the island and stop construction of the bridge, called the celebrations "a new and shabby way of debasing Roosevelt Island and dishonoring the memory of a great president."[38] To launch the pyrotechnics, part of the island required clearing. The blistering explosions would disrupt wildlife, particularly birds. Barnes warned that the event would "open the door to other inappropriate activities" in national parks. "The late president must be in a regular tizzy at the stupidity of the whole thing," one environmentalist remarked.[39]

The TRCC quickly responded to accusations that they had abandoned Roosevelt's conservation legacy, and it dispatched Hagedorn to defend the Independence Day plans. Hagedorn called Barnes "a little more papal than the Pope in protesting so loudly" and submitted that while Roosevelt "cherished every bird around his home," he nevertheless "set off firecrackers with his children" each year.[40] The festivities went ahead in 1958 but moved back to the Washington Monument in 1959. By the summer of 1960, construction had begun on Theodore Roosevelt Bridge, making it impossible to shoot off fireworks without interfering with traffic.

The engineers finally decided to locate the bridge across the southern expanse, a route that traversed only a small portion of the island, leaving the rest of the forested area untouched. The late change of plan gave conservationists faith that Olmsted's design would survive to some extent, but construction was not limited to the bridge. In exchange for the privilege to build the highway over the island, the government agreed to the TRA's demands for a new memorial at the northern plateau. Like the fireworks, the memorial would emphasize Roosevelt's Americanism and his reputation as an icon of responsible citizenship.

In collaboration with the TRCC, the TRA hired architect Eric Gugler, an artist most famous for remodeling interiors like the White House West Wing and Oval Office. Gugler presented an immense scheme that conformed to the centennial theme and satisfied those in the TRA who sought a monumental national memorial. It was a vast rectangular court surrounded by trees and twelve granite panels stretching ten feet tall and twenty feet wide. On the panels Gugler inscribed quotations from TR that emphasized his civic ideology. At the center of the plaza, in what

Hagedorn called "a stroke of imagination and perception," the architect inserted a giant bronze armillary sphere atop a granite plinth.[41] The orbicular object—designed by Paul Manship, who crafted the gilded bronze *Prometheus* at Rockefeller Center—was said to symbolize infinity. Within the celestial sphere rose a bronze flame, representative of Roosevelt's spirit and the eternal vigor of American freedom. Hagedorn told the TRCC that the bronze "betoken[ed] the free spirit" at a time when the United States was "fighting the menace of enslavement." How, Hagedorn asked, "can we better serve the memory of Theodore Roosevelt?"[42]

Gugler's design resembled nothing of Olmsted's. With the island's southern expanse destroyed by the capital's traffic and the only other recreational spot at the northern expanse being measured for a giant cement plaza, Olmsted's vision for a natural landscape and primeval forest vanished. Despite instructions from Congress to keep the island free of architectural memorials, the TRA and TRCC proceeded with their plan to build one. What jolted Hagedorn's plan to have the monument erected by 1958 was the audaciousness of the design, the cost (around $2.5 million), and the public's realization that the scheme made no explicit reference to Roosevelt. The only visible trace of TR appeared on the plinth of the armillary sphere, where Manship inserted a small bas-relief of the former president opposite a reflecting pool.

Hagedorn received endorsement from city planners and President Eisenhower, but, to his dismay, the design did not win congressional support.[43] Reportedly, when congressmen saw the scale models, "everybody laughed."[44] The public likewise ridiculed the design with clever nicknames for the armillary like "doughnuts in limbo," a "pantywaist contraption," "an onion ring fried in molten bronze," or the "radiator cap of Jack Benny's Maxwell."[45] Conservationists added to the chorus of opposition. After the House reluctantly passed a bill authorizing the design, Wilderness Society president Benton MacKaye appealed to the Senate and President Eisenhower to reject it on the grounds that it desecrated the memorial's original purpose. When the matter came before the Senate in 1960, conservationists enlisted TR's descendants to help their case.[46] Alice Roosevelt Longworth denounced the "metal geegaws" as a "globular jungle gym" and suggested that the "lovely, wild island should be left as it is."[47] Archie preferred the installation of Akeley's lion, and Ethel refused to endorse either design. TR's grandson Kermit called the armillary a "glorified gyroscope" and believed the memorial should, at least, depict some image of his grandfather.[48]

The defection of TR's family embarrassed the memorial association, and the Senate refused to vote on the appropriation until the family was satisfied, a decision that led TRA president Oscar Straus II, himself a descendant of a famous father (TR's secretary of commerce and the first Jewish cabinet member), to reach out to Alice. In spite of her barbed condemnation of Manship's armillary, she told Straus she was "not opposed to *a* memorial" on the island.[49] Straus revived the stalled legislation by accompanying Alice to Senator Kenneth Keating's (D-NY) office to lobby for an amendment that gave the Roosevelts veto power over future designs. With that provision, the bill passed in September 1960, and the TRA enlisted Gugler and Manship to redesign the northern plateau.

Within four months, a new design was revealed. Gugler reshaped the rectangular plaza into an oval space paved with flagstones and a circular reflecting pool with fountains and flower beds. The new plan reduced the amount of lighting, removed the contentious parking lot, and provided access to the island by a single footbridge. Conservationists applauded the new entrance because it removed the threat of automobile traffic. Still, the purists believed that any monument fell afoul of the island's original intention.

In place of the armillary, Manship crafted a controversial seventeen-foot bronze statue of Roosevelt with a raised arm. Alongside the statue, four twenty-foot-high granite monoliths—two on each side of the statue—loomed, bearing inscriptions to represent the major themes of Roosevelt's legacy. When the Roosevelt family first viewed the model of the memorial, they were disappointed, particularly with the statue. Ethel Roosevelt Derby changed her mind when she visited Manship's studio, where she discovered variations of the proposed likeness. Over the course of 1963, TR's children debated which of Manship's clay sculptures best captured the essence of their father.

Unexpectedly, Hagedorn publicly voiced his dissatisfaction. He reminded the TRA that Roosevelt opposed lifelike memorials and above all disliked the idea of a carved effigy. That an enormous one would grace the national memorial, Hagedorn said, contradicted TR's wishes.[50] The *Washington Post* published a satirical editorial in which Roosevelt, from the grave, denounced the statue as "unnatural, pompous tomfoolery."[51] All the same, TR's children agreed on a model by 1964, and the bronze went into production.

Another debate emerged over the inscriptions on the monoliths. Given Theodore Roosevelt's many public speeches and highly memorable quips,

choosing only four all-encompassing quotes seemed impossible. Gradually, the children and the TRA resolved to inscribe multiple quotes on the
panels, each of which related to a theme. Individually, the slabs evoked TR's
legacy as an advocate of "Manhood," "Nature," "The State," and "Youth."
Collectively, the quotes embraced the prevailing theme of Americanism.

While the alterations addressed major controversies, they adhered
to the original design. The use of geometric symbols on a massive scale
and across a vast expanse imitated Pope's design for the National Mall
in 1925; it was a "modernistic version" of the Beaux-arts memorials that
dominated the capital's landscape, a style that emphasized Americanism
over environment and masculinity over Mother Nature.[52]

The legacy theme of progressivism and reform, largely absent from the
granite panels, received ample representation at the dedication ceremony.
On October 27, 1967, TR's 109th birthday, President Lyndon Johnson
unveiled the memorial. Johnson, a progressive southern Democrat, cast
himself as the political descendant of Franklin Roosevelt and, thereby,
Theodore. Flanked by Secretary of the Interior Stewart Udall, the man
responsible for the most aggressive expansion of federal parks since the
Depression, and Chief Justice Earl Warren, a strong proponent of desegregation and equal voting rights, the president celebrated Roosevelt's
contribution to political liberalism. "He challenged our people to build,
not just for themselves, but for their children," Johnson related, "not
just for private gain, but for the public good." As if choosing words for
another granite panel, Johnson recited famous Roosevelt witticisms in
his undeniable Texas drawl. "Every man will have a fair chance to make
of himself, all that in him lies; to reach the highest point." "Equality of
opportunity means that the commonwealth will get from every citizen the
highest service." "Woe to the country where a generation arises which . . .
shrinks from doing the rough work of the world." Roosevelt, Johnson
said, was a symbol "for all times—for calm and for storm."[53] Udall called
TR a personal hero, and Warren praised his "trustbusting" and "integrity
in the Federal Service."[54] In sum, the three speakers rebranded the site
a memorial to progressive politics, while the TRCC emphasized Americanism. The island's natural beauty reminds visitors of his conservation
legacy. Although it took nearly fifty years to mature into a multifaceted
commemoration of a many-sided man, by 1967 it achieved this objective.

Hagedorn counted the national memorial a major success. Over the
course of thirty-eight years at the helm of the TRA, he could count several
important achievements. When the opportunity arose to lead the TRCC,

Hagedorn resigned his post as director of the TRA. He left a lasting mark on the association and contributed to Roosevelt's public memory through absent and erected memorials. He helped compile a vast collection of motion pictures and supported academic scholarship. Looking back, Hagedorn reflected on his achievements, counting the acquisition of a library, the commission of Morison's *Letters,* and the merger of the RMA and WRMA as significant triumphs, as well as the maintenance of the Oyster Bay memorial park and TR Island.

In retrospect, Hagedorn believed that one achievement stood apart from any other: the 1948 decision by the TRA to purchase Roosevelt's Long Island home, Sagamore Hill. The opportunity arose when Edith, cognizant of her increasingly poor health, commenced negotiations for a sale to avoid multiple heirs fighting to claim parts of the estate. She proposed that the TRA take ownership of the land, the house, and its contents before her death.[55] Aware that the association's budget could not afford the house, Hagedorn nevertheless stoked trustees to consider the prospect. "We took a deep breath," ignored the financial impediments, and put "faith in the Angel that has the daring in his keeping."[56]

Theodore Roosevelt had planned to build the house for his first wife Alice Lee and to call it Leeholm in her honor. Her untimely death in 1884 not long after the birth of their baby girl crushed his hopes and delayed construction, but gradually he decided to finish the house for his young daughter. Roosevelt absconded to the Dakota Badlands, and, in his absence, Leeholm was completed. Designed in the Queen Anne style, the asymmetrical house had thick brick walls on the ground floor, and the upper stories were covered in painted clapboards, giving the house a sturdy appearance. The high gabled roof was scattered with jutting dormers.

Roosevelt thought that the exterior design of the house acknowledged his commitment to social stability. The solid walls shielded his family from the whipping winds of Long Island Sound.[57] Roosevelt had "perfect definite views" on the interior as well.[58] He instructed the architects to build a library for work and a drawing room in which to welcome guests from the outdoor piazza. Excluding the staff quarters, the house had ten bedrooms, numerous fireplaces, an ample kitchen, and several washrooms. Leeholm was designed for a large family, and, compared with the Gilded Age mansions that showcased their owners' wealth in baroque opulence, Roosevelt's house was modest and built for comfort.[59]

Over the course of his three-year residence in the Badlands, Roosevelt made several trips back East to visit baby Alice, his siblings, and his childhood sweetheart Edith Kermit Carow, whom he married in 1886 after a quiet courtship. During this period, he began referring to the Oyster Bay property as Sagamore Hill, a name that honored local Native American chief Sagamore Mohannis. In 1887, Roosevelt moved in on a permanent basis with Edith and Alice, and five more children arrived, three of whom Edith delivered in the house. The eighty-three acres of woodland surrounding Sagamore made for a vast outdoor playground, and the energetic family took shelter in the many indoor nooks on inclement days. During Roosevelt's presidency, Sagamore was the "summer White House." He would go to Long Island to relax with family, welcoming cabinet members and dignitaries to join him. Business leaders and trade unionists met on the piazza and made historic progress on industrial relations. The library adjacent to the entrance became a conference room for Republican Party strategists.

Soon, Roosevelt recognized that while the house was perfect for family, it lacked a room grand enough for distinguished guests. In 1905, he added the North Room as a formal parlor. It showcased hunting trophies, presidential artifacts, and family heirlooms. After retiring from the presidency, Roosevelt returned to live full-time at Sagamore and throughout the Great War used the drawing room veranda to speak out against Woodrow Wilson. Sagamore was a base of operations throughout Roosevelt's life, and in the days before he died, he asked Edith, "I wonder if you will ever know how I love Sagamore Hill."[60]

Shortly after his death, memorializers approached Edith with schemes to transform the house into a shrine like Washington's Mount Vernon or Jefferson's Monticello. But she refused to leave, alluding to her own affection for the place. Edith lived there until her death in 1948 and although she died before the sale to the TRA closed, she established the framework for the purchase that formally allowed the association to take ownership in 1950.

The TRA bought the house for $104,000 and began the painstaking work of restoring it to its early twentieth-century grandeur and to what it looked like during Roosevelt's presidency. The association prioritized fireproofing. The wooden clapboard, shingled roof, and old electric wiring was particularly dangerous, and the trustees used the association's capital reserves to replace asbestos shingles, repaint the exterior, and rewire the entire house. To recreate the interior, the TRA removed electric fittings installed in the 1920s and mounted faux gas lighting. The lights operated off the new electrics, but the gas effect made the house radiate with nineteenth-century charm. Functional changes included a new heating system, a new staircase to simplify traffic through the house, and the replastering of sagging ceilings.[61]

The TRA's Mrs. Reginald P. Rose, a New York socialite, art collector, and interior design consultant, oversaw the interior restoration, relying on Edith's correspondence and the recollections of family members. She revarnished walls, identified original wallpaper patterns, reupholstered furniture, and repositioned the family's belongings as they would have appeared in the early twentieth century. Photographs helped Rose dress TR's desk and arrange the numerous artifacts that adorned the North Room, such as animal heads, a samurai sword and scabbard, a Rough Rider's hat, and a presidential flag. These returned to their original places as if the structural work had never disturbed the house.[62]

The cost for repairs and restoration piled up, putting considerable pressure on the TRA's finances. The association expected to recover its expenses in visitor fees, but when local residents of Cove Neck protested the site's effect on village privacy, the project almost collapsed. Sagamore as a public shrine, residents contested, would remove several acres of land from the tax roll and prompt tourists to invade nearby properties for picnics and parking. Most of all, residents believed the house's popularity would strain access roads not suitable for heavy traffic. The TRA raised enough funds to widen the road, and gradually local resistance receded.[63] On June 14, 1953, former president Herbert Hoover and sitting president Dwight Eisenhower opened Sagamore Hill "with a plea to all Americans to follow in the footsteps of the famous leader of the Rough Riders."[64] The last two living Republican presidents shook hands for the press before touring the house with TR's daughters Alice and Ethel.

Although Eisenhower deployed the Rough Rider image in his speech, Sagamore expressed little of the cowboy or soldier. Hermann Hagedorn branded the house as a symbol of Americanism, much as he had when he orchestrated the fireworks on TR Island, the rededication of the birthplace, and the centennial commission. "Why should busy men and women work their heads off to prepare the house for public visitation?" he asked. "The answer is simple. Theodore Roosevelt had something that we who are living here in America, a generation after his death, need for our security, even for our continuance as a free people." Deploying Cold War rhetoric, Hagedorn called for the house to celebrate "American ideals."[65] Yet, the TRA gave little consideration to this legacy theme. Only two features of the restoration epitomized Hagedorn's Americanism: returning the house to appear as it did in Roosevelt's presidential years and filling the North Room with artifacts that reminded visitors that Oyster Bay had been an epicenter of American power, a site where Roosevelt held court.

The rest of the house manifested alternative legacies. The Library, for example, where Roosevelt had written correspondence and books, depicted him as a scholarly figure, less presidential or quintessentially American. The Library recalled the man of letters who spoke multiple languages and appreciated world cultures. Relics of Roosevelt's state-craft adorn the room, and visitors could not help but notice the large oil painting of Roosevelt's father. Looking down on TR's desk, the portrait encouraged guests to think about family. Indeed, the entire house signi-fied TR's dedication to family life. His grandchildren believed his "kindly spirit" haunted the house, and tourists imagined the ghost of Theodore Roosevelt playing, shooting, riding, and racing with his kids along the grounds.[66]

The upstairs rooms told this story best. The marital bedroom and the bedrooms of the children humanized Roosevelt in a way the birthplace in New York City failed to. Roosevelt designed Sagamore; he longed to be there when away; he died there, in Ethel's bedroom overlooking Oyster Bay. The grounds that surrounded the house brought to mind his con-servationist legacy, whether visitors imagined him rowing on the bay or taking notes on bird species. The flora and fauna of his neighborhood captivated a man who knew the exotic species of Africa, Europe, and South America.[67] Sagamore subtly memorialized the many-sided man. "During the 1950s," Roosevelt biographer Kathleen Dalton observes, "Sagamore Hill was seen primarily as the home of a great man," in part due to the Americanism revival led by Hagedorn. Since then, however, a common interpretation has taken visitors beyond the patriotic message and emphasized American values as a code of simple living that tran-scends nationalism and includes a faith in God, "mutual consideration and caring" for humanity, respect for nature, and a mindful resistance to greed. At Sagamore, Roosevelt escaped the vanity of politics, the urban setting of New York or the capital, and the bickering in Congress, and he reconnected with the elements of life that mattered most to him.[68]

When the doors to Sagamore opened to visitors in 1953, only a few rooms on the ground floor were completely restored. Over the next ten years, the TRA invested considerably in the house. The bedrooms and the gun room upstairs were opened, a souvenir shop was installed, and a parking lot surfaced over the former vegetable garden. After three years,

Hagedorn enthusiastically reported that the house was financially self-sufficient. "The black ink bottle, in the office where the books are kept," he told the TRA executive, "was recently observed thumbing its nose at the red."[69] He was right to count the TRA's purchase of Sagamore as the association's greatest success. "It is the aura of Roosevelt's presence," historian Lewis Gould relates, "that makes his home still the place where visitors go to recapture the sense of the man and his vibrant times."[70] It displays a polygonal figure to successive generations in a way no other monument can.

Sagamore also symbolized a transition for communities responsible for memorializing TR. By 1960, their members had grown old, and although the merger of the men's and women's groups had made the TRA appear to be a new venture, its activists knew otherwise. The aging demographic of trustees prompted Hagedorn to declare it "no over-dramatization to point out [that] in the Association's life, an era has ended."[71]

The most prominent and active trustees, many of whom had sparked a friendship with TR while he was still alive, died in the late 1940s and 1950s, including TR's conservationist ally and governor of Pennsylvania Gifford Pinchot; journalist and preparedness advocate John Callan O'Laughlin, once commissioned to write TR's biography; and past RMA presidents James R. Garfield, who had secured the purchase of TR Island, and Frank Ross McCoy, who had led the charge for revival after the war. RMA assistant secretary Gisela Westhoff died in 1950, and librarian Nora Cordingly in 1951. Will Hays, the former Republican National Committee chair, Hollywood censor, and RMA activist, did not survive to see the centennial celebrations, and Edith Roosevelt took her place alongside her husband in Youngs Cemetery in 1948. Having lived to the advanced age of eighty-seven, she had personally overseen the safeguarding of TR's legacy by destroying, censoring, and withholding resources from prying historians, as well as by validating the activities of the memorial associations.

The passing of a generation of memorializers marked the transition to a new period of commemoration. "We stand at a point of new departures, new personalities, new leadership, new visions, new achievements," Hagedorn anticipated. Mrs. Roosevelt's death ended the long wait for enshrining Sagamore Hill. Likewise, the capital's redesigned highway scheme sparked reconsideration of TR Island. In 1960, the death of Ted's wife Eleanor Butler Roosevelt, who lived adjacent to Sagamore Hill in a property known as Old Orchard, heralded the most significant change to the TRA. When the association had determined to buy Sagamore, it also promised to purchase Old Orchard upon Eleanor's death; however, the value of the property, appraised at nearly $200,000, far exceeded the association's investment capital. Moreover, the TRA's spending in the 1950s left the association with a foreboding deficit. Still, the Old Orchard property drew considerable interest from the trustees, who imagined opening a museum to exhibit a raft of collected Rooseveltiana.

To raise the necessary resources for Old Orchard, TRA trustees discontinued the role of director, cut publicity funding, and even considered ending the annual dinner and presentation of a distinguished medal. (Eventually, they retreated from such drastic measures.) Recognizing the birthplace as its greatest expense, the association proposed divesting the site to city, state, or federal interest groups, such as the New York Historical Society. Horace Albright, a former NPS director who sat on the TRA executive committee, advised that no agency would acquire the replica building and its debt. The NPS, however, might be interested in taking the birthplace if the popular and profitable Sagamore Hill property accompanied it.[72]

Albright held several informal conversations about this proposition with his successor, NPS director Conrad Wirth. Wirth favored the plan and envisioned Sagamore and the birthplace as potential sites of interest for the imminent 1964 World's Fair in New York. He encouraged the TRA to purchase Old Orchard, and in turn the memorial association came to believe that an NPS takeover was "the only recourse . . . to protect the future of the properties" and secure the association's financial sustainability. Roosevelt's living children agreed with that assessment, and Wirth drafted a congressional bill to legally transfer the properties. In 1963 the association purchased Old Orchard and transferred ownership to the NPS, along with Sagamore Hill and the birthplace.

The future of the TRA, Hagedorn acknowledged, was unpredictable. From 1919 to 1963, the association had focused heavily on public memorials to express the legacy of Theodore Roosevelt. In years to come, the former TRA director presumed, "the actions that await doing will take more imagination to conceive, more vision and resolution to carry out."[73] A new generation of memorializers would need to find innovative modes of commemoration, based in their own contextual circumstances, without help from those with a living memory.

And they would have to do it without Hagedorn. The longest-serving patron of the association suffered a massive heart attack and died on

July 27, 1964. He was eighty-two. More persistent than any other activist, Hagedorn provided a vision for memorializers. He deployed images of Roosevelt through public events, academic publications, the erection of memorials, and a constant engagement through cultural mediums—whether film, television, radio, or art. His contribution was evident in nearly every aspect of the postwar revival, and his absence, along with the divestment of TRA properties, raised questions about the future of Roosevelt commemoration.

CHAPTER SEVEN

A SECOND DECLINE AND REVIVAL

Given the high tide of Roosevelt commemoration in the 1950s and 1960s, trustees expected a decline. Anticipation outpaced that eventuality until 1968, when once-firm Cold War assumptions eroded amid the Vietnam War and the collapse of the New Deal consensus that had defined American politics for more than a generation. Only then did Theodore Roosevelt's image suffer a return to Pringle's characterization of TR as an aggressive and juvenile bully. The shifting sociopolitical context of the late 1960s corresponded with the death of stalwart TRA trustees, and by the 1970s, few trustees had personal memories of Roosevelt. The general public, more than half a century removed from TR's presidency, retained only vague impressions of his character.

These circumstances had the potential to permanently disrupt the TRA's activities. After decades of activism, memorials to Theodore Roosevelt existed at all the pertinent sites of historical importance. A rich historiographical debate had matured beyond orthodoxy and revisionism. Visual depictions had infiltrated American culture in motion pictures, museums, and commercial advertisements. With such extensive work already complete, the association struggled to identify new modes of commemoration. Trustees wondered what was left to do, and without strong leadership from Roosevelt's contemporaries, membership waned. Finances dwindled. By the end of the decade, the association considered scrapping membership altogether and rebranding as a nonprofit foundation.[1]

A good example of the association's impotence was its inability to combat erroneous factoids in the public domain. For instance, the Schlitz Brewing Company created a series of print advertisements in the 1960s that boasted Roosevelt's appreciation of their beer. The brewer alleged that Roosevelt brought "a whole lot of Schlitz" on his 1909 African safari, despite there being no record of it. Rumors of a photograph of Roosevelt accepting a consignment of Schlitz in Mombasa circulated widely at the time, and the company encouraged the tall tale for years to come. In the 1970s, Schlitz exaggerated the fabrication in television ads in which actor Sorrell Booke (who played Boss Hogg in *The Dukes of Hazzard*) portrayed TR as a beer-guzzling adventurer. Booke, dressed in khakis and bellowing "bully," accepts a bottle of Schlitz in what appears to be Sagamore Hill's North Room. The TRA complained to Schlitz that Roosevelt seldom drank alcohol, but to no avail. TR's easily identifiable features and his reputation as an all-American icon made him a valuable symbol. Although Schlitz manufactured the myth that he drank their beer, the regular invocation gradually cemented the link. Accounts of the "Schlitz consignment" continue to appear without any shred of evidence.[2]

TRA trustees diligently attempted to contradict false images, yet the growing absence of those with personal memories of Roosevelt made it a difficult task. Roosevelt's legacy was up for grabs, and audacious stories stretched historical truths to suit the particular interests of those who invoked him. Some spurious portrayals of TR, like the Schlitz ads, caused minor frustration for TRA trustees. Others provoked outrage and, according to the TRA, profoundly injured Roosevelt's legacy.

In the world of politics, Roosevelt's image faced particular vulnerability. The year 1968 was significant in American political history. Domestic unrest, spurred by decades of racial tension and social inequality, exploded when civil-rights leader Dr. Martin Luther King was assassinated. Riots consumed the nation's capital and other major cities, and the Black Power movement gained momentum, encouraged by Olympians Tommie Smith and John Carlos and the Black Panther Party. The assassination of Democratic presidential hopeful Robert F. Kennedy, two months after King's death, compounded the crisis. Discord at home overlapped international chaos that amplified the Cold War. When North Korea captured an American naval vessel spying in its territorial waters, fear of another war on the Korean peninsula intensified. In Europe, the Prague Spring, a Czechoslovakian liberalization movement, collapsed when confronted with Soviet invasion, reaffirming the reality of an iron curtain. And the North Vietnamese Army and Viet Cong launched the Tet Offensive, an assault on South Vietnamese cities that permanently changed the nature of American involvement in Southeast Asia.

The 1968 presidential election revealed public dissonance and the splintered political consensus that would permanently transform the American party system. The New Deal coalition built by Franklin Roosevelt disintegrated, and so did the unanimous belief in a monolithic communist menace responsible for global conflicts. The Vietnam War invalidated the impression that American foreign policy put humanity ahead of strategic interests. Lyndon Johnson's dual wars, on communists abroad and poverty at home, estranged once-loyal liberals and fragmented the Democratic Party's fragile bonds. Cold War standpatters clashed with antiwar candidates, as did the party's civil-rights advocates and Southern segregationists. Hubert Humphrey, the Democrats' eventual candidate and Johnson's vice president, could not hold the "liberal-Labor-Negro" coalition together or distance himself from an unpopular administration.[3] One notable Democratic defection was Alabama governor George Wallace. Running for president as an independent, Wallace pledged victory in Vietnam within days of taking office and promised to use the presidency to nullify desegregation. He won five Deep South states, breaking the Democrats' traditional hold on that region.

The Republican Party faced its own existential crisis. The nomination of Barry Goldwater in 1964 inspired conservatives ideologically opposed to the New Deal, as well as vehement anti-communists uncomfortable with the changing nature of the Cold War. Goldwater urged Republicans to unapologetically pursue a conservative course, and although he did not seek the Republican nomination in 1968, his political opinions found representation in the presidential candidacy of former actor and California governor Ronald Reagan.

A political rookie, Reagan unexpectedly won the 1966 California governor's race with a mix of Hollywood charm and unpretentious rhetoric that promoted low taxes, a smaller state bureaucracy, and the persecution of welfare fraudsters and communists. Reagan did not actively campaign for the presidential nomination, but he accepted almost every speaking invitation outside California, raised money for the national committee, and encouraged the popular groundswell for a Reagan draft. It worked. In 1968 he stood alone as the party's leading conservative candidate. To his left, Nelson Rockefeller, the liberal Republican governor of New York, sunk millions of his personal wealth into a third and final campaign for the nomination. What Rockefeller lacked in popular enthusiasm, he made up for in party support, representing a bloc of northern Republicans unwilling to shift so dramatically to the right.[4]

While the party's extremities fought for control, Richard Nixon straddled the liberal and conservative wings of the party. Recognized early in the campaign as the frontrunner, the former vice president and 1960 presidential candidate attracted conservatives and moderates. His political apprenticeship as a congressman allowed Nixon to gravitate toward conservative issues, and he helped stoke the anti-communist witch-hunts of the late 1940s and early 1950s. Nixon also collaborated with Robert Taft to restrict trade unions. Over the course of his career, however, he called for less radical reforms to the New Deal and softened his bombastic foreign policy position. After Goldwater's crushing defeat in 1964, the Republicans considered a moderate like Nixon the only hope to reclaim the White House. Even if he lacked the magnetism of Reagan and could not garner the affection of northeastern liberals who worshiped Rockefeller, Nixon commanded the party's ideological center.[5]

To bolster his image and enhance his personal appeal, Nixon exploited Theodore Roosevelt's public memory, which was still in the midst of a revival.[6] When a reporter asked why he wanted the job, Nixon replied, "I think a lot of it is what I have called this Teddy Roosevelt thing. I'm not in this for the prestige or cheers. Hell, I've seen all that before. It might sound corny . . . But I think I have some fresh ideas."[7] Nixon made the comparison regularly, employing the popular and likable image of TR as a "doer of deeds," and trying to escape his reputation as "Tricky Dick," the smarmy politician all too eager to smear his opponents.

As early as 1960, Nixon explained that it was "not so much" that he had an affinity for Roosevelt's ideas. Rather, he told journalist Gary Wills, "I guess I am like him in one way only: I like to be in the arena."[8] Quoting Roosevelt's 1910 "man in the arena" speech became a hallmark of Nixon's political image. The speech celebrates the "man actually in the arena" as opposed to the critic "who points out how the strong man stumbles." Nixon used the speech to publicly concede his shortcomings, while presenting himself as a tireless statesman who worked well under pressure.[9] Claiming kinship with Roosevelt was meant to show that Nixon was a man of conviction and thrust.

The man-in-the-arena image also transcended the rhetoric of the campaign. Roger Ailes, Nixon's broadcast consultant, deployed the "arena concept" for commercials and press conferences in an effort to visually depict Nixon as Rooseveltian. Ailes hung a framed portion of Roosevelt's speech in his office and, inspired by it, staged Nixon's appearances accordingly. At public events, crowds of Nixon devotees surrounded the candidate, as if he stood alone in a boxing ring. Eager to ask potted questions, the friendly spectators made Tricky Dick appear approachable, well informed, and sharp.[10] At the 1968 Republican National Convention, despite his self-professed ambivalence to TR's ideas, Nixon portrayed himself as an ideological acolyte. "Like Theodore Roosevelt," Nixon began, then quoted roughly from a 1912 speech, saying that "this country will not be a good place for any of us to live in unless it is a good place for all of us to live in."[11] He revered Roosevelt's advocacy of civic duty and national security, as well as his convictions about government intervention in support of public welfare. He purposely echoed the Republican platform of law and order, targeted reform of the welfare state, and strong but diplomatic management of international relations.

Alternately, conservatives like Reagan and Goldwater disassociated TR's progressivism from his Americanism, marking them out as mutually exclusive legacies. Goldwater said that Roosevelt's progressive policies of public education and income tax were communist inroads that would inevitably lead to state command, but he favored the anti-communist, independent spirit or "what Teddy Roosevelt once called Americanism."[12] Ronald Reagan carried Goldwater's jingoistic anti–New Deal message to the 1968 Republican National Convention and on his speaking tour criticized LBJ's war on poverty with a twist on TR's famous quip, joking that Democrats "walk softly and carry a big sack."[13]

Rebranding himself as an affable character akin to Theodore Roosevelt helped Nixon in some small part to secure the Republican nomination. He used the same approach during the general election, lecturing crowds on what "Teddy Roosevelt often said."[14] When asked to explain his conception of the presidency, Nixon deferred to Roosevelt. At times he did this indirectly, by explaining TR's concept of the "bully pulpit," and in other instances he quoted Roosevelt directly. "The best executive is the one who has enough sense to pick good men to do what he wants done, and self-restraint enough to keep from meddling with them while they do it," Nixon pronounced.[15]

Co-opting Roosevelt may have appeared to be political posturing had Alice Roosevelt Longworth not endorsed Nixon so enthusiastically. "I seem to have known the Nixons ever since they came to Washington in the late forties," she reminisced, recalling her attraction to the young senator's staunch anti-communist position.[16] Alice considered Nixon a "competent" legislator (unlike Senator Joseph McCarthy) and regularly invited him to dinner.[17] Her public faith in him lent weight to Nixon's appropriation of her father in 1968. "It's really amazing to see what has happened to Dick," Alice related, "defeated by Kennedy and then by Pat Brown for Governor of California . . . He's come through all that." She "didn't think that it was the end of him at the time," believing he had a staying power much like her father's, but she admitted being "one of the few" who believed he could come back from two political drubbings.[18] On Election Day, her intuition was validated. Nixon carried thirty-two states and narrowly won a plurality of the popular vote.

As president, Nixon continued to invoke TR. Citing Roosevelt's legacy as a family man and proponent of child development, he revived the White House Conference on Children and Youth, an event that had originated in TR's second term. When designating a week in May "Small Business Week," Nixon referred to Roosevelt's appreciation of the entrepreneurial spirit. His 1970 Labor Day speech trotted out TR-isms to celebrate the milestone of $1 trillion in gross national product. Roosevelt, he said, gave the country the necessary momentum to deliver a minimum income for working families, and in his courtship of organized labor, Nixon remarked that Roosevelt had similarly supported employee-benefits protection. Quoting directly from TR's first annual message, Nixon elevated the working man as the government's "prime consideration" for economic recovery.[19] When choosing a vice president after Spiro Agnew's resignation, when applauding Vietnam veterans, or when making an appearance at a sporting event, Nixon quoted Roosevelt. The intensity and frequency of these invocations followed the same stylistic co-option he deployed during the 1968 election.[20]

Nixon's compulsion to emulate a more appealing character became most obvious when he advocated for conservation legislation. Hardly the outdoorsman, Nixon was inherently uninspired by the environmental movement. In fact, he called it "crap for clowns," but the surge of eco-activism in the 1960s represented an opportunity to capture the hearts and minds of a new electoral demographic. The "prospect of losing political ground" led Nixon to opportunistically advocate environmental protections.[21] John C. Whitaker, the deputy assistant for domestic affairs and a genuine nature enthusiast, encouraged Nixon to embrace Theodore Roosevelt as a presidential model. In a variety of legislative victories he summoned TR—making Earth Day a national holiday, signing the Clean Air and Water Act, signing the Endangered Species Act, establishing the Environmental Protection Agency, and publishing the Roadless Area Review, which audited national forests.[22] The president often purposely signed conservation legislation in the Roosevelt Room, musing that "if [TR] were here today," he would say, "This is a great time. This is an exciting time."[23]

Nixon's "green" record remains unparalleled. His administration legislated for more environmental protections than that of any other American president, including Roosevelt. However, these initiatives derived from political opportunity, whereas Roosevelt's personal affection for nature inspired his policies. Co-opting TR never entirely obscured this fact, but it did conceal Nixon's cunning.

Theodore Roosevelt's legacy also loomed large in Nixon's foreign policy. Nixon's chief counsel on international relations was National Security Advisor and Secretary of State Henry Kissinger, who relied on Roosevelt without continually invoking him in private diplomatic conversations or by boastful platitudes in public speeches. Instead, Kissinger celebrated Roosevelt as a historical figure of great importance. As a realist in foreign relations who valued the preponderance of American power as the foremost objective of diplomacy, Kissinger traced his thinking to past realists like Klemens von Metternich, Otto von Bismarck, and Theodore Roosevelt. Nixon's secretary of state credited Roosevelt with achieving America's rise to global influence by implementing discreet lines of diplomatic communication, deploying the military in a strictly strategic manner, and supporting international allies, regardless of human rights abuses. "No other president defined America's world role so completely in terms of national interest, or identified the national interest with the balance of power," Kissinger wrote. The only administration to come close, he believed, was Nixon's.[24]

Kissinger did not ignore the moral and ethical dimensions of international relations; he simply put national interests ahead of ideals.[25] Roosevelt and Nixon, Kissinger wrote, saw the role of the United States not as an interventionist state for global freedom and democracy but as a "great" power competing among other great powers for a share of the world's material resources and wealth. By emulating TR, Kissinger boasted a return to the balance of power politics among global actors, a situation evident in the decade-long period of détente (1969–79). Détente did not sideline antagonistic Cold War ideologies but rather accepted them as acknowledged differences and attempted to look beyond them to avoid military and nuclear conflict, and foster meaningful economic collaborations. Kissinger associated such realism with Roosevelt.

In all aspects of Nixon's administration, Roosevelt cropped up as an icon to be admired. It is not surprising, then, that Nixon relied on TR when the Watergate scandal destroyed his administration's credibility and drove him out of office. The disgraced president recycled the "man in the arena" allegory to explain his transgressions:

> For more than a quarter of a century in public life, I have . . . fought for what I believed in. I have tried, to the best of my ability, to discharge those duties and meet those responsibilities that were entrusted to me. Sometimes I have succeeded and sometimes I have failed, but always I have taken heart from what Theodore Roosevelt once said about the man in the arena, "whose face is marred by dust and sweat and blood, who strives valiantly, who errs and comes short again and again because there is not effort without error and shortcoming, but who does actually strive to do the deed, who knows the great enthusiasms, the great devotions, who spends himself in a worthy cause, who at the best knows in the end the triumphs of high achievements and who at the worst, if he fails, at least fails while daring greatly."[26]

After announcing his intention to resign, Nixon bade farewell to the White House with yet another invocation of Roosevelt:

> I had a little quote in the speech last night from T.R. As you know, I kind of like to read books. I am not educated, but I do read books and the T.R. quote was a pretty good one. Here is another one I found as I was reading, my last night in the White House, and this quote is about a young man. He was a young lawyer in New York. He had married a beautiful girl, and they had a lovely daughter, and then suddenly she died, and this is what he wrote. This was in his diary. He said, "She was beautiful in face and form and lovelier still in spirit . . . And when my heart's dearest died, the light went from my life forever." That was T.R. in his twenties. He thought the light had gone from his life forever—but he went on. And he not only became President but, as an ex-President, he served his country, always in the arena, tempestuous, strong, sometimes wrong, sometimes right, but he was a man. And as I leave, let me say, that is an example I think all of us should remember . . . We think that when someone dear to us dies, we think that when we lose an election, we think that when we suffer a defeat that all is ended. We think, as T.R. said, that the light had left his life forever. Not true. It is only a beginning, always.[27]

Nixon hoped the American public would remember him as the man in the arena, a figure defined by more than his failures, relentless even in defeat. The book Nixon read before his farewell speech was Noel Busch's *T. R.: The Story of Theodore Roosevelt and His Influence on Our Times*. Recognizing that TR's image was vulnerable to being appropriated through popular invocations like Nixon's, Busch declared the act of summoning "interpretive diagnoses of eminent personages long deceased" a greater risk to the "practitioner" than the historic figure. "Research along such lines is likely to be mistaken for an attempt to belittle or disparage," the biographer noted, "even though exactly the reverse may be the case."[28] In the case of Nixon and Roosevelt, both images suffered. Watergate irreparably damaged Nixon's reputation, but it also inadvertently infected the perception of Roosevelt. The Pringle-inspired portrait of an impetuous, juvenile, and imperial president returned to popular memory, refracted through the indiscretions of Nixon.

Reassessment of Roosevelt owes equal credit to the emergence of the New Social History movement, which placed a greater emphasis on race, gender, and class in the study of history. These historians incorporated the stories of those who, till then, had been excluded from the historical narrative. Moreover, these historians reacted to political hypocrisies in global affairs, and particularly to the rhetoric of the US government, which called for the world to recognize inalienable freedoms but did not practice what it preached. The human rights violations of the United States at home and abroad, exemplified by segregation and the war in Vietnam, inspired New Social History studies. For Roosevelt's image, the historical turn destroyed the consensus paradigm established by authors like Richard Hofstadter and John Morton Blum, who placed Roosevelt in a long tradition of American politics.

The New Social Histories of the 1960s and 1970s emphasized the dissociative nature of the American experience, as demonstrated in the lives of minorities and underprivileged populations. Common in these historical accounts was Roosevelt's penchant for self-preservation, a view that favored Henry Pringle's profile of an entitled man led by ego. When it came to minorities, historians like Roger Daniels and Willard Gatewood indicted Roosevelt for surrendering to racial bigotry in political decisions. For Daniels, Roosevelt's Japanese immigration policy kowtowed to the endemic anti-Asian racism in California, while Gatewood proclaimed that Roosevelt's management of "the Negro Question" instigated controversy and bowed to public pressure when doing so was useful to his career. The evolving historiography also took aim at the nation's labor struggle, declaring it a futile fight against a dominant, and always victorious, capitalist class. Gabriel Kolko condemned Roosevelt's trustbusting as little

more than managing the interests of capitalist oligarchs, referring to
his progressivism as selective regulation. Kolko declared the Pure Food
and Drug Act a legal modification to industrial standards that regulated
trade rather than rectifying labor conditions, a complaint activist Upton
Sinclair made regularly despite his support for Roosevelt's legal reforms.[29]

On international affairs, radical New Left historians disillusioned with
consensus history attempted to "brush aside the question of American exceptionalism" as an intellectually dishonest concept.[30] Roosevelt, in these
narratives, came under particular criticism. Historian Lloyd Gardner,
for example, argued that Roosevelt aimed "to bring law and order into
international relations," as George Kennan and Henry Kissinger judged,
and equally desired "to put American banks into underdeveloped areas
of the world . . . to expand trade and cultural influence into world mar-
ketplaces."[31] Prosperity, Gardner reasoned, derived neither from a divine
source nor the spatial uniqueness of American geography but from the
nation's willingness to dominate and impose its wishes. New Left historians cast the United States less as a city on a hill spreading democracy by
example than as a nontraditional empire expanding its sphere of influence by force. By expanding American power internationally Roosevelt
thereby became culpable for the policies of successive executives. The
New Left traced the failures of the Cold War—namely, interventions like
the one in Vietnam—to Theodore Roosevelt's nationalism, which stressed
the universality of American ideas spread by a gritty energy akin to that
of the mythical cowboy.

Hollywood produced comparable interpretations. Director John Milius's 1975 film *The Wind and the Lion* exemplifies the reemergence of
Pringle's Roosevelt. Set in colonial Morocco during TR's presidency, Milius's film creatively depicts the Perdicaris incident of 1904, when Berber
bandit and outlaw hero Mulai Ahmed er Raisuli kidnapped Ion Perdicaris,
a wealthy Greek-American living in Tangiers. Raisuli demanded a hefty
ransom, prompting Roosevelt to issue an ultimatum: safely return Perdicaris or expect swift military retaliation. The incident occurred during
TR's first presidential election, and Republicans used the ultimatum to
demonstrate his credentials as a tough international negotiator. At the
national convention, delegates chanted "Perdicaris Alive or Raisuli Dead,"
an epigrammatic message inspired by Secretary of State John Hay to
galvanize delegates. It worked, and Roosevelt won the nomination. The
threat of intervention, however, amounted to little more than a storm

in a teacup. The United States never seriously entertained the idea of a military strike because Morocco quickly conceded to Raisuli's demands. Perdicaris went free, and relations in the region returned to normal.[32]

Milius's reinterpretation, allegedly based on historian Barbara Tuchman's account, embellishes a minor diplomatic episode and portrays it as a major conflict. Instead of showing a quick resolution without a shot fired, *The Wind and the Lion* features a full-scale invasion of Morocco in retaliation for Perdicaris's abduction. Two bloody battles ensue: one in which American marines annihilate Moroccan palace guards, and another in which they valiantly recapture Perdicaris while fighting off French and German armies. Both episodes defy reality. The full extent of the distortion is revealed in the cast of characters. The Scottish-accented Sean Connery, best known in 1975 as James Bond, plays Raisuli, while the bald and grey-bearded Ion Perdicaris becomes Eden Pedecaris, played by young, blond Candice Bergen.

Television star Brian Keith played Roosevelt, and while he physically resembled the president, the movie rendered an extreme interpretation of TR's personality. Flamboyantly imperial and somewhat ignorant, Keith offers a caricature of the American cowboy. He proposes to personally attend Pedecaris's rescue, struggles to remember Raisuli's name, and sums up the essence of Americanism in a soliloquy that equates the United States to a grizzly bear: strong, intelligent, voracious, if not "a little blind and reckless at times." Keith portrays the United States as a nation without "real allies, only enemies," and his Roosevelt says, "The world will never love us. We have too much audacity. And we're a bit blind and reckless at times, too."[33] *The Wind and the Lion* depicts the cavalier attitude of "that damned cowboy" and returns to Pringle's image of an adolescent Roosevelt, a man incapable of reasoned statecraft, a sentimentalist driven by emotion. Aware of Milius's distortion, critic Kevin Thomas applauded it anyway. He believed Milius's presentation was "healthy" because it marked "the beginning of the end of a kind of lethal innocence" that characterized American military endeavors like the Vietnam War.[34]

The film's release came days after the Khmer Rouge captured the American container ship *Mayaguez*. Often considered the last significant battle in the Vietnam War, the kidnapping of the *Mayaguez* sailors eerily paralleled Perdicaris's capture, except that the Ford administration did send a detachment of marines to rescue the imprisoned Americans. The *Mayaguez* incident reminded audiences of the perils of Cold War intervention, and as the war in Vietnam concluded, Roosevelt became as culpable as contemporary politicians for the failures of American foreign policy. He had earned praise in the 1950s when patriotism and anti-communism increased in popularity, and when those sentiments abated in the 1960s and 1970s, esteem for Roosevelt receded. Milius told journalists, "You can take the politics to be any way you want, for or against the United States," but Keith's portrayal does little to hide the indictment of executive power and militarism that grew during the Cold War era. Keith's portrayal of Roosevelt, film critic Joy Gould Boyum said, "too easily caricatured" him as the architect of American imperialism.

Had Milius released *The Wind and the Lion* two years earlier, the TRA might not have responded to the historical inaccuracies. After Hermann Hagedorn's death, the association rarely reacted to New Left historians or negative portrayals in popular culture. Instead, trustees with busy schedules kept the association ticking over until, by 1973, membership ominously declined, and the association recognized the necessity of hiring a director to manage the day-to-day operations. In 1974, the trustees appointed John Allen Gable, an energetic PhD candidate from Brown University. One of Gable's first self-directed duties was a full-throated attack on Milius. He called *The Wind and the Lion* an outlandish lie and published scathing editorials in the *New York Times, Variety,* and *Newsweek.* Gable personally replied to hundreds of letters from moviegoers about the "true" Roosevelt, and while his efforts hardly stemmed the film's popular appeal, it did provide the only public rejoinder.[35]

As director, Gable defended Roosevelt with boundless enthusiasm. Trustees likened his tenacious drive to Hagedorn's. In fact, in the 1950s, Hagedorn had serendipitously inspired Gable to learn more about TR. At the age of twelve, Gable began corresponding with Hagedorn and three years later met him at a centennial event at the East 20th Street birthplace. The attention Hagedorn paid Gable sparked the teenager's collection of Rooseveltiana and instigated his ceaseless appetite for Roosevelt trivia. Gable visited memorial sites like Sagamore Hill, where he imagined leading the tours, imparting his vast knowledge. In adulthood, he elected to write his doctoral thesis on Roosevelt's 1912 Bull Moose presidential campaign and taught history courses at several universities. He developed an encyclopedic understanding of Roosevelt's life and times. When he applied for Hagedorn's job, he relayed "a bounty of ideas" to trustees and presented a vision for a modern, innovative commemoration campaign.[36]

Gable approached memorialization in a style much like Hagedorn's.

Legacy, the young enthusiast believed, derived from countless sources, and when commemoration opportunities arose, he hastened to act. Cultivating the myriad visual images of Roosevelt consumed a great deal of his time. A large bust of Roosevelt sculpted by William Ordway Partridge, once displayed at the New York Republican Club, went on sale in 1974, just as Gable's work as director began. He prepared a research paper detailing the artwork's value and located buyers. The same year, TRA trustees asked him to "pull together" an unwieldy show of artist Augustus Saint-Gaudens's work commissioned during TR's presidency. The exhibition opened in New York and toured the country. Gable frequently collaborated with educational institutions. Harvard's Roosevelt collection curator Wallace Finley Dailey organized a memorial exhibition with the TRA director, and Gable assisted Boston University's Mugar Library to organize a public exhibition of Rooseveltiana and research materials. Budding artists like painter Mort Künstler owed his success, in part, to the TRA and Gable, who allowed him to showcase art at Sagamore Hill.[37] Unsatisfied with the National Park Service's static welcome messages at sites of memory, Gable ordered the TRA's unique collection of celluloid film transferred to VHS, installed screening equipment at the birthplace and Sagamore Hill, and produced a welcome video to enhance the visitor experience. Enhanced visual depictions at sites of memory, he understood, provided an opportunity to shape the public perception.[38]

Gable also sought to influence the academic interpretation of Roosevelt. He conducted public lectures in New England and New York, encouraged scholarship in the archives at Sagamore Hill and the birthplace, and prompted the TRA to publish new editions of Roosevelt's books. Existing partnerships expanded, and new partnerships emerged. Harvard remodeled the first floor of Widener Library to include a TR alcove and also expanded space for manuscript material at Houghton Library. Long Island University (LIU) accepted a donation of more than three thousand books and rare manuscript materials from the birthplace, prompting the college to host regular academic symposia on TR. Gable called the LIU donation part of a "Library Program," or series of TRA contributions designed to stimulate scholarly analysis. Younger generations benefited from the program's donations to local public library and school collections, which were complemented by TRA outreach through annual essay prizes and speaking contests. Perhaps the most influential of Gable's academic initiatives was the *TRA Journal*. Less than six months after his appointment, he published a ten-page illustrated pamphlet and released new issues when trustees responded positively. The *TRA Journal* combined news of the association with meaningful historical analysis. The first issue tackled Roosevelt's intellectualism, his New York heritage, his economic record, and an account of the 1917 Illinois race riots, all of which situated Roosevelt in the New Social History.[39]

The journal provided a dual benefit to the TRA. As well as being a mechanism for scholarly reinterpretation, it incentivized membership. Part of Gable's remit as director was the growth of the association, and the journal offered a compelling perk to members. He also created a publicity kit with redesigned brochures and membership forms. The TRA began mass mailings, and at the birthplace and Sagamore Hill, Gable held promotional events that drew first-time visitors and inquisitive tourists to join the association. To elicit support outside New York, he endorsed regional chapters; consequently, a number of branches opened. Within three years of his appointment, the association's membership doubled.

When TRA president P. James Roosevelt had accepted leadership of the association in 1972, he remembered, there had been "some question as to whether [it] should be phased out." Leadership of the TRA changed multiple times, and without an executive director like Hagedorn, the workload of trustees became burdensome. "Fortunately," the president noted at the 1974 annual meeting—"and it is extraordinary how often fortune smiles on the Association," he joked—"we found a young man, Mr. John A. Gable . . . to assume the duties of Executive Director" and credited him with spawning a new era of memorial activity. The TRA's Executive Committee reported that for the first time in years the association "is going forward and succeeding on all fronts."[40]

Among Gable's many contributions to Roosevelt's legacy, one of his most important was building partnerships with local organizers to keep the association involved in memorialization projects. At Wilcox House in Buffalo, New York, where Theodore Roosevelt took the presidential oath of office after William McKinley's death, the Buffalo and Erie County Historical Society worked to preserve the property as a heritage center. It opened to tourists in 1971. The site was managed by the National Park Service and was sustained by the enthusiasm of local volunteers; when Gable joined the TRA, the association approved a subsidy for a publicity campaign to bring visitors to Buffalo. On the seventy-fifth anniversary of Roosevelt's 1901 inaugural, the association held commemorative ceremonies there, recognizing the importance of the site for Roosevelt's legacy. Awed by the anniversary and historical importance of the house, Gable told reporters in 1976 that in "a very real sense the 20th Century began in this house, in this room."[41]

In Roswell, Georgia, far from any previous memorial activity, Gable encouraged the TRA to support the acquisition and renovation of Bulloch Hall, the plantation home of Theodore Roosevelt's mother. The restoration was instigated by a local historical society that aimed to dedicate the house and grounds as a center for understanding antebellum history and heritage. Gable encouraged the Friends of Bulloch Hall to consider it an important site for twentieth-century history, as well, and prodded TRA trustees to finance a portion of the operating costs to keep the operation afloat.

In North Dakota, the TRA cheered Harold and Sheila Schafer's personal investment to preserve the town of Medora, a place Roosevelt patronized during his sojourn in the Badlands. The association awarded the Schafers the Distinguished Service Medal for preserving the memory of Roosevelt's cowboy image and western identity.[42] Medora, Bulloch Hall, and Wilcox House represented a second wave of memorial activity at new sites of memory. Although the association no longer had the financial power to instigate memorial projects on its own, by working with local enthusiasts, the TRA expanded the geographic reach of Roosevelt's legacy and demonstrated the resiliency of the association as a force for commemorative activity.

In addition to working with these sites, Gable led restoration projects for existing memorials. To enhance the neighborhood surrounding the birthplace in New York City, he organized the 20th Street Rehabilitation Project. Two local businessmen, working with Gable, arranged to have the sidewalks repaved, new trees planted, building facades cleaned, and street lighting repaired. As empty commercial space filled in response to the restoration and arriving businesses capitalized on the street's transformation, new partners sought to join the project. The restoration scheme culminated with a rededication of the birthplace, a ceremony held on Roosevelt's 119th birthday (October 27, 1977). At the event, the NPS revealed a variety of fresh exhibitions, including one on birthplace architect Theodate Pope Riddle. The TRA assisted with restoring draperies, wallpaper, carpets, and furniture, work that prompted visitors to say that the facelift had made the house's Rococo characteristics even more charming.[43]

Elsewhere, the association funded the restoration of Theodore Roosevelt Fountain at the Chicago Zoo, hired Thomas Pynchon (father of famed literary author) to make improvements at the Oyster Bay memorial park, and began converting Old Orchard House at Sagamore Hill into a museum. These activities, Gable concluded, marked "another chapter in the history of the joint efforts of the TRA." They also demonstrated the director's extensive leadership abilities.[44]

By the end of the 1970s, the number of TRA members had tripled since Gable's appointment. The association's income increased, and, most importantly, Gable energetically sheltered Roosevelt from being subject to any singular posthumous portrayal, fighting off false depictions and undesirable invocations. Through popular culture, revised scholarly publications, the association's journal, and work at sites of memory, the TRA kept Roosevelt accessible and many sided.

Intellectuals assisted the second revival. Irked by historical misrepresentations, scholars sought to correct them. Edmund Morris, a Kenyan-born writer who immigrated to the United States in 1968, began investigating TR's life after watching Richard Nixon deliver his farewell address. "I became curious," Morris said, about Nixon's melancholy references to Roosevelt, particularly his parting mention of Alice Lee. "What is he talking about?" Morris asked: "What does [losing one's wife] have to do with leaving the White House?"[45] Morris felt equally disgruntled with Milius's *The Wind and the Lion,* an "erroneously ridiculous" movie, "aimed at adolescents," that filled "their heads with phony history."[46] As a result, he started writing a screenplay about Roosevelt's youth and rise to high office. The project began in 1975, but foundered until Morris decided to develop it into a biography. Four years later, with an abundance of help from John Gable, the wider membership of the TRA, and surviving Roosevelt family members, he released *The Rise of Theodore Roosevelt,* a nearly 900-page treatment of TR's pre-presidential years.

The literary community quickly came to regard Morris's book as definitive. With access to the latest archival materials—including Harvard's expanding collection, the TRA library at Roosevelt's birthplace, and the restricted papers of family members—Morris crafted a vivid image of his subject. *The Rise of Theodore Roosevelt* conveyed a multifaceted profile, illustrating a man capable of being at once a New Yorker and a cowboy, a reformer and a conservative, a sickly asthmatic and an exuberant naturalist. The literati commended Morris for a synthetic reappraisal that combined early hagiography with Pringle's debunking. Columnist Nicholas von Hoffman called it the homecoming of "the Theodore Roosevelt of patriotic legend," who also displayed the priggish "boy scoutism" so criticized by past generations.[47]

Morris came closest of all biographers (until then, at least) to representing what Brander Matthews called the "polygonal" Roosevelt, a portrayal that academic reviewers either acclaimed or condemned. "Readers
seeking a monograph packed with information" discovered a depiction
of a complicated man, but, historian Gerald McFarland complains, "one
closes [the book] with the feeling that some central element . . . remains
unexplained." McFarland proclaims the biography "frustrating," a book
that fails "to fit the contrasting elements of Roosevelt's personality into a
portrait of the whole."[48] Generally, academics criticized Morris for taking
a simplistic approach to historical context; indeed, the context pales in
comparison to Morris's construction of a riveting personality. Historian
David Thelen thought that Morris's positioning of Roosevelt as a unique,
many-sided man of action in a timorous age was disingenuous because
the Gilded Age abounded with complex characters with equivalent en-
thusiasms. Elting Morison said Morris only just kept "all the diverse
attractive forces of the magnetic field in hand."[49] As an "old-fashioned,
event-centered" biography, *The Rise of Theodore Roosevelt* delivered a
familiar account of the period, academics judged, and Morris's frequent
use of histrionic language took certain license with the past. Yet, his
critics agreed that, as a nuanced portrait of a "great" man, Morris's book
succeeded.

Regardless of the reviews, the book's release came at an opportune moment. Unlike Pringle, who saw Roosevelt from a Depression-era vantage,
or the hagiographers who had celebrated Roosevelt in the wake of his
death, Morris approached him from an "ambivalent age," in which "there
are no untarnished heroes and few unredeemed villains."[50] *Newsweek*
sportswriter Pete Axthelm gave a similar assessment: "Once, we routinely
asked our kids who their heroes were. Today we fumble for answers when
they ask us if there are any heroes left. Vietnam and Watergate played
their part in all this, as we learned to beware our leaders and to scrutinize
them warts and all."[51] Apathy appeared to be the mood de rigueur. The
twenty-four-hour news media covering the ongoing hostage crisis in the
Middle East exhibited the impotence of US foreign policy and President
Carter's leadership. Public cynicism and antipathy for big projects like
Skylab quashed the kind of aspirational ventures that once had inspired
public interest. For Axthelm, "team-hopping" sports stars best expressed
his conviction that "modern heroism" was rare. Rather than keep an affiliation with a single club for life, sportsmen now gravitated to the highest
bidder. Literary phenom Tom Wolfe called the 1970s the "Me Decade."[52]

George Will, also writing for *Newsweek,* disagreed. The problem was public expectations and Axthelm's definition of heroics. Contemporary Americans expected "a rounded portrait of the person's ambiguities, doubts, and defects," Will pronounced. Yet this did "not mean that the person does not deserve to be thought of as heroic. It does mean that those people who want to have heroes must outgrow the desire for cartoon characters, or monumental bronze statues."[53] The media was bringing the public closer to political leaders in a way they had never experienced before. Warts-and-all assessments became standard and the heroic literature of hagiography less so. Seizing the moment, Morris produced his image of TR as an authentic "warrior," one who would become president with a string of entertaining adventures to his name. Set in this context, *The Rise of Theodore Roosevelt* allowed readers to engage with an individual's heroics while understanding the complex personality (defects and all) that propelled him to fame. His portrait made TR a figure relatable to modern audiences. Americans could empathize with TR on a personal basis and simultaneously celebrate his life as a politician worth emulating. Morris nourished the nation's appetite for leadership with his book, which earned the Pulitzer Prize.

Many-sided portraits had existed long before Morris's debut, but the trend to depict Roosevelt this way increased in the late twentieth century. In 1977, David McCullough won acclaim for his multifaceted depiction of TR in *The Path between the Seas,* a narrative account of the Panama Canal's acquisition and construction. It was released at a timely moment, as Congress debated the ratification of the Panama treaties designed to gradually rescind the lease on the Canal Zone, and McCullough's book became an instant best-seller. Roosevelt signed the original Panama treaty in 1903, and it so obviously favored American interests in the region that the lease became a source of constant diplomatic friction and, at times, violent protests. President Carter pledged to restore Panamanian ownership, as well as good relations. His opponents demanded that the United States retain Roosevelt's agreement. McCullough's book set the historical scene and related TR's political decisions in 1903 to modern circumstances. "I think of what Theodore Roosevelt might say if he were alive today," McCullough wrote in an open letter to Carter: "Change was inevitable, he knew, and necessary . . . the Panama Canal is a vast, heroic expression of that age-old desire to bridge the divide and bring people closer together."[54] Roosevelt, McCullough asserted, would have supported Carter's efforts to foster closer relations by amending the treaties. Carter, in turn, used

McCullough's book as evidence of his respect for the original intent of
Roosevelt's treaty.

The Path between the Seas won the 1978 National Book Award. Mc-
Cullough said that the book impelled him to investigate Roosevelt further, and in 1981 he penned Mornings on Horseback, a biography that
covered roughly the same period as The Rise of Theodore Roosevelt. "I was
interested in knowing what was involved in the metamorphosis of this
most conspicuous animate wonder," McCullough explained, contending
that Morris had left gaps that a more experienced writer—namely, himself—could expand on.[55] His examination of Roosevelt demonstrated the
diverse approaches available to biography writers at the time, method-
ologies that stemmed from academic scholarship in social history and
cultural studies. New subfields emerged in biographical narratives, like
psychological analysis, the study of the agency of women and minorities,
and the consideration of how factors like family, class, religion, and
geography influence personality. These subfields encouraged authors
to investigate how a "fixed core within an individual persona" developed
from multiple sources, giving fresh life to old stories. Erudite biographers
presented their subjects as complex personalities not easily reduced to a
single dimension or affected by one "primal event."[56] Pringle's emphasis
on Roosevelt's adolescent spirit as his dominant characteristic was out
of place in the 1970s, and even Edward Wagenknecht's description of a
man fixed in seven worlds seemed too limited.

McCullough was able to write an account that detailed the same period
of time covered in Morris's seminal biography but was not just a vague
echo of that book. Mornings on Horseback focused on Roosevelt's family,
recounting how his childhood experiences molded him into the man he
would become. Reform-minded Theodore Roosevelt Sr. tutored young TR
on politics and ethics, becoming his model for progressivism and moral
righteousness. Mittie, TR's southern mother, bestowed upon her son an
appetite for adventure and heroics, one source of his frontier spirit and
conservationist impulse. TR's competitive siblings, along with the diverse
environs of Manhattan, taught him to communicate with constituencies
and build a personal network. McCullough produced a fresh appraisal
of TR's early years, noted Kirkus Reviews: "Nothing that has appeared
before, including Edmund Morris' recent The Rise of Theodore Roosevelt,
diminishes its interest or freshness or emotional force."[57] Mornings on
Horseback won the National Book Award, McCullough's second in four
years, and demonstrated that more could sometimes be said on a seem-

ingly closed subject. Or, as Gore Vidal said in his review, "there can never be too much of a good thing."[58]

The second Roosevelt revival steadily grew, catalyzed by early 1980s political developments. The year McCullough published *Mornings on Horseback,* another cowboy politician rode into the White House, promising to "renew the American spirit and sense of purpose." Ronald Reagan swept Jimmy Carter out of office with assurances that the United States would "keep our rendezvous with destiny."[59] His pledge to facilitate national rejuvenation came in the wake of economic degradation and the collapse of American preeminence abroad. In the 1970s, oil cartels held the American economy hostage, just as Iranian terrorists held American citizens hostage. Social discontent with inequality and stagflation corresponded with rising crime rates and increased drug use. The Soviet Union invaded Afghanistan. The worst nuclear meltdown in American history occurred. Anti-Americanism surged. Historian William Chafe called the 1970s "a decade of transition—marked by confusion, frustration, and an overwhelming feeling that America had lost its direction."[60] Reagan blamed presidents Johnson, Nixon, Ford, and Carter for lackluster leadership that corroded the political system, and he promised a return to prosperity, to be achieved by adhering to old-fashioned values of individual liberty and American democracy. He promised to be the hero those presidents were not, a leader capable of returning the United States to "greatness" in an "unbelieving world."[61]

Reagan's conservative call harkened many to the political fold but simultaneously repulsed others. The American left attacked Reagan as a saber-rattling cold warrior willing to experiment with the economy and abandon hard-fought advances in social justice. Despite winning 51 percent of the popular vote and forty-four states, Reagan entered the White House with the lowest recorded approval rating of any incoming president, demonstrating that his brand of politics galvanized strong opinions. Yet, Americans could agree on one thing: Ronald Reagan "established a new national tone, shaping otherwise inchoate stirrings" that occurred independent of politics. At his inauguration Reagan urged Americans to believe in heroes.[62] "Those who say that we're in a time when there are not heroes . . . just don't know where to look," he lectured. "You meet heroes across a counter, and they're on both sides of that counter. There are entrepreneurs with faith in themselves and faith in an idea who create new jobs, new wealth and opportunity. They're individuals and families whose taxes support the government and whose voluntary gifts support church,

charity, culture, art, and education. Their patriotism is quiet, but deep."[63]
Vidal attributed the rise of Reagan's conservatism to the same cultural
swing that revived TR's heroic image in biographies like McCullough's
and Morris's. Likewise FDR biographer Geoffrey Ward suggested that it
was "not surprising that the Republican Roosevelt has been getting good
press lately . . . [he] now seems to suit the national mood."[64]

Although TR's historical reputation for progressive reform ran counter
to Reagan's supply-side economics and planned deregulation of big business, his status as the foremost champion of Americanism suited Reagan's
mantra of audacious patriotism.[65] In the early 1980s, Roosevelt became
a regular symbol for what historian Fred Halliday called the "second
Cold War."[66] Abandoning détente, the Reagan administration pursued
an aggressive anti-Soviet foreign policy, defined by increased military
spending, missile deployments, war games in Europe, and the Strategic
Defense Initiative or missile shield. Not since the Cuban Missile Crisis in
1962 had nuclear conflict seemed so possible. During the early Cold War,
Theodore Roosevelt had symbolized Americanism and national resolve,
and now he came to symbolize that civic ideology in the 1980s.

Two episodes underscored the primacy of Roosevelt's Americanism
during Reagan's presidency. First, the TRA invited Reagan to chair the
association's anniversary committee to celebrate Roosevelt's 125th birthday. The president obliged and opened commemorations with a luncheon at the White House, during which he judged Roosevelt a "fearless
American hero" and beckoned the country to "redouble our efforts to
confront adversity and promote the virtues and ideals of Americanism."[67]
Thematically, the centennial in 1957–58 bore striking resemblance to the
quasquicentennial in 1982–83. Set against the Cold War, both anniversaries remembered Roosevelt's patriotism, while paying less attention to
memorial themes like conservation.[68]

The second episode that emphasized Roosevelt's Americanism during
the Reagan administration was the US Navy's construction and commission of a fourth Nimitz-class nuclear-powered aircraft carrier, the USS
Theodore Roosevelt (CVN-71). On October 27, 1984 (Roosevelt's 126th
birthday), the one-thousand-foot vessel, nicknamed "The Big Stick," was
launched, and two years later it went into active service. The carrier was
a weaponized expression of Reagan's dedication to Americanism through
military spending and power. Jimmy Carter had aborted the Navy's plans
to build the ship because it did not fit the foreign policy of détente. As
policy changed, and détente fell out of favor, the funding for new vessels

became a military priority, one intimately connected to patriotism and national virility. Secretary of Defense Caspar Weinberger said at the commissioning, "We are gathered . . . to celebrate the legacy of a man whose very name is synonymous with vigor and strength . . . Theodore Roosevelt believed passionately that the surest road to peace for America was a strong America."[69] When the bottle of champagne christened the ship, a flood of red, white, and blue balloons drifted from the deck as F-14s soared overhead and a sixty-eight-foot-long American flag unfurled to cannon fire.

Although Reagan relied on co-opting Roosevelt's legacy far less than Nixon had, when he did he tended to emphasize the qualities of good citizenship and the civic ideology of Americanism. He brought Soviet military figures to the USS *Theodore Roosevelt* to show off American strength in a manner not unlike TR's demonstration of power when ordering the Great White Fleet to sea. In an attempt to inspire "pride in America," Reagan told the nation to observe its natural wonders and the environment, echoing Roosevelt conservationist legacy through the patriotic theme. As a pro-life advocate, Reagan championed adoption and referred to Roosevelt's vision for American domesticity. In his frequent calls for individuality, he directly quoted TR: "The foundation stone of national life is and ever must be the individual character of the individual citizen."[70] The president's rhetoric abetted his goal of casting the 1980s as a distinctly different decade from the 1970s, while still summoning elements of the past to demonstrate continuity.

Reagan once joked that he had known Theodore Roosevelt, a gag about his age. Born in 1911, Reagan was seven when Roosevelt died and had no actual memories of him. People of a similar age did remember Roosevelt, yet as the twentieth century neared its end, fewer of that generation existed. Many of TR's friends and colleagues had passed away in the 1950s and 1960s, and his surviving children Ethel, Archie, and Alice died in 1977, 1979, and 1980, respectively. Their absence eroded the remaining living link to the past, but conscious that such a day would come, Roosevelt's family had empowered the TRA to maintain their father's legacy. More than anyone, Ethel Roosevelt Derby protected her father's reputation by resisting the divestiture of TRA assets and enticing youth to join, believing they would lead the association with fresh ideas. Enlisting John Gable to be the association's executive director, she believed, did more than anything to help bridge the gap between the generations.

In 1981 the association founded a long-range planning committee to "exert an influence on contemporary society," a strategy that resulted in innovative new partnerships. For example, restaurateur Ed Engoron and Pepsico proposed building a casual-dining business called TR's. The TRA furnished Engoron with the blueprints of Sagamore Hill to help him replicate the exterior of the house for his restaurants. They also provided details about Roosevelt's favorite foods to help Engoron develop a menu inspired by Victorian-era cooking. TR's opened in Sunnyvale, California, and Wichita, Kansas, and until 1984, Pepsico considered extending the brand nationwide. The planning committee also strengthened existing partnerships. For instance, the TRA helped Harvard acquire private collections of papers to add to their already vast archive.[71]

The first generation of Roosevelt's descendants left their father's legacy in a strong position. Under John Gable's direction, the TRA flourished. Within three years of his appointment, membership in the association doubled, and it doubled again three years later. He revitalized the balance sheet, and the association no longer worried about its future. The context of the second Cold War buttressed their efforts, extended Roosevelt's legacy as a patriotic Republican, and fortified the heroic portrait. Amid changing contexts, Roosevelt's ghost, like the mythical phoenix, endured another cycle of decline and revival in public memory.

[CHAPTER EIGHT]

AN ICON EVERLASTING

The second revival of commemorative activity in the 1980s demonstrated the resiliency of Theodore Roosevelt's ghost and the potency of the legacy themes. Although his posthumous reputation had vacillated from deity to demagogue since his death, by the end of the twentieth century interpretations of Roosevelt calmed considerably. As the centennial of Roosevelt's death neared, public memory continued to portray TR as an American icon with unique and meaningful legacies, but it was less common to see extreme portraits. In addition, a new generation of memorializers cast him as an ambiguous personality, without concrete meaning.

Nowhere was this transition more apparent than in national politics. Every president since Warren G. Harding had invoked TR, and while Republicans did so more frequently than Democrats, Roosevelt tended to remain outside partisan disputes, representing apolitical values that evolved with the sociocultural context. As such, he became an icon for all politicians. George H. W. Bush frequently told audiences that "Teddy Roosevelt is among my favorite Presidents," summoning his predecessor's legacy to encourage environmental policies, a cause that Bush called a top priority and "not a conservative or liberal question." Bush also celebrated Roosevelt's "elite" Knickerbocker upbringing, comparing his own privileged background with TR's in an effort to shrug off the "wimp factor" that dogged his 1992 reelection campaign.[1] Bush's chair of the joint chiefs of staff Colin Powell hung a painting in his office of buffalo soldiers who joined TR's Rough Riders at San Juan Heights to remind him of the men who "made their sacrifices so that I could sit where I sit today."[2] House Speaker Newt Gingrich, an avid reader of Roosevelt biographies, regularly mentioned the former president; New York governor George Pataki called TR his political hero; and, in 2000, Arizona senator John McCain co-opted Roosevelt in his campaign for the Republican presidential nomination. McCain cast himself as a Republican maverick who challenged his party in much the same way Roosevelt did, and he referred to TR as his philosophical idol.[3] Republicans maintained a close allegiance to TR, treasuring him as one of the party's historic figures.

Democrats also drew from this well. House Majority Leader Dick Gephardt ran for president in 1988 as a "progressive pragmatist," using Bull Moose iconography on his campaign buttons and placards. In the 1992 vice-presidential campaign, Dan Quayle called Senator Al Gore's environmental policies "hysterical," and in response, to demonstrate the moderate and bipartisan nature of his policies, Gore cited TR's advocacy of ecological protection. The New Democrats, a centrist faction of the party led by Arkansas governor Bill Clinton, professed their admiration for Roosevelt in a manner unparalleled in preceding decades. FDR, Truman, Kennedy, and Johnson had paid respect to TR's progressivism and Americanism, but Clinton revered his "incrementalism," habitually invoking TR and making him a political icon for domestic policies like healthcare, welfare reform, and the management of natural resources. When Clinton moved into the White House, he also acclaimed Roosevelt's use of arbitration and revered his foreign policy as an antecedent to the contemporary ideology of liberal internationalism.[4] Clinton even brought to the Oval Office the bust of Roosevelt that had adorned his desk in the Little Rock governor's mansion, and he broke with White House decorative tradition by declining to swap TR's portrait in the Roosevelt Room with that of FDR, a typical practice of incoming Democrats. And in one of his last acts in office, Clinton awarded a posthumous Medal of Honor to TR for his heroic charge up San Juan Heights over a century earlier.[5] More than any Democrat since FDR, Clinton looked to TR as his political lodestar.

The frequent mention of Roosevelt in late twentieth-century politics influenced other vehicles of public memory, such as televised documentaries. In 1986, the ABC network broadcast *The Indomitable Teddy Roosevelt,* a patriotic film that celebrated TR's legacy of Americanism at the apex of the second Cold War. Actor Bob Boyd played Roosevelt in the film's flag-waving reenactments set against the chords of John Philip Sousa compositions like "Onward Christian Soldiers." The jingoistic score was accompanied by narrator George C. Scott, an actor best known for playing Gen. George S. Patton in *Patton* (1970) or Gen. Buck Turgidson in *Dr. Strangelove* (1964). Scott's voice conveyed a patriotic vibe because audiences associated him with the characters he played in these other films, and his narration of the documentary underscored its intrinsic anti-communist message. *The Indomitable Teddy Roosevelt* reflected the era's conservative political climate, making obvious parallels to Reagan's injunction that "government is not the solution to our problem, government is the problem." Quoting Roosevelt, Scott intoned that "government ought not to conduct the business of this country." The documentary's director, Harrison Engle, whitewashed Roosevelt's progressive legacy, omitting key moments that conflicted with the conservative image.[6] Absent from the film is the 1912 presidential election, Roosevelt's intervention on behalf of labor unions, and the federal regulation of industry, omissions that produce a thoroughly Republican image of TR consistent with the policies of the Reagan administration.

A decade later, at the peak of President Clinton's popularity, PBS released *TR: The Story of Theodore Roosevelt* (1996), a traditional documentary showing interviewed experts rather than reenactments. *TR* countered the conservative image that had developed in the 1980s, swinging to the opposite political pole by emphasizing Roosevelt's progressive policies as the historical precedent of contemporary liberalism. Director David Grubin detailed the domestic achievements of the Square Deal, the arbitration of labor issues, and the platform of Roosevelt's 1912 Progressive Party campaign. And by emphasizing the breakup of Northern Securities, the Pure Food and Drug Act, and Roosevelt's environmental-preservation initiatives, Grubin cast TR as the direct inspiration for FDR and depicted the Square Deal as "quite literally a forerunner to the New Deal, resting as it does upon a logic of government expansion and an activist state."[7] By focusing only on TR's progressive image, the documentary whitewashed the past, erasing Roosevelt's conservative legacy by skirting his advocacy of Americanism, imperialism, and Victorian social codes. Historian Matthew Frye Jacobson castigated Grubin for producing a movie that suffered from selective amnesia.

After Clinton's second term as president came to an end and another Bush occupied the White House, the politically polarized image of TR retreated. In 2002, the History Channel released *Teddy Roosevelt: An American Lion,* a synthesis documentary that combined elements of *The Indomitable Teddy Roosevelt* and *TR. Teddy Roosevelt* balanced the political perspective by giving both parties an opportunity to stake a claim to Roosevelt's legacy. Commentators included Clinton, Pataki, and Republican mastermind Karl Rove. Each invoked TR as an icon of the twentieth century, a figure beyond partisanship, and a symbol of the nation's political traditions. Employing a diverse group of historians from the left and right, the film produced a portrait of an ambiguous political leader, available to multiple interpretations and useful for all. Because it ran for over three hours, double the length of the previous documentaries, it covered a broader range of episodes in Roosevelt's life and thus avoided manipulating his image by omitting or overemphasizing particular historical events. Indeed, the broad coverage and differentiated analysis demonstrated what the political rhetoric of the age had already established: Theodore Roosevelt no longer belonged to any political party exclusively. By the end of the century, he was a figure as familiar as Uncle Sam, as inoffensive as apple pie, and as emblematic as the bald eagle.

Twenty-first-century presidents have summoned TR as readily as their predecessors. George W. Bush read the second volume of Edmund Morris's biography *Theodore Rex* and regarded Roosevelt as a "warrior for peace who faced the world without illusions."[8] At a White House reception in honor of TR's 150th birthday, Bush said that he meditated in front of a portrait of Roosevelt when contemplating "the character and courage that is necessary for any President" and predicted his successors would do the same.[9] Bush's successor Barack Obama, who regularly called on a team of historians to inform him how the achievements of past presidential administrations could advance his political agenda, invited comparison with Roosevelt in 2011. Speaking in Osawatomie, Kansas, where John Brown attempted to defend his men against pro-slavery forces in 1856 and where TR delivered his "New Nationalism" speech in 1910, Obama used the town's history to set the stage for his 2012 reelection campaign and his defense of the Affordable Care Act.[10] "I'm here in Kansas to reaffirm my deep conviction that we're greater together than we are on our own," Obama said, paraphrasing TR's Square Deal speech. He told the crowd and televised audiences that his progressive policies, like Roosevelt's, did not stem from "Democratic values or Republican values," but "American values."[11]

One exception to Roosevelt's seemingly universal political popularity came from the loosely organized libertarian Tea Party movement. Although closely associated with the GOP, the fringe Tea Party disowned Roosevelt as a "RINO" or Republican in name only. Acerbic FOX News commentator Glenn Beck denounced Roosevelt as a communist and beseeched the party to censure TR's type of Republican progressivism as entirely un-American.[12] The disdain for TR from right-wing conservatives should come as little surprise. Roosevelt had defined the divisions within the Republican Party since 1912, when his campaign against William Howard

Taft split the party's conservatives and progressives. After one hundred years, that division still persisted. In 2012, thirteen candidates battled for the Republican presidential nomination. Moderates like Newt Gingrich and eventual nominee Mitt Romney claimed TR as an inspirational forefather, but libertarians and far-right conservatives like Michele Bachmann, Rick Santorum, and Ron Paul repudiated Roosevelt's political ideology as too closely aligned with social democracy. The persistence of the Tea Party movement in American politics, and its members' contempt of Roosevelt, jeopardized the image that the TRA and moderate politicians of both major parties had invented.[13]

John Gable recognized the power of political co-option long before the Tea Party mobilized, and he acknowledged that relating the present with the past often takes comparison too far. The TRA director equally appreciated that the association could bring no force to bear on politicians intent on invoking Roosevelt. So, to combat renegade portrayals, Gable encouraged the production of a sustainable cultural image, grounded in the primary memorial themes the TRA had helped to construct decades earlier. To accomplish this, Gable supported academics who wrote innovative historical accounts, as well as the producers of visual representations and various strategic partners, including those who managed memorial sites. "Both critics and admirers of TR for many years debated the mythic Teddy," the TRA director observed, choosing to describe TR in a binary manner, either as a heroic overachiever or adolescent juggernaut. "Too often professional historians, no less glib journalists have helped perpetuate the debate," chiefly because "the mythic Teddy is easier to attack or defend, to dismiss or ignore, and to understand or categorize than the real Roosevelt."[14] The challenge, Gable told trustees, was to end the cycle of hagiography and revisionism—to stabilize but not standardize the image.

By the mid-1980s, the TRA redoubled its support for scholars willing to push against the boundaries of the mythical Roosevelt. "The field is active," historian Richard Collin observed in 1995; "the pot is simmering, and the possibility exists that a new paradigm might emerge."[15] In his own work, Collin attempted to understand Roosevelt's foreign-policy machinations through international cultural trends, disputing the New Left view that identified imperialism or hegemony as the defining characteristic of his statecraft. Collin rejects the discourse of American domination as an oversimplification of international relations. "It is impossible to dismiss Caribbean love of baseball as a Yankee plot," he argues, and explains the acquisition of the Panama Canal Zone as a collaborative venture. Collin designated Roosevelt's foreign policy as "symbiotic," one of compromise and partnership, and he invited the academy to publish a "no-fault historiography" in which scholars refrained from demonizing or uncritically celebrating Roosevelt.

Despite Collin's call, polemic histories continued to attract publishers, as did intensely political portrayals. But the tendency for uncompromising scholarly portraits about the mythic Teddy ebbed as the century closed, and the many-sided Roosevelt became even more polygonal. Lewis Gould's 1991 biography shows how Roosevelt redefined the White House, despite his being "a persistent source of fascination for admirers and detractors alike."[16] John Milton Cooper's comparative biography of Roosevelt and Wilson, aptly titled *The Warrior and the Priest,* presents two chief executives who shared common ground and similar tactics, yet established competing agendas and legacies. To the last page, Cooper's portrait obscures which personality type—the warrior or the priest—best fits Roosevelt. In many regards, he is both.[17] Late twentieth-century intellectual histories also maintained a balanced view. Reviewers credited Thomas Dyer with handling Roosevelt's racial ideology "dispassionately and judiciously," Gail Bederman's account of gender tropes identifies Roosevelt as a proponent of "civilized manliness" and "primitive masculinity," and William Tilchin's examination of TR's transatlantic statecraft approaches the past with "even-handedness . . . catching his bombastic tendencies" as well as his diplomatic tact.[18]

These books set Roosevelt in his Gilded Age and Progressive Era context without relying heavily on the late twentieth-century milieu, and in 2002 Kathleen Dalton's single-volume biography achieved a portrait of Roosevelt so immersed in his times that it stood out as comprehensive among many works in a distended field. John Gable called the 1990s a golden age of Roosevelt historiography and encouraged the TRA to actively support the academic renaissance through conferences and publications that explored Roosevelt from a range of angles, including the largely ignored topic of legacy.[19]

The torrent of scholarship continued into the twenty-first century. As the business community gave greater consideration to the idea of "executive leadership," Roosevelt became an example of an effective manager. James Strock describes Roosevelt's leadership style as indicative of what corporate America was aiming for in the modern workplace.[20] The increasing importance of ecology prompted Douglas Brinkley to revive the conservationist legacy, branding Roosevelt a "Wilderness Warrior" and exemplar for contemporary generations.[21] Building on McCullough's work, scholars revisited the Roosevelt family. Indeed, endless possibilities existed for contextual analysis, which led authors to examine Roosevelt's cooperation with the press, his meaning in urban and rural settings, his relationship with notable luminaries of his time, and his place in world history.[22] The centennials of the Treaty of Portsmouth (2004), the Great White Fleet (2009), and World War I (2014–18) stimulated reconsideration of old narratives and produced new collections of essays intended to capture the latest "turns" in the historical field.[23]

When, in 2010, Edmund Morris completed the third and final volume of his biography of Roosevelt, a book that chronicled the last ten years of TR's life, historian Jackson Lears pronounced the field of Roosevelt studies "as bloated as the man himself" and attributed the outpouring of scholarship to the political invocation that began during Bill Clinton's first term in office.[24] The TRA also deserved credit. The association had fostered academic conversations with their journal through reviews and in lectures and symposia held during annual meetings.

Besides adding to the written record, the association worked with new partners to ensure that Roosevelt transcended partisan interpretation at sites of memory. Franklin Delano Roosevelt's one-hundredth birthday was in 1982, and among the myriad legacy projects that year, the Four Freedoms Foundation conferred an eponymous award on individuals who exemplified the spirit of FDR's famous speech. The award recognized those who promoted freedom of speech, freedom of worship, freedom from want, and freedom from fear. Since then, awards have gone to Americans in odd-numbered years at the FDR Presidential Library in Hyde Park. Non-Americans have received the award in even-numbered years at Middelburg Abbey, the provincial capital of Zeeland in the Netherlands, and where the Roosevelt family traced its ancestral roots. Because 1982 also marked the bicentennial of official relations between the Netherlands and the United States, the foundation's debut ceremony honored five Dutch nationals for their service to global diplomacy, economics, and ecumenism. Princess Juliana, who had abdicated the Dutch throne in 1980 and who had often visited FDR during her World War II exile in Canada, accepted a special award for her role promoting democracy in Europe throughout the Cold War.[25]

The inaugural ceremony proved so inspirational that the Four Freedoms Foundation built an enduring relationship with the city of Mid-

delburg. Historian Arthur Schlesinger Jr. recommended the foundation
construct a permanent memorial by endowing an archival repository
in the city. It would, he believed, extend FDR's legacy internationally.
Cognizant that the Dutch award winners in 1982 had all enjoyed close
connections to the United States in their formative years, Schlesinger
suggested an educational program to assist future generations in realizing access to American academic resources without leaving the continent. He imagined an archive of modern American history that would
fortify a kindred spirit and, in 1984, the Four Freedoms Foundation and
the FDR Institute (a memorial community like the TRA) resolved to build
an archive in Middelburg. The provincial government of Zeeland hired
historian Cornelis van Minnen to lead an investigation into the archive's
feasibility.[26]

Until 1985, the study center idea only commemorated Franklin and
Eleanor Roosevelt. The Four Freedoms Foundation and the Roosevelt
Institute promoted the legacy of the Hyde Park clan, but as van Min-
nen discovered, the Oyster Bay faction required addressing, too. After
Schlesinger announced the plan to build a study center, US ambassador to
the Netherlands L. Paul Bremer, who was dispatched by President Reagan
to spearhead the deployment of American cruise missiles to northern
Europe, invited van Minnen to The Hague to discuss the proposed facility.
Bremer urged the director to include TR in the center's scheme. Doing so,
the ambassador said, would give the center a distinctly bipartisan appeal
and garner support from President Reagan. It would keep the Roosevelt
Study Center (RSC) above the political fray. Furthermore, TR's addition
increased the academic value of the center by extending the chronological
scope of the archive.

Van Minnen reported the ambassador's pitch to the president of the
Roosevelt Institute, William vanden Heuvel, who immediately expressed
an interest in the idea and reached out to Gable at the TRA. After a positive conversation between the directors, the idea of an all-Roosevelt
center took hold. Gable urged the trustees of the TRA to engage with
the project and personally visited the Netherlands in November 1985.
Funded by the United States Information Agency, he addressed students
and dignitaries at several Dutch universities, conducted advisory sessions
with van Minnen on how to incorporate the Republican Roosevelt at the
site, and, with the backing of the Oyster Bay family, pledged over $12,000
from the TRA to supply the center with a copy of TR's papers held at the
Library of Congress. The association also donated books that had been

held at the birthplace, an enormous portrait of TR, and a unique Dutch
Bible inscribed with the signature of Nicholas Roosevelt, the patriarch of
the Oyster Bay and Hyde Park families. Gable encouraged historians like
William Henry Harbaugh, biographers like Edmund Morris, and library
curators like Wallace Finley Dailey to provide assistance to van Minnen
as he developed the repository.[27]

When the study center opened on September 19, 1986, it exceeded
Bremer's aspirations. The first academic symposium featured Schlesinger,
who spoke about FDR's statecraft. Morris followed with a discussion on
TR's diplomatic legacy. Likewise, the center's first publications included
lectures by Gable and FDR scholar Leon Gordenker. An impressive collection of presidential papers and personal manuscripts from 1901 to
1962 complemented the extensive library. Set in the medieval Middelburg
Abbey, the center imparted to Europeans unmatched access to American
historical resources and tapped into the growth of American Studies programs across the continent. The RSC hosted academic events and funded
research trips. Most importantly, the center united the legacies of FDR
and TR, and, fortuitously, prompted the reconciliation of the Oyster Bay
and Hyde Park families.

The public displays of bitterness between the clans that dominated
family relations during FDR's life had receded by the 1950s. Nevertheless,
an underlying antipathy continued to simmer, and over the years the
families made few attempts to mend relations. It wasn't until the inaugural
of the RSC, held on the soil of their mutual ancestors, that the Roosevelt
cousins buried the hatchet. Over the course of an hour-long bus ride from
Amsterdam to Middelburg, the Roosevelt cousins began to appreciate
how much they had in common and concluded that the feud had endured
for long enough.[28]

"The Peace Treaty of Middelburg," as the family called it, inspired a
series of reunions.[29] The first, in the last weekend in June 1989, brought
descendants of Theodore and Franklin to Hyde Park, where they lunched
at Eleanor's Val-Kill estate, dined formally on the lawn outside Springwood house where FDR was born, and collectively prayed for the family's
patriarchs at St. James Episcopal Church. Initially, family members
reported, the atmosphere was stilted. FDR's grandson John Roosevelt
Boettiger said the events "were friendly," but cloaked "an underlying
sense of some tension, a tendency to gather in one's own more familiar
circles of family." That apprehension defined the festivities until two elder
Roosevelts broke the ice. FDR's son Elliott paid tribute to TR, and retired

TRA president P. James Roosevelt reciprocated with warm affection for FDR. Then the men recounted dueling war stories: "they got into a mock competition as to which one of them had the more serious wound. Elliott decided the only conclusive proof was in demonstration, and he proceeded to unbutton his jacket and pull up his shirt and undershirt. His startled cousin could not but do likewise. Both came out winners, for they brought the house down." Boettiger described the moment as "a historical turning point for the Roosevelts." The awkwardness evaporated over drinks and storytelling, and a non–family member who witnessed the spectacle called it "remarkable"; relatives, who for so long had remained unknown to each other, finally embraced without the acrimony of bygone years.[30]

Successive reunions proved equally positive. In 1991 the Roosevelts met in Oyster Bay, swapping the Springwood lawn for Sagamore's grassy pitch. A somber occasion, the second gathering followed the death of FDR's son James, a circumstance that contributed to a large turnout of more than one hundred Roosevelts. In 1997 the family met in Medora, North Dakota, where TR once ranched. The Hyde Park and Oyster Bay branches organized a lively vacation in the Badlands to mark the fiftieth anniversary of Theodore Roosevelt National Park. In 1999 the families gathered at Campobello Island in New Brunswick, Canada, where FDR vacationed, and celebrated the thirty-fifth anniversary of the preservation of his cottage there.[31] These gatherings, including the 1986 "peace" of Middelburg, ended the interfamily resentment and reinforced the nonpartisan image at sites of memory associated with the Roosevelt family. TR took on new meaning at sites once reserved for FDR's legacy, and vice versa.

The TRA capitalized on the era of good feelings by prioritizing the restoration of another site: TR's retreat at Pine Knot, Virginia, fifteen miles from Charlottesville. Adjacent to the northern Blue Ridge Mountains, Pine Knot sat deep in the Shenandoah watershed, cut off from electricity and without indoor plumbing. The *Washington Post* described the cabin's interior as "primitive," with a stark downstairs consisting of "a single large room." The two rooms upstairs were equally sparse, with "a meager complement of furniture—merely a double bed of cheap style, an oak bureau that cost a few dollars, a washstand of the plainest kind, probably worth a dollar and a half, and a goods box cheaply tricked out as a table."[32] When the Roosevelts took possession, they added a porch and fireplaces, but Edith and Theodore purposely avoided any other modern conveniences.

The cabin served as a place of respite, an escape from the commotion of Washington and the presidency. Its remoteness was the most important feature. Set amid a dense pine forest that inspired Edith to name the place Pine Knot, the family reconnected with nature; enjoyed hiking, hunting, and bird watching; and "discouraged reporters and visitors." Only "a few hearty souls" traversed the forest to disturb the president's vacation.[33]

In total, Theodore Roosevelt visited Pine Knot on eight occasions during his presidency. After his retirement to Sagamore Hill, he found no reason to return, and the value of Pine Knot as an outdoor retreat decreased. As a site of memory, however, it had tremendous value. As environmental issues acquired greater importance in the late twentieth century, Pine Knot grew in significance. It symbolized Roosevelt's conservation legacy and the simple rugged lifestyle he revered. On leave in the dense Virginia forest, TR had recorded the last sighting of a passenger pigeon in 1908 and had tested his survival skills by living off the land. Even after he stopped visiting, the cabin's surrounding seventy-five acres stood as an emblem of his ecological mindfulness.

That legacy inspired his great-grandson Theodore Roosevelt IV to purchase Pine Knot in 1990 and donate it to the TRA two years later. In 1993, the TRA enlisted historian William Henry Harbaugh to investigate a plan for conservation, and TR's grandson Theodore Roosevelt III issued a challenge grant to develop the property. He would match every dollar raised by the TRA for the repair and restoration, up to $100,000. By 1996 the association had successfully raised nearly $90,000 and installed structural supports for the cabin. With the help of retired Colonial Williamsburg managing director Roger Leclere, the site was completely renovated by 1998. However, the absence of a road connecting the cabin to the main highway left Pine Knot as isolated as it had been during Roosevelt's presidency.[34] Select tours visited the cabin in seasonable months, with guides pointing to where TR drew water, chopped firewood, and read on the porch. The cabin still attracts few tourists, a reality that adds to the site's authenticity and the theme of land conservation and ecological mindfulness. At Pine Knot, "I can see Roosevelt," Leclere told his wife; "I can just see him. I can feel him."[35]

The TRA spent considerable time and money conceptualizing and constructing memorials over the years. Pine Knot was the last major site the association restored. However, trustees continued to collaborate with partners to enhance existing memorial sites and invested in fresh exhibitions of Rooseveltiana. For example, the TRA worked with the National

Park Service to construct a boardwalk entrance to Theodore Roosevelt Island in 1998. The walkway ensured greater pedestrian access. In 2005 the town of Oyster Bay worked with the association to install an equestrian statue of Roosevelt along the roadside in memory of the village's veterans. In 2012 the American Museum of Natural History completed a long-overdue renovation of Theodore Roosevelt Memorial Hall, a TRA collaborative venture that depicted all the primary legacy themes. And in 2015 the NPS finished a four-year rehabilitation of Sagamore Hill in close cooperation with the TRA.

The TRA's decision to focus on existing sites of memory stemmed, at least in part, from the death of John Gable on February 18, 2005. Like his predecessor Hermann Hagedorn, whose passion drove enthusiasts to engage with Roosevelt's legacy, Gable attracted a new generation of disciples he called "Ted Heads." Friends recounted Gable's tireless activism, which often took the form of late-night phone calls imploring them to participate in commemorative events and membership drives. He single-handedly reinvigorated the association from obscurity and financial doom, and his death left a gaping vacancy. Gable's accumulated knowledge was unmatched, as was his energy. At the time of his death, the TRA counted over two thousand members, by far the most of any presidential fan club. The annual newsletter he founded had been transformed into a quarterly peer-reviewed journal. The increase in academic consciousness of Roosevelt and the relationships Gable had nurtured with partners like the National Park Service stood as testament to the director's influence. Remembering TR was Gable's life's work, and although he was buried in Massachusetts, the TRA placed a small cenotaph in Youngs Cemetery, near the twenty-six steps that lead to Roosevelt's grave. When younger, Gable had bounded up the steps, reciting the name of each president preceding his favorite. The stone memorial, placed halfway up that stairway, commemorates his unique devotion. Pilgrims can pay homage to both men in one visit.[36]

Gable's successors would lack his exhaustive expertise and zeal. Unfortunately, they also failed to match his integrity and plunged the association into scandal and turmoil. Edward Renehan, a historian, publisher, and Gable's interim replacement, stole from the birthplace library letters written by George Washington, Abraham Lincoln, and TR. The TRA did not know that the priceless documents, stored next to the executive director's office, were missing until Renehan attempted to sell the manuscripts for nearly $100,000 to a New York auction house. When endeavoring to identify the letters' provenance, the auction house contacted the association and sparked an NPS inquiry. Renehan was arrested, indicted, and sentenced to eighteen months in federal prison for theft and trafficking of stolen goods.[37]

In the midst of the fiasco, the TRA appointed James H. Bruns, a fundraising expert who claimed to have collected over $100 million as director of the national Postal Museum and the Smithsonian Institute's development program. He came to the TRA with decades of fundraising experience and fresh ideas about a Roosevelt museum in Oyster Bay, but his plans met with opposition from the town's residents. Locals had opposed the renovation of Sagamore Hill in the 1950s, and in the late 2000s they again feared the library and museum would turn their relatively quiet locale into a tourist trap. The TRA eventually recognized that the project was unworkable when the stream of donations never materialized. They pulled the plug on Bruns's plan and parted ways with him.[38] In sum, the two directors severely damaged the association's brand and drained its financial resources.

The enthusiasm of the TRA's earlier executive directors had directly correlated to the association's commemorative achievements, yet the high-profile debacles of Renehan and Bruns did not discourage memorialization. Others picked up where the association left off. In the last decades of the twentieth century, the cultural image of Roosevelt flourished independently, and memorializers naturally adopted the legacy themes established in preceding decades. Stage productions thrived. TheaterWorks USA, a troupe of actors and producers dedicated to entertaining young adults, sponsored a play about TR, "the adventuring young man." It toured New York for six weeks in 1984 and reached over fifty thousand public-school students. Jerome Alden's *Bully: An Adventure with Theodore Roosevelt,* a tale of heroic politics popularized in the 1970s, returned to the stage for an eighteen-state tour in 1998–99, with musical actor and host of TV's *Hollywood Squares* John Davidson as TR. Smaller, critically acclaimed productions ran in major American cities and depicted Roosevelt's conservationist record, oratorical talent, and progressive reputation.[39]

Literary portrayals multiplied as well. John Gable recognized the power of fiction as "a major phenomenon in terms of the history of Theodore Roosevelt's image," primarily because it complemented well-established legacy themes and extended them to a new generation.[40] The western cowboy image was depicted in Douglas C. Jones's *Remember*

Santiago (1988), a tale of the Rough Riders' campaign in Cuba, and Brian Garfield's *Manifest Destiny* (1989), a story about the North Dakota Badlands, both of which characterized Roosevelt as his generation's foremost frontiersman. Gore Vidal's *Empire* (1987), a book about the United States in the aftermath of the War of 1898, hinged on the negative cowboy image and fastened the discourse of imperialism to Roosevelt's frontier experience. Regardless of an author's judgment on the cowboy's virtues or deficiencies, the image of Roosevelt appeared as a symbol of the American West. "Given our current involvement with various Central American governments," a 1988 review of Jones's *Remember Santiago* noted, "there couldn't be a better time to turn the searchlight on America's turn-of-the-century adventure in imperial warfare."[41] Of course, previous remembrances had done the same thing at moments when US foreign policy had come under similar scrutiny.

Roosevelt's cowboy image proved so alluring that John Milius, the director of *The Wind and the Lion,* returned to it in his 1997 television miniseries *The Rough Riders.*[42] The ludicrous and bombastic portrayal of Roosevelt in Milius's 1975 story about Moroccan bandit Mulai er Raisuli was comparable to the uber-patriotic and reckless cowboy presented in *The Rough Riders.* The miniseries omits events, fabricates elements of Roosevelt's "crowded hour," and characterizes Roosevelt as an infantile jokester, annoying conversationalist, and sex-crazed husband. Milius's intention was to show Roosevelt's development from an immature patrician to a responsible leader, and in the final scenes, as the colonel ascends San Juan Hill, he is no longer a comedic figure. He sits on the deck of the Spanish blockhouse and sobs in front of his men. In the background waves a gleaming American flag; TR mutters, "It will never be the same," a reference to his life and the nation. Despite his intentions, Milius reduced one of Roosevelt's proudest moments to a charade, and *The Rough Riders* yields a portrait much like those in the 1980s novels that cast TR as the key actor of American empire. *New York Times* critic Caryn James noted that *The Rough Riders* is another "cookie-cutter" type of war film meant to entertain; it "does not improve on [Roosevelt's] cartoonish image or anyone's memory of a flat junior high school history lesson."[43]

The TRA, however, judged the miniseries a success because it drew on well-established memorial themes. Gable considered *The Rough Riders* "close to the mark" and "credible," if not entirely accurate, and he quoted from television critic Marvin Kitman's positive review to explain why the TRA recommended the miniseries. "When was the last time a

TV movie was accurate? Which one ever gave two sides of a story[?]" Kitman asked. "The fact that a crassly commercial cable TV network is doing something about an American hero is enough for me."[44] The TRA accepted such representations in popular culture. As long as the image was positive and adhered to one or more of the memorial themes, the association tended to approve. For instance, there were a number of crime novels that oversimplified Roosevelt's legacy as a progressive reformer by dramatizing aspects of his two-year term as president of New York City's police commissioner's board; these produced a mythical TR grounded in fact but shrouded in fiction. The most notable such mystery stories included Lawrence Alexander's *The Big Stick* (1986) and *Speak Softly* (1987), Caleb Carr's *The Alienist* (1994) and *The Angel of Darkness* (1997), and Victoria Thompson's *Murder in Little Italy* (2006) and *Murder in Chinatown* (2007). In each, Roosevelt starred as the city's crusading detective.[45]

Carr's *The Alienist* exemplifies this type of crime writing. His book reached number four on the *New York Times* best-seller list. It depicts Roosevelt as the dynamic force in New York City's police department and the foremost reformer of his time. Carr's Roosevelt inspires other urban agitators, like investigative journalist Lincoln Steffens and social-justice advocate Jacob Riis. In the novel, TR dominates the narrative, solves the mystery, bags the criminal, and restores order. Such books blur the lines of history and literature by blending information from primary sources with fictional tales—the facts are molded to suit the narrative. *New York Times* reviewer Matthew Purdy called *The Alienist* "history spun through a Cuisinart, garnished with a fictional killer."[46] But the TRA celebrated it as a positive portrayal that brought substantial attention to TR's progressive legacy.

Moderating their once-strict stance against inaccuracy in cultural depictions, the TRA encouraged nongovernmental organizations to join the commemorative chorus and invoke the core memorial themes. The rise of the religious right and social conservatism provoked public-service advertisements from Christian groups. The National Bible Association, a society dedicated to spiritual education, ran ads in the 1990s promoting Christianity by co-opting Roosevelt as a role model. "Before he had any ambition to be leader of our country," the Bible Association announced, "he had something else. His faith."[47] Groups like theirs led popular debates on family values and held nationwide religious events that reached millions of Americans, linking Roosevelt's religiosity with their cause.

TR's conservation legacy persisted along similar lines. The Nature Conservancy lobbied for heritage trails in New York, one of which celebrated Roosevelt's contribution to preserving the state's natural resources. The conservative think tank Republicans for Environmental Protection (now known as ConservAmerica) bestows an annual Theodore Roosevelt leadership award on individuals and institutions that promote sustainable energy and environmental awareness. And the Sierra Club celebrated the centenary of Roosevelt's camping trip with John Muir at Yosemite National Park in 2003.[48]

While the TRA habitually summoned the six primary legacy themes and encouraged others to do the same, portrayals incongruous with the themes also thrived. By the 1990s Roosevelt's image began to appear in a way that bestowed no appreciable meaning at all on his life. In 1993, IBM advertised its new PS/1 home computer with a pixilated image of Roosevelt, boasting that "it comes with a Teddy." The promotion referred to the computer's $800 software package that included Compton's Interactive Encyclopedia, a database of 33,000 articles, one of which was about Theodore Roosevelt. IBM drew TR from the catalog because his iconic expression provided a friendly, recognizable, and trustworthy image, but the computer company made no attempt to associate the former president's legacy with their product.[49] It was a marketing ploy, and other advertisements have done the same thing. After the financial crisis of 2008, Citigroup ran an advertising campaign to win back the trust of its customers. As the centenary of the Panama Canal's opening approached, the bank presented Roosevelt as the project's political champion and Citigroup as the financial sponsor. "When [Roosevelt] needed help with his monumental and perilous undertaking, Citi was there to support him."[50] Some commercial invocations do not ever mention Roosevelt by name. In 2015 when Cadillac ran a television, Internet, and print advertising campaign that pressed motorists to "dare greatly" and quoted from TR's "man in the arena" speech, the ads featured neither Roosevelt nor a Cadillac.[51]

According to *Advertising Age,* a leading magazine for marketing professionals, advances in technology—namely, the Internet—transformed American consumerism in the 1990s and, consequently, transformed advertising as well. Purchases could happen at midnight, and small retailers could reach global buyers, fragmenting consumer audiences and provoking businesses to adopt new approaches to attract customers. "Integrated marketing," or the consistent use of a brand over several media channels to reinforce a message, became necessary in publicity campaigns.[52] The almost incidental portrayal of Roosevelt by IBM, Citigroup, and Cadillac be-comes understandable in this context. Roosevelt was a brand ambassador but ultimately secondary to the product and the brand itself. In the brief moment a consumer gives attention to an advertisement, the image must generate immediate interest, and Roosevelt served that purpose. Outside the initial hook, his legacy mattered little. IBM concentrated on promot-ing their computer's specifications, Citigroup demonstrated its staying power as a financial institution, and Cadillac used its customary crest to sell luxury cars as a lifestyle choice. Roosevelt merely aided these ends.

Cyberspace, a term which already seems an outdated description of an Internet realm that changes rapidly, had wider consequences for Roose-velt's ghost. It democratized the projection of his image and allowed it to reach global audiences. Anyone able to access a chat room could discuss Roosevelt's legacy, and those with a basic knowledge of Web coding or the financial means to hire a website designer became memorializers. The first cyber-enthusiasts who posted content online did so as hobbyists, and these websites frequently misquoted TR, occasionally misappropriated his achievements, and, at times, concocted questionable historical analyses. Unlike professional publications, the amateur Roosevelt fan who circu-lated online information did so without copyeditors and fact-checkers. Accuracy suffered, and misrepresentations multiplied.

Entrepreneurs also embraced the early Internet and posted incorrect or absurd portrayals of TR. For example, in 1998, Keith McGough pur-chased the domain name www.theodoreroosevelt.com to advertise his Roosevelt reenactment business. According to the website, Theodore Roosevelt spent the late 1990s and early 2000s working as a leadership coach to help small and medium enterprises toil through "change" and boost company morale. McGough, dressed in costume moustache and pince-nez, made surprise visits as Roosevelt to corporate offices, sales meetings, or industry conventions. His appearance produced a spectacle that "secures immediate attention, generates excitement and soon creates an emotional bond with people." The aim of impersonation, McGough re-lated on his website, is to "inspire and move people from ideas to action," yet he did so by employing a superficial interpretation of Roosevelt's life and legacy.[53]

TRA trustees recognized the potential detriment the Internet could have on their "brand." After all, the idea of integrated marketing was hardly new to an association that had helped conceive and propagate six memorial themes across a range of media outlets. John Gable fought the proliferation of erroneous digital content by commissioning a revised Roosevelt *Cyclopedia,* released as a CD-ROM.[54] The disc provided an accurate digital record of Roosevelt quotes, cross-referenced with keywords, as well as several voice recordings. Gable also created a discussion forum on Yahoo! Groups, which served as a venue for public questions and conversations. Gable's efforts returned a modicum of control to the TRA, whose trustees provided precise answers to the most curious questions and used the discussion board to connect with enthusiasts, inviting them to attend annual meetings, join the association, read the *TRA Journal,* and combat falsehoods in the public domain, most notably by editing Roosevelt's Wikipedia pages.[55]

The technology revolution continued after Gable's death. The association digitized the Roosevelt Almanac, a database of dates and Roosevelt publications originally compiled in 1957 by the centennial commission. Rogina Louisa Jeffries, a TRA executive committee member, launched the first association website, which was redesigned in 2014. The association created complementary Facebook and Twitter accounts to extend the virtual conversation Gable had begun.[56] The TRA also brokered new relationships with digital partners. For example, trustees supported the Theodore Roosevelt Center, an academic institute located at Dickinson State University in North Dakota. The center organized in 2011 to promote TR scholarship through the digitization of "all Roosevelt-related items" and by July 2015 it had catalogued nearly fifty thousand items online, including Roosevelt's correspondence from more than a dozen manuscript archives in locations around the United States.[57]

Despite the abundance of authentic online content, absurd Internet depictions endure. For example, online magazine Nerve ranked TR the "sexiest" American president, "so sexy that if he slept with your girlfriend, you'd be flattered."[58] On YouTube, viewers can watch comedian Mallory Ortberg perform her scathing rant "Dirt Bag Teddy Roosevelt," in which she portrays a TR who abuses William Howard Taft in a variety of unexpected and ahistorical ways, including bench-pressing America's largest president.[59] One inventive blogger has imagined the outcome of a mass knife fight among forty-three presidents at their prime; TR nearly emerges victorious, succumbing only to the physical fury of "Old Hickory," Andrew Jackson.[60] And the viral sensation of the 2014 FIFA World Cup was a TR impersonator, affectionately nicknamed Teddy Goalsevelt, who became the de facto mascot of Team USA and ran for FIFA president in 2015.[61] These images, of course, bear little or no resemblance to the representations of past generations; they depict a Roosevelt neither grounded in fact nor interpreted through the legacy themes.

Perhaps the greatest example of the deterioration of the memorial themes is evident in the exceedingly successful film trilogy *Night at the Museum*.[62] The first film, released in 2006, takes place in the American Museum of Natural History, where the exhibits come to life at night and run amok. Ben Stiller, playing night watchman Larry Daley, attempts to keep order by reasoning with historical characters, prehistoric creatures, and formerly inanimate objects—a rational approach to an irrational situation that provides the film's comedy. Producers marketed *Night at the Museum* to adolescent audiences as a film that makes history "cool," if inaccurate. The statue of Theodore Roosevelt, played by comedian Robin Williams, comes to life as a patriarchal figure who helps Stiller's character maintain control over the out-of-control exhibits. Trace references to Roosevelt's conservation record and his preacher-of-righteousness image appear. As Roosevelt, Williams tells Larry, "Self-reliance is the key to a vigorous life. A man must look inward for his own answers." The film takes liberties with the past, of course, a fact the writers Robert Ben Garant and Thomas Lennon admit. The Roosevelt statue that comes to life inside the museum does not exist; Larry mistakenly refers to Roosevelt as the fourth president; and Williams as Roosevelt startlingly lusts after Sacagawea in the Lewis and Clark diorama. The film's popularity led to two sequels, released in 2009 and 2014, that take place in similar venues (the Smithsonian Institute and the British Museum, respectively). Neither, however, deviates from the first movie's characterization of Roosevelt. In fact, TR eventually wins the heart of Sacagawea in the last movie. But for all the silliness and absurdity, Robin Williams makes clear that he does not represent the real Roosevelt. Near the end of the first film, he admits that he is made of wax, a confession that distinguishes *Night at the Museum* from other false portrayals. It compels viewers to consider the fabrication inherent in fictional tales. Whether audiences choose to believe is entirely up to them.[63]

Night at the Museum proves that Roosevelt's posthumous image retains certain meanings yet can also exist as an arbitrary icon without clear definition.[64] The abundant portrayals of Roosevelt in the twenty-first century at once seem to threaten and fortify the coherent legacy themes constructed by various communities of commemoration. Indeed, John Gable said that cultural depictions have the ability to "magnify or distort the truth" and believed that fictional portrayals would "deepen or trivialize our understanding" of Roosevelt.[65] In actuality, these depictions do both things. They intensify the public perception of long-articulated memorial themes and concurrently implore us to question whether Roosevelt's legacy has any real, tangible meaning. Whatever his contemporary significance or future meaning, Roosevelt's ghost persists in the public imagination as an American icon, even if it is not always obvious why.

CONCLUSION

T he Washington Nationals clinched the National League East Division on October 2, 2012, and reached the playoffs for the first time in the baseball club's history. The following day, the last of the regular season, the Nationals played the Philadelphia Phillies and, after three and a half innings, the customary presidents' race began. A home-game tradition, the race pits caricatured mascots of George Washington, Thomas Jefferson, Abraham Lincoln, and Theodore Roosevelt in a sprint across the outfield toward the home-team dugout. Over seven years the presidents ran more than five hundred times, but "Teddy" never won. The team insists they do not fix the race.

In some measure, this is probably true. Teddy regularly trips, stumbles, falls, and inadvertently loses. As often, however, he is attacked. Fellow presidents, other mascots, fans dressed in costume, and even Nationals' players have tackled, struck, or clipped Teddy before he could cross the finish line. Cheating also plagues his record. The frustration of recurring losses has led Teddy to desperate stunts. On one occasion he zip-lined from the stadium's upper deck to outrun his competition; other times he drove a golf cart, rickshaw, scooter, or a Segway across the finish line, which led to disqualification.

Nationals' fans anticipate the fourth-inning entertainment, and in 2012 the vigilant activism of Scott Ableman, an obsessive fan who created a "Let Teddy Win" movement, brought the race to national attention. ESPN covered the races, and the network's features producer Michael Johns commissioned a short documentary about the longest losing streak in baseball history. Narrated by Ken Burns, the eminent documentary film director, the ESPN short starred Republican presidential nominee and self-professed TR admirer Senator John McCain. A spoof, the film whipped up public interest. McCain, tongue-in-cheek, called the race a distressing conspiracy that necessitated congressional hearings. The senator's outspokenness prompted White House spokesman Jay Carney to announce that President Obama concurred. The press joined the satirical protest. The *Wall Street Journal* and *Washington Post* described Teddy's streak as "shadowy," and Ableman compared it to famous Washington scandals like Teapot Dome and Watergate.[1]

On the final day of the 2012 season, after the Phillies left the field, the crowd chanted "Teddy" and waited for the mascots to emerge from the center-field bullpen. Expectations of a historic victory ran high, although fans had suffered disappointment so many times before. From the outset, Teddy's victory seemed improbable. Last out of the gate and in the back of the pack, Teddy charged ahead undaunted, wearing golden shoes gifted to him by Olympian Usain Bolt. George, Abe, and Tom struck out ahead and opened a gap. As the race reached its midpoint, however, an interloper jumped from the visitor's bullpen. The opposing team's mascot attacked the leading trio, and Teddy streaked away to his first "legitimate" win.[2]

The crowd erupted, jubilant that the streak had ended, and even the Nationals players seemed invigorated. When the real game resumed, third baseman Ryan Zimmerman hit a lead-off home run to right field to tie the game. Outfielder Michael Morse hit a looping double to deep right, and first baseman Tyler Moore doubled to bring Morse home, putting the home team ahead. In the sixth and eighth innings, the Nationals added three insurance runs, ending the year on a high and giving the team every hope for a successful postseason campaign.

Sports headlines the following day barely mentioned the team's victory over the Phillies. Instead, Teddy dominated the news. The *Washington Post* prepared a detailed infographic on the race's history; Twitter "exploded," according to the *Wall Street Journal*; and John McCain, relieved, said that Teddy's victory broke a "massive left-wing conspiracy."[3] Jordan Zimmermann, the Nationals' ace right-hand pitcher, said he was glad. Now "we can stop talking about Teddy. People get more excited for a mascot race than a game."[4] But fans delighted in the silliness. Teddy won all three of the 2012 playoff races, whereas the Nationals lost three of five games to the St. Louis Cardinals, ingloriously dropping out of the postseason in the first series.

Popular culture references to Roosevelt like the president's race may seem inconsequential or transient, but they have persistently shaped our sense of the past. They are expressions of our collective opinions, and they help define the past for future generations. As consumers of culture, we endorse these representations and encourage manufacturers to produce similar outputs. The presidents' race and the good-humored "Let Teddy Win" campaign is one of the most significant episodes in the history of Roosevelt's legacy, even if it might appear trivial. More than a Major League Baseball publicity stunt, it illustrates the legacy themes so often commemorated. The campaign recalled TR's Americanism, progressivism, conservation record, and cowboy persona, and used mass media, political figures, and popular culture to do so. Equally, the presidents' race produced an ambiguous representation that reflects the twenty-first-century tendency to portray Roosevelt in the abstract. The presidents' race itself makes no reference to memorial themes. Teddy is a vehicle for entertainment, and while audiences recognize his historical importance as a former president, the race offers no further insight on Roosevelt's legacy. In sum, the presidents' race displays the remarkable degree to which commemorative themes and methods remain consistent and how the relevance of Theodore Roosevelt endures. It affirms that Roosevelt's ghost still haunts our consciousness.

Roosevelt's legacy continues to pervade popular culture as we approach the centennial of his death. Movie producers have seized on his image for heroic epics, romantic dramas, and comedies. The Roosevelt image has appeared in over one hundred movies and hundreds of television shows since 1919. With a wide reach and an ability to present a visual likeness of the past, motion pictures and television generate a powerful source of public memory. Perhaps the best example of the enduring impact of film can be gleaned from the minor controversy surrounding Ken Burns's fourteen-hour documentary *The Roosevelts: An Intimate History* (2014), a film that traces the history of the Oyster Bay and Hyde Park clans over the course of the twentieth century. Aired on PBS, the documentary attracted 9 million viewers, despite running in direct competition with the Super Bowl. Burns and scriptwriter Geoffrey Ward earned critical acclaim for recounting well-worn legacy themes and casting TR, FDR, and Eleanor as political operatives cut from the same cloth. Although the film provided no new observations about the family, and actually omitted conspicuous moments of interest in spite of its length, it is the first popular documentary about TR since 2002 and thus represents a key source of memory for a new generation. That fact explains why the Theodore Roosevelt Association took umbrage at what it called a "defamatory misrepresentation" of Roosevelt's character, highlighting the inaccuracies in the film. William Tilchin, editor of the *Theodore Roosevelt Association Journal,* criticized Burns's choice of scholars who appeared in the documentary, the loose generalities in their commentary, and the hyperbolic depiction of Roosevelt's personality. The film, Tilchin said, will make a "contribution to the historical education" of audiences all over the world and therefore deserved to be criticized for any misrepresentations.[5]

Likewise, political invocations of Roosevelt have demonstrated the power of rhetorical co-option. Presidential homage in particular affected Roosevelt's legacy, be it Harding's phony imitation, FDR's aloof admiration, or Nixon's twisted worship. Today's generation of presidential candidates also tend to gaze to the past for inspiration and frequently seize upon Theodore Roosevelt as a poignant icon, and because the presidential election cycle now starts earlier than it used to, TR has enjoyed substantial exposure in 2016. (In fact, the first references to him in the 2016 election cycle appeared in 2014, two years after Obama won a second term.) Before the Super Tuesday primaries in February 2016, the *New Yorker* published Barry Blitt's sketch of a "consternated" TR, among other past presidents, watching Donald Trump's populist campaign gain momentum. And the Democratic nominee Hillary Clinton, after watching the Burns documentary, spoke about the similarities between 2016 and Roosevelt's Progressive era. Clinton praised "how he dealt with the imbalances that were in the economy and in society" and said she hoped to do the same.[6] No matter how tenuous a candidate's connection to TR, politicians of all parties and persuasions gravitate to him.

So do celebrities. Controversial pop-music sensation Miley Cyrus tattooed part of Roosevelt's "man in the arena" speech on her inner forearm; her boyfriend Liam Hemsworth tattooed a corresponding part of the speech on his arm months later.[7] Talk-show host Conan O'Brien, considered a "lifelong American president buff," admits he is awed by TR's accomplishments.[8] *The Daily Show* host Jon Stewart declared Roosevelt "a larger-than-life figure" and revealed his appreciation in several interviews with prominent biographers, historians, and documentarians.[9] Nick Offerman, the star of NBC's *Parks and Recreation,* regularly quotes from Roosevelt in interviews and dedicated a chapter of his 2015 book *Gumption* to TR, proclaiming a "healthy sense of rippling admiration."[10] These invocations make Roosevelt's appeal seem as boundless as ever.

Often these representations in popular culture occur independently, without the succor of memorial associations. Periodically, TRA trustees wonder if Roosevelt still needs a fan club. The RMA and WRMA internalized these questions before they merged in the 1950s, and after they formed the TRA, the new association considered on multiple occasions whether it should cease operating and leave Roosevelt's legacy to the masses. Indeed, the relevance of the association continues to worry trustees. "For a long time we were about buildings, saving memory and supporting historians," TRA president Tweed Roosevelt told me, but in the current context, "we need a cause."[11] Historically, the TRA has always been searching for a cause, and when it accomplishes one goal, another memorial scheme arises. As the centennial of Roosevelt's death and the foundation of the memorial campaign approaches (2019), the TRA is reflecting on how best to sustain its activities in an ever-changing world.

Perhaps the answer lies in its already remarkable history. The association has found innovative ways of celebrating Roosevelt's birthday and the anniversary of his death for more than a century. On several occasions, the TRA enlisted powerful partners to stoke public interest. The White House, for example, hosted receptions for TR's 100th, 125th, and 150th birthdays. The 1958 fireworks display on Theodore Roosevelt Island, while controversial, sparked attention, and the association has a long record of commissioning historians, biographers, fiction writers, filmmakers, and business people to depict Roosevelt. It has protested perceived inaccuracies, making the association a gatekeeper to TR's living memory. It bestows the Distinguished Service Medal on individuals with outstanding service to the nation, the Theodore Roosevelt Police Service Award on law enforcement officers in honor of exceptional service, and the Theodore Roosevelt Public Speaking Award on high school students with unique oratory skills. It also facilitates the Teddy Bears for Kids program, which delivers stuffed bears to hospitalized children. The work of the association has never been singular, and as a posthumous public relations team for Roosevelt, the TRA has utilized various methods of memorialization. It has evolved with advances in technology and marketing. Its longest-serving and most influential executive directors Hermann Hagedorn and John Allen Gable understood that the "cause" can remain the same (to perpetuate Roosevelt's memory and ideals), while the tactics must necessarily change to suit new generations.

Among the TRA's most valuable partners in this pursuit is the Roosevelt family. Edith Roosevelt contributed to her husband's memory by making political endorsements and by restricting access to his papers at the Library of Congress. Ted emulated his father and challenged Franklin as heir to the family's political dynasty, and Franklin did as much to extend his cousin's legacy through invocation and ideological adoption. Alice Roosevelt Longworth, TR's eldest daughter and a mainstay of beltway politics from 1905 to 1975, attributed her father's legacy to several leading political personalities. Son Archie produced histrionic and counterfactual publications that presumed to know his father's political position on issues of the day, and daughter Ethel worked to keep sites of memory open and the TRA functional. Because TR's immediate family had the most personal knowledge of the man, they played a vital role in his memorialization. They condoned the building of controversial monuments, swayed reluctant legislators, and became titular representatives of TR.

Successive generations of Roosevelts have also contributed to TR's public memory. Grandchildren Kermit Roosevelt Jr. and Archie Roosevelt Jr. led CIA operations that transformed American foreign relations in the Cold War. Historians and journalists compared their service to TR's in terms of global leadership. Cousin P. James Roosevelt directly affected memorial activities as president of the TRA, as does great-grandson Tweed Roosevelt, who acts in that capacity today. Namesakes Theodore Roosevelt III, IV, and V support environmental preservation projects, furthering the family's conservation legacy. Elizabeth Roosevelt, the granddaughter of W. Emlen Roosevelt, distant cousin of TR and an Oyster Bay native, contributes family artifacts to exhibitions commemorating the family's contribution to American history. As grandson Archie Roosevelt Jr. explained, TR's life gave his children and their children a legacy of public service to which to aspire.

Academics have contributed much to Roosevelt's legacy, even if their relationship to him comes from distant contemplation and painstaking research. What strikes me most about the historiographical record on Roosevelt—a shifting paradigm of consensus and hostility that has moved from deification, to demonization, to synthesis and the construction of multilayered portraits—is that it often has preceded popular perceptions. That is, scholarly accounts of Roosevelt led public memory, a fact that signifies just how insightful and pioneering the work of historians and biographers can be. Before writing *Arsenic and Old Lace,* Joseph Kesselring read Henry Pringle's biography. Historian Barbara Tuchman inspired John Milius to write and direct *The Wind and the Lion.* And speculation exists that Martin Scorsese is considering making a biopic adapted from Edmund Morris's *The Rise of Theodore Roosevelt,* starring Leonardo di Caprio as the Rough Rider.

Roosevelt's ghost appears in all quarters of American life. This book only presents the most important sightings as examples of the interpretations in public memory. The "mythical" Roosevelt, as John Allen Gable put it, surpassed the "real" Roosevelt almost instantly after he died in 1919. That myth, or ghost, has evolved continuously, a derivative of the personal ambitions of those who conjured TR. By considering Roosevelt from their various perspectives, we can clearly see how memorializers created legacy themes and, consequently, transformed TR's popular image again and again. The only apparent constant is Roosevelt's popularity. He remains as germane today as a century ago. Our impressions of him may change, but until the time when his memory is entirely insignificant—a scenario that seems utterly unlikely—Roosevelt's ghost will continue to inspire debate and interest. Like the Cheshire cat, the image of Roosevelt's pince-nez, mustache, and toothy smile flourishes in our imaginations, and even when they fade, the image leaves a lasting impression.

NOTES

ABBREVIATIONS USED IN NOTES

CRR	Corinne Roosevelt Robinson
EKR	Edith Kermit Roosevelt
FDR	Franklin Delano Roosevelt
FDRL	Franklin Delano Roosevelt Presidential Library
FRM	Frank Ross McCoy
GB	Gutzon Borglum
HH	Hermann Hagedorn
JRG	James R. Garfield
LOC	Library of Congress
RMA	Roosevelt Memorial Association
TR	Theodore Roosevelt
TRA	Theodore Roosevelt Association
TRA-EXEC	Theodore Roosevelt Association Executive Committee
TRB	Theodore Roosevelt Birthplace, National Park Service, Manhattan Sites
TRCC	Theodore Roosevelt Centennial Commission
TRC-H	Theodore Roosevelt Collection, Houghton Library, Harvard University
TRC-W	Theodore Roosevelt Collection, Widener Library, Harvard University
TRJ	Theodore Roosevelt Jr.
WRMA	Woman's Roosevelt Memorial Association
WRT	William Roscoe Thayer

INTRODUCTION

1. *F.D.R.: His Personal Letters,* ed. Elliott Roosevelt, vol. 2 (New York: Kraus Reprint, 1970), 477.

2. "Supreme Court Adjourns as Mark of Respect," *New York Times,* January 7, 1919; "Washington Mourns," *Belleville News Democrat,* January 6, 1919; Hamlin Garland, *My Friendly Contemporaries: A Literary Log* (New York: Macmillan, 1932), 214.

3. Olivia Cutting to Anna Roosevelt Cowles, January 7, 1919, MS Am 1834.1: 242, Anna Roosevelt Cowles Papers, TRC-H; Nationwide Tributes Paid to America's Great Citizen," *New York Tribune,* January 7, 1919; James Roosevelt Roosevelt to Anna Roosevelt Cowles, January 7, 1919, MS Am 1834.1: 242, Anna Roosevelt Cowles Papers, TRC-H; "Whole Country is Mourning," *El Paso Herald,* January 7, 1919.

4. JRG diary, January 8, 1919, box 12, JRG Papers, LOC; Ethel Roosevelt Derby to Richard "Dick" Derby, January 8, 1919, 87M-100, Ethel Roosevelt Derby Papers, TRC-H.

5. "Assorted Clippings," box 36, James Earle and Laura Fraser Papers, Syracuse University; Frank Owen Payne, "Theodore Roosevelt in Sculpture," *Art and Archaeology* 8, no. 2 (April 1919): 113.

6. John Dewey, "Theodore Roosevelt," *Dial,* February 8, 1919.

7. Lawrence Abbott, *Impressions of Theodore Roosevelt* (Garden City, NY: Doubleday, Page, 1919), 313–4; Ethel Roosevelt Derby to Richard "Dick" Derby, January 8, 1919, 87M-100, Ethel Roosevelt Derby Papers, TRC-H; JRG diary, January 8, 1919, box 12, JRG Papers, LOC; Garland, *My Friendly Contemporaries,* 216.

8. Ferdinand Iglehart, *Theodore Roosevelt: The Man as I Knew Him* (New York: The Christian Herald, 1919), 349.

9. Geoffrey Cubitt, *History and Memory* (Manchester: Manchester University Press, 2007), 79.

10. Michael Kammen, *Mystic Chords of Memory: The Transformation of Tradition in American Culture* (New York: Knopf, 1991), 9.

11. Brander Matthews, "Theodore Roosevelt as a Man of Letters," *Munsey's Magazine,* March 1919, 252.

12. Henry Pringle, *Theodore Roosevelt: A Biography* (New York: Harcourt Brace, 1956), vii; Edmund Morris, "Theodore Roosevelt, the Polygon," in *Theodore Roosevelt: Many-Sided American,* ed. Natalie A. Naylor, Douglas Brinkley, and John A. Gable (Interlaken, NY: Heart of the Lakes, 1992), 25; David McCullough, *Mornings on Horseback: The Story of an Extraordinary Family, a Vanished Way of Life, and the Unique Child Who Became Theodore Roosevelt* (New York: Simon and Schuster, 1981), 11.

13. Henry Fairfield Osborn, "Theodore Roosevelt, Naturalist," *Natural History* 19, no. 1 (January 1919): 7.

14. Charles Towne, ed., *Roosevelt as the Poets Saw Him* (New York: Charles Scribner's Sons, 1923), 204.

15. J. N. "Ding" Darling, "America's Darling," 1955 interview, Marvo Entertainment Group, http://marvoentertainmentgroup.com/music/archival_audio2.html.

16. Minutes of the RMA, Permanent Committee on Memorials, March 24, 1919, TRA-EXEC Minutes, TRC-H.

17. This book takes an interdisciplinary approach inspired by a growing body of critical scholarship on memory and presidential history. Among the best work in this growing field are Merrill D. Peterson, *Lincoln in American Memory* (New York: Oxford University Press, 1994); David Greenberg, *Nixon's Shadow: The History of an Image* (New York: W. W. Norton, 2003); Phillip G. Payne, *Dead Last: The Public Memory of Warren G. Harding's Scandalous Legacy* (Athens: Ohio University Press, 2009); Edward G. Lengel, *Inventing George Washington: America's Founder, in Myth and Memory* (New York: Harper, 2011); Jason R. Jividen, *Claiming Lincoln: Progressivism, Equality, and the Battle for Lincoln's Legacy in Presidential Rhetoric* (DeKalb: Northern Illinois University Press, 2011); Joan Waugh, *U. S. Grant: Ameri-*

can Hero, American Myth (Chapel Hill: University of North Carolina Press, 2013); Mark White, *Kennedy: A Cultural History of an American Icon* (London: Bloomsbury, 2013); Paul H. Santa Cruz, *Making JFK Matter: Popular Memory and the Thirty-Fifth President* (Denton: University of North Texas Press, 2015). For examples of this trend in transnational presidential studies, see Richard Carwardine and Jay Sexton, eds., *The Global Lincoln* (New York: Oxford University Press, 2011). A diverse range of posthumous biographies and legacy studies also inform this research, including Anne C. Loveland, *Emblem of Liberty: The Image of Lafayette in the American Mind* (Baton Rouge: Louisiana State University Press, 1971); David W. Blight, *Race and Reunion: The Civil War in American Memory* (Cambridge, MA: Belknap Press of Harvard University Press, 2001); Merrill D. Peterson, *John Brown: The Legend Revisited* (Charlottesville: University of Virginia Press, 2002); Robert Cook, *Troubled Commemoration: The American Civil War Centennial, 1961–1965* (Baton Rouge: Louisiana State University Press, 2007); Amber Roessner, *Inventing Baseball Heroes: Ty Cobb, Christy Mathewson, and the Sporting Press in America* (Baton Rouge: Louisiana State University Press, 2014).

18. Ed Engoron, interview with author, March 30, 2015.

19. Alon Confino, "Collective Memory and Cultural History: Problems of Method," *American Historical Review* 102, no. 5 (December 1997): 1386.

20. Clifford Geertz, *The Interpretation of Cultures: Selected Essays* (New York: Basic Books, 1973), 14.

21. Lynn Hunt, *Writing History in the Global Era* (New York: W. W. Norton, 2014), 88, 110.

22. Archie Roosevelt Jr., *For Lust of Knowing: Memoirs of an Intelligence Officer* (Boston: Little, Brown, 1988), 4.

23. Ibid., 9.

1. CONSTRUCTING A LEGACY

1. Rudyard Kipling, "Great-Heart," in *Roosevelt as the Poets Saw Him*, ed. Charles Towne (New York: Charles Scribner's Sons, 1923), 113–4; "Roosevelt to Live in History as Agitator like Isaiah and Elijah," *Savannah (GA) News,* October, 28, 1926.

2. Rudyard Kipling, *The Letters of Rudyard Kipling, 1911–19,* ed. Thomas Pinney (Iowa City: University of Iowa Press, 1990), 527.

3. "Cable Messages by King and Pope Mourn Roosevelt," *Chicago Daily Tribune,* January 9, 1919; Henry Pringle, *Theodore Roosevelt: A Biography* (New York: Harcourt Brace, 1956), 422; Edmund Morris, *Colonel Roosevelt* (New York: Random House, 2010), 725–6.

4. "Death of Mr. Roosevelt," *La Democratie Nouvelle,* January 7, 1919, TRC-W.

5. Kipling, *The Letters of Rudyard Kipling,* 540. For a lengthier treatment of Roosevelt's death set in the context of the 1919 peace negotiations, see Michael Patrick Cullinane, "Roosevelt in the Eyes of the Allies," *Journal of the Gilded Age and Progressive Era* 15, no. 1 (January 2016): 80–101.

6. Rabbi Jos. Krauskopf, "A Discourse at Temple Keneseth Israel," February 2, 1919, TRC-W.

7. "Greatest since Lincoln," *New York Sun,* January 7, 1919; "Roosevelt Family Gets Condolences," *Washington Times,* January 7, 1919.

8. Leighton Parks, "Address at St. Bartholomew's Church," January 12, 1919, TRC-W.

9. Walter I. Smith to William Howard Taft, January 6, 1919, reel 203, William Howard Taft Papers, LOC.

10. "Bryan who Politically Opposed T.R., Pays him High Tribute," *Washington Times,* January 6, 1919.

11. Eugene Thwing, *The Life and Meaning of Theodore Roosevelt* (New York: Current Literature, 1919), 350.

12. Chauncey M. Depew, "Speech before the Methodist Ministers' Association," January 13, 1919, TRC-W.

13. Leroy Dorsey, *We Are All Americans, Pure and Simple: Theodore Roosevelt and the Myth of Americanism* (Tuscaloosa: University of Alabama Press, 2007), 12, 6–7.

14. Rev. Daniel H. Clare, "Theodore Roosevelt, an American," TRC-W; Johannes V. Jensen, "An Estimate of Mr. Roosevelt," *Hamburger Nachrichten,* n.d., TRC-W; "Theodore Roosevelt, His Death," *La Nacion,* March 7, 1919, bMS Am 1785.4, CRR Papers, TRC-H; "How Twelfth Street Hailed its New Name," *Chicago Tribune,* July 3, 1919; "Calls Roosevelt Greatest Citizen," *Boston Globe,* July 5, 1919; Edwin Marcus, "American," 1919, TRB.

15. For the debate on Roosevelt as a pan-sectional American, see Edward P. Kohn, *Heir to the Empire City: New York and the Making of Theodore Roosevelt* (New York: Basic Books, 2014).

16. John A. Barsness, "Theodore Roosevelt as Cowboy: The Virginian as Jacksonian Man," *American Quarterly* 21, no. 3 (1969): 609–19; Richard Slotkin, *Gunfighter Nation: The Myth of the Frontier in Twentieth Century America* (New York: Atheneum, 1992); David Hamilton Murdoch, *The American West: The Invention of a Myth* (Reno: University of Nevada Press, 2001); David M. Wrobel, *The End of American Exceptionalism: Frontier Anxiety from the Old West to the New Deal* (Lawrence: University Press of Kansas, 1993); Beverly J. Stoeltje, "Making the Frontier Myth: Folklore Process in a Modern Nation," *Western Folklore* 46, no. 4 (October 1987): 235–53.

17. Louis S. Warren, *Buffalo Bill's America: William Cody and the Wild West Show* (New York: Vintage, 2006); Owen Wister, *The Virginian: A Horseman of the Plains* (New York: Macmillan, 1902); Frederick Jackson Turner, *The Significance of the Frontier in American History* (London: Penguin, 2008).

18. Sarah Watts, *Rough Rider in the White House: Theodore Roosevelt and the Politics of Desire* (Chicago: University of Chicago Press, 2003), 144–8; Ray Allen Billington, *Frederick Jackson Turner: Historian, Scholar, Teacher* (Oxford: Oxford University Press, 1973), 176–7; Warren, *Buffalo Bill's America,* 462.

19. Michael Patrick Cullinane, "Imperial 'Character': How Race and Civilization Shaped Theodore Roosevelt's Imperialism," in *America's Transatlantic Turn: Theodore Roosevelt and the "Discovery" of Europe,* ed. Hans Krabbendam and John M. Thompson (New York: Palgrave Macmillan, 2012), 31–49.

20. Warren G. Harding, "The Most Courageous American," January 29, 1919, TRC-W.

21. J.A.H., "The Great, Wild, Free Soul," in Towne, *Roosevelt as the Poets Saw Him,* 133.

22. Slotkin, *Gunfighter Nation,* 1–28.

23. Schurz originally made this statement in the Senate when debating patriotism in 1872. He reiterated it when opposing US foreign policy in the Philippines. Carl Schurz, "The Policy of Imperialism," *Speeches, Correspondence and Political Papers of Carl Schurz,* ed. Frederic Bancroft (New York: G. P. Putnam's Sons, 1913): 6, 119–20.

24. For treatment of the progressive movement see, Michael McGerr, *A Fierce Discontent: The Rise and Fall of the Progressive Movement in America, 1870–1920* (Oxford: Oxford University Press, 2003). On Roosevelt's role in the progressive movement, see Michael Wolraich, *Unreasonable Men: Theodore Roosevelt and the Republican Rebels Who Created Progressive Politics* (New York: St. Martin's, 2014).

25. "Good Bye, Teddy," *New Appeal,* February 8, 1919 (emphasis in original).

26. Harding, "The Most Courageous American," TRC-W.

27. Harold L. Ickes, "Roosevelt Eulogy," box 407, Harold L. Ickes Papers, LOC.

28. Merle D. Vincent, "Roosevelt Memorial Address," January 12, 1919, box 713, Gifford Pinchot Papers, LOC.

29. Boone and Crockett Club, "Roosevelt Tribute," January 1919, TRC-W.

30. David Starr Jordan, "Personal Glimpses of Theodore Roosevelt," *Natural History* 19, no. 1 (January 1919): 13.

31. Henry C. Wallace, "Roosevelt, Preacher of Righteousness," box 713, Gifford Pinchot Papers, LOC.

32. *The Autobiography of William Allen White* (New York: Macmillan, 1946), 552.

33. Brander Matthews, "Theodore Roosevelt as a Man of Letters," *Munsey's Magazine,* March 1919, 254.

34. Leighton Parks, William Henry Huber, and William E. Barton, "Tributes to Theodore Roosevelt," February 9, 1919, TRC-W.

35. George Henry Payne, "Roosevelt the Moralist in Action," February 9, 1919, in TRC-W.

36. James Roscoe, "Speech in the New York Legislature," February 9, 1919; Charles Kerr, "Roosevelt Memorial," Lexington, Kentucky, February 9, 1919; F. H. Norcross, "Theodore Roosevelt, a Tribute," February 9, 1919; and Frank Springer, "Theodore Roosevelt Memorial Service Held in the New Museum, Santa Fe, New Mexico," February 9, 1919, TRC-W.

37. "Honor Roosevelt at Westminster," *New York Times,* February 10, 1919; "Memorial Service for Mr. Roosevelt," *London Times,* February 10, 1919; "Nation Bows at Memorials to Roosevelt," *New York Tribune,* February 10, 1919.

38. Henry Cabot Lodge, "Address in Honor of Theodore Roosevelt" (Washington, DC: Government Printing Office, 1919), 5–7, 40–5, 56. See, also, "In Honor of Theodore Roosevelt," *Outlook,* January 22, 1919; "Tears Flow as Lodge Pays Tribute to His Old Friend," *New York Tribune,* February 10, 1919.

39. Investigating Committee of the Woman's Roosevelt Memorial Committee, January 21, 1919, folder 29, box 1, WRMA Papers, TRB.

40. John R. Lancos, "Theodore Roosevelt Birthplace: Study in Americanism," in *Theodore Roosevelt Many-Sided American,* ed. Natalie A. Naylor, Douglas Brinkley, and John A. Gable (Interlaken, NY: Heart of the Lakes Publishers, 1992), 518.

41. WRMA charter and by-laws, 1919–1920, folder 8, box 1, WRMA Papers, TRB.

42. Mrs. Charles Austin Bryan, "The Early History of the Theodore Roosevelt House," *Roosevelt House Bulletin* (1950): 7–8; "Annual Report of the State Organization Committee," January 6, 1920, folder 6, box 1, WRMA Papers, TRB.

43. Thompson's reputation for using personal finances to kick-start campaigns swung many former Roosevelt associates to support his bid for the leadership of the RMA. For Thompson, the chairmanship offered an opportunity to raise his profile among Republican power brokers, a motive that led to speculation that he took the job in the hope of a future

political appointment. "The Roosevelt Memorial Association: A Historical Sketch," box 712, Gifford Pinchot Papers, LOC; Scott M. Cutlip, *Fund Raising in the United States: Its Role in America's Philanthropy* (New Brunswick, NJ: Rutgers University Press, 1965), 265, 293n.

44. Minutes of the RMA Roosevelt Permanent National Memorial Committee, March 24, 1919, TRA-EXEC Minutes, TRC-H.

45. "Memorials to Roosevelt: A Book of Suggestions," Roosevelt Permanent Memorial National Committee, 1919, TRC-H.

46. Cutlip, *Fund Raising in the United States,* 242-65.

47. "18 States Now Have Chairmen," *Woman's Roosevelt Memorial Bulletin* 1, no. 1 (December 1919); WRMA Executive Board Minutes, October 9 and 28, 1919, minute books, WRMA Papers, TRB.

48. Minutes of the RMA's Executive Committee of the Committee of One Hundred, April 30, 1919, TRA-EXEC Minutes, TRC-H.

49. Campaign of the Executive Committee, Exhibit A: Suggested Plan of Publicity, TRA-EXEC Minutes, TRC-H.

50. WRMA Executive Board minutes, April 11, 1919, minute books, WRMA Papers, TRB; Minutes of the RMA's Campaign Executive Committee, TRA-EXEC Minutes, TRC-H.

51. WRMA Executive Board minutes, May 23, 1919, minute books, WRMA Papers, TRB.

52. Hermann Hagedorn, *The Boys' Life of Theodore Roosevelt* (New York: Harper and Brothers, 1918), 2-3.

53. Hermann Hagedorn, *Roosevelt in the Bad Lands* (Boston: Houghton Mifflin, 1921).

54. *Throughout Roosevelt Country with Roosevelt's Friends,* directed by Hermann Hagedorn (1919), Theodore Roosevelt Digital Library, Dickinson State University, www.theodore rooseveltcenter.org.

55. Ibid. See, also, *The Roosevelt Country: Hermann Hagedorn, Theodore Roosevelt and Dakota, 1919,* produced by the Theodore Roosevelt Center, Dickinson State University, 2011.

56. *The Fighting Roosevelts* or *Our Teddy,* directed by William Nigh (McClure's Productions, 1919); "Enduring Memorial to Roosevelt in Picture of his Life's Activities," *Pittsburg Press,* January 19, 1919. For those Americans unable to make it to the cinema, Charles Hanson Towne published a series of nationally syndicated articles that mirrored the film's content. See Charles Hanson Towne and Daniel Henderson, "The Fighting Roosevelts," *McClure's Magazine* 51 (November 1919).

57. "The Screen: The Fighting Roosevelts," *New York Times,* January 20, 1919.

58. "Roosevelt Exhibit Opens at Columbia," *New York Times,* May 10, 1919.

59. Frank Owen Payne, "More Roosevelt Sculptures," *Art and Archaeology* 8, no. 4 (August, 1919): 197.

60. "Columbia to Have Roosevelt Exhibit," *New York Sun,* April 13, 1919; "Many Roosevelt Mementos to be Shown in Columbia's Americanization Drive," *New York Times,* April 13, 1919; "Notes on Current Art," *New York Times,* May 4, 1919; Hermann Hagedorn, *Theodore Roosevelt: A Biographical Sketch* (New York: Roosevelt Memorial Exhibition Committee and Columbia University, 1919), 9.

61. "Relics Reveal Wide Scope of Roosevelt's Life," *New York Tribune,* May 9, 1919.

62. Minutes of the RMA Executive Committee, February 2, 1920, TRA-EXEC Minutes, TRC-H.

2. PROMETHEUS UNBOUND

1. "A Presidential Biography," scrapbooks, reel 459, Theodore Roosevelt Papers, LOC.

2. William Roscoe Thayer, *Theodore Roosevelt: An Intimate Biography* (Boston: Houghton Mifflin, 1919), 449; William Howard Taft's introduction to William Lewis, *The Life of Theodore Roosevelt* (Philadelphia: John C. Winston, 1919); Sylvia Jukes Morris, *Edith Kermit Roosevelt: Portrait of a First Lady* (New York: Coward McCann and Geoghegan, 1980), 436.

3. Edmund Gosse, "The Custom of Biography," *Anglo-Saxon Review* 8 (March 1901): 204–5.

4. David Nasaw, "AHR Roundtable: Historians and Biography—Introduction," *American Historical Review* 114, no. 3 (June 2009): 574; Oscar Handlin, *Truth in History* (Cambridge, MA: Belknap Press of Harvard University Press, 1979), 276.

5. "Some Canal Problems," *New York Times,* August 31, 1913; "Critical Reviews of the Season's Latest Books," *New York Sun,* August 30, 1913.

6. Joseph Bucklin Bishop, *Notes and Anecdotes of Many Years* (New York: Scribner's, 1925), 146.

7. Joseph Bucklin Bishop, *Theodore Roosevelt and His Time* (New York: Charles Scribner's Sons, 1920), vii; Chip Bishop, *The Lion and the Journalist: The Unlikely Friendship of Theodore Roosevelt and Joseph Bucklin Bishop* (Guilford, CT: Lyons, 2012), 267.

8. Lawrence Abbott, *Impressions of Theodore Roosevelt* (New York: Doubleday, Page, 1919).

9. Ferdinand Iglehart, *Theodore Roosevelt: The Man as I Knew Him* (New York: The Christian Herald, 1919), vii, 91, 196.

10. William Wingate Sewall, *Bill Sewall's Story of T.R.* (New York: Harper and Brothers, 1919), 16, 113–4.

11. Richard H. Collin, "The Image of Theodore Roosevelt in American History and Thought, 1885–1965" (PhD diss., New York University, 1966), 264; Frederick Drinker, *Theodore Roosevelt: His Life and Work* (Washington, DC: National Publishing, 1919); Lewis, *The Life of Theodore Roosevelt;* Thayer, *Theodore Roosevelt, an Intimate Biography.*

12. Drinker, *Theodore Roosevelt,* vi; Collin, "The Image of Theodore Roosevelt in American History and Thought," 266.

13. H. L. Mencken, *Prejudices: Second Series* (New York: Alfred A. Knopf, 1920), 106.

14. "How Our List of '1919's Best' Was Made Up," *New York Sun,* December 7, 1919.

15. J. A. James, "Review of *Theodore Roosevelt* by William Roscoe Thayer, *The Life of Theodore Roosevelt* by William Draper Lewis, and *Theodore Roosevelt's Letters to His Children* by Joseph Bucklin Bishop," *Mississippi Valley Historical Review* 7, no. 1 (June 1920): 76–9; M. A. De Wolfe Howe, *James Ford Rhodes: American Historian* (New York: D. Appleton, 1929), 313.

16. EKR correspondence with Lawrence Abbott, June 10–15, 1919, R110.Ab2p3, TRC-H.

17. TRJ diary, October 26, 1921, TRJ Papers, LOC.

18. CRR to WRT, March 18, 1919, bMS Am 1081: 1515, WRT Papers, TRC-H.

19. Ibid.; HH to WRT, March 27, 1919, bMS Am 1081: 726, WRT Papers.

20. Lawrence Abbott to WRT, March 31, 1919, bMS Am 1081: 5, WRT Papers; WRT to CRR, February 28, 1919, CRR Papers, bMS Am 1785: 1366, TRC-H.

21. William Roscoe Thayer, "Recent American Biographies and Letters," *North American Review* 213, no. 786 (May 1921): 686–8.

22. Hiram Bingham, "Theodore Roosevelt," *Yale Law Review* 9 (1921–2): 438–44.

23. Thayer, "Recent American Biographies and Letters," 686–7.

24. Nathaniel W. Stephenson, *Nelson W. Aldrich, A Leader in American Politics* (New York: Charles Scribner's Sons, 1930), 281; William Allen White to TRJ, February 26, 1921, box 31, TRJ Papers, LOC.

25. Bishop, *The Lion and the Journalist,* 270; "Once Again One Marvels at Roosevelt's Manifold Activities," *New York Tribune,* December 5, 1920.

26. WRT to CRR, August 19, 1919, bMS Am 1785: 1366, CRR Papers, TRC.

27. Lord Charnwood, *Theodore Roosevelt* (London: Constable, 1923), 211–2; James Amos, *Theodore Roosevelt: Hero to His Valet* (New York: John Day, 1927), 8; J. Walker McSpadden, *The Story of Theodore Roosevelt* (New York: Barse and Hopkins, 1923), 4–5, 126.

28. "Letters Reveal a Many-Sided Roosevelt," *New York Times,* October 3, 1920.

29. Alice Roosevelt Longworth, *Crowded Hours: Reminiscences of Alice Roosevelt Long-worth* (New York: Charles Scribner's Sons, 1933), 304.

30. William Harbaugh, *Power and Responsibility: The Life and Times of Theodore Roosevelt* (New York: Farrar, Straus and Cudahy, 1961), 479.

31. Edmund Morris, *Colonel Roosevelt* (New York: Random House, 2010), 548; Henry F. Pringle, *Theodore Roosevelt: A Biography* (New York: Harcourt Brace, 1956), 424.

32. "Choice of Roosevelt," *Washington Post,* January 21, 1920.

33. John Holme, *The Life of Leonard Wood* (Garden City, NY: Doubleday, Page, 1920), 15–43.

34. John Milton Cooper, *The Warrior and the Priest: Woodrow Wilson and Theodore Roosevelt* (Cambridge, MA: Harvard University Press, 1997), 277–80.

35. Longworth, *Crowded Hours,* 304.

36. CRR, "My Reasons for Wishing that General Leonard Wood may be the Next President of the United States," bMS Am 1785.3: 4, CRR Papers. Emphasis in original.

37. William Howard Taft to Horace D. Taft, February 7, 1920, Letter books, William Howard Taft Papers, LOC.

38. George Rothwell Brown, "Labor Scans Booms," *Washington Post,* February 16, 1920; Oswald Garrison Villard, "The Truth About Leonard Wood," *Nation,* May 29, 1920; "Wood Undecided About Resigning," *New York Times,* February 6, 1920.

39. A. Lincoln, "Theodore Roosevelt, Hiram Johnson, and the Vice-Presidential Nomination of 1912," *Pacific Historical Review* 28, no. 3 (1959): 269.

40. Spencer C. Olin, "Hiram Johnson, the California Progressives, and the Hughes Campaign of 1916," *Pacific Historical Review* 31, no. 4 (November 1, 1962): 403–12.

41. Clinton Wallace Gilbert, *The Mirrors of Washington* (New York: G. P. Putnam's Sons, 1921), 183–4.

42. Richard Coke Lower, "Hiram Johnson: The Making of an Irreconcilable," *Pacific Historical Review* 41, no. 4 (November 1972): 519. Johnson referred to Wilson's authorization of American expeditionary forces in Russia as an example of the executive's ability to commit troops to undeclared wars. 65 Cong. Rec. 2261–3 (January 29, 1919).

43. "Claim T.R.'s Toga is a Legacy to Hiram Johnson," *Chicago Tribune,* February 25, 1920; "Johnson's Right to Teddy Mantle," *Atlanta Constitution,* February 25, 1920; "Claims Roosevelt Shoes for Johnson," *New York Times,* February 25, 1920.

44. "Johnson Backers Publish 'T.R.' Written in '16 to Prove Leadership Claim," *Washington Post,* February 25, 1920.

45. "Johnson Cites Roosevelt," *New York Times,* July 10, 1919; "Get U.S. Out of Whole Rotten Mess—Johnson," *Chicago Tribune,* September 21, 1919; Michael A. Weatherson and

Hal Bochin, *Hiram Johnson: Political Revivalist* (Boston: University Press of America, 1995), 116.

46. Longworth, *Crowded Hours*, 277.

47. William Hutchinson, *Lowden of Illinois: The Life of Frank O. Lowden* (Chicago: University of Chicago Press, 1957), 269; "Lowden Takes Governor Oath; Asks New Deal," *Chicago Tribune,* January 9, 1917.

48. Walter Lippmann, "The Logic of Lowden," *New Republic,* April 14, 1920; Hutchinson, *Lowden of Illinois,* 249.

49. "TR for Lowden, Right Off Bat," *Chicago Tribune,* October 27, 1916.

50. Hutchinson, *Lowden of Illinois,* 388-9.

51. "Lowden Latest Heir to Mantle of Roosevelt," *Chicago Tribune,* March 1, 1920.

52. Randolph C. Downes, *The Rise of Warren Gamaliel Harding, 1865-1920* (Columbus: Ohio State University Press, 1970), 293.

53. "Nominating Speech of Warren G. Harding," *Official Report of the Fifteenth Republican National Convention* (New York: Tenny, 1912), 379.

54. David Pietrusza, *1920: The Year of the Six Presidents* (New York: Basic Books, 2007), 76.

55. "Senate Debate Spirited," *New York Times,* April 29, 1917.

56. Downes, *Rise of Warren Gamaliel Harding,* 395.

57. Ibid., 294-5. See, also, Harding's correspondence with Harry Daugherty, January 6-11, 1919, reel 28, Warren G. Harding Papers, Ohio Historical Society.

58. Warren G. Harding, "The Most Courageous American," January 29, 1919, TRC-W.

59. *The Autobiography of William Allen White* (New York: Macmillan, 1946), 587; M. McGeary, "Gifford Pinchot's Years of Frustration, 1917-1920," *Pennsylvania Magazine of History and Biography* 83, no. 3 (1959): 339-40; Desha Breckinridge to CRR, June 15, 1920, bMS Am 1785: 148, CRR Papers, TRC-H.

60. Downes, *Rise of Warren Gamaliel Harding,* 434-6, 682; McGeary, "Gifford Pinchot's Years of Frustration," 341.

61. "Gifford Pinchot Backs Harding to Shield Nation," *Chicago Tribune,* August 31, 1920.

62. "The Democratic Opportunity," *Boston Globe,* June 28, 1920.

63. "Bars Big Donations," *Washington Post,* June 26, 1920; TRJ to Alice Roosevelt Longworth, May 20, 1920, box 8, TRJ Papers, LOC.

64. Downes, *Rise of Warren Gamaliel Harding,* 434; "Roosevelt's Widow Indorses Harding," *New York Times,* October 1, 1920.

65. Joe Chapple, *Warren G. Harding: The Man* (Boston: Chapple, 1920), 84-5, 95-6; Harding, "The Most Courageous American," TRC-W.

66. "Hughes Declares Harding the Best Man," *New York Times,* August 25, 1920; "Ragtimers Visit Front Porch," *Bakersfield Californian,* August 31, 1920.

67. James A. Hollomon, "Politics at Random," *Atlanta Constitution,* September 16, 1920.

68. Eustace Hall Ball, "Roosevelt at Harvard," *New York Times,* July 18, 1920, in FDR Papers as Vice-Presidential Candidate 1920, FDRL.

69. Geoffrey C. Ward, *A First-Class Temperament: The Emergence of Franklin Roosevelt* (New York: Harper and Row, 1989), 37-8; Peter Collier and David Horowitz, *The Roosevelts: An American Saga* (New York: Simon and Schuster, 1994), 21.

70. "Memorandum of Conversation between Dr. Adolph C. Miller and Sidney Hyman," Washington, DC, April 22, 1949, FDR Memorial Foundation Papers, FDRL.

71. Ward, *A First-Class Temperament*, 119, 152–3; J. Simon Rofe, "'Under the Influence of Mahan': Theodore and Franklin Roosevelt and Their Understanding of American National Interest," *Diplomacy and Statecraft* 19, no. 4 (December 2008): 736–40.

72. Alice Roosevelt Longworth and Michael Teague, *Mrs. L.: Conversations with Alice Roosevelt Longworth* (Garden City, NY: Doubleday, 1981), 159.

73. Ward, *A First-Class Temperament*, 510–1; Stephen Early to FDR HQ, August 11 and October 3, 1920, box 6, Papers as Vice-Presidential Candidate, FDRL; Stephen Early to Louis Howe, August 11, 1920, box 2, Papers as Vice-Presidential Candidate, FDRL. On the use of Franklin's rhetoric in the 1920 campaign, and particularly the use of TR's image, see Grady Jackson Gravlee, "A Rhetorical Study of Franklin Delano Roosevelt's 1920 Campaign" (PhD diss., Louisiana State University, 1963), 383–4, 396–8, 415–6, 452–3, 526–7.

74. Stephen Early to FDR HQ, August 19, 1920, box 6, Papers as Vice-Presidential Candidate, FDRL.

75. FDR, speech at Chicago, August 11, 1920, Master Speech File, FDRL.

76. FDR, speeches at Helena (August 18), Cincinnati (October 16), and Cumberland, WV (October 27), Master Speech File, FDRL; newspaper scrapbooks, boxes 13–14, Papers as Vice-Presidential Candidate, FDRL.

77. Collier and Horowitz, *The Roosevelts*, 258–60; TRJ to CRR, August 24, 1920, box 8, TRJ Papers, LOC; Ward, *A First-Class Temperament*, 530; "A Cousin or Something," *Bismarck Tribune*, August 23, 1920; Gerald Holdridge to FDR, July 14, 1920, box 7; Calvin Goss to FDR, August 19, 1920, box 6, Papers as Vice-Presidential Candidate, FDRL.

78. "One Half of One Percent Roosevelt," *Barnes (ND) Weekly Times Record*, August 26, 1920; "Mr. F. D. Roosevelt," *Princeton Union*, August 19, 1920; Ward, *A First-Class Temperament*, 531.

79. Joseph P. Lash, *Eleanor and Franklin: The Story of Their Relationship* (New York: W. W. Norton, 1971), 254; TRJ to CRR, August 24, 1920, box 8, TRJ Papers, LOC. Several newspaper clippings on Ted's speeches and the reaction of the general public were saved by FDR's campaign and preserved at his presidential library; see box 16, Papers as Vice-Presidential Candidate, FDRL.

80. William H. Anderson to Charles McCarthy (FDR HQ), August 16, 1920, box 2, Papers as Vice-Presidential Candidate, FDRL.

81. Lash, *Eleanor and Franklin*, 254; "An Unfortunate Admission," *New York Times*, August 28, 1920. "Much has been made, by our Democratic opponents, of the fact that Senator Harding's Newspaper in 1912, criticized Colonel Roosevelt," Corrine Roosevelt Robinson acknowledged, but she attested that all "differences of opinion between Senator Harding and my Brother were wiped out completely in their common patriotic endeavor to prepare this country for its obvious duty to the . . . great war." CRR, speech given in Portland, Maine, 1920, bMS Am 1785.3: 2, CRR Papers, TRC-H.

82. "Republicans Won War Says Col. Roosevelt," *New York Times*, August 31, 1920. See, also, Gravlee, "A Rhetorical Study of Franklin Delano Roosevelt's 1920 Campaign," 526; memo from FDR HQ to Senator Harrison, September 2, 1920, box 2, Papers as Vice-Presidential Candidate, FDRL.

83. WRT to CRR, November 6, 1920, bMS Am 1785: 1366, CRR Papers, TRC-H. Emphasis in original.

84. Kathleen Dalton, *Theodore Roosevelt: A Strenuous Life* (New York: Vintage, 2004), 521.

3. THE FIRST MONUMENTS

1. Sites of memory come in a variety of forms, most typically artistic monuments, a form of public memory made through the display of symbols, landscape, or architecture representing the past in a creative interpretation. Alternatively, utilitarian memorials such as libraries, hospitals, roads, or airports memorialize the past in name. There is also a distinction to be made between monuments to national experiences, like war, and those erected to individuals. For detailed analysis of these types of memorials, the agency of memorial communities, and the general contributions that sites of memory make to public consciousness, see John E. Bodnar, *Remaking America: Public Memory, Commemoration, and Patriotism in the Twentieth Century* (Princeton: Princeton University Press, 1991), 15–16; Jay M. Winter, *Sites of Memory, Sites of Mourning: The Great War in European Cultural History* (New York: Cambridge University Press, 1995), 1–12; Paul A. Shackel, *Myth, Memory, and the Making of the American Landscape* (Gainesville: University Press of Florida, 2001), 1–16.

2. For a comprehensive account of Akeley's work on the lion sculpture, see WRMA files in FRM Papers, LOC; minutes of the RMA Executive Committee, April 19, 1921, TRA-EXEC Minutes, TRC-H.

3. Albert H. Yoder, "The Proposed Roosevelt Memorial Park," TRC-W; "Proposed Roosevelt Sequoia National Park," *National Parks Bulletin* 45 (October 24, 1925): 3; "The Plans for the Great Roosevelt Memorial Park," TRC-W; Alden H. Hadley, "Roosevelt Memorial Bird Fountain," *Maryland Conservationist* 4, no. 4 (Fall 1927); W. Emlen Roosevelt to William Loeb, n.d., minutes of the RMA Executive Committee, February 6, 1922, TRA-EXEC Minutes, TRC-H.

4. Janet Stewart, "The Proposed Pilgrimage of 1922," *The Roosevelt Pilgrimage* (Privately printed, 1922), xiv–xv.

5. "Dedication of Mount Theodore Roosevelt," *Outlook*, July 16, 1919; US Department of Agriculture, "Mount Roosevelt Friendship Tower Virtual Tour," YouTube, www.youtube.com/watch?v=J_ix94pBV0A.

6. "Guide through Montana: Over T.R. Highway, 1921," reprinted by the Montana Department of Transportation and Montana Historical Society, www.mdt.mt.gov/photogallery/docs/trhwy1.pdf.

7. Catawba College in North Carolina proposed renaming itself Roosevelt University in 1920. Roosevelt scholarships existed for many New York City public high schools, and individual colleges and universities adopted Roosevelt grants. Minutes of the RMA Executive Committee, October 27, 1926, TRA-EXEC Minutes, TRC-H; Charles G. Washburn, *Address upon the Unveiling of a Tablet to Mark No. 38 Winthrop Street, Cambridge, Where Theodore Roosevelt Lived While a Student at Harvard University* (Boston: Privately printed, 1923); "Dedication of a Tablet in Memory of Theodore Roosevelt," *Harvard Alumni Bulletin* 26 (November 1, 1923): 131–2; "Memorial to Theodore Roosevelt, '80," *Harvard Alumni Bulletin* 24 (June 2, 1921): 301–5. The class of 1880 erected a memorial to their graduating year, marking out Theodore Roosevelt and Robert Bacon as the most distinguished members. "Portrait of Robert Bacon Given Harvard," *Cambridge Tribune*, November 25, 1922; Langdon P. Marvin to WRT, June 12, 1919, and "Minutes in Memory of Theodore Roosevelt and Robert Bacon 1880," bMS Am1081: 1184, WRT Papers, TRC-H.

8. "Roosevelt Memorial Dedicated by Bishop Burgess at Forest Hills," *Forest Hills Bulletin* 8, no. 18/19 (June 30, 1923): 1–2.

9. Commemorators dedicated several memorials to Roosevelt in the 1920s, and while many have fascinating backstories, there are too many to mention. The Roosevelt Distinguished Service Medals deserve special mention as "living monuments" awarded to those who embodied the values and virtues Roosevelt championed. In the first years that awards were issued, the RMA gave medals annually at a ceremony in the White House. Another interesting monument that suggests that Roosevelt's memorialization went far beyond the domestic United States was a replica of James Earle Fraser's bust erected in Santiago, Cuba. The Theodore Roosevelt Collection in Widener Library includes an extensive collection of documents on the various memorial projects, including these.

10. TR to William D. Murphy, October 17, 1905, *The Letters of Theodore Roosevelt* (hereafter cited as *Letters*), ed. Elting E. Morison et al. (Cambridge, MA: Harvard University Press, 1952): 5, 60.

11. Report on Organization Work, January 27, 1919, folder 6, box 1, WRMA Papers, TRB.

12. According to the *Roosevelt House Annual* (1950), Edith Roosevelt related her desire to see the house become a memorial, but she and the rest of the Roosevelt family provided little input and took no active part in the decision immediately after TR's death. "The Early History of Theodore Roosevelt House," *Roosevelt House Annual* (1950): 7–8; WRMA Executive Board minutes, May 23 and 29, 1919, minute books, WRMA Papers, TRB.

13. WRMA minutes, January 27, 1919, WRMA Papers, minute books, TRB.

14. John R. Lancos, "Theodore Roosevelt Birthplace: Study in Americanism," *Theodore Roosevelt: Many-Sided American,* ed. Natalie A. Naylor, Douglas Brinkley, and John A. Gable (Interlaken, NY: Heart of the Lakes Publishers, 1992), 517–26; Richard J. Melnick, "The Theodore Roosevelt Birthplace," *Historian* 58, no. 2 (1996): 289–94; Judith Paine, *Theodate Pope Riddle: Her Life and Work* (New York: Theodore Roosevelt Birthplace National Park Site, 1979), 24–5; Roosevelt Home Club Pamphlet (New York: Hallenbeck, Crawford Co.), TRC-W; Report of the Investigating Committee, folder 29, box 1, WRMA Papers, TRB.

15. WRMA Minutes, November 14, December 12 and 30, 1919, folder 7, box 1, WRMA Papers, TRB; Tara Callahan, *Theodate Pope Riddle: A Pioneer Woman Architect* (Fort Washington, PA: Eastern National, 1998), TRB.

16. "Each Room Has Many Memories," *Woman's Roosevelt Memorial Bulletin* 1, no. 3 (April 1920): 2; "Contributions Total More than $110,00," *Woman's Roosevelt Memorial Bulletin* 1, no. 1 (December 1919): 1; "Architect is Chosen to Restore Roosevelt House," *Woman's Roosevelt Memorial Bulletin* 1, no. 2 (February 1920): 1.

17. "Each Room Has Many Memories," 2; WRMA Executive Board minutes, May 23, 1919, WRMA Papers, minute books, TRB.

18. "Series of Text Books Planned," *Woman's Roosevelt Memorial Bulletin* 1, no. 4 (June 1920): 3.

19. "Scholarships are to be a Feature of the House Educational Work," *Woman's Roosevelt Memorial Bulletin* 1, no. 4 (June 1920): 2.

20. "Cornerstone of Roosevelt House Set in Place," *Woman's Roosevelt Memorial Bulletin* 1, no. 6 (February 1921): 1–2; "Cornerstone of New Roosevelt House is Laid," *New York Tribune,* January 7, 1921.

21. Ibid.

22. "Appealed to Mankind," *Woman's Roosevelt Memorial Bulletin* 1, no. 5 (October 1920): 3.

23. "Cornerstone of Roosevelt House Set in Place," 1–2.

24. "Report on Decorations and Furnishings," April 13 and May 11, 1923, folder 28, box 1, WRMA Papers, TRB; "Mrs. Lambert Tells of Her Quest for Roosevelt House Furnishings," *Roosevelt House Bulletin* 2, no. 1 (Summer 1923): 3.

25. Minutes of the conferences of the WRMA and RMA, February–March 1922, folder 1, box 3, WRMA Papers, TRB.

26. Ibid.

27. RMA, "Annual Report" (1921), TRC-W; Alan Havig, "Presidential Images, History, and Homage: Memorializing Theodore Roosevelt, 1919–1967," *American Quarterly* 30, no. 4 (October 1978): 514–32.

28. "Exhibit A: Suggested Plan of Publicity for the Roosevelt Memorial Campaign," TRA-EXEC Minutes, TRC-H.

29. Minutes of the RMA Executive Committee, October 16, 1920, January 17, 1921, TRA-EXEC Minutes, TRC-H.

30. Richard H. Collin, "The Image of Theodore Roosevelt in American History and Thought, 1885–1965," (PhD diss., New York University, 1966), 399.

31. Minutes of the RMA Executive Committee, May 30, 1923, TRA-EXEC Minutes, TRC-H.

32. Minutes of the RMA Executive Committee, February 8, 1924, TRA-EXEC Minutes, TRC-H.

33. 68 Cong. Rec. 7737 (May 3, 1924); minutes of the RMA Executive Committee, February 8, 1924, TRA-EXEC Minutes, TRC-H.

34. HH to JRG, August 22, 28, October 9, 1925, box 150, JRG Papers, LOC; "Old Hostilities Still Live," *New York World*, October 3, 1925; "Roosevelt vs. Wilson: Fourth Round," *Nation*, January 20, 1926.

35. "Creating Reputations, Ltd.," *American Mercury* 4, no. 16 (April 1925): 385–9; "Denies Making Halo for Col. Roosevelt," *New York Times*, March 23, 1925.

36. 68 Cong. Rec. 1007 (December 30, 1924); 68 Cong. Rec. 2897 (February 2, 1925).

37. Roosevelt Memorial Association, *Program of a Competition to Select the Artist or Group of Artists who will be Commissioned to Design and Direct the Construction of a Monumental Memorial to Theodore Roosevelt in the City of Washington* (1925), TRC-W.

38. "Prize Winning Design, Competition for a Memorial to Theodore Roosevelt in Washington, D.C.," *American Architect* 129, no. 2489 (January 20, 1926): plate 2.

39. JRG to HH, October 14 and 30, 1925, box 150, JRG Papers, LOC.

40. "Great Roosevelt Memorial Planned in Washington," *Exporters and Importers Journal* 34, no. 12 (March 5, 1926): 11.

41. In addition to Pope's winning bid, the competition inspired more than a dozen designs for the Tidal Basin. Of the submissions, four drafted memorial arches, two had rotundas, and two envisioned temples. The RMA also entered Carl Akeley's lion on his behalf and at the request of the Roosevelt family. The lion sculpture was judged without prejudice to any other entries.

42. Alfred Granger, "The Roosevelt Memorial," *Architect* 5, no. 4 (January 1926): 387.

43. Henry Stoddard to JGR, November 2, 1925; JRG to HH, November 6, 1925; HH to JRG, November 7, 1925, box 150, JRG Papers, LOC.

44. Minutes of the RMA Executive Committee, November 14, December 21, 1925, TRA-EXEC Minutes, TRC-H; "Memorial for Roosevelt to Grace Potomac," *Chicago Tribune*, December 13, 1925; HH to JRG, October 14, 1925, box 150, JRG Papers, LOC; Hermann Hagedorn, "The Roosevelt Memorial," *New York Times*, November 24, 1925.

45. "A Misplaced Memorial," *New York World,* December 15, 1925; "Residence of Woodrow Wilson May Become National Shrine," *Atlanta Constitution,* August 6, 1925; "Division over Roosevelt," *New York Times,* December 7, 1925.

46. 29 Cong. Rec. 919–20 (December 16, 1925); "Senator Questions Memorial Site," *Christian Science Monitor,* December 21, 1925.

47. Hermann Hagedorn, "The Roosevelt Memorial," *New York Times,* December 15, 1925. See, also, A.B., "Division over Roosevelt," *New York Times,* December 7, 1925; "Roosevelt Memorial Stirs up a Dispute," *New York Times,* November 22, 1925.

48. Havig, "Presidential Images, History, and Homage," 529–30; "Jefferson Monument to Have Precedence," *New York Times,* July 4, 1926; "Halt Memorial to Roosevelt," *New York Times,* May 14, 1926.

49. Gilbert C. Fite, *Mount Rushmore* (Norman: University of Oklahoma Press, 1952), 22–8; John Taliaferro, *Great White Fathers: The Story of the Obsessive Quest to Create Mount Rushmore* (New York: Public Affairs, 2002), 58.

50. Calvin Coolidge, "Address at the Opening of Work on Mount Rushmore in Black Hills, August 10, 1927," *American Presidency Project,* www.presidency.ucsb.edu.

51. Doane Robinson, "Notes on the Inception and Development of the Rushmore Idea," box 163, Peter Norbeck Papers, South Dakota University; GB to William Boyce Thompson, August 27, 1919, folder: Theodore Roosevelt Memorial, box 113, GB Papers, LOC; Taliaferro, *Great White Fathers,* 58.

52. The credit for Roosevelt's place on the mountain often goes to Borglum. Rex Allan Smith credits Borglum with mentioning Roosevelt as a potential figure for Rushmore in October 1924, but Borglum also wrote to friends about including Cleveland and McKinley at that point, and not until Norbeck's insistence in January 1925 did the prospect of adding Roosevelt become a reality. Rex Alan Smith, *The Carving of Mount Rushmore* (New York: Abbeville, 1985), 130.

53. Peter Norbeck to C. M. Henry, January 25, 1925, box 133, Peter Norbeck Papers, South Dakota University.

54. Fite, *Mount Rushmore,* 6–7.

55. Ibid., 8–9.

56. Peter Norbeck to GB, May 1926, box 163, Peter Norbeck Papers, South Dakota University.

57. This came about after Catawba College proposed renaming itself Roosevelt University. The college requested an endorsement from the RMA, but the committee refused. All other requests received identical responses, including Rushmore. Minutes of the RMA Executive Committee, October 27, 1926, TRA-EXEC Minutes, TRC-H.

58. Mary Borglum, "Notes on Borglum/Roosevelt Relationship," n.d., box 38, GB Papers, LOC.

59. GB, "Notes on Roosevelt," 1919, box 38, GB Papers, LOC.

60. Mary Borglum, "Notes on Borglum/Roosevelt Relationship."

61. GB, "Diary Notes, February 18, 1919," box 113, GB Papers, LOC.

62. Howard Shaff and Audrey Karl Shaff, *Six Wars at a Time: The Life and Times of Gutzon Borglum, Sculptor of Mount Rushmore* (Sioux Falls, SD: Center for Western Studies, Augustana College, 1985), 181. Borglum led a local branch of the RMA in Connecticut. He maintained a close correspondence with leaders of the association, including William Howard Taft and William Boyce Thompson. See, Borglum's correspondence with the RMA, box 86, GB Papers, LOC.

63. Joseph Fulford Folsom, "The Bust of Roosevelt," box 113, GB Papers, LOC.

64. "Random Impressions in Current Exhibitions," *New York Tribune,* November 2, 1919; "Pictorial Section," *New York Sun,* November 9, 1919; "City Tribute to Roosevelt Launched at Sub-Treasury," *New York Tribune,* October 21, 1919.

65. Fite, *Mount Rushmore,* 22–6; Taliaferro, *Great White Fathers,* 55–8.

66. Mary Borglum, "From the Beginning," *Mount Rushmore National Memorial: A Monument Commemorating the Conception, Preservation, and Growth of the Great American Republic* (Mount Rushmore National Memorial Commission, 1941).

67. GB to William Boyce Thompson, copied by Mary Borglum in 1951, box 86, GB Papers, LOC.

68. HH to JRG, November 19, 1925, box 150, JRG Papers, LOC.

4. THE OTHER ROOSEVELT

1. Edmund Morris, *Colonel Roosevelt* (New York: Random House, 2010), 565.

2. Geoffrey C. Ward, *A First-Class Temperament: The Emergence of Franklin Roosevelt* (New York: Harper and Row, 1989), 558–9.

3. Ibid., 633–8.

4. "Want Roosevelt Put in Coolidge's Place," *New York Times,* April 4, 1923.

5. H. N. Brailsford, "A New Technique of Peace," *New Republic,* November 30, 1921; H. Paul Jeffers, *In the Rough Rider's Shadow* (New York: Ballantine, 2003), 132–5; Eleanor Butler Roosevelt, *Day Before Yesterday: The Reminiscences of Mrs. Theodore Roosevelt, Jr.* (Garden City, NY: Doubleday, 1959), 144–5.

6. Laton McCartney, *The Teapot Dome Scandal: How Big Oil Bought the Harding White House and Tried to Steal the Country* (New York: Random House, 2008), 85–6.

7. Eleanor Butler Alexander-Roosevelt, *Day Before Yesterday,* 141.

8. "Stevenson Insists Roosevelt Should Go," *New York Times,* March 19, 1924; "Roosevelt Hurls Lie at Stevenson," *Atlanta Constitution,* March 18, 1924; "Stevenson's Charges Challenged in House," *Washington Post,* March 18, 1924.

9. Eleanor Butler Alexander-Roosevelt, *Day Before Yesterday,* 147–8.

10. Ward, *A First-Class Temperament,* 689–9.

11. FDR, "Nomination of Al Smith at Democratic National Convention," June 26, 1924, Master Speech File, FDRL.

12. "Mr. Davis' Speech of Acceptance," *Washington Post,* August 12, 1924; "I Have to Quit Wall Street," *Chicago Tribune,* August 12, 1924.

13. Joseph P. Lash, *Eleanor and Franklin: The Story of Their Relationship* (New York: W. W. Norton, 1971), 287–8.

14. Ibid., 291.

15. Peter Collier and David Horowitz, *The Roosevelts: An American Saga* (New York: Simon and Schuster, 1994), 298; "Round About with M. E. Hennessy," *Boston Globe,* November 9, 1924; Eleanor Butler Alexander-Roosevelt, *Day Before Yesterday,* 163; Anna Eleanor Roosevelt, *This I Remember* (New York: Harper and Brothers, 1949), 32; "3 Women Debate Campaign Issues," *New York Times,* November 2, 1924.

16. "F. D. Roosevelt Hits Theodore's Record," *New York Times,* October 31, 1924.

17. FDR, Campaign Speech (1924) on Harding Administration Scandals, box 41, FDR Family Business and Personal Papers, FDRL.

18. Ward, *A First-Class Temperament*, 700–1.

19. Henry F. Pringle, *Big Frogs* (New York: Vanguard, 1928), 247.

20. Ted's wife, Eleanor (not to be confused with FDR's wife), believed Smith and Tammany stole the election by fraud. She blamed the lack of voting machines in New York City, where Smith won overwhelmingly. Alexander-Roosevelt, *Day Before Yesterday*, 165–6.

21. Alice Roosevelt Longworth and Michael Teague, *Mrs. L.: Conversations with Alice Roosevelt Longworth* (Garden City, NY: Doubleday, 1981), 159.

22. CRR to Anna Eleanor Roosevelt, October 5, 1928, box 9, Anna Eleanor Roosevelt Papers, FDRL.

23. Charles R. Lingley, "Review of Theodore Roosevelt: A Biography by Henry F. Pringle," *American Historical Review* 37, no. 3 (April 1932): 570–72.

24. Richard H. Collin, "The Image of Theodore Roosevelt in American History and Thought, 1885–1965" (PhD diss., New York University, 1966), 266, 306.

25. Owen Wister, *Theodore Roosevelt: The Story of a Friendship, 1880–1919* (London: Macmillan, 1930); Lewis Einstein, *Roosevelt: His Mind in Action* (Boston: Houghton Mifflin, 1930), 243.

26. Harold Brackman, "'Biography Yanked down out of Olympus': Beard, Woodward, and Debunking Biography," *Pacific Historical Review* 52, no. 4 (November 1983): 403–27.

27. Edward G. Lengel, *Inventing George Washington: America's Founder, in Myth and Memory* (New York: Harper, 2011), 101, 140–5; William E. Woodward, *George Washington, the Image and the Man* (New York: Boni and Liveright, 1926).

28. Beverly W. Smith Jr., "A Genuine Study of Al," *New York Evening Post*, October 8, 1927.

29. Pringle, *Big Frogs;* Richard H. Collin, "Henry Pringle's Theodore Roosevelt: A Study in Historical Revisionism," *New York History* 52, no. 2 (April 1971): 158.

30. "Pulitzer Prize Won by Musical Show," *Washington Post*, May 3, 1932; "Review of Theodore Roosevelt: A Biography by Henry F. Pringle," *International Affairs* 12, no. 2 (March 1933): 284; "Review of Theodore Roosevelt: A Biography by Henry F. Pringle," *American Political Science Review* 26, no. 2 (April 1932): 363.

31. Henry F. Pringle, *Theodore Roosevelt, A Biography* (New York: Harcourt Brace, 1956), 13, 144, 149–50, 180.

32. Ibid., 4.

33. Henry F. Pringle, "Roosevelt's Vigorous Mind in Action," *New York Times*, November 30, 1930.

34. "Advertisement," *Saturday Review of Literature*, November 7, 1931.

35. Collin, "The Image of Theodore Roosevelt in American History and Thought," 319.

36. Pringle, *Theodore Roosevelt, A Biography*, 41.

37. Ibid., 68.

38. Matthew C. Gunter, *The Capra Touch: A Study of the Director's Hollywood Classics and War Documentaries, 1934–1945* (Jefferson, NC: McFarland, 2011), 46.

39. Eric Johnson, "The Character of Teddy Brewster in *Arsenic and Old Lace*" (MFA thesis, Mankato State University, 1989), 32.

40. RMA, "1934 Annual Report," box 2, TRA Papers, TRB.

41. Collier and Horowitz, *The Roosevelts*, 322.

42. Betty Caroli, *The Roosevelt Women* (New York: Basic Books, 1998), 129–31.

43. William E. Lemanski, *Lost in the Shadow of Fame* (Camp Hill, PA: Sunbury, 2012), 118–9.

44. Alexander-Roosevelt, *Day Before Yesterday*, 240; Caroli, *The Roosevelt Women*, 361.

45. Ted Morgan, *FDR: A Biography* (New York: Simon and Schuster, 1985), 323–4.

46. Ibid., 342.

47. The Basil O'Connor Papers at the Franklin Roosevelt Presidential Library contain an extensive collection of political cartoons from 1932 to 1943. "Another Roosevelt Rides the Range," *Philadelphia Public Ledger,* March 18, 1932; "Brewerton's Billboard of Current Events," *Atlanta Journal,* March 27, 1932; "A New Roosevelt Invades the West," *New York Herald Tribune,* April 21, 1932, boxes 1–4, Basil O'Connor Papers, FDRL.

48. Parker La Moore, "Roosevelt—Good Citizen," *Oklahoma Oklahoman,* March 25, 1932, box 1, Basil O'Connor Papers, FDRL.

49. Steve Neal, *Happy Days Are Here Again* (New York: William Morrow, 2004), 273–94; Russell M. Posner, "California's Role in the Nomination of Franklin D. Roosevelt," *California Historical Society Quarterly* 39, no. 2 (June 1960): 121–39.

50. James MacGregor Burns and Susan Dunn, *The Three Roosevelts: The Leaders Who Transformed America* (London: Atlantic, 2001), 56, 78, 231; FDR, Address Accepting the Presidential Nomination at the Democratic National Convention in Chicago, July 2, 1932, www.presidency.ucsb.edu.

51. FDR, Campaign Address on Progressive Government at the Commonwealth Club in San Francisco, September 23, 1932, www.presidency.ucsb.edu. In correspondence with Ted, Walter Lippmann credited FDR with achieving what TR did not in 1912. Walter Lippmann to TRJ, November 22, 1932, box 29, TRJ Papers, LOC.

52. Arthur M. Schlesinger, *The Coming of the New Deal, 1933–1935* (New York: Houghton Mifflin Harcourt, 2003), 92, 180, 189, 347, 357; Memorandum of a Conversation between Sidney Hyman and Rexford Tugwell, Spring 1949, box 26, FDR Memorial Foundation Papers, series I, FDRL.

53. "Cool Head is Called Roosevelt Asset," *New York Times,* July 29, 1932.

54. Longworth and Teague, *Mrs. L.,* 158–9.

55. "Arena Throng Hears Roosevelt Decry Fear," *Boston Globe,* November 1, 1932; EKR to TRJ, June 29, 1932, box 4, TRJ Papers, LOC; EKR to TRJ, August 14, 1932, TRA Papers, TRB.

56. Allen Churchill, *The Roosevelts* (London: Frederick Muller, 1966), 291; EKR to CRR, August 9, 1932, bMS Am 1785: 1169, CRR Papers, TRC-H.

57. "Text of Col. Theodore Roosevelt's Broadcast from Manila," *New York Times,* October 28, 1932.

58. "The Copyright Owners," *New York American,* August 22, 1932, box 3, Basil O'Connor Papers, FDRL.

59. Sylvia Morris, *Edith Kermit Roosevelt: Portrait of a First Lady* (New York: Coward McCann and Geoghegan, 1980), 477.

60. Churchill, *The Roosevelts,* 291.

61. Kathleen Dalton, *Theodore Roosevelt: A Strenuous Life* (New York: Vintage, 2004), 521; Alan Havig, "Theodore and Franklin: F.D.R.'s Use of the Theodore Roosevelt Image, 1920–1936," *TRA Journal* 5, no. 2 (Spring 1979): 6–10.

62. Morgan, *FDR,* 378.

63. FDR, "Second Fireside Chat," May 7, 1933, Master Speech File, FDRL.

64. "President Scored by Col. Roosevelt," *New York Times,* September 15, 1935; "Col. Roosevelt Says President Violated Oath," *Chicago Tribune,* September, 15, 1935.

65. EKR to JRG, September 29, 1933, box 119, JRG Papers, LOC.

66. Stacy A. Cordery, *Alice: Alice Roosevelt Longworth, from White House Princess to Washington Power Broker* (New York: Penguin, 2008), 374–5, 382–3.

67. Collin, "The Image of Theodore Roosevelt in American History and Thought," 333–41; Alan Nevins, "If Roosevelt Looks Back at Roosevelt," *New York Times,* October 22, 1933.

68. FDR, speech given at New York State Theodore Roosevelt Memorial, dedicated January 19, 1936, prepared by George N. Pindar, box 6, Theodore Roosevelt Memorial and Exhibitions Papers, American Museum of Natural History, New York.

69. Ibid.; "'Teddy' is Lauded as Square Dealer," *Atlanta Constitution,* January 20, 1936; "Roosevelt Pays 'T.R.' Great Honor as Patriot," *Chicago Tribune,* January 20, 1936; "President Links his Policies and that of T.R." *Washington Post,* January 20, 1936; "President Extolls 'T.R.' as Defender of Social Justice," *New York Times,* January 20, 1936; Longworth and Teague, *Mrs. L.,* 159.

70. Henry Fairfield Osborn, "History, Plan, and Design of the New York State Roosevelt Memorial" (1928), box 6, Theodore Roosevelt Memorial and Exhibitions Papers, American Museum of Natural History, New York. The New York State memorial took sixteen years to plan and design. The Roosevelt Memorial Association planned to connect the legacy of TR with Franklin at the dedication, but bad blood between the Oyster Bay and Hyde Park clans sunk the plan. See minutes of the RMA Executive Committee, May 13, 1934, TRA-EXEC Minutes, TRC-H.

71. Arthur M. Schlesinger, *The Politics of Upheaval: 1935–1936* (New York: Houghton Mifflin Harcourt, 2003), 529.

72. William Allen White to TRJ, February 1, 1933, and December 5, 1933, box 31, TRJ Papers, LOC; *The Autobiography of William Allen White* (New York: Macmillan, 1946), 639–40.

73. FDR, "Informal Extemporaneous Remarks at a Luncheon in Dallas, Texas, June 12, 1936," *The Public Papers and Addresses of Franklin D. Roosevelt* (New York: Random House, 1948): 5, 214–5.

74. FDR, "Address at Chicago, Illinois, October 14, 1936"; "Address at Wilkes-Barre, Pennsylvania, October 29, 1936"; "Final Campaign Radio Speech of the 1936 Presidential Campaign, November 2, 1936," www.presidency.ucsb.edu. During the campaign, surrogates for Hyde Park and Oyster Bay jousted over legacy matters. Sen. Vic Donahey (D-OH) compared TR and FDR, and RMA president James R. Garfield refuted the parallel.

75. Theodore Roosevelt, "The Conditions of Success: A Speech Delivered at the Cambridge Union, May 26, 1910," www.theodore-roosevelt.com.

76. Colin Schindler, *Hollywood in Crisis: Cinema and American Society, 1929–1939* (New York: Routledge, 2005), 160.

77. Ibid., 161.

78. Gregory D. Black, "Hollywood Censored: The Production Code Administration and the Hollywood Film Industry, 1930–1940," *Film History* 3, no. 3 (January 1989): 184–5.

79. "Movie Review: Road Gang," *New York Times,* February 24, 1936.

80. Lester D. Friedman, *Hollywood's Image of the Jew* (New York: Fredrick Ungar, 1982), 82.

81. Colin Shindler, *Hollywood Goes to War: Films and American Society, 1939–1952* (New York: Routledge, 2014), 9; Schindler, *Hollywood in Crisis,* 203.

82. Charles L. Telford, writer, *The Monroe Doctrine,* directed by Crane Wilbur (Warner Bros., 1939).

83. *Teddy the Rough Rider,* directed by Ray Enright (Warner Bros., 1940); *Yankee Doodle Dandy,* directed by Michael Curtiz (Warner Bros., 1942); Michael Patrick Cullinane, "The

Memory of Theodore Roosevelt through Motion Pictures," *A Companion to Theodore Roosevelt,* ed. Serge Ricard (Malden, MA: Wiley-Blackwell, 2012), 506–7.

84. Alice Roosevelt Longworth to TRJ, August 26, 1939, box 3, TRJ Papers, LOC.

85. Edward Renehan, *The Lion's Pride: Theodore Roosevelt and His Family in Peace and War* (New York: Oxford University Press, 1998), 228.

86. Charlie Hamilton, "Excerpts from the Press Conference, December 2, 1941," www .presidency.ucsb.edu.

87. FDR, "Campaign Address in Boston, October 30, 1940," www.presidency.ucsb.edu; John Lamberton Harper, *American Visions of Europe: Franklin D. Roosevelt, George F. Kennan, and Dean G. Acheson* (Cambridge: Cambridge University Press, 1996), 61, 32.

88. Archibald Bulloch Roosevelt to FDR, 1942–1945, box 17, FDR Family Papers, FDRL.

89. The Belle and Kermit Roosevelt Papers at the Franklin Roosevelt Presidential Library detail the extent to which the president and first lady orchestrated Kermit's transfer to Alaska. Archie also wrote the president on the matter. See Belle Willard Roosevelt correspondence with Eleanor Roosevelt and FDR, Kermit and Belle Roosevelt Papers, FDRL.

90. Morris, *Edith Kermit Roosevelt,* 511.

91. TRJ to FDR, May 7, 1942, box 20, Roosevelt Family Papers, FDRL.

92. "Politics Losing Hatred's Spice, Alice Laments," *Chicago Tribune,* June 23, 1944.

93. Stimson got the year wrong. The twenty-fifth anniversary was in 1944. See Henry L. Stimson Diary, January 6, 1945, reel 9, Henry Stimson Papers, Roosevelt Study Center, Middelburg, The Netherlands. See, also, F. Trubee Davison, Theodore Roosevelt Association Oral History Project (1953–1955), Columbia University Center for Oral History.

5. COLD WAR REVIVAL

1. EKR to JRG, January 24, 1941, box 119, JRG Papers, LOC.

2. HH to JRG, June 12, 1941, letter in the minutes of the RMA Executive Committee, September 19, 1941, July 31, 1942, TRA-EXEC Minutes, TRC-H.

3. Minutes of the RMA Executive Committee, May 14, July 31, October 26, 1942, March 15, 1943, TRA-EXEC Minutes, TRC-H. See, also, Nora Cordingly's correspondence with the RMA and Harvard University Faculty in TRA-Harvard College Library Administrative Files, TRC-H.

4. Nora Cordingly to HH, September 14, 1944, TRC Archival Correspondence, TRC-H.

5. Albert Bushnell Hart to HH, October 27, 1926, folder 1, box 3, HH Papers, TRC-H; Minutes of the RMA Executive Committee, April 14, 1926, May 6, 1927, February 17, May 30, 1928, TRA-EXEC Minutes, TRC-H.

6. Minutes of the RMA Executive Committee, May 30, 1928, TRA-EXEC Minutes, TRC-H.

7. Minutes of the RMA Executive Committee, May 13, 1934, May 28, 1939, October 7, 1940, TRA-EXEC Minutes, TRC-H.

8. Minutes of the RMA Executive Committee, October 27, 1944, TRA-EXEC Minutes, TRC-H.

9. Ferleger took note of the most important correspondence during the *Cyclopedia* work in the hope that an edited collection of Roosevelt's correspondence would follow. RMA Annual Report 1939–1940, box 2, TRA Papers, TRB; RMA Minutes of the RMA Executive Committee, May 10, 1940, TRA-EXEC Minutes, TRC-H.

10. Minutes of the RMA Executive Committee, October 7, 1940, September 19, December 23, 1941, April 17, 1942, TRA-EXEC Minutes, TRC-H; Herbert Ferleger to HH, January 2, 1943, April 25, 1944, folder 6, box 3, HH Papers, TRC-H.

11. Minutes of the RMA Executive Committee, October 27, 1945, September 17, 1946, September 30, October 27, December 23, 1947, March 16, 1948, TRA-EXEC Minutes, TRC-H. Colleagues of Morison and Blum advised them to avoid the project believing that, like the *Cyclopedia,* it would never amount to much. Ferleger was angry about Morison's appointment. He had expected to take up the editorial role after the war, although the RMA had made no formal commitment to give him the position. John Morton Blum, *A Life with History* (Lawrence: University Press of Kansas, 2004), 76. See, also, correspondence between Ferleger and HH, January 1941–November 1945, folder 6, box 3, HH Papers, TRC-H.

12. Mark Sullivan to HH, September 19, 1951, minutes of the RMA Executive Committee, October 2, 1951, October 27, 1952, TRA-EXEC Minutes, TRC-H.

13. "Introduction," *Letters,* 1:xv; John A. Garraty, "Review of The Letters of Theodore Roosevelt," *New England Quarterly* 24, no. 3 (September 1951): 390; Robert S. Maxwell, "Review of *The Letters of Theodore Roosevelt,* Vol. I and II," *Mississippi Valley Historical Review* 38, no. 2 (September 1951): 335–7; Howard K. Beale, "Review of *The Letters of Theodore Roosevelt,* Vol. I and II," *American Historical Review* 57, no. 1 (October 1951): 184–7.

14. Dewey W. Grantham Jr., "Review of *The Letters of Theodore Roosevelt,* Volumes I and II," *Journal of Southern History* 17, no. 4 (November 1951): 568.

15. George E. Mowry is an exception to the post-revisionist scholarship. He "reopened" the history of TR's post-presidential years and began to scrutinize his progressive legacy before Morison published the *Letters.* Yet, as Richard Collin rightly points out, his book "cannot be taken as the start of the rediscovery moment." George Mowry, *Theodore Roosevelt and the Progressive Movement* (Madison: University of Wisconsin Press, 1946); Richard H. Collin, "The Image of Theodore Roosevelt in American History and Thought, 1885–1965" (PhD diss., New York University, 1966), 360.

16. Richard Hofstadter, *The American Political Tradition and the Men Who Made It* (New York: Knopf, 1948), 271, 296; David S. Brown, *Richard Hofstadter: An Intellectual Biography* (Chicago: University of Chicago Press, 2006), xvi.

17. Beale to Hofstadter, February 6, 1948, in Brown, *Richard Hofstadter,* 61.

18. It should be noted that Hofstadter's review of Morison's *Letters* did not predict the reversal he eventually made. Roosevelt, Hofstadter argued, was "consistently interesting but consistently unlikable . . . nothing that has since come to light—certainly nothing I can find in this mass of correspondence—goes very far to rehabilitate him." Richard Hofstadter, "Review of *The Letters of Theodore Roosevelt,* Volumes I and II," *Commentary,* September 1, 1951.

19. Richard Hofstadter, *The Age of Reform: From Bryan to FDR* (New York: Knopf, 1954), 13, 236–7, 252–3.

20. Richard Hofstadter, *Anti-Intellectualism in American Life* (New York: Knopf, 1962), 193, 196, 207. See, also, Blum, *A Life with History,* 90–1.

21. John Blum, *The Republican Roosevelt* (Cambridge, MA: Harvard University Press, 1954), 22–3.

22. John Higham, "The Cult of the American Consensus: Homogenizing Our History," *Commentary,* February 1, 1959; George E. Mowry, *The Era of Theodore Roosevelt, 1900–1912* (New York: Harper and Brothers, 1958).

23. See Dewey W. Grantham Jr., "Theodore Roosevelt in American Historical Writing, 1945–1960," *Mid-America* 43, no. 1 (January 1961): 3–35. See, also, Collin, "The Image of Theodore Roosevelt in American History and Thought."

24. Carleton Putnam, *Theodore Roosevelt: The Formative Years, 1858–1886* (New York: Charles Scribner's Sons, 1958); Grantham, "Theodore Roosevelt in American Historical Writing, 1945–1960," 6.

25. Blum, *A Life with History,* 76. The RMA planned to commission a new wave of hagiographies and enlisted journalist and former assistant secretary of state John Callan O'Laughlin to produce a biography of that sort. O'Laughlin's death in 1949 led the association to abandon the idea, but they eagerly supported Putnam's idea for a multivolume biography. Minutes of the RMA Executive Committee, December 23, 1947, and March 16, 1949, TRA-EXEC Minutes, TRC-H.

26. See Oscar E. Anderson, *The Health of a Nation: Harvey W. Wiley and the Fight for Pure Food* (Chicago: University of Chicago Press, 1958); Robert J. Cornell, *The Anthracite Coal Strike of 1902* (Washington: Catholic University of America Press, 1957); William Behl, "The Rhetoric of Theodore Roosevelt" (PhD diss., Northwestern University, 1942); Howard K. Beale, "Theodore Roosevelt's Ancestry: A Study in Heredity," *New York Genealogical and Biographical Record* 85 (October 1954): 196–205; G. Wallace Chessman, "Theodore Roosevelt, Governor" (PhD diss., Harvard University, 1950); Peter R. Levin, *Seven by Chance: The Accidental Presidents* (New York: Farrar, Straus, 1948); Ari Hoogenboom, "The Pendleton Act and the Civil Service," *American Historical Review* 64, no. 2 (January 1959): 301–18; Dewey W. Grantham Jr., "Dinner at the White House: Theodore Roosevelt, Booker T. Washington, and the South," *Tennessee Historical Quarterly* 17, no. 2 (June 1958): 130. For histories that detail Roosevelt's relationship to American regions or particular historical episodes written in the 1950s, see Grantham, "Theodore Roosevelt in American Historical Writing, 1945–1960."

27. Introduction to *Letters,* 1:xxviii.

28. Howard K. Beale, *Theodore Roosevelt and the Rise of America to World Power* (Baltimore: Johns Hopkins Press, 1956), vii–viii, xi, 448–62. It is worth noting that Beale did not use Morison's *Letters,* although he did rely on the same archives Morison mined. William Tilchin, "The Rising Star of Theodore Roosevelt's Diplomacy: Major Studies from Beale to the Present," *TRA Journal* 15, no. 3 (Summer 1989): 2.

29. Michael J. Hogan and Thomas G. Paterson, *Explaining the History of American Foreign Relations* (New York: Cambridge University Press, 2004), 3.

30. George F. Kennan, *American Diplomacy, 1900–1950* (Chicago: University of Chicago Press, 1951), 13, 18, 43–4, 47.

31. George Kennan, "Policy Planning Staff Memorandum 53, United States Foreign Policy toward Formosa and the Pescadores," *Foreign Relations of the United States: The Far East, China* 8 (Washington, DC: Government Printing Office, 1949), 358.

32. "Roosevelt Medalist Annual Dinner," *Roosevelt House Annual* (1950), 9–11; "Big Stick Urged to Repel Red Foes," *New York Times,* October 28, 1949.

33. "My Uncle Teddy," *Boston Globe,* October 26, 1958.

34. Theodore Roosevelt, *The Free Citizen: A Summons to Service of the Democratic Ideal,* ed. Hermann Hagedorn (New York: Macmillan, 1956).

35. See correspondence between the TRA and NYPD, "Police Exhibit—New York Police Force and Theodore Roosevelt," folder 5, box 7, TRA Papers, TRB.

36. "Theodore Roosevelt Stamp, February 1–December 8, 1955," folder 12, box 7, TRA Papers, TRB; Theodore Roosevelt Association Oral History Project (1953–1955), Columbia University Center for Oral History.

37. HH to John A. Gade, June 22, 1955, box 1, HH Papers, TRC-H.

38. Joint Committee of RMA and WRMA Meeting minutes, February 21, 1938, TRA-EXEC Minutes, TRC-H. See, also, folders 1–3: "Joint Conference," "Consideration of a Merger," and "Correspondence 1920–1940," box 3, WRMA Papers, TRB.

39. When the RMA divested its portion of the library to Harvard, the WRMA protested. The women wanted to keep the archive in New York and refused to relinquish their small collection. Emily Eaton Hepburn, the WRMA treasurer, strongly opposed the merger and claimed that the RMA had misappropriated funds and frivolously overspent. Finance committee member Mrs. Frederick Longfellow also spread rumors that the RMA had mismanaged investments. WRMA Meeting with RMA and Minutes of the RMA Executive Committee, October 13, 1937, April 4, 1938, April 17, 1942, TRA-EXEC Minutes in TRC-H; WRMA Financial Committee Minutes, March 13, 1942, and JGR to Mrs. Frederick Longfellow, March 13, 1942, folder 2, box 3, WRMA Papers, TRB.

40. Minutes of the RMA Executive Committee, October 27, 1951, April 29, 1952, TRA-EXEC Minutes, TRC-H.

41. "Suggested Program for Theodore Roosevelt House" and memorandum to the Special Committee on the Theodore Roosevelt Association, box 6, TRA Papers, TRB.

42. Consolidation agreement between WRMA and TRA, signed January 6, 1955, approved by Congress, March 29, 1955, and by New York Supreme Court, May 3, 1956, box 1, TRCC Papers, TRB. See, also, Formation of the TRCC and Congressional Resolutions, box 1, TRCC Papers, TRB.

43. "Suggested Program for Theodore Roosevelt House" and memorandum to the Special Committee on the Theodore Roosevelt Association, box 6, TRA Papers, TRB.

44. Report of the TRA House Committee, November 14, 1956, box 1, WRMA Papers, TRB.

45. TRCC Proposals, box 1, TRCC Papers, TRB. Hagedorn rewrote his pitch several times. This excerpt is taken from the original draft.

46. The commission's ex officio members included Senators Karl Mundt (R-SD) and Joseph O'Mahoney (D-WY), and Representatives Steven Derounian (R-NY) and Leo O'Brien (D-NY). At-large commissioners included Senator Hazel Abel (R-NE), Governor C. Norman Brunsdale (R-ND), Hal Davies, Mrs. Sherman Post Haight, Herbert Miller, Lowell Stockman, and TRA president Oscar Straus II.

47. "Statement of Purpose," Appendix A from minutes of TRCC meeting, January 18, 1956, box 2, TRCC Papers, TRB.

48. Ibid.

49. Elaine Tyler May, *Homeward Bound: American Families in the Cold War Era* (New York: Basic Books, 2008), 21–2.

50. Script for radio broadcast, "The Night there was No President," *Cavalcade of America* (January 2, 1951–March 17, 1952), folder 15, box 5, TRA Papers, TRB. Archie wrote several books in the 1950s that adapted TR's legacy to fit mainstream American mores of the era. Archie also imagined how TR would react to civil rights debates and social issues like capital punishment, welfare, and judicial review. See Theodore Roosevelt, *Theodore Roosevelt on Race, Riots, Reds, Crime,* ed. Archibald B. Roosevelt (Metairie, LA: Sons of Liberty, 1968);

Archibald B. Roosevelt, *Manual for American Action* (New York: The Alliance, 1956); Zygmund Dobbs, *Red Intrigue and Race Turmoil* (New York: The Alliance, 1958).

51. Tom Engelhardt, *The End of Victory Culture: Cold War America and the Disillusioning of a Generation* (Amherst: University of Massachusetts Press, 2007), 135.

52. "The Dude Rides: A True Story," box 3, TRCC Papers, TRB; *The Rough Riders,* December 1, 1957, Classics Illustrated; *Dennis the Menace* 21 (March 1957), Pines Comics; *Adventures of Mighty Mouse,* February 1957, Pines Comics; *Adventures of Winky Dink* 75 (March 1957), Pines Comics; "Teddy Roosevelt and his Rough Riders," Avon Periodicals, 1 August 1950); "Jesse James: Gunplay at Gallatin," Avon Periodicals, 18 (July 1950).

53. *Arbor and Wildlife Day* (Albany: New York State Education Department, 1958), box 4, TRCC Papers, TRB.

54. S. Doc. 36, *Final Report of the Theodore Roosevelt Centennial Commission relating to a Celebration of the Hundredth Anniversary of the Birth of Theodore Roosevelt, 1858–1958,* (hereafter *TRCC Final Report*), 86th Cong., 1st sess. (1959), 30; Dwight D. Eisenhower, Remarks at the Theodore Roosevelt Centennial Conservation Ceremony, May 8, 1958, www.presidency.ucsb.edu.

55. *TRCC Final Report,* 43.

56. TRCC placard, folder 4, box 4, TRCC Papers, TRB.

57. John F. Kennedy, "The Moral and Spiritual Imperatives of Free Government," speech given April 12, 1958, at the 1958 Theodore Roosevelt Symposium in Dickinson, North Dakota, available at www.theodorerooseveltcenter.org.

58. *TRCC Final Report,* 19–23.

59. TRCC "Statement of Purpose" (proposed), n.d., box 1, TRCC Papers, TRB.

60. Richard Slotkin, *Gunfighter Nation: The Myth of the Frontier in Twentieth-Century America* (New York: Atheneum, 1992), 347–8; Stanley Corkin, *Cowboys as Cold Warriors: The Western and U.S. History* (Philadelphia: Temple University Press, 2004), 2.

61. Corkin, *Cowboys as Cold Warriors,* 9–10; John H. Lenihan, *Showdown: Confronting Modern America in the Western Film* (Urbana: University of Illinois Press, 1980), 4–5.

62. Tony Shaw, *Hollywood's Cold War* (Edinburgh: Edinburgh University Press, 2007), 202–6.

63. Richard Slotkin, *The Fatal Environment: The Myth of the Frontier in the Age of Industrialization, 1800–1890* (Norman: University of Oklahoma Press, 1985), 28–9.

64. *In Old Oklahoma* (re-released as *War of the Wildcats*), directed by Albert S. Rogell (Republic Pictures, 1943).

65. Three years later, Republic Pictures released *Sun Valley Cyclone,* which also showed Roosevelt as an arbitrator. He was played by Ed Cassidy, who would act as Roosevelt in two other Westerns. *Sun Valley Cyclone* follows the trials of a young recruit to the Rough Riders who, at Roosevelt's urging, helps realize national ambitions on the frontier. *Sun Valley Cyclone,* directed by R. G. Springsteen (Republic Pictures, 1946).

66. Ella Taylor, *Prime-Time Families: Television Culture in Post-War America* (Berkeley: University of California Press, 1989), 36.

67. "Rough and Ready," episode 24 of *My Friend Flicka,* season 1, CBS, March 9, 1956.

68. Michael Patrick Cullinane, "The Memory of Theodore Roosevelt through Motion Pictures," *A Companion to Theodore Roosevelt,* ed. Serge Ricard (Malden, MA: Wiley-Blackwell, 2012), 508–13; Matthew J. Costello, "Rewriting High Noon: Transformations in American

Popular Political Culture during the Cold War, 1952–1968," in *Hollywood's West: The American Frontier in Film, Television, and History,* ed. John E. O'Connor and Peter Rollins (Lexington: University Press of Kentucky, 2005), 176; Dan Gagliasso, "Rough Riders, Moviemakers, and History: Hollywood Images of Theodore Roosevelt and the First U.S. Volunteer Cavalry," *Journal of Arizona History* 41, no. 3 (October 2000): 307–30; Slotkin, *Gunfighter Nation,* 351.

69. *My Girl Tisa,* directed by Elliott Nugent (United States Pictures, 1948).

70. Richard L. Coe, "Such a Nice Picture," *Washington Post,* February 20, 1948.

71. Edwin Schallert, "Wanamaker, Lilli Palmer Well Matched in 'Tisa,'" *Los Angeles Times,* February 7, 1948.

72. Gary Gerstle, "Theodore Roosevelt and the Divided Character of American Nationalism," *Journal of American History* 86, no. 3 (1999): 1281.

6. UNFINISHED BUSINESS

1. Advertisement, Lincoln Motor Company, http://mascola.com/insights/luxury-auto mobile-advertising-retro-ad-week-lincoln-1924; advertisement, Lincoln National Life Insurance Company, http://sites.oxy.edu/special-collections/lincoln-legacies/memorials.htm; "History of John E. Fowler's Cherry Smash," www.cherry-smash.com/history-of-john-e-fowlers-cherry-smash.html; advertisement, Anheuser Busch, Budweiser Great Contributions to Good Taste, http://envisioningtheamericandream.com/2014/02/18/mac-cheese-and-the-pursuit-of-happiness; advertisement, Old Crow Bourbon, www.decodog.com/inven/sports/sp28940.jpg; advertisement, Grant's Tobacco, http://images.fineartamerica.com/images-medium-large-5/grants-tobacco-studio-artist.jpg.

2. "T.R. Madison Avenue Pitchman," Almanac of Theodore Roosevelt, https://m2.facebook.com/notes/almanac-of-theodore-roosevelt/tr-madison-avenue-pitchman; advertisement, Sinclair Oil, *Time* (1958), box 55, TRCC Papers, TRB; advertisement, Hammermill Bond, Subject Files: Advertising, TRC-H; Minutes of the TRA Executive Committee, September 7, 1955, TRA-EXEC Minutes, TRC-H.

3. "Great Ideas of Western Man: Walter and Elizabeth Paepcke and the CCA," *Codex 99,* www.codex99.com/design/great-ideas.html; additional advertising images from the CCA available in box 49, TRCC Papers, TRB.

4. Gregory A. Wynn, "The Little-Known Sculptor Vincenzo Miserendino," *TRA Journal* 33, no 4 (Fall 2012): 25–31; Theodore Roosevelt Portrait Bust Advertisement, box 3, TRCC Papers; S. Doc. 36, *Final Report of the Theodore Roosevelt Centennial Commission relating to a Celebration of the Hundredth Anniversary of the Birth of Theodore Roosevelt, 1858–1958,* 86th Cong., 1st sess. (1959), 157–60.

5. William Davison Johnston, *TR: Champion of the Strenuous Life* (New York: Theodore Roosevelt Association, 1958); Edward Wagenknecht, *The Seven Worlds of Theodore Roosevelt* (Guilford, CT: Lyons, 2009).

6. Ambrose Flack, *Room for Mr. Roosevelt* (Boston: Thomas Y. Crowell, 1951); "Make Way for Teddy," episode of *Schlitz Playhouse of Stars,* CBS, 1952. See, also, Ambrose Flack, "Theodore Roosevelt and My Green-Gold Fountain Pen," *New Yorker,* May 22, 1948.

7. Will Henry, *San Juan Hill* (New York: Random House, 1962); Oakley Hall, *The Bad Lands* (New York: Scribner, 1978); H. Paul Jeffers, *The Further Adventures of Sherlock Holmes: The Stalwart Companions* (London: Titan Books, 2010); Marjorie Barrows, *Along*

Blazed Trails (Chicago: Spencer, 1953); Edd Winfield Parks, *Teddy Roosevelt, All Around Boy* (Indianapolis: Bobbs-Merrill, 1961).

8. The RMA did not change its name to the TRMA until 1946; it became the TRA in 1953. In this chapter, I refer to the TRA to maintain a chronological consistency despite the association's transition over the course of many years. It was the men (the RMA or TRMA) and not the women (WRMA or WTRMA) who instigated the purchase of Analostan Island and Sagamore Hill. In 1931, the RMA reported, entirely implausibly, that Analostan Island appeared "far more promising than the original site" at the Tidal Basin. "RMA Annual Report, 1931," and "RMA 25 Year Report, 1944," box 2, TRA Papers, TRB.

9. Kay Fanning, *National Register of Historic Places Registration Form: Theodore Roosevelt Island* (Washington, DC: U.S. Department of the Interior, National Park Service, 1999), 1–5, 33–42.

10. Ibid., 45–6; *Historic American Landscapes Survey: Theodore Roosevelt Island* (Washington, DC: US Department of Interior, National Park Service, 2007), 47–8; Minutes of the RMA Executive Committee, January 3, 1931, May 21, 1931, September 21, 1931, TRA-EXEC Minutes, TRC-H.

11. Henry Vincent Hubbard to Olmsted Brothers, "Notes on Certain Considerations Affecting the Design," December 22, 1932, Theodore Roosevelt Island National Memorial Archive, Theodore Roosevelt Center Digital Library, Dickinson State University.

12. 75 Cong. Rec. 9397–8 (May 2, 1932); "House Approves Analostan Plan," *Washington Star,* May 16, 1932.

13. "Roosevelt Shrine Deeded to Nation," *New York Times,* December 13, 1932.

14. "Analostan Island, Named Roosevelt, Accepted by U.S.," *Washington Post,* December 13, 1932.

15. "Theodore Roosevelt Island Now," *New York Times,* February 15, 1933.

16. "Summary of Mr. Olmsted's Progress Report," May 13, 1934, TRA-EXEC Minutes, TRC-H.

17. Ibid.

18. "Wild Park Made to Honor T.R.," *New York Times,* November 7, 1937. Olmsted complained that the CCC destroyed some trees and plants he intended to keep, but overall they completed the work as ordered.

19. HH to FRM, March 22, 1938, box 85, FRM Papers, (Women's) Roosevelt Memorial Association, LOC.

20. Minutes of the TRA Executive Committee, September 3, 1943, TRA-EXEC Minutes, TRC-H. See, also, minutes of the TRA Executive Committee, September 19, 1941, May 25, 1943, October 18, 1943, TRA-EXEC Minutes, TRC-H.

21. Fanning, *Theodore Roosevelt Island,* 54; Frederick Law Olmsted to FRM, in the minutes of the TRA Executive Committee, May 25, 1943, TRA-EXEC Minutes, TRC-H.

22. Ibid., 55; minutes of the TRA Executive Committee, April 17, 1942, TRA-EXEC Minutes, TRC-H. See, also, Olmsted Associates Records, reel 104, Analostan Island, folder 4, LOC.

23. Ulysses S. Grant III to FRM, October 20 and 27, 1947, letters in the TRA-EXEC Minutes, TRC-H. See, also, Minutes of the TRA Executive Committee, December 18, 1951, TRA-EXEC Minutes, TRC-H.

24. "Cent Boost in Gas Tax Urged to Pay Off Part of Bill," *Washington Post,* February 1, 1952; "First Response to Road Survey is Favorable," *Washington Post,* February 2, 1952.

25. "Fight Promised on Any Plan to Run Bridge over Island," *Washington Post,* May 29, 1953.

26. Irston R. Barnes, "T.R.'s Island has Two Purposes," *Washington Post*, August 2, 1953.

27. Jean White, "Roosevelt Island Saga, 'Only Unspoilt Spot' of Kind," *Washington Post*, August 7, 1953; "Leader of the Theodore Roosevelt Memorial Arrives to Wage Battle against E St. Span," *Washington Post*, January 23, 1953.

28. Minutes of the TRA Executive Committee, July 11, 1953, TRA-EXEC Minutes, TRC-H. On the TRA's opposition, see minutes of the TRA Executive Committee, March–July 1955, TRA-EXEC Minutes, TRC-H.

29. "Roosevelt Island Clear as Bridge Site," *Washington Post*, July 14, 1953; "Interior Dept. Sees Bar to E St. Bridge," *Washington Post*, August 8, 1953.

30. Fanning, *Theodore Roosevelt Island*, 74–5; *Historic American Landscapes Survey*, 85; minutes of the TRA Executive Committee, March 17, 1955, TRA-EXEC Minutes, TRC-H.

31. Minutes of the TRA Executive Committee, June 16, 1955, TRA-EXEC Minutes, TRC-H.

32. "Cohesion to Beauty," *Washington Post*, July 9, 1955.

33. Minutes of the TRA Executive Committee, June 16, 1955, TRA-EXEC Minutes, TRC-H.

34. Ibid. The TRA continued to favor a tunnel over a bridge and lobbied when appropriate but to little avail. See minutes of the TRA Executive Committee, October 17, 1957-January 31, 1958, TRA-EXEC Minutes, TRC-H.

35. Minutes of the TRA Executive Committee, July 7, 1955, TRA-EXEC Minutes, TRC-H; Fanning, *Theodore Roosevelt Island*, 58.

36. Fanning, *Theodore Roosevelt Island*, 59.

37. "July 4 Celebrations Viewed by 215,000," *Washington Post*, July 5, 1958.

38. "Would Fireworks Honor Theodore Roosevelt?" *Washington Post*, June 29, 1958.

39. Ethel Quillian Bixby, "Editorial," *Washington Post*, June 23, 1958.

40. Hermann Hagedorn, "TR and Fireworks," *Washington Post*, June 28, 1958.

41. Minutes of TRCC meeting, January 1956, box 1, TRCC Papers, TRB.

42. Minutes of the TRA Executive Committee, January 12, 1956, TRA-EXEC Minutes, TRC-H.

43. Ibid. Hagedorn invited foreign democracies to contribute granite plaques to the site showing how "freedom fighters" shaped their nation.

44. *Historic American Landscapes Survey*, 91.

45. "Apply the Big Stick," *Washington Post*, August 8, 1960; "Is this Memorial Really Necessary?" *Washington Post*, August 11, 1960; "Theodore Roosevelt Memorial Nears Actuality but Battle Still Rages on Design," *Washington Star*, August 14, 1960.

46. Benton MacKaye, "Island Outrage," *Washington Post*, August 11, 1960.

47. "TR Memorial Plans Would Desecrate Anyone's Memory, Daughter Says," *Washington Post*, August 19, 1960.

48. Minutes of the TRA Executive Committee, September 14, 1960, TRA-EXEC Minutes, TRC-H; "TR Glorified Gyroscope Memorial Rouses Scorn of Grandson Kermit," *Washington Post*, August 5, 1960.

49. Minutes of the TRA Executive Committee, September 14, 1960, TRA-EXEC Minutes, TRC-H. Emphasis in original.

50. Minutes of the TRA Executive Committee, January 20, 1963, TRA-EXEC Minutes, TRC-H.

51. "A Wraith Flails a Big Stick against the TR Memorial," *Washington Post*, June 19, 1966.

52. Fanning, *Theodore Roosevelt Island*, 61.

53. Lyndon Johnson, "Remarks at the Dedication of the Theodore Roosevelt Memorial in Washington, October 27, 1967," www.presidency.ucsb.edu.

54. Stewart Udall, "Theodore Roosevelt Memorial Dedication Address, October 27, 1967," www.library.arizona.edu; "Rough Rider Rides Again," *Washington Post,* October 28, 1967.

55. Minutes of the RMA Executive Committee, December 23, 1947, March 16, 1948, TRA-EXEC Minutes, TRC-H.

56. Minutes of the TRA Executive Committee, February 28, 1957, TRA-EXEC Minutes, TRC-H.

57. Hermann Hagedorn and Gary G. Roth, *Sagamore Hill: An Historical Guide* (Oyster Bay, NY: Theodore Roosevelt Association, 1977), 10.

58. TR to Henry H. Saylor, October 3, 1915, in Gary G. Roth, "The Roosevelt Memorial Association and the Preservation of Sagamore Hill, 1919–1953" (MA thesis, Wake Forest University, 1980), 4.

59. Hermann Hagedorn, *The Roosevelt Family of Sagamore Hill* (New York: Macmillan, 1954), 7.

60. Ibid., 424.

61. Marie Carden and Richard Crisson, *Historic Structure Report: Sagamore Hill, Home of Theodore Roosevelt, Sagamore Hill National Historic Site* (Boston: US Department of the Interior, National Park Service, 1997); RMA annual reports, 1948–1949, box 2, TRA Papers, TRB.

62. Reginald P. Rose, "The Sagamore Story," *Long Island Courant* 1, no. 2 (October, 1965): 23–36. See, also, TRA Committee for the Development of Sagamore Hill, box 4, TRA Papers, TRB.

63. The RMA resisted widening the road and attempted to have the area rezoned by Nassau County in order to avoid a protracted debate about traffic. Residents appealed to the Roosevelt family, who considered cancelling the RMA's contract to purchase the house. Doing so would have put the house on the open market and, presumably, relisted it as a private residence capable of paying tax to the city. To avoid this, the RMA capitulated, but rather than build a new road that extended to most of the residences, as locals hoped for, the RMA paid to have it widened. The road issue came up periodically in town debates over the site. See Minutes of the RMA Executive Committee, 1948–1952, TRA-EXEC Minutes, TRC-H.

64. James A. Hagerty, "Theodore Roosevelt's Home Made Shrine by Eisenhower," *New York Times,* June 15, 1953.

65. Hermann Hagedorn, *A Guide to Sagamore Hill: The Place, the People, the Life, the Meaning* (New York: Theodore Roosevelt Association, 1953), 72–3.

66. Archie Roosevelt Jr., *For Lust of Knowing: Memoirs of an Intelligence Officer* (Boston: Little, Brown, 1988), 4–5.

67. Kathleen Dalton, "The Strenuous Outdoor Life," *Theodore Roosevelt and his Sagamore Hill Home: Historic Resource Study* (Oyster Bay, NY: US Department of the Interior, National Park Service, 2007), 65–78.

68. Ibid., 29, 65.

69. TRA Annual Report 1956, box 6, TRA Papers, TRB.

70. Lewis L. Gould, "'The House is Overrun with Political People:' Sagamore Hill after the Presidency," *Theodore Roosevelt and His Sagamore Hill Home,* 64.

71. TRA "Annual Report 1956," box 6, TRA Papers, TRB.

72. The women's association considered donating the house to the New York Historical Society or New York State Department of Education, but neither showed interest. The men's association also considered donating the birthplace at the time of the merger but believed doing so would risk the unity of the group. Despite determining that it was "financially no longer in a position to maintain the house," the TRA continued to keep it open. See min-

utes of the RMA/TRA Executive Committee, July 18, 1950, April 29, 1952, January 15, 1953, October 4, 1954, June 25, 1959, TRA-EXEC Minutes, TRC-H.

73. Minutes of the TRA Executive Committee, September 14, November 30, 1960, January 9 and 27, 1961, TRA-EXEC Minutes, TRC-H.

7. A SECOND DECLINE AND REVIVAL

1. Minutes of the TRA Executive Committee, February 9, 1974, TRA-EXEC Minutes, TRC-H.

2. Schlitz television commercial, 1977, www.youtube.com/watch?v=sT3NZ-UMXI0; J. Travis Smith, "Malted Madness: A Quick Drunk History of Milwaukee," http://gearpatrol .com/2014/03/27/the-history-of-milwaukee-beer; Harva Hachten and Teresa Allen, *The Flavor of Wisconsin: An Informal History of Food and Eating in the Badger State* (Madison: Wisconsin Historical Society Press, 2013), 122–3. For an accurate account of the advertising campaign, see, Jay Brooks, *Brookston Beer Bulletin,* http://brookstonbeerbulletin.com/ beer-in-ads-1503-teddy-roosevelts-african-safari.

3. Lewis L. Gould, *1968: The Election That Changed America* (Chicago: Ivan R. Dee, 1993), 3–4, 89–91, 94–5.

4. Ibid., 99–102, 106–7.

5. Robert Mason, *Richard Nixon and the Quest for a New Majority* (Chapel Hill: University of North Carolina Press, 2004), 5–30.

6. Democrats utilized TR's progressive legacy as well. In an attempt to strengthen Humphrey's campaign, President Johnson signed landmark legislation in 1968 for safe poultry, water conservation, and national parks. In each instance he invoked TR as the inspiration. In the final days of the election, Johnson quoted Roosevelt directly, insisting that Humphrey was "fit to hold the position of President" because he "feels that he represents no party but the people as a whole." See "Remarks Broadcast on a Program Sponsored by the Democratic Victory Committee, November 3, 1968," www.presidency.ucsb.edu.

7. Robert B. Semple Jr., "It's Time Again for the Nixon Phenomenon," *New York Times,* January 21, 1968.

8. Garry Wills, *Nixon Agonistes: The Crisis of the Self-Made Man* (New York: Mariner Books, 2002), 17.

9. John Robert Greene, "The Men in the Arena: Presidential Co-Option of the Image of Theodore Roosevelt, 1916–1989," *Theodore Roosevelt: Many-Sided American,* ed. Natalie A. Naylor, Douglas Brinkley, and John A. Gable (Interlaken, NY: Heart of the Lakes, 1992), 603.

10. Rick Perlstein, *Nixonland: The Rise of a President and the Fracturing of America* (New York: Simon and Schuster, 2008), 330–2.

11. "Address Accepting the Presidential Nomination at the Republican National Convention in Miami Beach, Florida," August 8, 1968, www.presidency.ucsb.edu; Merlo J. Pusey, "Will GOP Respond to Modern Temper," *Washington Post,* August 6, 1968.

12. Rick Perlstein, *Before the Storm: Barry Goldwater and the Unmaking of the American Consensus* (New York: Hill and Wang, 2001), 108.

13. "Reagan Denies He's In," *Boston Globe,* July 21, 1968.

14. "Nixon Visits Negro Slum and Warns White Suburbs," *New York Times,* September 22, 1968.

15. "Excerpts from Text of Speech by Nixon," *New York Times,* September 20, 1968; "Nixon Breaking with Ike Policies," *Washington Post,* October 9, 1968; Nixon Keys His Pitch to Promise Change," *Washington Post,* October 20, 1968.

16. Alice Roosevelt Longworth and Michael Teague, *Mrs. L.: Conversations with Alice Roosevelt Longworth* (Garden City, NY: Doubleday, 1981), 197.

17. Stacy Cordery, *Alice: Alice Roosevelt Longworth, from White House Princess to Washington Power Broker* (New York: Viking, 2007), 440.

18. Ibid., 469. The cozy relationship between Alice Roosevelt Longworth and Nixon was captured on White House recordings, including their candid remarks about TR. See Nixon Tapes, Alice Roosevelt Longworth telephone call to Nixon, November 11, 1972, Camp David Study Table, tape 153, conversation 1, www.nixonlibrary.gov.

19. "Statement Announcing the White House Conference on Children and Youth," October 26, 1969; "Proclamation 3961—Small Business Week," February 12, 1970; "Special Message to the Congress on Employee Benefits Protection," March 13, 1970; "Labor Day Statement," August 25, 1970; "Remarks at a Ceremony Marking Attainment of a Trillion Dollar Gross National Product," December 15, 1970, www.presidency.ucsb.edu.

20. Nixon's public papers abound with examples of political co-option. On topics mentioned, see "News Conference," July 27, 1972; "Statement about the Vietnam Veteran," March 24, 1973, www.presidency.ucsb.edu.

21. J. Brooks Flippen, *Nixon and the Environment* (Albuquerque: University of New Mexico Press, 2000), 1–4; Paul Charles Milazzo, "Nixon and the Environment," *A Companion to Richard M. Nixon,* ed. Melvin Small (Malden, MA: Wiley-Blackwell, 2013), 270–1.

22. David Greenberg, *Nixon's Shadow: The History of an Image* (New York: W. W. Norton, 2003), 324.

23. See "Remarks at the Swearing in of Rogers C. B. Morton as Secretary of the Interior," January 29, 1971, www.presidency.ucsb.edu.

24. Henry Kissinger, *Diplomacy* (New York: Simon and Schuster, 1994), 29–55; Kissinger has continued to depict his diplomacy as Rooseveltian, an ideology he contrasts with Wilsonianism. See Henry Kissinger, *Does America Need a Foreign Policy?* (New York: Simon and Schuster, 2001), 240–3; Anne-Marie Slaughter, "How to Fix America's Foreign Policy," *New Republic,* November 18, 2014.

25. Jussi M. Hanhimäki, *The Flawed Architect: Henry Kissinger and American Foreign Policy* (New York: Oxford University Press, 2004), 30–1, 489–92.

26. "Address to the Nation Announcing Decision to Resign the Office of President of the United States," August 8, 1974, www.presidency.ucsb.edu. Nixon would title his memoir *In the Arena* and in it made several references to Roosevelt after his departure from the White House. See Richard Nixon, *In the Arena: A Memoir of Victory, Defeat, and Renewal* (New York: Simon and Schuster, 1990).

27. "Remarks on Departure from the White House," August 9, 1974, www.presidency.ucsb.edu.

28. Noel Busch, *T.R.: The Story of Theodore Roosevelt and His Influence on Our Times* (New York: Reynal, 1963), 3–4, 9.

29. Roger Daniels, *The Politics of Prejudice: The Anti-Japanese Movement in California, and the Struggle for Japanese Exclusion* (Berkeley: University of California Press, 1962); Willard B. Gatewood, *Theodore Roosevelt and the Art of Controversy: Episodes of the White House Years* (Baton Rouge: Louisiana State University Press, 1970); Gabriel Kolko, *The Tri-*

umph of Conservatism: A Reinterpretation of American History, 1900–1916 (New York: Free Press, 1977), 57–97, 103.

30. John Higham, "Changing Paradigms: The Collapse of Consensus History," *Journal of American History* 76, no. 2 (September 1989): 461–5.

31. Lloyd C. Gardner, "American Foreign Policy, 1900–1921: A Second Look at the Realist Critique of American Diplomacy," in *Towards a New Past: Dissenting Essays in American History,* ed. Barton J. Bernstein (New York: Pantheon, 1968), 202–31.

32. Barbara W. Tuchman, "Perdicaris Alive or Raisuli Dead," *American Heritage* 10, no. 5 (August 1959); Michael Patrick Cullinane, "The Memory of Theodore Roosevelt through Motion Pictures," *A Companion to Theodore Roosevelt,* ed. Serge Ricard (Malden, MA: Wiley-Blackwell, 2012), 512–3.

33. *The Wind and the Lion,* directed by John Milius (Metro-Goldwyn-Mayer, 1975).

34. Kevin Thomas, "The Thinking Man's Spectacle," *Los Angeles Times,* May 22, 1975.

35. Minutes of the TRA Executive Committee and Executive Director's Report, July 9, 1975, TRA-EXEC Minutes, TRC-H.

36. Ibid., March 30, 1974.

37. Minutes of the TRA Executive Committee, March 30, May 4, June 6, 1974, TRA-EXEC Minutes, TRC-H.

38. Ibid., May 4, 1974, TRA-EXEC Minutes, TRC-H.

39. See *TRA Journal* 1, no. 1 (Winter/Spring 1975): 5–14.

40. "President's Annual Report: The Work of the T.R.A. in 1974," *TRA Journal* 1, no. 1 (Winter/Spring 1975): 2; minutes of the TRA Executive Committee, April 24, 1976, December 17, 1977, TRA-EXEC Minutes, TRC-H; John Allen Gable, "Report to the Sagamore Hill Anniversary Committee," May 23, 1978, TRC-H.

41. Ralph Dibble, "TR's Personal Check Kicks off Drive to Save Wilcox Mansion," *Buffalo Evening News,* September 14, 1976.

42. "The 59th Annual Meeting of the Theodore Roosevelt Association," *TRA Journal* 5, no. 1 (Winter 1979): 2–3.

43. Minutes of the TRA Executive Committee, July 9, 1975, October 26, 1977, TRA-EXEC Minutes, TRC-H; "Teddy Roosevelt Would Have Been Pleased," *Wallcoverings* (1977), TRC-W.

44. Report to Sagamore Hill Anniversary Committee, May 23, 1978, TRA-EXEC Minutes, TRC-H; "Lecture Series Will Mark 25th Anniversary of Sagamore Hill," *Oyster Bay Guardian,* March 17, 1978.

45. "Roosevelts Rise to the Occasion," *Washington Post,* September 21, 1979; Q&A with Edmund Morris, C-SPAN, November 4, 2010, www.c-span.org/video/?296436-1/qa-edmund-morris; Edmund Morris, *This Living Hand: And Other Essays* (New York: Random House Paperbacks, 2013), 128–9.

46. Edmund Morris, "The Distortion of History: 'The Wind and the Lion,'" *TRA Journal* 1, no. 2 (Summer/Fall 1975): 9–10, 12.

47. Nicholas von Hoffman, "A Bully Portrait of the Legendary Teddy," *Chicago Tribune,* March 25, 1979.

48. Gerald W. McFarland, "Review: The Rise of Theodore Roosevelt," *American Historical Review* 84, no. 5 (December 1979): 1492.

49. David P. Thelen, "Review: The Rise of Theodore Roosevelt," *Wisconsin Magazine of History* 63, no. 3 (April 1980): 239–40; Elting Morison, "Rough Riding on the Road to the Presidency," *New York Times,* March 25, 1979.

50. Miles F. Shore, "On Action and Affect," *Journal of Interdisciplinary History* 11, no. 2 (October 1980): 287–94.

51. Pete Axthelm, "Where Have All the Heroes Gone?" *Newsweek,* August 6, 1979.

52. Tom Wolfe, "The 'Me' Decade and the Third Great Awakening," *New York,* August 23, 1976.

53. George Will, "Fashions in Heroes," *Newsweek,* August 6, 1979.

54. "Book Notes," *TRA Journal* 4, no. 1 (Winter 1978): 18–9; Address to the Nation on the Panama Canal Treaties, February 1, 1978, www.presidency.ucsb.edu.

55. Geoffrey C. Ward, "The Making of Theodore Roosevelt," *New York Times,* July 26, 1981. McCullough admitted that he aimed to resurrect Roosevelt from the kind of 1930s depictions that began with Henry Pringle and culminated in the Frank Capra adaptation of Joseph Kesselring's play *Arsenic and Old Lace.* See "Book Notes," *TRA Journal* 7, no. 3 (Summer 1981): 22–3.

56. Lois W. Banner, "Biography as History," *American Historical Review* 114, no. 3 (June 2009): 579–86. The cultural turn also gave rise to the postmodern turn, a theoretical approach that denied that biography, or indeed histories, could locate meaning and truth from the resources available to researchers. Biographers were affected by this, but as Nigel Hamilton relates, with "no credible alternative to the *grand récit* of life chronicling," the writing of biography continued to churn over human existence. Nigel Hamilton, *Biography: A Brief History* (Cambridge, MA: Harvard University Press, 2007), 206–12.

57. Kirkus Reviews, June 22, 1981, www.kirkusreviews.com.

58. Gore Vidal, "An American Sissy," *New York Review of Books,* August 13, 1981.

59. "Address Accepting the Presidential Nomination at the Republican National Convention in Detroit, July 17, 1980," www.presidency.ucsb.edu.

60. William H. Chafe, *The Unfinished Journey: America since World War II* (New York: Oxford University Press, 1986), 430.

61. Ronald Reagan, "Announcement of Presidential Candidacy," www.reagan.utexas .edu.

62. Gil Troy, *Morning in America: How Ronald Reagan Invented the 1980s* (Princeton: Princeton University Press, 2005), 51.

63. Ronald Reagan, "Inaugural Address, January 20, 1981," www.presidency.ucsb.edu.

64. Gore Vidal, "An American Sissy," *New York Review of Books,* August 13, 1981; Geoffrey Ward "The Making of Theodore Roosevelt," *New York Times,* July 26, 1981.

65. Reagan rarely invoked TR as a national hero except to relish his predecessor's use of the bully pulpit. Like Roosevelt, Reagan crafted a political image through memorable parables and adept salesmanship, detaching himself from entangling scandals while crediting himself with steering popular culture. For that reason most, he admired TR. "Interview with Representatives of Western European Publications," May 21, 1982, and "Remarks at the First Annual Commemoration of the Days of Remembrance of Victims of the Holocaust," April 30, 1981, www.presidency.ucsb.edu.

66. Fred Halliday, *The Making of the Second Cold War* (London: Verso, 1983).

67. "Proclamation 4992—Theodore Roosevelt Day," October 27, 1982 www.presidency .ucsb.edu.

68. Reagan visited Theodore Roosevelt Island in 1984 to sign an environmental quality report, for example. "Reagan Cites 'Solid Progress' Toward Clean Air, Water," *Washington Post,* July 12, 1984.

69. "The Launching of the U.S.S. Theodore Roosevelt," *TRA Journal* 11, no. 1 (Winter 1985): 3; "USS Theodore Roosevelt Joins Active Service as 15th Carrier," *Washington Post,* October 26, 1986.

70. Ronald Reagan, "Remarks at the National Convention of the American Legion in Louisville, Kentucky," September 6, 1988; "Remarks at the Presentation Ceremony for the Take Pride in America Awards," July 26, 1988; "Proclamation 5746—National Adoption Week," November 19, 1987; "Proclamation 5757—National Day of Excellence," December 23, 1987, www.presidency.ucsb.edu.

71. Ethel Roosevelt Derby's death in 1977 led to a sizable donation to the Harvard University Library system. Included in the gift was the Burroughs Torrey portrait of Roosevelt, which currently hangs in Houghton Library's Reading Room. Executive Director's Report, July 1978, TRA-EXEC Minutes, TRC-H; "Annual Meeting of T.R. Collection Committee at Harvard," *TRA Journal* 4, no. 4 (Fall 1978): 4–5; Ed Engoron, interview with author, March 30, 2015.

8. AN ICON EVERLASTING

1. George H. W. Bush, "Remarks at the Swearing-in Ceremony for Manuel Lujan, Jr., as Secretary of the Interior," February 8, 1989; "Remarks at the Congressional Fire Services Institute Dinner," April 12, 1989; "Remarks at the Associated Press Business Luncheon in Chicago, Illinois," April 24, 1989, www.presidency.ucsb.edu.

2. "A Tribute to America's Buffalo Soldiers," *Los Angeles Times,* July 29, 1990.

3. Michael Patrick Cullinane, "Invoking Teddy: The Inspiration of John McCain's Foreign Policy," *Diplomacy and Statecraft* 19, no. 4 (December 2008): 767–86.

4. John Morton Blum, *A Life with History* (Lawrence: University Press of Kansas, 2004), 123. See also Nigel Hamilton, *Bill Clinton: An American Journey* (Random House, 2011), 338.

5. William Jefferson Clinton, "Remarks on Presenting the Medal of Honor," January 16, 2001, www.presidency.ucsb.edu; Tweed Roosevelt, "The Second Battle of San Juan Hill," *TRA Journal* 21, nos. 1 and 2 (2002): 8-21.

6. *The Indomitable Teddy Roosevelt,* dir. Harrison Engle (ABC, 1986); Michael Patrick Cullinane, "The Memory of Theodore Roosevelt through Motion Pictures," *A Companion to Theodore Roosevelt,* ed. Serge Ricard (Malden, MA: Wiley-Blackwell, 2012), 513–4. It is interesting to note that George C. Scott campaigned for George McGovern in 1972.

7. *T.R.: The Story of Theodore Roosevelt,* dir. David Grubin (PBS, 1996); Matthew Frye Jacobson, "Imperial Amnesia: Teddy Roosevelt, the Philippines, and the Modern Art of Forgetting," *Radical History Review* 1999, no. 73 (Winter 1999): 124.

8. George W. Bush, "Remarks at a United States Reception in New York City," September 23, 2003; "Remarks Welcoming General Tommy R. Franks and an Exchange with Reporters in Crawford, Texas," December 28, 2001, www.presidency.ucsb.edu.

9. George W. Bush, "Remarks Honoring President Theodore Roosevelt's 150th Birthday," October 27, 2008, www.presidency.ucsb.edu.

10. For analysis of Obama's Osawatomie speech, see Ben Soskis, "How Pundits Are Misreading Obama's Speech—and Teddy Roosevelt's," *New Republic,* December 7, 2011; John Cassidy, "Invoking Teddy Roosevelt, Obama Finds his Voice," *New Yorker,* December 6, 2011. The same week Obama spoke in Osawatomie, Newt Gingrich called himself a "Theodore

Roosevelt Republican." For his remarks, see transcript of Newt Gingrich interview with Glenn Beck, Mercury Radio, December 6, 2011, www.glennbeck.com.

11. Barack Obama, "Remarks at Osawatomie High School in Osawatomie," December 6, 2011, www.presidency.ucsb.edu.

12. Glenn Beck, Mercury Radio, December 7, 2011, www.glennbeck.com/2011/12/07/ who-was-teddy-roosevelt-and-why-do-progressives-love-him-so-much; Edmund Morris, "The Tea Party Last Time," *New York Times,* October 31, 2010.

13. Jeffery Lord, "The Hundred Year GOP War," *American Spectator,* January 10, 2012.

14. John Allen Gable, "The Two TR's- Mythic and Real," *TRA Journal* 11, no. 4 (Fall 1985): 7.

15. Richard H. Collin, "Symbiosis versus Hegemony: New Directions in the Foreign Relations Historiography of Theodore Roosevelt and William Howard Taft," *Diplomatic History* 19, no. 3 (July 1995): 473.

16. Lewis L. Gould, *The Presidency of Theodore Roosevelt* (Lawrence: University Press of Kansas, 1991).

17. John Milton Cooper, *The Warrior and the Priest: Woodrow Wilson and Theodore Roosevelt* (Cambridge, MA: Harvard University Press, 1997).

18. Willard B. Gatewood, "Theodore Roosevelt and the Shaping of the Modern Presidency," *Reviews in American History* 20, no. 4 (December 1992): 512–17; Carl R. Osthaus, "Review: Theodore Roosevelt and the Idea of Race," *Journal of Southern History* 47, no. 1 (February 1981): 129–30; Gail Bederman, *Manliness and Civilization: A Cultural History of Gender and Race in the United States, 1880–1917* (Chicago: University of Chicago Press, 1995); Richard H. Collin, "Review: Theodore Roosevelt and the British Empire: A Study in Presidential Statecraft," *International History Review* 20, no. 4 (December 1998): 999–1000.

19. See Natalie A. Naylor, Douglas Brinkley, and John Allen Gable, eds., *Theodore Roosevelt Many-Sided American* (Interlaken, NY: Heart of the Lakes, 1992). On Kathleen Dalton's biography, see James Chace, "TR and the Road Not Taken," *New York Review of Books,* July 17, 2003; Tom Lansford, "Review: Theodore Roosevelt: A Strenuous Life," *Pennsylvania Magazine of History and Biography* 128, no. 2 (April 2004): 218–19. Wallace Finley Dailey, the long-serving curator of the Theodore Roosevelt Collection at Harvard University, also credited Dalton with producing the most well-rounded single-volume account of Roosevelt's life. Wallace Finley Dailey, interview with author, July 24, 2012.

20. James M. Strock, *Theodore Roosevelt on Leadership: Executive Lessons from the Bully Pulpit* (Roseville, CA: Forum, 2001).

21. Douglas Brinkley, *The Wilderness Warrior: Theodore Roosevelt and the Crusade for America* (New York: HarperCollins, 2009).

22. Stacy Cordery, *Alice: Alice Roosevelt Longworth, from White House Princess to Washington Power Broker* (New York: Viking, 2007); Douglas Brinkley, *The Wilderness Warrior: Theodore Roosevelt and the Crusade for America* (New York: HarperCollins, 2009); H. Paul Jeffers, *In the Rough Rider's Shadow: The Story of a War Hero--Theodore Roosevelt Jr.* (New York: Ballantine, 2003); Betty Caroli, *The Roosevelt Women* (New York: Basic Books, 1998); David Fromkin, *The King and the Cowboy: Theodore Roosevelt and Edward VII* (New York: Penguin, 2008); *America's Transatlantic Turn: Theodore Roosevelt and the "Discovery" of Europe,* ed. Hans Krabbendam and John M. Thompson (New York: Palgrave Macmillan, 2012); Leroy Dorsey, *We Are All Americans, Pure and Simple: Theodore Roosevelt and the Myth of Americanism* (Tuscaloosa: University of Alabama Press, 2007); Edward P. Kohn,

Heir to the Empire City: New York and the Making of Theodore Roosevelt (New York: Basic Books, 2014); Richard Zacks, *Island of Vice: Theodore Roosevelt's Doomed Quest to Clean Up Sin-Loving New York* (New York: Doubleday, 2012); Doris Kearns Goodwin, *The Bully Pulpit: Theodore Roosevelt, William Howard Taft, and the Golden Age of Journalism* (New York: Viking, 2013); Chip Bishop, *The Lion and the Journalist: The Unlikely Friendship of Theodore Roosevelt and Joseph Bucklin Bishop* (Guilford, CT: Lyons, 2012); Serge Ricard, *A Companion to Theodore Roosevelt* (Malden, MA: John Wiley and Sons, 2011).

23. Steven J. Ericson and Allen Hockley, eds., *The Treaty of Portsmouth and Its Legacies* (Hanover, NH: Dartmouth College Press, 2008); Henry J. Hendrix, *Theodore Roosevelt's Naval Diplomacy: The U.S. Navy and the Birth of the American Century* (Annapolis, MD: Naval Institute Press, 2009); J. Lee Thompson, *Theodore Roosevelt Abroad: Nature, Empire, and the Journey of an American President* (New York: Palgrave Macmillan, 2010); J. Lee Thompson, *Never Call Retreat: Theodore Roosevelt and the Great War* (New York: Palgrave Macmillan, 2013).

24. Jackson Lears, "A Boy's Own Story," *New Republic,* April 7, 2011.

25. A. L. Oosthoek, *Roosevelt in Middelburg: The Four Freedoms Awards, 1982–2008,* ed. Christina Polderman, trans. Diederik van Werven (Vlissingen, Netherlands: Olive Press, 2010).

26. Cornelis van Minnen, interview with the author, January 8, 2015.

27. "News and Notes," *TRA Journal* 11, no. 4 (Fall 1985): 14–5; "The Roosevelt Study Center in the Netherlands," *TRA Journal* 12, no. 1 (Winter 1986): 13; "Roosevelt Study Center Opens in Netherlands," *TRA Journal* 13, no. 4 (Fall 1986): 18–22; Minutes of the TRA Executive Committee, March 2, 1985, May 11, 1985, August 8, 1985, August 5, 1986, TRA-EXEC Minutes, TRC-H.

28. Cornelis van Minnen, interview with the author, January 8, 2015; Tweed Roosevelt, interview with the author, July 4, 2015.

29. "Some have called it the peace treaty of Utrecht as they were coming from Utrecht on their way to Middelburg and others call it the peace treaty of Middelburg as that was their destination," van Minnen relates.

30. Boettiger recounted this story in an authentication letter to the president of the Franklin D. Roosevelt American Heritage Center in Worcester, Massachusetts. See John Roosevelt Boettiger to Dr. Joseph Plaud, September 23, 2003, historical.ha.com/common/images/inthenews/boettiger_provenance_letter.pdf. See, also, Peter Collier and David Horowitz, *The Roosevelts: An American Saga* (New York: Simon and Schuster, 1994), 482.

31. "Roosevelt Reunion in Oyster Bay," *TRA Journal* 18, no. 3 (Summer 1991): 16–7; "Roosevelt Family Reunion in North Dakota," *TRA Journal* 22, nos. 1 and 2 (Fall 1997): 28–9; "Roosevelts Gather at Campobello," *Bangor Daily News,* August 7, 1999.

32. "President's Quiet Day," *Washington Post,* May 20, 1907.

33. DeeGee Lester, "The Public Presentation of Theodore Roosevelt at American Historic Sites and Museums, 1919–1998" (MA thesis, Middle Tennessee State University, 1999), 92.

34. Ibid., 94–108.

35. "Pine Knot's Preserver," *Daily Progress,* October 8, 2008. While Pine Knot took commemoration of Roosevelt's conservation legacy to a new high, and the increasing importance of environmental issues prompted parks and nature preserves to name sites in honor of Roosevelt, Pennsylvania decided to delist Theodore Roosevelt State Park along the Delaware Canal.

36. Marcelle S. Fischler, "The Legacies they Left," *New York Times,* January 1, 2006; "Obituary: John Allen Gable," *Glen Cove Record Pilot,* February 25, 2005; Edward Renehan,

"John Allen Gable: Tribute by his Friends," History News Network, http://historynewsnet work.org/article/9769; "Cenotaph Stone at Youngs Cemetery Dedicated to the Memory of John Allen Gable," *TRA Journal* 26, no. 4 (2005): 30.

37. Larry Neumeister, "18-month Sentence in NY Presidential Letters Theft," *USA Today,* September 19, 2008; Dagmar Fors Karppi, "A New Office for the TRA," *Oyster Bay Enterprise-Pilot,* June 20, 2008.

38. Bill Blyer, "Theodore Roosevelt Group Seeks New Leader," *Newsday,* September 17, 2012.

39. *Teddy: The Musical,* lyrics by Marshall B. Breeden, directed by Stan Raiff (New York: Power Productions, 1981); *Teddy Roosevelt,* by Jonathan Bolt, directed by John Henry Davis (TheaterWorks USA, Theodore Roosevelt Birthplace, 1986); *Bully: An Adventure with Teddy Roosevelt,* by Jerome Alden, directed by Joe Leonardo (touring show, 1998–99); *Teddykins,* by W. Frank, directed by James Tasse (Broadway Theater Center, Milwaukee, WI, 2000).

40. John Allen Gable, "TR in Fiction," *TRA Journal* 15, no. 4 (Fall 1989): 8.

41. Kirkus Reviews, "Remember Santiago," October 26, 1988; Douglas C. Jones, *Remember Santiago* (New York: H. Holt, 1988); Brian Garfield, *Manifest Destiny* (New York: Penzler Books, 1989); Gore Vidal, *Empire: A Novel* (New York: Random House, 1987).

42. *Rough Riders,* directed by John Milius (TNT, 1997).

43. Caryn James, "A Roosevelt who Exulted in Bully War," *New York Times,* July 19, 1997.

44. Marvin Kitman, *Newsday,* July 20, 1997, quoted in John Allen Gable, "The Return of the Rough Riders," *TRA Journal* 22, nos. 1 and 2 (Fall 1997): 25.

45. Lawrence Alexander, *The Big Stick* (Garden City, NY: Doubleday, 1986); Lawrence Alexander, *Speak Softly* (Garden City, NY: Doubleday, 1987); Caleb Carr, *The Alienist* (New York: Random House, 1994); Caleb Carr, *The Angel of Darkness* (New York: Random House, 1997); Victoria Thompson, *Murder in Little Italy: A Gaslight Mystery* (New York: Berkley Prime Crime, 2006); Victoria Thompson, *Murder in Chinatown: A Gaslight Mystery* (New York: Berkley Prime Crime, 2007). The murder mystery genre continues to use Roosevelt's image. In 2014, Gerry O'Brien created a steampunk thriller in which Vice President Roosevelt foils an international conspiracy. Gerry O'Brien, *1901: Theodore Roosevelt, Robot Fighter,* http://1901robotfighter.com.

46. Matthew Purdy, "On the Lower East Side with Caleb Carr: Writing to Flee the Past," *New York Times,* May 19, 1994.

47. Layman's National Bible Association Advertisement, *TRA Journal* 17, no. 1 (Winter 1991): 23.

48. New York State Open Space Conservation Plan (2009), 135; National Park Service press release: "100th Anniversary of Theodore Roosevelt and John Muir's Visit to Yosemite", www.nps.gov; ConservAmerica Leadership Awards, http://conservamerica.org.

49. IBM print advertisement, "PS/1: Power Made Easy" (1993).

50. Citigroup print and television advertisement: "1904: Citi Meets Roosevelt, Atlantic Meets Pacific" (2014). Ironically, Citigroup attempted to win back public trust with a gross exaggeration. J. P. Morgan organized the financing in 1904, and Morgan enlisted Citigroup (then National City Bank) as a subsidiary along with seven other lenders.

51. Cadillac print and television advertisement, "Dare Greatly" (2015).

52. "Encyclopedia: History, 1990s," *Advertising Age,* September 15, 2003; "1990s Information Superhighway," *Advertising Age,* March 28, 2005.

53. Keith McGough, "Front Page," *Theodore Roosevelt . . . Today,* www.theodoreroosevelt .com, available on the Internet Archive's Way Back Machine, https://archive.org/web. John Allen Gable barred TR impersonators from attending TRA meetings or sponsored events when dressed in character. For a commentary on "imposters," see Tweed Roosevelt, "Forgotten Fragments: Impostors!" *TRA Journal* 35, nos. 1 and 2 (Winter–Spring 2014): 27–31.

54. The CD-ROM also included TR's public papers as New York governor. *Cyclopedia with Supplements* [CD-ROM], TRA and New York State's Temporary Commission to Commemorate the Centennial of the Governorship of Theodore Roosevelt (1989).

55. TR Moderated Discussion Board, *Yahoo! Groups,* founded November 18, 1999, https:// groups.yahoo.com/neo/groups/tr-m/info; TR Moderated Discussion Board, "2 New Wikipedia Articles on Roosevelts," and "Re: TR and Other Roosevelt Articles on Wikipedia," *Yahoo! Groups,* https://groups.yahoo.com/neo/groups/tr-m/conversations/messages/1316 and https://groups.yahoo.com/neo/groups/tr-m/conversations/messages/1297.

56. Almanac of Theodore Roosevelt, www.theodore-roosevelt.com; Almanac of Theodore Roosevelt Facebook account, www.facebook.com/RooseveltAlmanac; TRA website www .theodoreroosevelt.org; TRA Twitter account, https://twitter.com/TRooseveltAssoc; TRA Facebook account, https://www.facebook.com/pages/Theodore-Roosevelt-Association.

57. Theodore Roosevelt Center at Dickinson State University, "About Us," www.theodore-rooseveltcenter.org/About-Us.aspx.

58. "The Top 43 Sexiest U.S. Presidents," *Nerve,* February 15, 2015, www.nerve.com/ dispatches/the-top-43-sexiest-us-presidents.

59. Mallory Ortberg, "Dirtbag Teddy Roosevelt," *The Toast,* http://the-toast.net/ 2014/09/16/dirtbag-teddy-roosevelt; Mallory Ortberg and Rachel Fershleiser, "Dirtbag Teddy Roosevelt," https://www.youtube.com/watch?v=nfKSa0MCrg0.

60. "In a Mass Knife Fight to the Death between Every American President, Who Would Win and Why?" *Face in the Blue,* https://faceintheblue.wordpress.com/2012/08/22/in-a-mass-knife-fight-to-the-death-between-every-american-president-who-would-win-and-why.

61. "Roosevelt Lookalike Goes Viral in Show of Rising US Soccer Power," *Guardian,* June 30, 2014; "Teddy Goalsevelt Throws Hat in FIFA Presidential Ring," *Chicago Tribune,* July 20, 2015.

62. *Night at the Museum* is a variation of Milan Trenc's *The Night at the Museum,* although Roosevelt does not feature in the original children's book. *Night at the Museum,* directed by Shawn Levy (2006); *Night at the Museum: Battle of the Smithsonian,* directed by Shawn Levy (2009); *Night at the Museum: Secret of the Tomb,* directed by Shawn Levy (2014).

63. Cullinane, "The Memory of Theodore Roosevelt through Motion Pictures," 517.

64. Several other contemporary motion picture productions accomplish this. Popular shows like *The Simpsons* and *Drunk History* produced unorthodox depictions of Roosevelt but still adhered to the traditional memorial themes. "Bart Stops to Smell the Roosevelts," directed by Stephen Dean Moore, written by Tim Long, episode 2 of *The Simpsons,* season 23, FOX (2011); "Wild West," directed by Jeremy Konner, written by Derek Waters, episode 8 of *Drunk History,* season 1, Comedy Central, 2013.

65. John Allen Gable, "Best Selling Novel Features TR," *TRA Journal* 19, no. 4 (Spring and Summer 1993–1994): 9–10; John Allen Gable, "TR in Fiction," *TRA Journal* 15, no. 4 (Fall 1989): 8.

CONCLUSION

1. Scott Ableman, *Let Teddy Win,* http://blog.letteddywin.com; Neil King Jr., "In this Presidential Race, the Fans are Crying Foul," *Wall Street Journal,* September 28, 2012; Paul Orzulak, "Seriously, Nats: It's Time for Teddy to Win," *Washington Post,* August 3, 2012.

2. Scott Ableman, "Teddy Wins his First Presidents Race on Historic Day at Nationals Park," *Let Teddy Win,* http://blog.letteddywin.com/2012/10/03/teddy-wins-first-presidents-race.

3. "Finally Teddy Wins," *Washington Post,* October 3, 2012; Dan Steinberg, "Teddy Wins First Presidents Race," *Washington Post,* October 3, 2012; Mike Foss, "Nationals Mascot Claims Historic Victory," *USA Today,* October 3, 2012; Scott Cacciola, "No Bull: Roosevelt Prevails at Last," *Wall Street Journal,* October 3, 2012.

4. Howard Fendrich, "Teddy Mascot Finally Wins Nats' Presidents Race," *Huffington Post,* October 3, 2012.

5. *The Roosevelts,* directed by Ken Burns (PBS, 2014); William N. Tilchin, "Exceptional Artistry, Uneven History," *TRA Journal* 36, nos. 1, 2, and 3 (2015): 27.

6. Barry Blitt, "Cover Story," *New Yorker,* January 25, 2016; Annie Karni, "Hillary Clinton Talks Parallels with Former President Theodore Roosevelt," *Daily News,* November 21, 2014.

7. Rebecca Macatee, "Miley Cyrus' New Tattoo Channels Theodore Roosevelt," *E! News Online,* July 10, 2012, http://eonline.com/news; "Liam Hemsworth Gets Tattoo to Match Miley Cyrus' Theodore Roosevelt Quote," *Us Weekly,* October 12, 2012.

8. Conan O'Brien, "Serious Jibber Jabber with Presidential Biographer Edmund Morris," September 6, 2012, http://teamcoco.com/video/edmund-morris-serious-jibber-jabber.

9. See *The Daily Show,* http://thedailyshow.cc.com, September 15, 2014 (with Ken Burns), November 12, 2013 (with Doris Kearns Goodwin), December 9, 2010 (with Edmund Morris), and August 18, 2010 (with Edward Kohn).

10. Nick Offerman, *Gumption: Relighting the Torch of Freedom with America's Gutsiest Troublemakers* (New York: Dutton, 2015), see Roosevelt chapter; Miriam Coleman, "Watch Nick Offerman Deliver a Lesson on the Second Amendment," *Rolling Stone,* June 15, 2014. Offerman fielded questions from online fans on Reddit, and quoted Roosevelt twice. See "Nick Offerman, Funambulist, Returning for More," Reddit, April 4, 2014, www.reddit.com/r/IAmA.

11. Tweed Roosevelt, interview with the author, July 4, 2015.

BIBLIOGRAPHY

MANUSCRIPT COLLECTIONS

Gutzon Borglum Papers, Library of Congress
Doris A. and Lawrence H. Budner Collection, DeGolyer Library, Southern
    Methodist University
James Earle and Laura Fraser Papers, Syracuse University
James R. Garfield Papers, Library of Congress
Hermann Hagedorn Papers, Library of Congress
Hermann Hagedorn Papers, Syracuse University
Warren G. Harding Papers, Ohio Historical Society
Harold L. Ickes Papers, Library of Congress
Frank O. Lowden Papers, University of Chicago
Frank Ross McCoy Papers, Library of Congress
Peter Norbeck Papers, South Dakota University
Basil O'Connor Papers, FDR Presidential Library
Olmsted Associates Records, Library of Congress
Gifford Pinchot Papers, Library of Congress
Anna Eleanor Roosevelt Papers, FDR Presidential Library
FDR Memorial Foundation Papers, FDR Presidential Library
Franklin Delano Roosevelt Papers, FDR Presidential Library
Theodore Roosevelt Association Oral History Project, Columbia University
Theodore Roosevelt Association Papers, Theodore Roosevelt Birthplace
Theodore Roosevelt Centennial Commission Papers, Theodore Roosevelt
    Birthplace
Theodore Roosevelt Collection, Houghton Library, Harvard University
        Joseph Bucklin Bishop Letters
        Anna Roosevelt Cowles Papers
        Ethel Roosevelt Derby Papers
        Hermann Hagedorn Papers
        John J. Leary Papers
        Henry F. Pringle Papers

Corinne Roosevelt Robinson Papers
Edith Kermit Roosevelt Papers
Letters to Kermit Roosevelt
Theodore Roosevelt Association Executive Committee Minutes
Theodore Roosevelt Association Papers
Theodore Roosevelt Association—Harvard College Library Administrative Files
Edwin Van Valkenburg Papers
Subject files including Advertising, Carl Akeley, Dossier on Medical
    History, Memorials, Morris Chronology, Movies/Television, Plays,
    Portraits, Portraits Sculpture, Presidential Ranking, Roosevelt
    Centennial, Sesquicentennial, TRA Reports, and TR Island
Theodore Roosevelt Papers, Library of Congress
Theodore Roosevelt Jr. Papers, Library of Congress
Theodore Roosevelt Memorial and Exhibitions Papers, American Museum of
    Natural History, New York
Henry L. Stimson Papers, Roosevelt Study Center, the Netherlands
William Roscoe Thayer Papers, Houghton Library, Harvard University
Woman's Roosevelt Memorial Association Papers, Theodore Roosevelt Birthplace

NEWSPAPERS AND PERIODICALS

Advertising Age
American Mercury
American Spectator
Atlanta Constitution
Boston Globe
Cambridge Tribune
Chicago Tribune
Christian Science Monitor
Commentary
Dial
Guardian
Harvard Alumni Bulletin
London Times
Los Angeles Times
McClure's Magazine
Munsey's Magazine
Nation
New Republic
New York Review of Books

New York Sun
New York Times
New York Tribune
New York World
New Yorker
Newsweek
North American Review
Outlook
Rolling Stone
Roosevelt House Annual
Roosevelt House Bulletin
Roosevelt Quarterly
Theodore Roosevelt Association Journal
TIME
Washington Post
Washington Star
Washington Times
Women's Roosevelt House Bulletin

SELECT FILMOGRAPHY

Fancy Pants. Directed by George Marshall. 1950.
The Indomitable Teddy Roosevelt. Directed by Harrison Engle. 1986.
The Monroe Doctrine. Directed by Crane Wilbur. 1939.
My Girl Tisa. Directed by Elliott Nugent. 1948.
Night at the Museum. Directed by Shawn Levy. 2006.
Night at the Museum: Battle of the Smithsonian. Directed by Shawn Levy. 2009.
Night at the Museum: Secret of the Tomb. Directed by Shawn Levy. 2014.
Our Teddy or *The Fighting Roosevelts*. Directed by William Nigh. 1919.
The Roosevelts: An Intimate History. Directed by Ken Burns. 2014.
The Rough Riders. Directed by Victor Fleming. 1927.
The Rough Riders. Directed by John Milius. 1997.
Sun Valley Cyclone. Directed by R. G. Springsteen. 1946.
Teddy the Rough Rider. Directed by Ray Enright. 1940
Through the Roosevelt Country. Directed by Hermann Hagedorn. 1919.
TR: An American Lion. Directed by David de Vries. 2003.
TR: The Story of Theodore Roosevelt. Directed by David Grubin. 1996.
War of the Wildcats. Re-released as *In Old Oklahoma*. Directed by Albert S. Rogell. 1943.
The Wind and the Lion. Directed by John Milius. 1975.
Yankee Doodle Dandy. Directed by Michael Curtiz. 1942.

BOOKS AND ARTICLES

Abbott, Lawrence. *Impressions of Theodore Roosevelt*. Garden City, NY: Doubleday Page, 1919.

Akeley, Carl. "Theodore Roosevelt in Africa." *Natural History* 19, no. 1 (January 1919): 12–14.

Alexander, De Alva Stanwood. *Four Famous New Yorkers: The Political Careers of Cleveland, Platt, Hill, and Roosevelt*. New York: H. Holt, 1923.

Alexander, Lawrence. *The Big Stick*. Garden City, NY: Doubleday, 1986.

———. *Speak Softly*. Garden City, NY: Doubleday, 1987.

Amos, James. *Theodore Roosevelt: Hero to His Valet*. New York: John Day, 1927.

Anderson, Oscar E. *The Health of a Nation: Harvey W. Wiley and the Fight for Pure Food*. Chicago: University of Chicago Press, 1958.

Anderson, Robert. *Leader of Men: Theodore Roosevelt*. New York: G. P. Putnam's Sons, 1920.

Arnold, Peri. *Remaking the Presidency: Roosevelt, Taft, and Wilson, 1901–1916*. Lawrence: University Press of Kansas, 2009.

Auchincloss, Louis. *Theodore Roosevelt*. New York: Times Books, 2001.

Auerbach, Joseph. *Theodore Roosevelt, an Appreciation*. New York: Longmans Green, 1923.

Bailey, Thomas. *Theodore Roosevelt and the Japanese-American Crises*. Gloucester, MA: P. Smith, 1964.

Banner, Lois W. "Biography as History." *American Historical Review* 114, no. 3 (June 2009): 579–86.

Barrows, Marjorie. *Along Blazed Trails*. Chicago: Spencer, 1953.

Barsness, John A. "Theodore Roosevelt as Cowboy: The Virginian as Jacksonian Man." *American Quarterly* 21, no. 3 (Autumn 1969): 609–19.

Beale, Howard. *Theodore Roosevelt and the Rise of America to World Power*. Baltimore: Johns Hopkins Press, 1956.

Bederman, Gail. *Manliness and Civilization: A Cultural History of Gender and Race in the United States, 1880–1917*. Chicago: University of Chicago Press, 1996.

Beers, Henry A. *Four Americans: Roosevelt, Hawthorne, Emerson, Whitman*. Freeport, NY: Books for Libraries Press, 1968.

Behl, William Auburn. "The Rhetoric of Theodore Roosevelt." PhD diss., Northwestern, 1942.

Benson, W. Todd. *President Theodore Roosevelt's Conservation Legacy*. Haverford, PA: Infinity, 2003.

Berman, Jay Stuart. *Police Administration and Progressive Reform: Theodore Roosevelt as Police Commissioner of New York*. New York: Greenwood, 1987.

Bingham, Hiram. "Theodore Roosevelt." *Yale Law Journal* 9 (January 22, 1921).

Bingham, Mary. "The Administration of the Civil Service under Theodore Roosevelt, 1889–1924." PhD diss., Smith College, 1924.

Bishop, Charles O. *The Lion and the Journalist: The Unlikely Friendship of Theodore Roosevelt and Joseph Bucklin Bishop.* Guilford, CT: Lyons, 2012.

———. *Quentin and Flora: A Roosevelt and a Vanderbilt in Love during the Great War.* CreateSpace, 2014.

Bishop, Joseph Bucklin. *Notes and Anecdotes of Many Years.* New York: Scribner's, 1925.

———. *Theodore Roosevelt and His Time.* New York: Charles Scribner's Sons, 1920.

Blackorby, E. C. "Theodore Roosevelt's Conservation Policies and Their Impact upon America and the American West." *North Dakota History* 25, no. 4 (October 1958): 107–17.

Blake, Nelson Manfred. "Ambassadors at the Court of Theodore Roosevelt." *Mississippi Valley Historical Review* 42, no. 2 (September 1955): 179–206.

Blight, David W. *Race and Reunion: The Civil War in American Memory.* Cambridge, MA: Belknap Press of Harvard University Press, 2001.

Blum, John Morton. *A Life with History.* Lawrence: University Press of Kansas, 2004.

———. "The Presidential Leadership of Theodore Roosevelt." *Michigan Alumnus* 65, no. 10 (Autumn 1958).

———. *The Progressive Presidents: Roosevelt, Wilson, Roosevelt, Johnson.* New York: Norton, 1980.

———. *The Republican Roosevelt.* Cambridge, MA: Harvard University Press, 1954.

Bodnar, John E. *Remaking America: Public Memory, Commemoration, and Patriotism in the Twentieth Century.* Princeton: Princeton University Press, 1991.

Brackman, Harold. "'Biography Yanked down out of Olympus': Beard, Woodward, and Debunking Biography." *Pacific Historical Review* 52, no. 4 (November 1983): 403–27.

Brands, H. W. *T. R.: The Last Romantic.* New York: Basic Books, 1997.

Bridges, Robert. *Theodore Roosevelt as Author and Contributor.* New York: Charles Scribner's Sons, 1919.

Brinkley, Douglas. *The Wilderness Warrior: Theodore Roosevelt and the Crusade for America.* New York: HarperCollins, 2009.

Brooks, Sydney. *Theodore Roosevelt.* London: Hodder and Stoughton, 1910.

Brough, James. *Princess Alice: A Biography of Alice Roosevelt Longworth.* Boston: Little, Brown, 1975.

Brown, David S. *Richard Hofstadter: An Intellectual Biography.* Chicago: University of Chicago Press, 2006.

Brumbaugh, Martin. *The Story of Theodore Roosevelt.* Dansville, NY: F. A. Owen, 1922.

Buehler, Daniel O. "Permanence and Change in Theodore Roosevelt's Conservation Jeremiad." *Western Journal of Communication* 62, no. 4 (December 1998): 439–58.

Burns, James MacGregor, and Susan Dunn. *The Three Roosevelts: The Leaders Who Transformed America.* London: Atlantic, 2001.

Burton, David H. "The Influence of the American West on the Imperialist Philosophy of Theodore Roosevelt." *Arizona and the West* 4, no. 1 (1962): 5–26.

———. *The Learned Presidency: Theodore Roosevelt, William Howard Taft, Woodrow Wilson*. Rutherford, NJ: Fairleigh Dickinson University Press, 1988.

———. *Taft, Roosevelt, and the Limits of Friendship*. Madison, NJ: Fairleigh Dickinson University Press, 2005.

———. *Theodore Roosevelt*. New York: Twayne, 1972.

———. *Theodore Roosevelt, American Politician: An Assessment*. Madison, NJ: Fairleigh Dickinson University Press, 1997.

———. "Theodore Roosevelt and His English Correspondents: A Special Relationship of Friends." *Transactions of the American Philosophical Society* 63, no. 2 (January 1973): 1–70.

———. *Theodore Roosevelt: Confident Imperialist*. Philadelphia: University of Pennsylvania Press, 1969.

———. "Theodore Roosevelt's Social Darwinism and Views on Imperialism." *Journal of the History of Ideas* 26, no. 1 (1965): 103–18.

Busch, Noel. *T.R.: The Story of Theodore Roosevelt and His Influence on Our Times*. New York: Reynal, 1963.

Callahan, Tara. *Theodate Pope Riddle: A Pioneer Woman Architect*. Fort Washington, PA: Eastern National, 1998.

Campbell, John P. "Taft, Roosevelt, and the Arbitration Treaties of 1911." *Journal of American History* 53, no. 2 (September 1966): 279–98.

Carlton, Mabel. *Theodore Roosevelt: The Man of Action*. Boston: John Hancock Mutual Life Insurance, 1923.

Caroli, Betty. *The Roosevelt Women*. New York: Basic Books, 1998.

Carr, Caleb. *The Alienist*. New York: Random House, 1994.

———. *The Angel of Darkness*. New York: Random House, 1997.

Carwardine, Richard, and Jay Sexton, eds. *The Global Lincoln*. New York: Oxford University Press, 2011.

Chapple, Joe. *Warren G. Harding: The Man*. Boston: Chapple, 1920.

Charnwood, Godfrey Rathbone Benson. *Theodore Roosevelt*. London: Constable, 1923.

Chessman, G. Wallace. *Governor Theodore Roosevelt: The Albany Apprenticeship, 1898–1900*. Cambridge, MA: Harvard University Press, 1965.

———. *Theodore Roosevelt and the Politics of Power*. Boston: Little, Brown, 1969.

Churchill, Allen. *The Roosevelts*. London: Frederick Muller, 1966.

Collier, Peter, and David Horowitz. *The Roosevelts: An American Saga*. New York: Simon and Schuster, 1994.

Collin, Richard H. "Henry Pringle's Theodore Roosevelt: A Study in Historical Revisionism." *New York History* 52, no. 2 (April 1971): 151–68.

———. "The Image of Theodore Roosevelt in American History and Thought, 1885–1965." PhD diss., New York University, 1966.

———. *Theodore Roosevelt and Reform Politics*. Lexington, MA: Heath, 1972.

——. *Theodore Roosevelt's Caribbean: The Panama Canal, the Monroe Doctrine, and the Latin American Context.* Baton Rouge: Louisiana State University Press, 1990.

——. *Theodore Roosevelt, Culture, Diplomacy, and Expansion: A New View of American Imperialism.* Baton Rouge: Louisiana State University Press, 1985.

——. "Symbiosis Versus Hegemony: New Relations in the Historiography of Theodore Roosevelt and William Howard Taft." *Diplomatic History* 19, no. 3 (June 1995): 473–97.

Collins, Michael. *That Damned Cowboy: Theodore Roosevelt and the American West, 1883–1898.* New York: P. Lang, 1989.

Confino, Alon. "Collective Memory and Cultural History: Problems of Method." *American Historical Review* 102, no. 5 (1997): 1386–1403.

Cook, Robert. *Troubled Commemoration: The American Civil War Centennial, 1961–1965.* Baton Rouge: Louisiana State University Press, 2007.

Cooper, John. *The Warrior and the Priest: Woodrow Wilson and Theodore Roosevelt.* Cambridge, MA: Belknap Press of Harvard University Press, 1983.

Cordery, Stacy. *Alice: Alice Roosevelt Longworth, from White House Princess to Washington Power Broker.* New York: Viking, 2007.

Corkin, Stanley. *Cowboys as Cold Warriors: The Western and U.S. History.* Philadelphia: Temple University Press, 2004.

Cornell, Robert J. *The Anthracite Coal Strike of 1902.* Washington, DC: Catholic University of America Press, 1957.

Cotton, Edward. *The Ideals of Theodore Roosevelt.* New York: D. Appleton, 1923.

——. *Theodore Roosevelt, the American.* Boston: Beacon, 1926.

Cross, Whitney R. "Ideas in Politics: The Conservation Policies of the Two Roosevelts." *Journal of the History of Ideas* 14, no. 3 (June 1953): 421–38.

Cubitt, Geoffrey. *History and Memory.* Manchester: Manchester University Press, 2007.

Cullinane, Michael Patrick. "Imperial 'Character': How Race and Civilization Shaped Theodore Roosevelt's Imperialism." *America's Transatlantic Turn: Theodore Roosevelt and the "Discovery" of Europe,* edited by Hans Krabbendam and John M. Thompson. New York: Palgrave Macmillan, 2012.

——. "Invoking Teddy: The Inspiration of John McCain's Foreign Policy." *Diplomacy and Statecraft* 19, no. 4 (December 2008): 767–86.

——. "The Memory of Theodore Roosevelt through Motion Pictures." *A Companion to Theodore Roosevelt,* edited by Serge Ricard. Malden, MA: Wiley-Blackwell, 2012.

——. "Theodore Roosevelt in the Eyes of the Allies." *Journal of the Gilded Age and Progressive Era* 15, no. 1 (January 2016): 80–101.

Cuncannon, Paul. "The Political Philosophy of Theodore Roosevelt." PhD diss., Princeton University, 1925.

Cutlip, Scott M. *Fund Raising in the United States: Its Role in America's Philanthropy.* New Brunswick, NJ: Rutgers University Press, 1965.

Cutright, Paul Russell. *Theodore Roosevelt, the Making of a Conservationist.* Urbana: University of Illinois Press, 1985.

Dalton, Kathleen. "Finding Theodore Roosevelt: A Personal and Political Story." *Journal of the Gilded Age and Progressive Era* 6, no. 4 (October 2007): 363–84.

———. *Theodore Roosevelt: A Strenuous Life.* New York: Vintage, 2004.

Daniels, Roger. *The Politics of Prejudice: The Anti-Japanese Movement in California, and the Struggle for Japanese Exclusion.* Berkeley: University of California Press, 1962.

Dawson, Warrington. *Opportunity and Theodore Roosevelt.* Chicago: Honest Truth, 1924.

Dennett, Tyler. *Roosevelt and the Russo-Japanese War.* Garden City, NY: Doubleday Page, 1925.

DeStefano, Susan, and Antonio Castro. *Theodore Roosevelt, Conservation President.* New York: Twenty-First-Century Books, 1993.

Dewey, John. *The Middle Works of John Dewey, 1899–1924: Journal Articles, Essays, and Miscellany Published in the 1918–1919 Period.* Carbondale: Southern Illinois University Press, 2008.

DiSilvestro, Roger. *Theodore Roosevelt in the Badlands: A Young Politician's Quest for Recovery in the American West.* New York: Walker, 2011.

Dobbs, Zygmund. *Red Intrigue and Race Turmoil.* New York: The Alliance, 1958.

Donald, Aïda. *Lion in the White House: A Life of Theodore Roosevelt.* New York: Basic Books, 2007.

Donn, Linda. *The Roosevelt Cousins: Growing Up Together, 1882–1924.* New York: Alfred A. Knopf, 2001.

Dorsey, Leroy G. "The Frontier Myth in Presidential Rhetoric: Theodore Roosevelt's Campaign for Conservation." *Western Journal of Communication* 59, no. 1 (Winter 1995): 1–19.

———. *We Are All Americans, Pure and Simple: Theodore Roosevelt and the Myth of Americanism.* Tuscaloosa: University of Alabama Press, 2007.

Downes, Randolph C. *The Rise of Warren Gamaliel Harding, 1865–1920.* Columbus: Ohio State University Press, 1970.

Drinker, Frederick. *Theodore Roosevelt: His Life and Work.* Washington, DC: National, 1919.

Dyer, Thomas. *Theodore Roosevelt and the Idea of Race.* Baton Rouge: Louisiana State University Press, 1980.

Egan, Timothy. *The Big Burn: Teddy Roosevelt and the Fire That Saved America.* New York: Houghton Mifflin Harcourt, 2009.

Einstein, Lewis. *Roosevelt: His Mind in Action.* Boston: Houghton Mifflin, 1930.

Emerson, Edwin. *Adventures of Theodore Roosevelt.* New York: E. P. Dutton, 1928.

Engel, Jeffrey. "The Democratic Language of American Imperialism: Race, Order, and Theodore Roosevelt's Personifications of Foreign Policy Evil." *Diplomacy and Statecraft* 19, no. 4 (December 2008): 671–89.

Engelhardt, Tom. *The End of Victory Culture: Cold War America and the Disillusioning of a Generation.* Amherst: University of Massachusetts Press, 2007.

Ericson, Steven J., and Allen Hockley, eds. *The Treaty of Portsmouth and Its Legacies.* Hanover, NH: Dartmouth College Press, 2008.

Esthus, Raymond. *Theodore Roosevelt and Japan.* Seattle: University of Washington Press, 1967.

Fehn, Bruce. "Theodore Roosevelt and American Masculinity." *OAH Magazine of History* 19, no. 2 (2005): 52–59.

Felsenthal, Carol. *Alice Roosevelt Longworth.* New York: Putnam, 1988.

Finger, Charles. *Life of Theodore Roosevelt.* Girard, KS: Haldeman-Julius, 1924.

Fite, Gilbert Courtland. *Mount Rushmore.* Norman: University of Oklahoma Press, 1952.

Flack, Ambrose. *Room for Mr. Roosevelt.* Boston: Thomas Y. Crowell, 1951.

Flippen, J. Brooks. *Nixon and the Environment.* Albuquerque: University of New Mexico Press, 2000.

Frantz, Joe Bertram, and Julian Ernest Choate, eds. *The American Cowboy: The Myth and the Reality.* Norman: University of Oklahoma Press, 1955.

Friedenberg, Robert V. *Theodore Roosevelt and the Rhetoric of Militant Decency.* New York: Greenwood, 1990.

Friedlander, Robert A. "A Reassessment of Roosevelt's Role in the Panamanian Revolution of 1903." *Western Political Quarterly* 14, no. 2 (June 1961): 535–43.

Fromkin, David. *The King and the Cowboy: Theodore Roosevelt and Edward VII.* New York: Penguin, 2008.

Gable, John. *The Bull Moose Years: Theodore Roosevelt and the Progressive Party.* Port Washington, NY: Kennikat, 1978.

Gagliasso, Dan. "Rough Riders, Moviemakers, and History: Hollywood Images of Theodore Roosevelt and the First U.S. Volunteer Cavalry." *Journal of Arizona History* 41, no. 3 (October 2000): 307–30.

Gardner, Joseph. *Departing Glory: Theodore Roosevelt as Ex-President.* New York: Scribner, 1973.

Garfield, Brian. *Manifest Destiny.* New York: Penzler, 1989.

Garland, Hamlin. *My Friendly Contemporaries: A Literary Log.* New York: Macmillan, 1932.

———. *Theodore Roosevelt.* New York: Mentor Association, 1920.

Gatewood, Willard B. *Theodore Roosevelt and the Art of Controversy: Episodes of the White House Years.* Baton Rouge: Louisiana State University Press, 1970.

———. "Theodore Roosevelt and the Shaping of the Modern Presidency." *Reviews in American History* 20, no. 4 (December 1992): 512–17.

Geertz, Clifford. *The Interpretation of Cultures: Selected Essays.* New York: Basic Books, 1973.

Gerstle, Gary. "Theodore Roosevelt and the Divided Character of American Nationalism." *Journal of American History* 86, no. 3 (December 1999): 1280–1307.

Gilbert, Clinton Wallace. *The Mirrors of Washington*. New York: G. P. Putnam's Sons, 1921.

Gilman, Bradley. *Roosevelt, the Happy Warrior*. Boston: Little, Brown, 1921.

Goodwin, Doris Kearns. *The Bully Pulpit: Theodore Roosevelt, William Howard Taft, and the Golden Age of Journalism*. New York: Viking, 2013.

Gosse, Edmund. "The Custom of Biography." *Anglo-Saxon Review* 8 (March 1901).

Gould, Lewis L. *Four Hats in the Ring: The 1912 Election and the Birth of Modern American Politics*. Lawrence: University Press of Kansas, 2008.

———. *Grand Old Party: A History of the Republicans*. New York: Oxford University Press, 2012.

———. *1968: The Election That Changed America*. Chicago: Ivan R. Dee, 1993.

———. *The Presidency of Theodore Roosevelt*. Lawrence: University Press of Kansas, 2011.

———. *Theodore Roosevelt*. New York: Oxford University Press, 2012.

———. "Theodore Roosevelt, Woodrow Wilson, and the Emergence of the Modern Presidency: An Introductory Essay." *Presidential Studies Quarterly* 19, no. 1 (January 1989): 41–50.

Granger, Alfred. "The Roosevelt Memorial." *Architect* 5, no. 4 (January 1926).

Grantham, Dewey W. "Dinner at the White House: Theodore Roosevelt, Booker T. Washington, and the South." *Tennessee Historical Quarterly* 17, no. 2 (June 1958): 112–30.

———. "Theodore Roosevelt in American Historical Writing, 1945–1960." *Mid-America* 43, no. 1 (January 1961): 3–35.

Gravlee, Grady Jackson. "A Rhetorical Study of Franklin Delano Roosevelt's 1920 Campaign." PhD diss., Louisiana State University, 1963.

Greenberg, Irving. *Theodore Roosevelt and Labor, 1900–1918*. New York: Garland, 1988.

Hagedorn, Hermann. *The Boys' Life of Theodore Roosevelt*. New York: Harper and Brothers, 1918.

———. *A Guide to Sagamore Hill: The Place, the People, the Life, the Meaning*. New York: Theodore Roosevelt Association, 1953.

———. *The Roosevelt Family of Sagamore Hill*. New York: Macmillan, 1954.

———. *Roosevelt in the Bad Lands*. Boston: Houghton Mifflin, 1921.

———. *Theodore Roosevelt: A Biographical Sketch*. New York: Roosevelt Memorial Association and Columbia University, 1919.

Hagedorn, Hermann, and Gary G. Roth. *Sagamore Hill: A Historical Guide*. Oyster Bay, NY: Theodore Roosevelt Association, 1977.

Haglund, David G. "Roosevelt as 'Friend of France'—But Which One?" *Diplomatic History* 31, no. 5 (November 2007): 883–908.

Hall, Oakley. *The Bad Lands*. New York: Scribner, 1978.

Halliday, Fred. *The Making of the Second Cold War*. London: Verso, 1983.

Hamilton, Nigel. *Biography: A Brief History*. Cambridge, MA: Harvard University Press, 2007.

———. *Bill Clinton: An American Journey.* New York: Random House, 2011.

Handlin, Oscar. *Truth in History.* Cambridge, MA: Belknap Press, 1979.

Hanhimäki, Jussi M. *The Flawed Architect: Henry Kissinger and American Foreign Policy.* New York: Oxford University Press, 2004.

Harbaugh, William H. *Power and Responsibility: The Life and Times of Theodore Roosevelt.* New York: Farrar, Straus and Cudahy, 1961.

Harper, John Lamberton. *American Visions of Europe: Franklin D. Roosevelt, George F. Kennan, and Dean G. Acheson.* New York: Cambridge University Press, 1996.

Havig, Alan. "Presidential Images, History, and Homage: Memorializing Theodore Roosevelt, 1919–1967." *American Quarterly* 30, no. 4 (October 1978): 514–32.

Hawley, Joshua. *Theodore Roosevelt: Preacher of Righteousness.* New Haven: Yale University Press, 2008.

Hendrix, Henry J. *Theodore Roosevelt's Naval Diplomacy: The U.S. Navy and the Birth of the American Century.* Annapolis, MD: Naval Institute Press, 2009.

Henry, Will. *San Juan Hill.* New York: Random House, 1962.

Higham, John. "Changing Paradigms: The Collapse of Consensus History." *Journal of American History* 76, no. 2 (September 1989): 460–66.

Hodge, Carl Cavanagh. "A Whiff of Cordite: Theodore Roosevelt and the Transoceanic Naval Arms Race, 1897–1909." *Diplomacy and Statecraft* 19, no. 4 (December 2008): 712–31.

Hofstadter, Richard. *The Age of Reform: From Bryan to FDR.* New York: Knopf, 1954.

———. *The American Political Tradition and the Men Who Made It.* New York: Knopf, 1948.

———. *Anti-Intellectualism in American Life.* New York: Knopf, 1962.

Holme, John. *The Life of Leonard Wood.* Garden City, NY: Doubleday Page, 1920.

Holmes, James R. *Theodore Roosevelt and World Order: Police Power in International Relations.* Washington, DC: Potomac Books, 2006.

Hoogenboom, Ari. "The Pendleton Act and the Civil Service." *American Historical Review* 64, no. 2 (January 1959): 301–18.

Howe, M. A. De Wolfe. *James Ford Rhodes, American Historian.* New York: D. Appleton, 1929.

Howland, Harold. *Theodore Roosevelt and His Times: A Chronicle of the Progressive Movement.* New Haven: Yale University Press, 1921.

Hunt, Lynn. *Writing History in the Global Era.* New York: W. W. Norton, 2014.

Hutchinson, William. *Lowden of Illinois: The Life of Frank O. Lowden.* Chicago: University of Chicago Press, 1957.

Iglehart, Ferdinand. *Theodore Roosevelt: The Man as I Knew Him.* New York: The Christian Herald, 1919.

Jacobson, Matthew Frye. "Imperial Amnesia: Teddy Roosevelt, the Philippines, and the Modern Art of Forgetting." *Radical History Review* 1999, no. 73 (Winter 1999): 117–27.

Jeffers, H. Paul. *Colonel Roosevelt: Theodore Roosevelt Goes to War, 1897–1898.* New York: J. Wiley and Sons, 1996.

———. *Commissioner Roosevelt: The Story of Theodore Roosevelt and the New York City Police, 1895–1897.* New York: J. Wiley and Sons, 1994.

———. *The Further Adventures of Sherlock Holmes: The Stalwart Companions.* London: Titan Books, 2010.

———. *In the Rough Rider's Shadow: The Story of a War Hero—Theodore Roosevelt Jr.* New York: Ballantine, 2003.

Jividen, Jason R. *Claiming Lincoln: Progressivism, Equality, and the Battle for Lincoln's Legacy in Presidential Rhetoric.* DeKalb: Northern Illinois University Press, 2011.

Johnson, Eric. "The Character of Teddy Brewster in *Arsenic and Old Lace.*" MFA thesis, Mankato State University, 1989.

Johnston, William Davison. *TR: Champion of the Strenuous Life.* New York: Theodore Roosevelt Association, 1958.

Jones, Douglas C. *Remember Santiago.* New York: H. Holt, 1988.

Jordan, David Starr. "Personal Glimpses of Theodore Roosevelt." *Natural History* 19, no. 1 (January 1919).

Judis, John. *The Folly of Empire: What George W. Bush Could Learn from Theodore Roosevelt and Woodrow Wilson.* New York: Scribner, 2004.

Judson, Clara. *Theodore Roosevelt, Fighting Patriot.* Chicago: Wilcox and Follett, 1953.

Kammen, Michael. *Mystic Chords of Memory: The Transformation of Tradition in American Culture.* New York: Knopf, 1991.

Karsten, Peter. "The Nature of 'Influence': Roosevelt, Mahan and the Concept of Sea Power." *American Quarterly* 23, no. 4 (October 1971): 585–600.

Kennan, George F. *American Diplomacy, 1900–1950.* Chicago: University of Chicago Press, 1951.

Kipling, Rudyard. *The Letters of Rudyard Kipling: 1911–19.* Edited by Thomas Pinney. Iowa City: University of Iowa Press, 1990.

Kissinger, Henry. *Diplomacy.* New York: Simon and Schuster, 1994.

———. *Does America Need a Foreign Policy?* New York: Simon and Schuster, 2001.

Kohn, Edward P. *Heir to the Empire City: New York and the Making of Theodore Roosevelt.* New York: Basic Books, 2014.

———. *Hot Time in the Old Town: The Great Heat Wave of 1896 and the Making of Theodore Roosevelt.* New York: Basic Books, 2010.

Kolko, Gabriel. *The Triumph of Conservatism: A Reinterpretation of American History, 1900–1916.* New York: Free Press, 1977.

Kraft, Betsy Harvey. *Theodore Roosevelt: Champion of the American Spirit.* New York: Houghton Mifflin Harcourt, 2003.

Larner, Jesse. *Mount Rushmore: An Icon Reconsidered.* New York: Nation Books, 2002.

Lash, Joseph P. *Eleanor and Franklin: The Story of Their Relationship.* New York: W. W. Norton, 1971.

Leary, John J. *Talks with T.R.: From the Diaries of John J. Leary, Jr.* Boston: Houghton Mifflin, 1920.

Lengel, Edward G. *Inventing George Washington: America's Founder, in Myth and Memory.* New York: Harper, 2011.

Lenihan, John H. *Showdown: Confronting Modern America in the Western Film.* Urbana: University of Illinois Press, 1980.

Lester, DeeGee. "The Public Presentation of Theodore Roosevelt at American Historic Sites and Museums, 1919–1998." MA thesis, Middle Tennessee State University, 1999.

Levin, Peter R. *Seven by Chance: The Accidental Presidents.* New York: Farrar, Straus, 1948.

Levine, Stephen L. "'Forces Which Cannot Be Ignored': Theodore Roosevelt's Reaction to European Modernism." *Revue Francaise D'Etudes Americains* 2, no. 116 (2008): 5–19.

Lewis, William. *The Life of Theodore Roosevelt.* Philadelphia: John C. Winston, 1919.

Lincoln, A. "Theodore Roosevelt, Hiram Johnson, and the Vice-Presidential Nomination of 1912." *Pacific Historical Review* 28, no. 3 (August 1959): 267–83.

Link, Arthur. "Theodore Roosevelt and the South in 1912." *North Carolina Historical Review* 23, no. 3 (July 1946): 313–24.

Longworth, Alice Roosevelt. *Crowded Hours: Reminiscences of Alice Roosevelt Longworth.* New York: Charles Scribner's Sons, 1933.

Longworth, Alice Roosevelt, and Michael Teague. *Mrs. L.: Conversations with Alice Roosevelt Longworth.* Garden City, NY: Doubleday, 1981.

Lorant, Stefan. *The Life and Times of Theodore Roosevelt.* Garden City, NY: Doubleday, 1959.

Loveland, Anne C. *Emblem of Liberty: The Image of Lafayette in the American Mind.* Baton Rouge: Louisiana State University Press, 1971.

Lowenthal, David. "The Timeless Past: Some Anglo-American Historical Preconceptions." *Journal of American History* 75, no. 4 (March 1989): 1263–80.

Lower, Richard Coke. "Hiram Johnson: The Making of an Irreconcilable." *Pacific Historical Review* 41, no. 4 (November 1972): 505–26.

Mallan, John P. "Roosevelt, Brooks Adams, and Lea: The Warrior Critique of the Business Civilization." *American Quarterly* 8, no. 3 (October 1956): 216–30.

Markham, Lois. *Theodore Roosevelt.* New York: Chelsea House, 1985.

Marks, Frederick W. "Morality as a Drive Wheel in the Diplomacy of Theodore Roosevelt." *Diplomatic History* 2, no. 1 (January 1978): 43–62.

———. *Velvet on Iron: The Diplomacy of Theodore Roosevelt.* Lincoln: University of Nebraska Press, 1979.

Marolda, Edward J. *Theodore Roosevelt, the U.S. Navy, and the Spanish-American War.* New York: Palgrave Macmillan, 2001.

Mason, Robert. *Richard Nixon and the Quest for a New Majority.* Chapel Hill: University of North Carolina Press, 2004.

Mattison, Ray H. "Roosevelt and the Stockmen's Association." *North Dakota History* 17, no. 2 (April 1950): 73–95.

May, Elaine Tyler. *Homeward Bound: American Families in the Cold War Era.* Basic Books, 2008.

McCaleb, Walter. *Theodore Roosevelt.* New York: A. and C. Boni, 1931.

McCartney, Laton. *The Teapot Dome Scandal: How Big Oil Bought the Harding White House and Tried to Steal the Country.* New York: Random House, 2008.

McCullough, David. *Mornings on Horseback.* New York: Simon and Schuster, 1981.

———. *The Path Between the Seas: The Creation of the Panama Canal, 1870–1914.* New York: Simon and Schuster, 1978.

McFarland, Philip James. *Mark Twain and the Colonel: Samuel L. Clemens, Theodore Roosevelt, and the Arrival of a New Century.* New York: Rowman and Littlefield, 2012.

McGeary, M. "Gifford Pinchot's Years of Frustration, 1917–1920." *Pennsylvania Magazine of History and Biography* 83, no. 3 (1959).

McGerr, Michael. *A Fierce Discontent: The Rise and Fall of the Progressive Movement in America, 1870–1920.* Oxford: Oxford University Press, 2003.

McIntyre, Niel. *Great-Heart: The Life Story of Theodore Roosevelt.* New York: William Edwin Rudge, 1919.

McSpadden, J. Walker. *The Story of Theodore Roosevelt.* New York: Barse and Hopkins, 1923.

Melnick, Richard J. "The Theodore Roosevelt Birthplace." *Historian* 58, no. 2 (December 1996): 289–94.

Meltzer, Milton. *Theodore Roosevelt and His America.* New York: F. Watts, 1994.

Mencken, H. L. *Prejudices: Second Series.* New York: Alfred A. Knopf, 1920.

Metcalf, Victor. *Personal Recollections of Theodore Roosevelt.* Berkeley: University of California Press, 1919.

Milazzo, Paul Charles. "Nixon and the Environment." In *A Companion to Richard M. Nixon,* edited by Melvin Small. Malden, MA: Wiley-Blackwell, 2013.

Milkis, Sidney. *Theodore Roosevelt, the Progressive Party, and the Transformation of American Democracy.* Lawrence: University Press of Kansas, 2009.

Millard, Candice. *River of Doubt: Theodore Roosevelt's Darkest Journey.* New York: Doubleday, 2005.

Miller, Kelly. *Roosevelt and the Negro.* Washington, DC: Hayworth, 1907.

Morgan, James. *Theodore Roosevelt, The Boy and the Man.* New York: Grosset and Dunlap, 1919.

Morgan, Ted. *FDR: A Biography.* New York: Simon and Schuster, 1985.

Morris, Edmund. *Colonel Roosevelt.* New York: Random House, 2010.

———. *The Rise of Theodore Roosevelt.* New York: Random House, 1979.

———. *Theodore Rex.* New York: Random House, 2001.

———. *This Living Hand: And Other Essays.* New York: Random House Paperbacks, 2013.

Morris, Sylvia. *Edith Kermit Roosevelt: Portrait of a First Lady.* New York: Coward McCann and Geoghegan, 1980.

Mowry, George E. *The Era of Theodore Roosevelt, 1900–1912.* New York: Harper and Brothers, 1958.

———. *Theodore Roosevelt and the Progressive Movement.* Madison: University of Wisconsin Press, 1946.

Murdoch, David Hamilton. *The American West: The Invention of a Myth.* Reno: University of Nevada Press, 2001.

Murphy, Gary. "'Mr. Roosevelt Is Guilty': Theodore Roosevelt and the Crusade for Constitutionalism, 1910–1912." *Journal of American Studies* 36, no. 3 (December 2002): 441–57.

Murphy, John. "'Back to the Constitution': Theodore Roosevelt, William Howard Taft and Republican Party Division, 1910–1912." *Irish Journal of American Studies* 4 (January 1995): 109–26.

Nasaw, David. "AHR Roundtable: Historians and Biography—Introduction." *American Historical Review* 114, no. 3 (May 2009): 573–78.

Naylor, Natalie A., Douglas Brinkley, and John A. Gable, eds. *Theodore Roosevelt: Many-Sided American.* Interlaken, NY: Heart of the Lakes, 1992.

Neal, Steve. *Happy Days Are Here Again.* New York: William Morrow, 2004.

Neu, Charles E. "Theodore Roosevelt and American Involvement in the Far East, 1901–1909." *Pacific Historical Review* 35, no. 4 (November 1966): 433–49.

———. *An Uncertain Friendship: Theodore Roosevelt and Japan, 1906–1909.* Cambridge, MA: Harvard University Press, 1967.

Ninkovich, Frank. "Theodore Roosevelt: Civilization as Ideology." *Diplomatic History* 10, no. 3 (July 1986): 221–45.

Nixon, Richard M. *In the Arena: A Memoir of Victory, Defeat, and Renewal.* New York: Simon and Schuster, 1990.

———. *RN: The Memoirs of Richard Nixon.* New York: Grosset and Dunlap, 1978.

Noll, Mark A. "William Jennings Bryan, Theodore Roosevelt, Woodrow Wilson, and the King James Version of the Bible." *Theology* 114, no. 4 (July 2011): 251–59.

Norcross, Frank. *Theodore Roosevelt: A Tribute.* Carson City, NV: State Printing Office, 1920.

Olin, Spencer C. "Hiram Johnson, the California Progressives, and the Hughes Campaign of 1916." *Pacific Historical Review* 31, no. 4 (November 1962).

Oliver, Lawrence J. "Theodore Roosevelt, Brander Matthews, and the Campaign for Literary Americanism." *American Quarterly* 41, no. 1 (March 1989): 93–111.

Oosthoek, A. L. *Roosevelt in Middelburg: The Four Freedoms Awards, 1982–2008.* Edited by Christina Polderman. Vlissingen, Netherlands: Olive Press, 2010.

Osborn, Henry Fairfield. "Theodore Roosevelt, Naturalist." *Natural History* 19, no. 1 (January 1919): 9–11.

O'Toole, Patricia. *When Trumpets Call: Theodore Roosevelt after the White House.* New York: Simon and Schuster, 2005.

Oyos, Matthew M. "Theodore Roosevelt, Congress, and the Military: U.S. Civil-Military Relations in the Early Twentieth Century." *Presidential Studies Quarterly* 30, no. 2 (June 2000): 312–31.

Parks, Edd Winfield. *Teddy Roosevelt, All Around Boy.* Indianapolis: Bobbs-Merrill, 1961.

Payne, Frank Owen. "More Roosevelt Sculptures." *Art and Archaeology* 8, no. 4 (August 1919): 197-202.

———. "Sculptures of the Late Theodore Roosevelt." *Art and Archaeology* 8, no. 2 (April 1919): 109-13.

Payne, Phillip G. *Dead Last: The Public Memory of Warren G. Harding's Scandalous Legacy.* Athens: Ohio University Press, 2009.

Pearson, Edmund Lester. *Theodore Roosevelt.* New York: Macmillan, 1920.

Perlstein, Rick. *Before the Storm: Barry Goldwater and the Unmaking of the American Consensus.* New York: Hill and Wang, 2001.

———. *Nixonland: The Rise of a President and the Fracturing of America.* New York: Simon and Schuster, 2008.

Peterson, Merrill. *The Jefferson Image in the American Mind.* New York: Oxford University Press, 1960.

———. *John Brown: The Legend Revisited.* Charlottesville: University of Virginia Press, 2002.

———. *Lincoln in American Memory.* New York: Oxford University Press, 1994.

Pietrusza, David. *1920: The Year of the Six Presidents.* New York: Basic Books, 2009.

Pinals, Robert S. "Theodore Roosevelt's Inflammatory Rheumatism." *Journal of Clinical Rheumatology* 14, no. 1 (February 2008): 41–44.

Ponder, Stephen. "Publicity in the Interest of the People: Theodore Roosevelt's Conservation Crusade." *Presidential Studies Quarterly* 20, no. 3 (July 1990): 547–55.

Posner, Russell M. "California's Role in the Nomination of Franklin D. Roosevelt." *California Historical Society Quarterly* 39, no. 2 (June 1960): 121–39.

Powell, Jim. *Bully Boy: The Truth about Theodore Roosevelt's Legacy.* New York: Crown Forum, 2006.

Pringle, Henry Fowles. *Big Frogs.* New York: Vanguard, 1928.

———. *Theodore Roosevelt: A Biography.* 2nd ed. New York: Harcourt Brace, 1956.

Putnam, Carleton. *Theodore Roosevelt: The Formative Years, 1858–1886.* New York: Charles Scribner's Sons, 1958.

Rego, Paul. *American Ideal: Theodore Roosevelt's Search for American Individualism.* Lanham, MD: Lexington Books, 2008.

Renehan, Edward. *The Lion's Pride: Theodore Roosevelt and His Family in Peace and War.* New York: Oxford University Press, 1998.

Ricard, Serge. "An Atlantic Triangle in the 1900s: Theodore Roosevelt's 'Special Relationships' with France and Britain." *Journal of Transatlantic Studies* 8, no. 3 (June 2010): 202–12.

——. A Companion to Theodore Roosevelt. Malden, MA: John Wiley and Sons, 2011.

——. "The Roosevelt Corollary." *Presidential Studies Quarterly* 36, no. 1 (March 2006): 17–26.

——. *Theodore Roosevelt: et la Justification de l'Impérialisme.* Aix-en-Provence: Université de Provence, 1986.

——. "Theodore Roosevelt: Imperialist or Global Strategist in the New Expansionist Age?" *Diplomacy and Statecraft* 19, no. 4 (December 2008): 639–57.

Riis, Jacob. *Theodore Roosevelt, the Citizen.* New York: Outlook, 1904.

Robinson, Corinne Roosevelt. *My Brother, Theodore Roosevelt.* New York: Charles Scribner's Sons, 1921.

Roessner, Amber. *Inventing Baseball Heroes: Ty Cobb, Christy Mathewson, and the Sporting Press in America.* Baton Rouge: Louisiana State University Press, 2014.

Rofe, J. Simon. "'Under the Influence of Mahan': Theodore and Franklin Roosevelt and Their Understanding of American National Interest." *Diplomacy and Statecraft* 19, no. 4 (December 2008): 732–45.

Roosevelt, Anna Eleanor. *This I Remember.* New York: Harper and Brothers, 1949.

Roosevelt, Archibald B. *Manual for American Action.* New York: The Alliance, 1956.

Roosevelt, Archie, Jr. *For Lust of Knowing: Memoirs of an Intelligence Officer.* Boston: Little, Brown, 1988.

Roosevelt, Eleanor Butler. *Day before Yesterday: The Reminiscences of Mrs. Theodore Roosevelt, Jr.* Garden City, NY: Doubleday, 1959.

Roosevelt, Franklin D. *F.D.R.: His Personal Letters.* Edited by Elliott Roosevelt. 2 vols. New York: Kraus Reprint, 1970.

Roosevelt, Kermit. *The Happy Hunting-Grounds.* New York: Charles Scribner's Sons, 1920.

——. *War in the Garden of Eden.* New York: Charles Scribner's Sons, 1919.

Roosevelt, Theodore. *The Free Citizen: A Summons to Service of the Democratic Ideal.* Edited by Hermann Hagedorn. New York: Macmillan, 1956.

——. *The Letters of Theodore Roosevelt.* Edited by Elting E. Morison, John Blum, Hope W. Wigglesworth, and Sylvia Rice. 8 vols. Cambridge, MA: Harvard University Press, 1951–54.

——. *Theodore Roosevelt: An Autobiography.* New York: Da Capo, 1985.

——. *Theodore Roosevelt Cyclopedia.* Edited by Albert Bushnell Hart and Herbert Ronald Ferleger. New York: Roosevelt Memorial Association, 1941.

——. *Theodore Roosevelt on Race, Riots, Immigration, and Crime.* Washington, DC: Scott-Townsend, 1996.

——. *Theodore Roosevelt on Race, Riots, Reds, Crime.* Edited by Archibald B. Roosevelt. Metairie, LA: Sons of Liberty, 1968.

——. *The Winning of the West.* New York: Putnam's, 1889.

——. *The Works of Theodore Roosevelt.* National ed. New York: Charles Scribner's Sons, 1926.

Roosevelt, Theodore, and Joseph Bucklin Bishop. *Theodore Roosevelt's Letters to His Children*. New York: Charles Scribner's Sons, 1919.

Roth, Gary G. "The Roosevelt Memorial Association and the Preservation of Sagamore Hill, 1919–1953." MA thesis, Wake Forest University, 1980.

Russell, Thomas. *Life and Work of Theodore Roosevelt*. Chicago: Homewood, 1919.

Scheiner, Seth M. "President Theodore Roosevelt and the Negro, 1901–1908." *Journal of Negro History* 47, no. 3 (July 1962): 169–82.

Schindler, Colin. *Hollywood in Crisis: Cinema and American Society, 1929–1939.* New York: Routledge, 2005.

Schlesinger, Arthur M. *The Coming of the New Deal, 1933–1935.* New York: Houghton Mifflin Harcourt, 2003.

———. *The Cycles of American History*. New York: Houghton Mifflin Harcourt, 1999.

———. *The Politics of Upheaval, 1935–1936*. New York: Houghton Mifflin Harcourt, 2003.

Sewall, William Wingate. *Bill Sewall's Story of T.R.* New York: Harper and Brothers, 1919.

Shackel, Paul A. *Myth, Memory, and the Making of the American Landscape.* Gainesville: University Press of Florida, 2001.

Shaff, Howard, and Audrey Karl Shaff. *Six Wars at a Time: The Life and Times of Gutzon Borglum, Sculptor of Mount Rushmore.* Sioux Falls, SD: Center for Western Studies, Augustana College, 1985.

Shaw, Tony. *Hollywood's Cold War*. Edinburgh: Edinburgh University Press, 2007.

Shore, Miles F. "On Action and Affect." *Journal of Interdisciplinary History* 11, no. 2 (October 1980): 287–94.

Skidmore, Max J. "Theodore Roosevelt on Race and Gender." *Journal of American Culture* 21, no. 2 (Summer 1998): 35–45.

Slotkin, Richard. *The Fatal Environment: The Myth of the Frontier in the Age of Industrialization, 1800–1890.* Norman: University of Oklahoma Press, 1985.

———. *Gunfighter Nation: The Myth of the Frontier in Twentieth-Century America.* New York: Atheneum, 1992.

Smith, Rex Alan. *The Carving of Mount Rushmore*. New York: Abbeville, 1985.

Stephenson, Nathaniel W. *Nelson W. Aldrich, A Leader in American Politics.* New York: Charles Scribner's Sons, 1930.

Stoeltje, Beverly J. "Making the Frontier Myth: Folklore Process in a Modern Nation." *Western Folklore* 46, no. 4 (October 1987): 235–53.

Strock, James M. *Theodore Roosevelt on Leadership: Executive Lessons from the Bully Pulpit.* Roseville, CA: Forum, 2001.

Taliaferro, John. *All the Great Prizes: The Life of John Hay, from Lincoln to Roosevelt.* New York: Simon and Schuster, 2013.

———. *Great White Fathers: The Story of the Obsessive Quest to Create Mount Rushmore.* New York: PublicAffairs, 2002.

Taylor, Ella. *Prime-Time Families: Television Culture in Post-War America*. Berkeley: University of California Press, 1989.

Teichmann, Howard. *Alice: The Life and Times of Alice Roosevelt Longworth*. Englewood Cliffs, NJ: Prentice-Hall, 1979.

Testi, Arnaldo. "The Gender of Reform Politics: Theodore Roosevelt and the Culture of Masculinity." *Journal of American History* 81, no. 4 (March 1995): 1509–33.

Thayer, William Roscoe. *Theodore Roosevelt, an Intimate Biography*. Boston: Houghton Mifflin, 1919.

Thelen, David. "Memory and American History." *Journal of American History* 75, no. 4 (March 1989): 1117–29.

Thompson, J. Lee. *Never Call Retreat: Theodore Roosevelt and the Great War*. New York: Palgrave Macmillan, 2013.

———. *Theodore Roosevelt Abroad: Nature, Empire, and the Journey of an American President*. New York: Palgrave Macmillan, 2010.

Thompson, Victoria. *Murder in Chinatown: A Gaslight Mystery*. New York: Berkley Prime Crime, 2007.

———. *Murder in Little Italy: A Gaslight Mystery*. New York: Berkley Prime Crime, 2006.

Thwing, Eugene. *The Life and Meaning of Theodore Roosevelt*. New York: Current Literature, 1919.

Tilchin, William. *Theodore Roosevelt and the British Empire: A Study in Presidential Statecraft*. New York: St. Martin's Press, 1997.

———. "Theodore Roosevelt, Anglo-American Relations, and the Jamaica Incident of 1907." *Diplomatic History* 19, no. 3 (June 1995): 385.

Tilchin, William N., and Charles E. Neu, eds. *Artists of Power: Theodore Roosevelt, Woodrow Wilson, and Their Enduring Impact on U.S. Foreign Policy*. Westport, CT: Greenwood, 2006.

Towne, Charles, ed. *Roosevelt as the Poets Saw Him*. New York: Charles Scribner's Sons, 1923.

Troy, Gil. *Morning in America: How Ronald Reagan Invented the 1980s*. Princeton: Princeton University Press, 2005.

Tuchman, Barbara W. "'Perdicaris Alive or Raisuli Dead.'" *American Heritage* 10, no. 5 (August 1959).

Turk, Richard W. *The Ambiguous Relationship: Theodore Roosevelt and Alfred Thayer Mahan*. New York: Greenwood, 1987.

Vidal, Gore. *Empire: A Novel*. New York: Random House, 1987.

Vries, George de. "Theodore Roosevelt: An American Synthesis." *Midcontinent American Studies Journal* 9, no. 2 (October 1968): 70–80.

Wagenknecht, Edward. *The Seven Worlds of Theodore Roosevelt*. Guilford, CT: Lyons, 2009.

Walker, Dale. *The Boys of '98: Theodore Roosevelt and the Rough Riders*. New York: Forge, 1998.

Ward, Geoffrey C. *A First-Class Temperament: The Emergence of Franklin Roosevelt*. New York: Harper and Row, 1989.

Warren, Louis S. *Buffalo Bill's America: William Cody and the Wild West Show*. New York: Vintage, 2006.

Washburn, Charles. *Theodore Roosevelt*. Boston: Houghton Mifflin, 1919.

Watterson, John S., III. "Political Football: Theodore Roosevelt, Woodrow Wilson, and the Gridiron Reform Movement." *Presidential Studies Quarterly* 25, no. 3 (July 1995): 555–64.

Watts, Sarah. *Rough Rider in the White House: Theodore Roosevelt and the Politics of Desire*. Chicago: University of Chicago Press, 2003.

Waugh, Joan. *U.S. Grant: American Hero, American Myth*. Chapel Hill: University of North Carolina Press, 2013.

Weatherson, Michael A., and Hal W. Bochin. *Hiram Johnson: Political Revivalist*. Lanham, MD: University Press of America, 1995.

Wertheim, Stephen. "Reluctant Liberator: Theodore Roosevelt's Philosophy of Self-Government and Preparation for Philippine Independence." *Presidential Studies Quarterly* 39, no. 3 (September 2009): 494–518.

White, Mark. *Kennedy: A Cultural History of an American Icon*. London: Bloomsbury, 2013.

White, Richard. *Roosevelt the Reformer: Theodore Roosevelt as Civil Service Commissioner, 1889–1895*. Tuscaloosa: University of Alabama Press, 2003.

White, William Allen. *The Autobiography of William Allen White*. New York: Macmillan, 1946.

Wills, Garry. *Nixon Agonistes: The Crisis of the Self-Made Man*. New York: Mariner Books, 2002.

Wimmel, Kenneth. *Theodore Roosevelt and the Great White Fleet: American Seapower Comes of Age*. Washington, DC: Brassey's, 1998.

Winter, Jay M. *Sites of Memory, Sites of Mourning: The Great War in European Cultural History*. New York: Cambridge University Press, 1995.

Wister, Owen. *Theodore Roosevelt: The Story of a Friendship, 1880–1919*. London: Macmillan, 1930.

Wolraich, Michael. *Unreasonable Men: Theodore Roosevelt and the Republican Rebels Who Created Progressive Politics*. New York: St. Martin's Press, 2014.

Wood, Frederick S. *Roosevelt as We Knew Him: The Personal Recollections of 150 of His Friends and Associates*. Philadelphia: John C. Winston, 1927.

Woods, Frederick Adam. *Genius of Theodore Roosevelt and His Place among Historic Personalities*. Washington, DC: American Genetic Association, 1919.

Woodward, William E. *George Washington, the Image and the Man*. New York: Boni and Liveright, 1926.

Wrobel, David M. *The End of American Exceptionalism: Frontier Anxiety from the Old West to the New Deal*. Lawrence: University Press of Kansas, 1993.

Zacks, Richard. *Island of Vice: Theodore Roosevelt's Doomed Quest to Clean Up Sin-Loving New York*. New York: Doubleday, 2012.

Zyskind, Harold. "A Case Study in Philosophic Rhetoric: Theodore Roosevelt." *Philosophy and Rhetoric* 1, no. 4 (October 1968): 228–54.

INDEX

Facebook, 210
Fall, Albert, 82
Ferleger, Herbert, 129, 239n, 240n
Fleming, Victor, 65
Folsom, Joseph Fulford, 76
Ford, Gerald, 180–81, 189
Ford, John, 144
Four Freedoms Foundation, 199–200
Frankfurter, Felix, 106
Fraser, James Earle, 2, 4, 27, 76, 155, 232n
Friendship Tower, 56

Gable, John Allen, 181–84, 185, 191, 192,
    197, 198, 200–201, 204, 205, 206, 209–
    10, 211–12, 217, 218–19, 256n
Garant, Robert Ben, 211
Gardner, Lloyd, 179
Garfield, Brian, 206
Garfield, James A., 10
Garfield, James R., 66–67, 69–70, 79, 154, 167
Gatewood, Willard, 178
Gephardt, Richard, 194
Gingrich, Newt, 193, 197
Goldwater, Barry, 172–73, 174
Gordenker, Leon, 201
Gore, Albert, Jr., 194
Gosse, Edmund, 31
Gould, Lewis, 167, 198
Grant, Cary, 91
Grant, Ulysses S., 10, 149
Grant, Ulysses S., III, 157
Grantham, Dewey, 130
Great Depression, 7, 92–93, 97–98, 102, 162
Grubin, David, 195
Gugler, Eric, 159–60, 161

Hagedorn, Hermann, 20–22, 25–26, 27, 28,
    35, 57, 64–67, 69–71, 79, 92, 127–29, 135–
    40, 141, 155, 157, 158–63, 165–69, 181–82,
    183, 204, 217, 246n
Hanna, Marcus Alonzo, 14–15
Harbaugh, William Henry, 201, 203
Harding, Warren Gamaliel, 6, 14, 16, 37,
    43–48, 49–50, 51–52, 53, 61, 80–82, 97,
    193, 216, 230n
Hart, Albert Bushnell, 128–29

Harvard University, xii, 11, 38, 47, 56–57,
    127–30, 150, 182, 185, 192, 231n, 242n,
    252n
Hay, John, 179
Hays, Will H., 167
Heuvel, William vanden, 200
Hill, Harvey J., 23
Hillard, Mary, 59–60
Hofstadter, Richard, 131–32, 178, 240n
Hoover, Herbert, 51, 53, 81–82, 86, 88, 93,
    96–97, 153–54, 165
Hoover, J. Edgar, 135
Houghton Library. *See* Harvard University
Howe, Louis, 84–85, 93, 94
Huber, William Henry, 18
Hughes, Charles Evans, 40, 44, 75, 81
Humphrey, Hubert, 172, 248n
Hyde Park, NY, 47, 199, 201

IBM, 150, 208–9
Ickes, Harold L., 16, 50, 95
Iglehart, Ferdinand, 3, 33
Indomitable Teddy Roosevelt, The (film),
    194–95
In Old Oklahoma (film), 145
irreconcilables, 40, 41, 45
Ives, Irving, 139

Jackson, Andrew, 11, 17, 149, 210
Jefferson, Thomas, 11, 66, 71–72, 73–74, 77,
    78, 149, 164, 213
Jeffries, Rogina Louisa, 210
Johnson, Hiram, 37–38, 39–42, 43, 45, 228n
Johnson, Lyndon Baines, 162, 172, 189,
    194, 248n
Jolson, Al, 46–47
Jones, Douglas C., 205–6
Jordan, David Starr, 17
Juliana, Princess (Wilhelmina), 199
Jusserand, Jules, 61

Keating, Kenneth, 161
Keith, Brian, 180–81
Kennan, George, 134, 179
Kennedy, John F., 142, 174, 194
Kennedy, Robert F., 171

www.ingramcontent.com/pod-product-compliance
Lightning Source LLC
Chambersburg PA
CBHW032344280326
41935CB00008B/448